In Search of
Coronary-Prone
Behavior:
Beyond Type A

In Search of
Coronary-Prone Behavior:

Beyond Type A

edited by

Aron W. Siegman
Theodore M. Dembroski

University of Maryland

LEA LAWRENCE ERLBAUM ASSOCIATES, PUBLISHERS
1989   Hillsdale, New Jersey   Hove and London

Lawrence Erlbaum Associates, Inc., Publishers
365 Broadway
Hillsdale, New Jersey 07642

Library of Congress Cataloging-in-Publication Data

In search of coronary-prone behavior.

Bibliography: p.
Includes indexes.
1. Coronary heart disease—Psychosomatic aspects.
2. Type A behavior. I. Siegman, Aron Wolfe.
II. Dembrowski, Theodore.
RC685.C615 1988   616.1′23071   88-11171
ISBN 0-8058-0341-6

#17873553

Printed in the United States of America
10 9 8 7 6 5 4 3 2 1

Contents

Introduction

A decade ago, the accumulation of research findings bearing on the epidemiological validity of the Type A behavior pattern (TABP) was sufficiently positive to convince a NIH-sponsored scientific review panel to conclude that it was an independent risk factor for coronary heart disease (CHD). Positive findings regarding the TABP stimulated a second decade of retrospective and prospective epidemiological, biobehavioral, and biomedical research. The second decade of research has produced an expanding body of negative findings, which has called into serious question the risk factor status of globally-defined TABP and has suggested that the earlier conclusion of the review panel was premature.

Despite the growing body of evidence against global TABP as a risk factor for CHD, research has continued to examine whether some of the components of the multidimensional TABP are related to clinical manifestations of CHD. Such research is guided by the distinction between the construct of TABP and the concept of coronary-prone behavior; a distinction that recognizes that many of the attributes contained in the conceptual definition of the global TABP may not be related to CHD and as such are simply benign correlates of the pattern. In fact, some elements of TABP may even be protective and only a few, even perhaps one, may be "toxic" in its effects. In addition, the concept of coronary-prone behavior raises the possibility that behavioral attributes not included in the traditional definition of TABP may qualify as coronary-prone tendencies.

There are standard epidemiological criteria for establishing any variable as a risk factor for CHD. When the latter criteria are reasonably satisfied, a risk factor is identified. But the scientific search for the pathogenic component of the established risk factor continues to proceed. For example, following the identification of cholesterol as a risk factor, various fractions of the lipid were examined to determine which conferred the most risk. Similarly, there is mounting evidence that the hostility component of the TABP confers risk for CHD. Scientific search is currently underway to determine whether some facets of hostility confer more risk than other components. This current state of scientific inquiry heavily influenced our decision to select the present title of this volume.

The lead chapter by Suls and Sanders begins with an assumption that there are particular behaviors or patterns of behavior that are risk factors for CHD. They address the important issue of the role of potential mechanisms or processes by which a behavioral risk factor may be translated into CHD. They devote considerable attention to three processes that may be associated with a behavioral risk factor: inborn structural weakness, proneness to physiologic hyperresponsivity, and a tendency to be exposed to dangerous situations.

Dembroski and Czajkowski (Chapter 2) trace the historical development of the TABP and describe the evolution of the component analyses of the TABP in efforts to identify the "virulent" component that confers risk. The results appear to suggest that the hostility component probably is a risk factor for CHD. Costa, McCrae, and Dembroski (Chapter 3) examine hostility in the broader framework of theoretical and empirical advances associated with a comprehensive five-factor model of personality in an attempt to show how a certain facet of hostility can be integrated into one of the five major domains, namely, the Agreeableness vs. Antagonism dimension. Integration of hostility with a broader theory of personality should promote conceptual clarification of present notions of hostility and other personality predictors of disease in psychosomatic research.

Siegman (Chapter 4) takes the position that hostility is no less multidimensional than the TABP construct, with probably only some dimensions of hostility being related to CHD. One distinction, suggested by earlier studies, is between the *experience* of anger and hostility, or covert hostility, and the *expression* of anger and hostility, or overt hostility and aggression (also see Costa et al., Chapter 3). The evidence suggests a positive correlation between the expression of hostility and the severity of coronary artery disease (CAD). Some evidence suggests that expressed hostility also correlates positively with cardiovascular reactivity and with the production of testosterone. On the other hand, the evidence suggests a *negative* correlation between the experience of hostility, or covert hostility, and CAD, cardiovascular reactivity and testosterone production in challenging situations.

In discussing how overt anger and hostility become translated into CHD, Siegman emphasizes the role of expressive manifestations of overt anger and hostility, especially that of loud (rapid) and interruptive speech. Of interest from a prophylactic and rehabilitative perspective is the finding that by instructing people to speak softly and slowly, one can significantly reduce their cardiovascular reactivity. The chapter includes a biobehavioral model that proposes a synergistic interaction between expressed anger and hostility, loud, rapid and interruptive speech, and cardiovascular reactivity during angry interactions. Finally, Sieg-man suggests that objective, computer-scorable, expressive correlates of expressed hostility (e.g., loud and interruptive speech) may have significant advantages over paper-and-pencil measures such as the JAS, and the subjective, SI-derived judgments for assessing coronary-prone behavior.

The methodological problems associated with the SI for assessing the TABP is the focus of Chapter 6 by Scherwitz. He introduces the issue with a detailed historical review of the SI, in which he shows that over the years there have been important changes in the administration of the SI—from a moderately reflective, to a provocative, back to a more reflective interviewing strategy—and that such variations in interviewer behavior affect the interviewee's behavior type (evidence for the latter conclusion is also presented in Siegman's chapter). Most disturbing is the evidence presented by Scherwitz that although extraordinary efforts were made in the MRFIT study to ensure standard administration and scoring of the SI, there remained wide variations in both its administration and scoring. These findings plus a statistical reanalysis of the published data on the SI's reliability, lead Scherwitz to conclude that these data overestimate the reliability of SI-derived TABP scores obtained in the field.

Assessment issues are also the focus of Friedman's chapter (Chapter 7). The results of a meta-analysis of 79 coronary-prone behavior studies showed that the combined effect size of the relationship between TABP measures and coronary heart disease outcomes was .16, which is significant but small. A comparison of the results obtained for the two primary measures of TABP—the SI and the JAS—revealed that the SI has a much stronger association with disease outcome than does the JAS. Finally, and most importantly, it showed that only some of the components of the TABP construct, specifically, aggressive hostility and competitiveness, are related to disease endpoints and that others, such as job involvement and speed, are not. Another interesting result of that meta-analysis is that depression correlated significantly with disease endpoints, and at a higher level than the global Type-A coronary disease relationship ($.21, p < .001$). It may very well be that, in our preoccupation with global Type-A, we have neglected other potential coronary-prone behaviors. That depression may play such a role is not that surprising given recent findings that depressed attributional style is related to a number of other disease outcomes (Peterson & Seligman, 1987). We need to distinguish, however, between behaviors that are related to *self-reported* symptoms, to objectively verified diseases of all sorts and to specific CHD endpoints (e.g., angina documented myocardial infarction).

Another personality dimension whose role in CHD needs further clarification is anxiety and neuroticism. Friedman reports a small but significant positive relationship between anxiety and CHD. This seems contrary to a widely held assumption, based on clinical impressions, that coronary-prone individuals are not anxious (e.g., Chesney, Black, Chadwick, & Rosenman, 1981), and to empirical evidence of a significant negative correlation between anxiety-neuroticism and severity of CAD (Costa et al., Chapter 3; Siegman, Chapter 4).

Perhaps the most intriguing point in Friedman's chapter is his distinction between vigorous expressive behavior (the charismatic personality) that is not coronary prone, and expressive anger and hostility which may be a coronary-prone tendency. A further distinction is between the "true," relaxed Type B and an individual who lacks expressiveness because of repression or depression. It remains to be seen whether such refinements will improve the ability of the Type-A construct to predict disease outcome. In a study by Friedman it did, when the TABP was indexed by the JAS but not when indexed by the SI.

Chapter 5 by Timothy W. Smith attempts to place the research on coronary-prone behavior within the broader context of current thinking in personality theory. From the very beginning, Rosenman and Friedman (1974) have pointed out that they do not conceive of Type-A as a static personality trait. Instead, their conception of Type-A is consistent with the person-by-situation interaction model of personality. According to this model, overt Type-A behavior and pathogenic physiological reactions occur *only* when Type-As encounter situations involving difficult tasks, threats to self-esteem, threats to control or interpersonal conflict. Smith, however, suggests that rather than simply responding to challenges and demands, Type-A persons seem to create them (see Suls & Sanders, Chapter 1). Through their characteristic ways of choosing situations, thinking and behaving toward others, Type-As increase the frequency, severity, and durations of stressors in their daily lives. Moreover, challenging and demanding situations are likely to reinforce and maintain predispositions toward Type-A behavior, rather than simply eliciting or activating them. This formulation is consistent with the currently in vogue, dynamic interactional, or transactional, approach to personality (Snyder & Ickes, 1985; Bandura, 1977; Magnusson & Endler, 1977; Mischel, 1977). Of course, a similar dynamic interactional approach can be applied to the hostility-CHD relationship.

Most importantly, Smith clearly articulates the methodological implications of the three major approaches to the Type-A-CHD relationship (the classical "trait" approach vs. the statistical interactional approach, vs. the dynamic interactional approach). It would seem to be the case, however, that there is a discrepancy between researchers' theoretical positions on the Type-A-CHD relationship and their actual research paradigms. Although theoretically most researchers seem to espouse an interactional approach (statistical or dynamic), most actual research paradigms reflect the classical "trait" approach. Clearly, we need to develop research paradigms that are more consistent with current thinking in personality theory.

The work place should provide an ideal setting for testing the transactional hypothesis that Type-A or hostile personalities may by their behavior shape their environment so that it is conducive to emotional arousal and CHD. In Chapter 8, Ganster, Sime, and Hayes review the relevant field research, as well as a recent study of their own on the moderating effect of the TABP on perceived work stress and reactivity in stressful work situations. Although they found a number of significant differences between Type As and Bs, they do not all fit neatly into a simple hyper-reactivity model. For example, Type Bs were physiologically more responsive than As to role conflict and ambiguity. Type As, on the other hand, tend to show higher cardiovascular responses when they perceive that their work load is high. Such data seem most consistent with a person-environment fit model that assumes that Type As prefer some work environments and Bs other ones, and that both will show emotional and physiological strain in inappropriate (for them) work environments.

One interesting finding, reported by Ganster, Sime, and Hayes, is that individual components of global Type-A related differentially to the appraisal of specific sources of work stress. Thus, the competitiveness and hostility components were primarily related to interpersonal work stressors such as role conflict, role ambiguity, and responsibility without authority. On the other hand, intense speech patterns and impatience were associated with stress resulting from work demands requiring effort and adjustment (work load and variability). Again and again, the empirical findings reinforce the need to go beyond global Type-A. We need to look at its individual components and beyond that at other potential coronary-prone behaviors.

Williams (Chapter 9) discusses various static and dynamic physiological processes including neuroendocrine activity that may be associated with pathophysiological mechanisms whereby behavior may participate in the development of CHD. His work on the subject represents some of the most advanced thinking in this complex and critically important area. The final chapter by Manuck (Chapter 10) presents some of the latest and most exciting work using animal models to illustrate how physiologic processes similar to those observed in humans can be related to the extent of CHD in animals. If this work proves successful, it will provide a methodology of enormous potential for examining the relationship between behavioral variables and basic pathophysiological mechanisms.

REFERENCES

Bandura, A. (1977). *Social learning theory.* Englewood Cliffs, NJ: Prentice-Hall.

Chesney, M., Black, G., Chadwick, J., & Rosenman, R. (1981). Psychological correlates of the coronary-prone behavior pattern. *Journal of Behavioral Medicine, 24,* 217–220.

Magnusson, D., & Endler, N. S. (1977). Interactional psychology: Present status and future prospects. In D. Magnusson & N. S. Endler (Eds.), *Personality at the crossroads: Current issues in interactional psychology* (pp. 3–31). Hillsdale, NJ: Lawrence Erlbaum Associates.

Mischel, W. (1979). On the interface of cognition and personality. *American Psychologist, 34,* 740–754.

Peterson, C., & Seligman, M. E. P. (1987). Explanatory style and illness. *Journal of Personality, 55,* 237–265.

Rosenman, R. H., & Friedman, M. (1974). Neurogenic factors in pathogenesis of coronary heart disease. *Medical Clinics of North America, 58,* 269–279.

Snyder, M., & Ickes, W. (1985). Personality and social behavior. In G. Linzey & E. Aronson (Eds.), *Handbook of social psychology, third edition.* New York: Random House.

1 Why Do Some Behavioral Styles Place People at Coronary Risk?

Jerry Suls and Glenn S. Sanders
State University of New York at Albany

Over three decades of empirical study suggest that certain behavior patterns place people at greater risk of developing coronary heart disease. In 1981 the Review Panel on Coronary-Prone Behavior and CHD (Cooper, Detre, & Weiss, 1981) concluded that people exhibiting a pattern of behavior called Type A were twice as likely to acquire premature CHD as those, called Type Bs, who did not exhibit this pattern. The Type A pattern is an environmentally provoked syndrome consisting of excessive competitiveness, impatience, and hostility. Actually, as many of the chapters in this volume indicate, the conclusions of the Review Panel may have been premature. More recent studies suggest that only certain components of the behavioral complex may be predictive of CHD. For example, data point to the importance of hostility (Dembroski, et al., 1985; Williams, Barefoot, & Shekelle, 1985) and self-involvement (Scherwitz, Berton, & Leventhal, 1978; Scherwitz et al., 1983; also see chapters by Dembroski, Scherwitz, & Williams in this volume).

Whether it is global Type A or some subcomponents of Type A that carry the associative burden with CHD, the question concerns how a behavioral style can place a person at coronary risk. The purpose of this chapter is to review potential mechanisms or processes by which behavior might facilitate the development of CHD. By proposing a taxonomy of causes, reviewing relevant past literature and pointing to gaps in the empirical literature, we hope to provide a framework for future efforts on coronary-prone behavior. To anticipate our general thesis, we observe that one causal explanation has received much more empirical attention than two other alternatives. In lieu of several considerations that are described in this chapter, it may be profitable for researches to give the other possibilities more attention.

1

THREE BEHAVIORAL ROUTES TO CHD

There are three logical ways in which a behavior pattern might be associated with CHD or sudden cardiac death risk status. First, the behavior pattern might be a marker of some underlying *inborn structural weakness* that makes CHD or sudden cardiac death more likely. The second mechanism, which has been widely discussed and researched, is the behavior pattern's possible association with exaggerated psychophysiological reactivity to certain situational circumstances, the *hyperresponsitivity hypothesis*, and this reactivity may in turn increase the atherosclerotic process. The third possibility, the *dangerous situations hypothesis*, is that Type A's are exposed or expose themselves to inherently more risky circumstances dangerous to cardiovascular health. For example, they may delay in seeking medical attention after experiencing angina symptoms. Of course, these three possibilities are not mutually exclusive; all may plausibly contribute to the higher risk status of certain individuals. In the following sections, we present a review of the literature regarding each of these explanations. Because our purpose is to point out problems, provide a taxonomy, and suggest new research directions, the review is selective.

Structural Weakness

The first possibility we examine is one of an overt behavior pattern, which may be an indicator of some inborn physical weakness or abnormality of the cardiovascular or related systems that increases the development of atherosclerosis or sudden death. For example, perhaps Type A's possess arterial walls that are physiologically more conducive to the occurrence of lesions; or perhaps Type A's have a genetically acquired tendency toward ECG abnormality. This hypothesis suggests that the so-called risky behavior is itself harmless, merely serving to indicate the presence of some preexisting abnormality.

An inborn structural explanation for the link between Type A and CHD has generally been given little credence. In fact, it is rarely mentioned as a potential causal mechanism. Lack of interest in this avenue of explanation is a result in part of early study of Type A's prospective role as a predictor of premature CHD mortality and morbidity. Rosenman et al. (1975) found that Type A was related to a twofold risk for CHD even when controlling for traditional risk factors, such as basal level blood pressure, diabetes, parental CHD history, and serum levels of cholesterol, triglyceride, and lipoproteins. These data suggested that Type A is an independent risk factor that exerts its pathogenic influence via mechanisms other than the standard risk factors.

In particular, the finding that Type A remains a significant risk factor after controlling for parental CHD history appears to be a strong argument against the role of genetic–structural differences. Also, recent evidence suggests that family history of CHD does not account for the association between hostility and degree of arterial occlusion (MacDougall, Dembroski, Dimsdale, & Hackett, 1985). However, it is possible that there were some false negatives (i.e., parents with angina or even MIs that went undetected) in these data sets. Also, the fact that parents did not have a history of CHD does not rule out more distant genetic influences.

This raises the issue of the heritability of Type A behavior. Unfortunately, there is a limited amount of information on the heritability of Type A behavior, but what is available suggests that at least some aspects of the pattern may indeed be inherited. Rosenman et al. (1974) administered the Structured Interview and the Jenkins Activity Survey to monozyotic and dyzygotic twin pairs. The results showed no significant heritability of global Type A as assessed by the SI. Analysis of the JAS data suggested that only the Speed/Impatience component of the scale appeared to be heritable.

In a related study, Matthews and Krantz (1976) administered the JAS to college-aged twins. The investigators found that only the Hard-driving component of the JAS was heritable. This result contradicts the positive findings for Speed–impatience reported by Rosenman et al. (1974). However, any results on heritability using the JAS should be interpreted cautiously because the JAS and its sub-scales do not predict CHD after controlling for other risk factors (Dembroski & Costa, 1987; Matthews & Haynes, 1986).

In a reanalysis of the Rosenman et al. data set, Matthews, Rosenman, and Dembroski (1984) coded a number of dimensions of the SI data for the mz and dz twin pairs. The results showed that the mz correlations for loudness of speech, competition for control of the interview, and potential for hostility were twice the size of the comparable dz correlations. Matthews and Rakaczny (in press) observe that all these dimensions share a common element—a general hyperresponsivity to challenge. Thus, it is possible that the cardiovascular hyperreactivity to environmental challenge that characterizes the Type A may have a heritable base.

Krantz and Durel (1983) have also proposed that there may be a constitutional basis for A–B differences in cardiovascular reactivity. They point to a study by Kahn and his associates (1980), finding that even while under general anesthesia for coronary artery bypass surgery, before maintenance on the heart-lung pump, Type A's evidenced greater increases over hospital admission blood pressure than Type B's. Krantz and Durel propose that Type A hyperresponsivity may be non-consciously mediated and constitutional in nature. They also note, however, that Kahn's use of admission baseline to calculate increases is somewhat problematic because one cannot determine whether increases were accounted for by elevations occurring during surgery when patients were anesthetized, as opposed to increases over admission blood pressure occurring prior to surgery when patients were fully awake.

Krantz, Arabian, Davia, and Parker (1982) conducted a replication and extension study that took an additional measure of blood pressure at onset of surgery. Their results showed that intensity of Type A behavior was positively related to intraoperative increases in systolic blood pressure occurring during surgery when patients were anesthetized. In contrast, Type A behavior was not related to blood pressure changes occurring prior to surgery. Krantz et al. concluded that there may be an underlying psychobiological basis for SI-defined Type A behavior because increased cardiovascular responses were observed under conditions where conscious perceptual mediation was minimized. Krantz and Durel also argue that the constitutional responsivity may be antecedent to Type A behaviors. Specifically, the underlying SNS responsivity may be the cause of impatience, hostility, and speech patterns exhibited by Type A individuals.

If Type A's are constitutionally, physiologically hyperresponsive, the greater SNS and adrenomedullary activity may result in increased coronary atheroslerosis and subsequent CHD. In this sense, Type A behavior may only be a marker of a physiologic process that increases coronary risk status. Krantz and Durel's proposal does have some problems. The major one is most studies (reviewed in the next section) find that Type A's and B's differ on physiologic parameters only in situations perceived to be stressful by the individual and do not differ in resting levels. If there is a constitutional difference in responsivity, why is it not exhibited during baseline periods? Also, though conscious mediation is minimized under anesthesia, the controversy (see Lazarus, 1984; Leventhal, 1982, Zajonc, 1984) about what constitutes a conscious versus a nonconscious state makes it very difficult to evaluate the Kahn and Krantz experiments. Additional research assessing A–B differences in other kinds of situations involving nonconscious mediation are needed to evaluate the Krantz–Durel proposal.

Aside from the possibility of constitutional differences in responsivity, there have been no systematic studies of structural differences in physiological systems between A's and B's (or hostile vs. nonhostile persons). Note that certain ECG abnormalities have been identified as risk factors for CHD (Kannel & Schatzkin, 1983; Verrier, DeSilva, & Lown, 1983), but, to our knowledge, their relationship to Type A has not been studied. This is important because about 50% of the deaths from CHD are sudden, and, of these sudden deaths, in only 25% is there an acute coronary thrombosis that precipitated the event (Perper, Kuller, & Cooper, 1975). As Pickering (1985) observes "This means that in the other 75%, death is due to a transient event, which is usually presumed to be an arrhythmia" (p. 209). It remains for future study to determine whether Type A's are more likely to exhibit cardiac arrhythmias than Type B's.

Another way in which the risk of sudden death might be increased involves platelet aggregation. There is evidence that the average clotting time of Type A's is significantly faster than B's (e.g., Friedman & Rosenman, 1959). This is not necessarily a manifestation of a structural difference because the discharge of catecholamines is believed to potentiate platelet aggregation, and stress increases the secretion of catecholamines. Hence, faster clotting times may be a reaction to the stressful lives Type A's create for themselves rather than an inborn structural physiologic tendency. Nonetheless, more empirical attention should be given to careful study of A–B differences in platelet aggregation. Of course, a major stumbling block to this type of study is that detection of structural weakness in Type A's does not mean it is necessarily inborn. This makes the inborn structural explanation a difficult one to prove.

To summarize, there is little evidence that supports the notion that Type A behavior is a marker and the result of some underlying structural defect that increases the coronary risk of Type A's. In fact, the only reasonably direct support consists of indications of heritability for some parts of the Type A pattern. But even after controlling for known physiologic risk factors such as blood pressure and family history, Type A and hostility remain significant risk factors. Nonetheless, the inborn weakness hypothesis cannot be dismissed with any confidence. Only direct comparative studies of the hemodynamic and structural properties of the cardiovascular system and related systems (such as the neuroendocrine system) in Type A's and B's can provide a strong test of the structural hypothesis. And only a further series of genetic analyses can determine if any such structural differences exist prior to and independently of overt behavioral style.

Such research will require a closer collaboration between the medical and psychological disciplines than is usually seen. We recognize that this line of research may be viewed with considerable cynicism because there is no obvious or cogent reason to explain why a structural defect of the cardiovascular system would be associated with a behavior pattern characterized by impatience, competitiveness, and hostility. Only the proposal made by Krantz regarding responsivity explains plausibly how responsivity can be a risk factor *and* also produce (or at least contribute to) the expression of Type A behavior. In any case, the structural defect explanation is a logical possibility and has been understudied. We think that researchers put this explanation aside once they were assured that Type A was not exerting its effects through the conventional physiologic risk factors. This may have been a premature judgment.

HYPERRESPONSIVITY

The most popular working hypothesis linking Type A or hostility to heart disease is that coronary-prone individuals exhibit higher levels of cardiovascular and neuroendocrine arousal that increase the atherosclerotic process and/or the incidence of life-threatening cardiac arrhythmias. To validate this hypothesis one needs to show: (1) that reactivity creates physiologic changes that eventuate in coronary disease; and (2) that persons who are high on a behavioral risk factor for CHD (such as Type A or hostility) show higher levels of reactivity.

There is a growing body of evidence relevant to the first point. For example, we know that in the face of stress, SNS arousal produces increases in blood pressure that may produce damage to the inner lining of arterial vessels due to turbulence and shear stress (Ross & Glomset, 1976). In addition, SNS arousal appears to produce alterations in the metabolism of myocardial cells and increases the deposition and incorporation into coronary artery plaques of thromboembolitic components of the blood. There is also evidence that SNS arousal facilitates the necrosis, calcification, and rupture of placques, which in turn could produce thrombosis and myocardial infarction. Furthermore, catecholamines can interact with existing atherosclerosis to result in ventricular fibrillation and sudden coronary death.

The pituitary–adrenocortical system may also play a contributing role because stress leads to prolonged elevations of plasma corticosteroids (Bronson & Eleftheriou, 1965). Positive associations between elevated plasma cortisol and early atherosclerosis have been shown by coronary angiography (Troxler, et al., 1977).

Although these converging lines of evidence make a case for the role of physiologic reactivity in CHD, the *critical level* of stress or reactivity that translates into disease pathology is not known. Nor is it clear how this could be established empirically at the present time. There is provocative evidence that reactivity considered on a molar level contributes to cardiovascular pathology. Manuck, Kaplan, and Clarkson (1983) identified male cynomologus monkeys, fed a moderately atherogenic diet, as either high- or low-heart rate reactive animals (upper or lower 35%), based on their cardiac responses to a laboratory stressor (threat of capture). Following necropsy, the high-heart rate reactive animals had developed nearly twice the coronary artery atherosclerosis of their low-heart rate reactive counterparts. These data are certainly quite consistent with a reactivity-CHD linkage; however, note that heart rate measurement was recorded on only a single occasion and at a time shortly before termination of the animals so the study cannot be considered prospective. Another factor complicating interpretation of the results is that the animals were fed a high-risk diet. Was diet, reactivity, and/or the combination of diet and reactivity responsible for the greater degree of atherosclerosis in the high reactors?

Only *prospective* studies can demonstrate that autonomic, sympathetic, and related neuroendocrine reactivity is a risk factor for the development of CHD. Given the cost, complexity, and present limitations of measurement procedures for studying this multifaceted process in humans, it is likely that animal models will have to suffice for some time. Nonetheless, behavioral scientists have found the existing evidence sufficiently convincing to make the tentative assumption of a reactivity–disease linkage (Dembroski, MacDougall, Herd, & Shields, 1983). This has encouraged research on the second critical assumption—do individuals with high-risk status exhibit hyperreactivity?

Physiologic Reactivity in Type A's and B's

In the last decade, a considerable number of studies have examined potential differences in Type A–B reactivity. These studies have been reviewed by Matthews (1982), Dembroski et al. (1983), Houston (1983), Holmes (1983), and more recently by Contrada, Wright, and Glass (1985). There is a general consensus that Type A's do not differ from B's in casual physiologic levels (baseline: no stressor). However, A's are characterized by more extreme sympathetic reactivity when confronted by challenging or demanding situations (Houston, 1983). There would be little reason for us to reiterate these points if the reliability and size of this relationship were not a matter of some debate. In fact, there is dissensus in this literature (Contrada et al., 1985; Holmes, 1983).

In his review, Houston (1983) claimed that Type A's manifest greater psychophysiological arousal than Type B's in solitary as well as interpersonal situations in which there is a moderate incentive and an intermediate probability of success. Holmes (1983) pointed out, however, that Houston did not take into account the many null effects in the studies he reviewed. For example, if a study measured three reactivity indices under two task conditions, there were six possible comparisons between A's and B's. If any one of the comparisons yielded a significantly larger mean for Type A's, Houston counted the study as an instance of greater reactivity in Type A's, in spite of the five null comparisons. Retabulating Houston's data with null effects, Holmes found that 25% of the studies had reliable A/B differences in heart rate (HR), 22% found differences in diastolic blood pressure (DBP), and 65% reported Type A's reacted with significantly higher systolic blood pressure (SBP) than Type B's. Holmes concluded that the only reliable difference between A's and B's was in terms of systolic blood pressure reactivity, and it was quite modest in size.

Recently, Contrada, Wright, and Glass (1985) have commented on these previous reviews, pointing out that Holmes did not distinguish between various methods of assessing Pattern A (i.e., the Structured Interview versus the JAS). In their review, they find greater support for A/B effects on SBP by distinguishing findings associated with the SI from those obtained using the JAS, and by excluding studies with methodological problems. Contrada et al. also note that inconsistency in SI findings for HR and DBP do not necessarily weaken support for an association between Pattern A and heightened sympathetic responsiveness. For example, sympathetic effects on HR may be offset by cardiac-inhibiting parasympathetic influences that have a greater influence on HR than SBP. With these considerations in mind, Contrada et al. conclude: "At minimum the data are consistent with the hypothesized role of sympathetic reactivity in mediating the relationship between Type A behavior and coronary disease" (p. 25).

Although the Contrada et al. review makes some finer distinctions than its predecessors, we still find all the reviews somewhat problematic because they rely on the vote-counting narrative review, where the extent of support for a hypothesis is trichotomized into positive, null, or negative findings. Such an approach is unable to detail the strength of support for a hypothesis. Findings that do not reach statistical significance may be taken as evidence that a variable has no effect, but this ignores the impact of statistical power (Hedges & Olkin, 1985). Moreover, a narrative approach can only provide a very approximate notion of the magnitude of a variable's effect (i.e., effect size) and cannot determine whether the effect sizes from different studies come from a common population, that is, are homogeneous. Only if effect sizes are homogeneous is it appropriate to average the magnitude of effects across studies and generalize across studies (see Hedges, 1982). Because narrative reviews cannot provide such quantitative information, an alternative way was sought to evaluate existing findings on Type A/B reactivity.

A Meta-analytic Approach

Recent advances in research synthesis, mainly meta-analytic techniques, can provide the kinds of quantitative information that are needed (e.g., G. Glass, 1977;

Hedges & Olkin, 1985; Rosenthal, 1984). A recent dissertation by one of our students, Barbara A. Fletcher, was a meta-analysis of the literature on A/B reactivity. Sixty-one studies examining Type A/B reactivity to stressors were located through *Psychological Abstracts* and *Index Medicus*. For each outcome in a study, an effect size d was computed. Cohen (1977) and Hedges (1982) define d as:

$$d = \frac{Ma - Mb}{SD}$$

where Ma and Mb are the means of the two groups (Type A's and Type B's). SD is the pooled within-group standard deviation. The d was given a positive value if Type A was associated with higher CVR; a negative value, if Type B was associated with higher CVR. Before computing an average $\bar{d}$ across studies, a chi-square statistic, H, was used to test whether the study d's were homogeneous (i.e., came from a common population). If the study set effect sizes were homogeneous, then an average effect size, $\bar{d}$, was computed and the null hypothesis tested (i.e., Is the average effect size significantly greater than zero?). If study effect sizes were heterogeneous, no inferential statistics were calculated. However, clustering procedures were then used to try to identify homogeneous study subsets (Hedges & Olkin, 1983).

The basic hypothesis tested, for each of 12 physiologic indices, was that Type A's exhibit greater reactivity than Type B's.[1] Table 1.1 shows the results of these analyses. For 10 of the 12 indices, the effect sizes were homogeneous (indicated by a nonsignificant H), thus permitting an average $\bar{d}$ to be calculated. Six of the 10 homogeneous measures had significant $\bar{d}$'s, that is, were statistically different from zero. Type A's showed greater reactivity across studies on heart rate, diastolic blood pressure, serum epinephrine, and serum norepinephrine. The two significant negative $\bar{d}$'s indicated that Type B's showed higher forearm vascular resistance and urinary epinephrine. It is worth emphasizing that, because the effect sizes for these 10 parameters were homogeneous, they would not be altered by further partitioning of study subsets, for example, breakdowns by gender or age of sample.

The findings for HR are interesting because Contrada et al's review suggested that HR differences in A's and B's occur only when Pattern A was measured with the SI. In contrast, the homogeneity of the HR outcome subset indicates that partitioning by type of A/B instrument (or any other variable) would not yield different $\bar{d}$'s. The meta-analysis also found an A/B effect for diastolic blood pressure, whereas neither Houston, Holmes, or Contrada et al. reported such an effect. The size of the effect is small ($\bar{d} = .07$) and was probably detected because of the greater precision of the meta-analytic method. There were several other significant $\bar{d}$'s, suggesting there are A/B differences on more parameters than previous reviews indicate. Conclusions should be cautious, however, because there

---

[1]Some studies used additional measures, but they were not included here if the measures were used too infrequently (e.g., pulse pressure) or are not obviously implicated in the pathogenesis of coronary disease (e.g., finger pulse volume).

TABLE 1.1.
Type A versus Type B by CVR Measure

Variable	H	p	$\bar{d}$	C.I.	p
			Heterogeneity		
1. Heart rate	—	ns	.12	.07 − .12	.001
2. Systolic blood pressure	316.3	.0001	.32	— —	—
3. Diastolic blood pressure	—	ns	.07	.02 − .12	.05
4. Pulse transit time	—	ns	.01	− 18 − .20	ns
5. Forearm bloodflow	15.6	.05	.04	— —	—
6. Forearm vascular resistance	—	ns	− .40	− .69 − − .11	.005
7. Serum epinephrine	—	ns	.21	.06 − .36	.005
8. Serum norepinephrine	—	ns	.14	− .01 − .29	.05
9. Urinary epinephrine	—	ns	.01	− .23 − .24	ns
10. Urinary norepinephrine	—	ns	− .33	− .56 − − .09	.005
11. Heart rate variability	—	ns	.00	− .13 − .12	ns
12. Cortisol	—	ns	.03	− .18 − .23	ns

Note: *H* represents the approximate chi-square value for the test of effect size homogeneity. A significant *H* indicates the effect sizes were heterogeneous. $\bar{d}$ is the average effect size. C.I. is the effect size 95% confidence interval. When the effect size subset is heterogeneous, it is not appropriate to calculate a confidence interval for the effect size.

are relatively few data points for some of the CVR parameters.

The unexpected result was the heterogeneity of the SBP outcomes that takes on added importance because blood pressure is one of the few parameters that experts agree is quite meaningful as an index of reactivity and presents few measurement problems (Schneiderman & Pickering, 1986). Moreover, though they disagreed on other points, Houston, Holmes, and Contrada et al. claimed there were consistent effects of A/B on SBP. Our meta-analytic results suggest there is considerable heterogeneity across studies, rendering such a conclusion premature.

To explore the source of the heterogeneity, we considered the possibility that it might be the result of aggregating the results of studies using the SI and the JAS. A number of biobehavioral researchers propose that the SI is a better measure of coronary proneness than the JAS, so reactivity may be more strongly related to SI-assessed Type A behavior (e.g., Dembroski et al., 1983). Perhaps the combining strong effects of the SI with weak effects associated with the JAS was responsible for the heterogeneous effect sizes. To test this notion, the subset of SI studies reporting SPB values was compared to the subset of JAS studies with SBP outcomes. Contrary to our speculation, both these subsets yielded highly heterogeneous effect sizes ($H = 121.83$; $p < .0001$ for the SI group; $H = 131.76$, $p < .0001$ for the JAS group).

Another possibility contributing to SBP heterogeneity may be that only certain stressors elicit consistent levels of reactivity from SI-assessed Type A's. Indeed, a number of theorists suggest that reactivity differences are most likely to occur when the Type A finds the task moderately challenging or when some

TABLE 1.2.
Analyses of Type A-SBP Outcomes Cross-Classified by SI/JAS
and the Presence/Absence of Harassment

Variable	H	p	d	C.I.	p
SI/no harassment	104.2	.0001	.50	— —	—
SI/harassment	—	ns	.13	−.11 − .36	ns
JAS/no harassment	125.0	.0001	.20	— —	—
JAS/harassment	—	ns	.17	−.08 − .43	ns

Note: H represents the approximate chi-square value for the test of effect size homogeneity. A significant H indicates the effect sizes were heterogeneous. $\bar{d}$ is the average effect size.
C.I. is the effect size 95% confidence interval. When the effect size subset is heterogeneous,
it is not appropriate to calculate a confidence interval for the effect size.

social harassment is involved (e.g., Glass, 1977; Houston, 1983; Matthews, 1982).
Perhaps the preceding analyses for SBP are heterogeneous because tasks and measurement were collapsed across high or low challenge or high or low harassment.
To examine this possibility, a number of study subsets were identified, which,
from a theoretical perspective, should elicit consistent reactivity differences. One
subanalysis was based on the hypothesis that subjects classified as Type A by
the SI would be more reactive to situations having components of harassment
because the SI classification depends heavily on the individual's response to interviewer provocation. In contrast, it was predicted that subjects classified as Type
A by the JAS would not be as reactive to harassment. Presumably, if we are correct, homogeneous effect sizes should emerge for each study subset.

Four subsets of studies were identified: SI—harassment, SI—no harassment,
JAS—harassment, JAS—no harassment. Table 1.2 shows the results of the meta-
analytic partitioning. Chi-square tests for heterogeneity were performed on each
study subset. The two subsets of studies involving harassment each had homogeneous effect sizes but their mean $\bar{d}$'s were nonsignificant, suggesting that whether
the SI or JAS was used to classify subjects makes little difference in this case.
The two subsets that included no harassment were heterogeneous (SI: $H = 105.18$,
$p < .0001$; JAS: $H = 124.97$, $p < .0001$). It appears that partitioning in terms
of assessment device and harassment was unsuccessful in identifying the source
of the heterogeneity. In any case, when homogeneous subsets were found, the
average $\bar{d}$'s were statistically nonsignificant.

The preceding analyses show that the heterogeneity associated with systolic
blood pressure remains even after partitioning studies along theoretical lines.
Several other attempts were made to identify homogeneous study subsets: partitioning according to gender, age of subjects, and stressor type, but heterogeneity
was found consistently. We also used a purely exploratory approach involving
clustering procedures developed by Hedges and Olukin (1985) (analogous to
posthoc comparisons used after analysis of variance). These attempts also failed
to identify any meaningful homogeneous study clusters.

There appears to be considerable variability in the results of studies comparing Type A/B reactivity in terms of SBP. As a result, at the present time, it is

inappropriate to make any strong statements about the relationship between SBP reactivity and Type A. Perhaps as additional research becomes available, a readily interpretable pattern and explanation for the heterogeneity will be found. Specifically, study of reactivity as a function of Type subcomponent behaviors such as potential for hostility or self-involvement may reveal homogeneous effects. Currently, there are too few studies available to assess these possibilities. Also, ambulatory monitoring of reactivity in coronary-prone individuals during normal daily activities may provide insights into this problem (Pickering et al., 1982).

Magnitude of the Effects

The reader may agree that the heterogeneity associated with the SBP outcomes is problematic but still point to the homogeneous and significant effects for such parameters as DBP and HR. However, the size of these effects should be kept in mind. To put them in perspective, it is worth mentioning that Jacob Cohen (1977) proposes that d's of .2 to .49 be considered small, .5 to .79 moderate, and .8 and above large. On the basis of this somewhat arbitrary classification scheme, the reactivity associated with Pattern A appears quite modest (d's ranged from .01 to .32). In a similar vein, Holmes (1983) calculated a median difference of 6 mm. Hg. between A's and B's on SBP. He questioned, as do we, whether this small difference could have pathogenic significance.

Even though the magnitude of reported differences between Pattern A and reactivity is small, the difference could be consequential if Type A's exceed B's with respect to the frequency and/or duration of hyperresponsive episodes over the course of a lifetime (Contrada et al., 1983). This notion has been discussed at length by Smith and Rhodewalt (1986). They make a distinction between two models of reactivity. The first, underlying much of the research in this area, has been labeled the *recurrent activation model* (Krantz & Manuck, 1984). This model claims that the highly reactive Type A individual responds to laboratory or real-life stressors with greater increases in reactivity than does the less reactive Type B individual. Smith and Rhodewalt argue that this model is limited because its focus is on differential responses to specific situations that are equivalent for Type A and B persons. More recent personality approaches (e.g., Cantor & Kilhstrom, 1981) suggest that persons and situations interact actively. Hence, according to Smith and Rhodewalt (1986), ''Rather then merely possessing a set of stressful coping behaviors that are elicited by challenging situations, Type As through their choices, appraisals and self-evaluations actively operate upon their environments in ways that should influence the frequency, duration and intensity of stressors, and, as a result, episodes of cardovascular reactivity.'' This approach, which they call the *transactional model*, contends that Type A's show greater reactivity and greater overall arousal because not only do they respond more strongly, but they also create more frequent sources of stress for themselves.

Smith and Rhodewalt cite a number of studies showing that Type A's choose or make situations stressful. For example, they carry more credit hours and spend more time in unpaid activities while expecting a higher grade point average than

Type B students (Ovcharchyn, Johnson, & Petzel, 1981). They also choose to work on problems of greater difficulty (Holmes, McGilly, & Houston, 1984), perceive their partners as more hard driving and competitive (Smith & Brehm, 1981), are more distracted by the presence of others when working (Gastorf, Suls, & Sanders, 1980), and refuse to delegate control to another person even when that person is better able to perform the task (Miller, Lack, & Asroff, 1985; Strube, Berry, & Moegen, 1985). We have also found that Type A's report more stressful life events than B's, presumably the result of A's more active life-styles (Byrne, 1981; see also Rhodewalt, Hayes, Chemers, & Wysocki, 1984; Suls, Gastorf, & Witenberg, 1979).

Although the transactional model is consistent with the published literature, the evidence suggesting that Type A's tend to create stressful environments comes mainly from studies using the JAS as the assessment tool. However, as already noted, the association between the JAS and CHD, after controlling for the traditional risk factors, is small and nonsignificant (see Dembroski & Costa, 1987; Matthews & Haynes, 1986). Whether Type A's assessed by the SI create stressful circumstances for themselves across time and situations needs more empirical attention.

The related question of whether *hostility* is relatively stable across situations has also received little attention in the literature. There are two instruments used most often in coronary-prone research to assess hostility: subcomponent scoring of the SI and the Cook and Medley (1954) Hostility scale (Ho) SI-ratings of hostility are made on the basis of subject behaviors (mainly verbal and nonverbal stylistics) in response to interviewer provocation. This measure presumably taps environmentally provoked hostility. In contrast, the Cook-Medley is a scale derived from the Minnesota Multiphasic Personality Inventory (MMPI) and presumably is a trait measure because it inquires about relatively stable tendencies of the individual. Correlations between the two measures are modest (MacDougall et al., 1985) so they do not appear to be measuring the same thing. Clearly, the two measures should not be used interchangeably. Whether the differences are the result of the trait versus situational focus remains to be examined. Again, the question for the consistency and stability of hostile behaviors is critical, especially if the magnitude of the reactivity differences between high- and low-hostile individuals is small.

Of course, even if one shows that Type A individuals are chronically reactive, this still does not answer the more critical questions: What frequency and duration of reactivity is "toxic" and is it characteristic of Type A individuals? Only a very costly, time-consuming program of research can answer these questions. It is not even clear that the methods are available at the present time to mount such a study. This does not mean that the hyperresponsivity hypothesis should be discarded. However, given the difficulty of obtaining conclusive data, it may be wise to consider other explanations for the association of behavioral risk factors and CHD, for example, the structural weakness hypothesis or the alternative discussed in the next section.

DANGEROUS SITUATIONS EXPLANATION

The dangerous situations hypothesis proposes that individuals high in Type A or hostility are at greater risk because they are exposed to inherently more risky circumstances more often than are Type B's. It is important to distinguish this view from the hyperresponsivity hypothesis. The dangerous situations approach does not contend or require that Type A's or hostile persons are coronary prone because they are more physiologically reactive to stress than people low in risk status. Rather, it is hypothesized that Type A risk is the result of routine physiological reactivity to abnormally stressful situations.

Like the Structural Weakness hypothesis, this notion has received little attention. We suspect the reason is that exposure to some inherently dangerous situations, such as smoking, has been controlled for statistically and the association between Type A (or Hostility) and CHD remains (see Dembroski et al., 1985; Rosenman et al., 1975). Hence, it appears that the behavioral style per se makes its own independent contribution. However, the tendency of this behavioral style to expose people to inherently dangerous situations may still be involved in the coronary risk carried by Type A.

One "dangerous situation" candidate is the tendency to delay seeking medical attention. There is a fairly consistent body of evidence showing that Type A's tend to underreport the severity of physical symptoms under conditions of challenge (Carver, Coleman, & Glass, 1976; Weidner & Matthews, 1978). Some years ago, Friedman and Rosenman (1974) hypothesized that Type A's might delay seeking medical attention until symptoms become quite severe. As Matthews (1982) observed "If this should occur during the development of atherosclerosis in the coronary arteries, then Type A's might wait until the symptoms of the disease become incapacitating, rather than seeking treatment early when alteration of behaviors to less stress-inducing forms would be beneficial" (p. 314). From this perspective, Type A's and B's might have the same underlying disease, but the former fail to take appropriate measures, thus increasing their risk status.

The preceding explanation fails to acknowledge the findings of angiography studies showing that Type A's have more coronary artery occlusion than Type B's, suggesting there is a real underlying physiological difference. However, there are two problems with the angiography data. First, a number of recent replications fail to show greater occlusion among A's and B's (e.g., Dimsdale et al., 1979). Of course, some researchers argue that it is hostility and not global Type A that carries the associative burden with CHD (Dembroski et al., 1985; Williams et al., 1980). Indeed, recent data do show a stronger relationship between hostility and occlusion than for global Type A (McDougall et al., 1985). However, there is a second objection to the basic methodology of all occlusion studies conducted up to the present. Pickering (1985) points out that some portion of the samples contain individuals who show no evidence of physical disease as indicated by negative coronary angiograms, but nonetheless report chest pain. Many of these individuals, who insist on having an angiogram despite no preliminary evidence of CHD, may be highly neurotic and exhibit an exaggerated level of somatic concern (cf. Costa & McCrae, 1985). Inclusion of these persons in the comparison of A and B or hostile/nonhostile persons renders any obtained angiographic differences difficult to interpret.

Some unpublished data from angiographic studies excluding neurotic subjects appear to show that there is greater coronary occlusion in hostile individuals (Dembroski & Costa, 1987), so there may be a real underlying physical difference between hostile and nonhostile persons. Nonetheless, one cannot discount the possibility that a particular *combination* of factors is necessary to produce the increased risk of certain individuals; that is, Type A's may have a higher risk of premature CHD death because they are more reactive to stress (hyperresponsivity)—eventuating in greater atherosclerosis—*and* more likely to delay in seeking medical attention about symptoms (dangerous situations).

There are other situations that anecdote suggests can confer risk status. A common conception is that the chances of sudden death from cardiac arrhythmias are more likely after a person engages in strenuous exercise. However, Verrier et al. (1983) point out (in Spain, 1964) that:

> Although witnessing someone die suddenly during exercise leaves an indelible impression, this is a most unusual sequence. To date there have been no persuasive reports linking sudden death with strenuous physical exertion or work. Nearly 75% of all sudden deaths occur at home, 8 to 12% at work (Kuller, 1966; 1967; Wikland, 1968), and only 2–5% have been preceded by vigorous physical effort. (p. 126)

On the other hand, there are some data suggesting that acute psychological stress is associated with sudden cardiac death (SCD). Myers and Dewar (1975) examined the deaths of 100 British men due to CAD, which occurred so suddenly and unexpectedly as to merit necropsy. The researchers compared the circumstances associated with the deaths with a group of control patients who survived myocardial infarctions. The control patients and/or relatives of the deceased or witnesses to the deaths were interviewed about the circumstances occurring before the incident. Myers and Dewar (1975) found that 23 of the sudden death group experienced a significant degree of psychological stress in the 30 minutes before death as compared with eight of the nonfatal MI group ($p < .02$). The kinds of stress varied greatly—some appeared to have been uncontrollable (e.g., being attacked by dogs; or after a traffic accident), whereas others were provoked by the person's actions (e.g., after driving in a motor race for the first time in his life). It is worth noting that no patient died soon after or during coitus.

Epidemiological evidence as well as animal experimental studies tend to support the view that SCD is due to electrical disorder of the heart beat that is not provoked by strenuous physical exertion but by an event of some neural origin (Lown, Verrier, & Rabinowitz, 1977; Verrier et al., 1983). Indeed, there is evidence that induction of stresses such as public speaking, loud sounds, and a clinical interview can evoke ventricular premature beats. The obvious implication is that Type A's or hostile persons may be more reactive to such stresses and this increases their risk status. Of course, this evidence appears to be supportive of the hyperresponsivity hypothesis and not the dangerous situations alternative.

There is yet another pattern in the literature that is suggestive of particular situations being dangerous. In the study discussed previously, Myers and Dewar (1975) found an association of sudden death within the hour after a meal, with a large consumption of alcohol, and also with Saturday (when social drinking is at its maximum in N.E. England). Each of these independently increased risk status. This finding suggests that some clusters of circumstances are especially risky. It is worth adding that Myers and Dewar did not find a difference in habitual alcohol consumption between the sudden deaths and the nonfatal MI's, so it may be the pattern of drinking in the context of other events and behaviors that is important. In any case, one possibility that needs examination is that Type A's tend to be involved more frequently than B's in this potentially dangerous eating/drinking situation.

Also consider that past studies finding few specific situations related to the onset of coronary events (such as MI or SCD) typically inquire only about the events and activities of the preceding 24 hours. But information about various combinations of situations and how frequently or actively people are involved in them has not been obtained or correlated with cardiac risk.

Finally, Type A or hostile persons may place themselves in a "dangerous situation" because they create inadequate social support resources for themselves. It has long been contended that persons lacking social support systems of friends or relatives are more vulnerable to a wide variety of physical and/or psychological problems (Cassel, 1976; Cobb; 1976). Presumably, social support buffers the effects of stress, encourages preventive health measures, and so forth, and hence serves to protect the individual from illness. In this regard, the common stereotype of Type A individuals suggests such persons would have a difficult time forming or maintaining close bonds with others because of their competitiveness and their intense work schedules. In support of this idea, there is some evidence that marital relationships involving Type A males are somewhat strained (Burke, Weir, & DuWors, 1979), as are dating relationships (Becker & Byrne, 1984). Suls, Becker, and Mullen (1981) found that A's and B's reported having the same number of good friends, but A's preferred keeping their problems to themselves. Strube, Berry, Goza, and Fennimore (1985) found that A's had larger social support networks, but the larger networks were no more emotionally supportive than those of Type B's.

The data with respect to hostility are more consistent. Though the relationship between SI-Potential for Hostility and social support has not yet been reported, there are data available for the Medley-Cook Hostility scale. Smith and Frohm (1985) found that individuals with high-hostility scores reported fewer and less satisfactory social supports. This is quite consistent with systematic examination of the items making up the Ho scale suggesting that high scorers are more likely to experience anger often, to be bitter and resentful, and to view others with distrust and resentment, but not necessarily likely to be overtly aggressive and assaultive (Barefoot, Dahlstrom, & Williams, 1983; Smith & Frohm, 1985).

These comments suggest that hostile individuals may act and think in ways that eventuate in deficient social supports, which in turn increases their risk status. It is relevant that lack of social support provides the most parsimonious explanation for the fact that high levels of hostility are also prospectively linked to premature death from malignant neoplasms and from all other causes (Barefoot et al., 1983; Shekelle, Gale, Ostfeld, & Paul, 1983). In nonvascular diseases, hyperresponsivity seems less convincing as a mediating mechanism.

Of course, the exact processes by which deficient social support translates into disease are still unknown (Cohen & Wills, 1985). Moreover, it is also unclear whether social support always has positive effects on health (see Heller, 1979; Suls, 1982; Wortman & Dunkel-Schetter, 1979). Nevertheless, the possibility that Type A's or hostile persons may act or think in ways that lead to a lack of social support is one possibility consistent with the Dangerous Situations approach. Given the paucity of research concerning the activities and daily living situations of coronary-prone individuals, research on the role of social support, delay in medical seeking, and combinations of potentially risky activities (such as drinking/eating in conjunction with strenuous exercise) should be a top priority for researchers.

CONCLUSION

In the preceding pages three possible explanations for the association between behavioral style and CHD were discussed in light of recent research. By proposing a conceptual taxonomy, we hope to provide more structure to past efforts as well as to future ones. We share with others (Contrada et al., 1985; Glass, 1977; Matthews, 1982) the concern that the study of coronary-prone behavior has been perhaps too inductive. Though the conceptual scheme we provide is clearly simplistic, it does help to distinguish between different types of mechanisms. Moreover, it points to critical gaps in the empirical literature.

Our review found few data supporting the notion that people who exhibit Type A behavior or some component of the pattern, such as hostility, possess any underlying structural weaknesses that render them more vulnerable to heart disease. Of course, with the exception of study of the relationship between the major traditional risk factors and Type A (or hostility), there has been little study of possible underlying physiological differences between A's and B's. There is a small body of evidence suggesting that responsivity to stress may be heritable and this may increase coronary risk. However, in general, it is not possible to confirm or deny the potential importance of structural–genetic differences between A's and B's. There is clearly a need for more research concerning structural weaknesses leading to coronary risk for which Type A behavior, or hostility, may be only a marker.

In contrast, the hyperresponsivity hypothesis has clearly captured the imaginations of many biobehavioral researchers. We have pointed out, however, that a quantitative analysis of the available research literature on reactivity in A's and B's shows that effects are inconsistent across studies and relatively small in magnitude. It is, of course, possible that the small differences are consequential when they occur over the course of a lifetime (Contrada et al., 1985). At this empirical stage, we do not know what level of reactivity is toxic or whether hostile or Type A persons consistently exhibit the critical threshold in real-life situations.

The dangerous situations hypothesis has been given less attention than either of the others. This is unfortunate because clearly a tendency to delay in seeking medical attention could lead to premature CHD death. Although evidence suggests that strenuous exercise is not associated with coronary incidents, certain patterns of eating and drinking are apparently risky. In any case, the study of daily activities and living situations of coronary-prone individuals has received little systematic attention. Finally, we do not know the degree to which coronary-prone individuals act in ways to create deficient social support networks that may render them more susceptible to serious illness.

The hyperresponsivity hypothesis remains the best supported explanation for the connection between Type A or hostility and CHD. But the findings to date are neither so strong or compelling that this hypothesis should receive single-minded attention. Biobehavioral researchers may best be advised at this stage to give considerably more attention to the possibilities that structural weaknesses or a tendency to place oneself in dangerous situations contribute to the coronary risk associated with certain behavioral styles.

REFERENCES

Barefoot, J. C., Dahlstrom, W. G., & Williams, R. B. (1983). Hostility, CHD incidence and total mortality: A 25-year follow-up study of 255 physicians. *Psychosomatic Medicine, 45*, 59–63.

Becker, M. A., & Byrne, D. (1984). Type A behavior and daily activities of young married couples. *Journal of Applied Social Psychology, 14*, 82–88.

Bronson, F. H., & Eleftheriou, B. E. (1965). Adrenal responses to fighting in mice: Separation of physical and psychological causes. *Science, 147*, 627–628.

Burke, R. J., Weir, T., & DuWors, R. E. (1979). Type A behavior of administrators and wives' reports of marital satisfaction and well-being. *Journal of Applied Psychology, 64*, 57–65.

Byrne, D. G. (1981). Type A behavior, life events and myocardial infarction: Independent or related risk factors? *British Journal of Medical Psychology, 54*, 371–377.

Cantor, N., & Kihlstrom, J. F. (1981). *Personality, cognition, and social interaction.* Hillsdale, NJ: Lawrence Erlbaum Associates.

Carver, C. S., Coleman, A. E., & Glass, D. C. (1976). The coronary-prone behavior pattern and the suppression of fatigue on a treadmill test. *Journal of Personality and Social Psychology, 33*, 460–466.

Cassell, J. (1976). The contribution of the social environment to host resistance. *American Journal of Epidemiology, 104*, 107–123.

Cobb, S. (1976). Social support as a moderator of life stress. *Psychosomatic Medicine, 38*, 300–314.

Cohen, J. (1977). *Statistical power for the behavioral sciences* (2nd ed.) New York: Academic Press.

Cohen, S., & Wills, T. A. (1985). Stress, social support, and the buffering hypothesis. *Psychological Bulletin, 98*, 310–357.

Contrada, R. J., Wright, R. A., & Glass, D. C. (1985). Psychophysiological correlates of Type A behavior: Comments on Houston (1983) and Holmes (1983). *Journal of Research in Personality,* *19,* 12–30.

Cook, W. W., & Medley, D. M. (1954). Proposed hostility and pharisaic scales for the MMPI. *Journal of Applied Psychology, 38,* 414–418.

Cooper, T., Detre, T., & Weiss, S. M. (1981). Coronary-prone behavior and coronary heart disease: A critical review. *Circulation, 63,* 1199–1215.

Costa, P., & McCrae, R. R. (1985). Hypochondriasis, neuroticism, and aging: When are somatic complaints unfounded? *American Psychologist, 40,* 19–28.

Dembroski, T. M., & Costa, P. (1987). Coronary-prone behavior: Components of the Type A pattern and hostility. *Journal of Personality, 55,* 211–236.

Dembroski, T. M., MacDougall, J. M., Herd, J. A., & Shields, J. L. (1983). Perspectives on coronary-prone behavior. In D. S. Krantz, A. Baum, & J. E. Singer (Eds.), *Handbook of psychology and health: Cardiovascular disorders and behavior* (Vol. 3, pp. 57–84). Hillsdale, NJ: Lawrence Erlbaum Associates.

Dembroski, T. M., MacDougall, J. M., Williams, R. B., Haney, T. L., & Blumenthal, J. A. (1985). Components of Type A, hostility, and anger-in: Relationship to angiographic findings. *Psychosomatic Medicine, 4,* 219–233.

Dimsdale, J. E., Hackett, T. P., Hutter, A. M., Block , P. C., Catanzano, D. M., & White, P. J. (1979). Type A behavior and angiographic findings. *Journal of Psychosomatic Research, 23,* 273–276.

Friedman, M., & Rosenman, R. M. (1959). Association of a specific overt behavior pattern with increases in blood cholesterol, blood clotting time, incidence of arcus senilis and clinical coronary artery disease. *Journal of the American Medical Association, 169,* 1286–1296.

Friedman, M., & Rosenman, R. H. (1974). *Type A behavior and your heart.* New York: Knopf.

Gastorf, J. W., Suls, J., & Sanders, G. S. (1980). Type A coronary-prone behavior pattern and social facilitation. *Journal of Personality and Social Psychology, 38,* 773–780.

Glass, D. C. (1977). *Behavior patterns, stress and coronary disease.* Hillsdale, NJ: Lawrence Erlbaum Associates.

Glass, G. V. (1977). Integrating findings: The meta-analysis of research. *Review of Research in Education, 5,* 351–379.

Hedges, L. V. (1982). Estimation of effect size from a series of independent experiments. *Psychological Bulletin, 92,* 490–499.

Hedges, L. V., & Olkin, I. (1985). *Statistical methods for meta-analysis.* Orlando: Academic Press.

Heller, K. (1979). The effects of social support: Prevention and treatment implications. In A. P. & F. H. Kanfer (Eds.), *Maximizing treatment gains: Transfer-enhancement in psychotherapy* (pp. 353–382). New York: Academic Press.

Holmes, D. S. (1983). An alternative perspective concerning the differential responsivity of persons with the Type A and Type B behavior patterns. *Journal of Research in Personality, 17,* 40–47.

Holmes, D. S., McGilley, B. M., & Houston, B. K. (1984). Task-related arousal of Type A and Type B persons: Level of challenge and response specificity. *Journal of Personality and Social Psychology, 46,* 1322–1327.

Houston, B. K. (1983). Psychophysiological responsivity and the Type A behavior pattern. *Journal of Research in Personality, 17,* 22–39.

Kahn, J. P., Kornfeld, D. S., Frank, K. A., Heller, S. S., & Hoar, P. F. (1980). Type A behavior and blood pressure during coronary artery bypass surgery. *Psychosomatic Medicine, 42,* 407–414.

Kannel, W. B., & Schatzkin, A. (1983). Risk factor analysis. *Progress in Cardiovascular Diseases, 26,* 309–332.

Krantz, D. S., Arabian, J. M., Davia, J. E., & Parker, J. S. (1982). Type A behavior and coronary artery bypass surgery: Intraoperative blood pressure and perioperative complications. *Psychosomatic Medicine, 44,* 273–284.

Krantz, D. S., & Durel, L. A. (1983). Psychobiological substrates of the Type A behavior pattern. *Health Psychology, 2,* 393–411.

Krantz, D. S., & Manuck, S. B. (1984). Acute psychophysiologic reactivity and risk of cardiovascular disease: A review and methodological critique. *Psychological Bulletin, 96*, 453-464.

Kuller, L. (1966). Sudden and unexpected nontraumatic deaths in adults: A review of epidemiological and clinical studies. *Journal of Chronic Diseases, 19*, 1165-1192.

Lazarus, R. S. (1984). On the primacy of cognition. *American Psychologist, 39*, 124-130.

Leventhal, H. (1982). The integration of emotion and cognition: A view from the Perceptual-Motor Theory of Emotion. In M. S. Clark & S. T. Fiske (Eds.), *Affect and cognition* (pp. 121-156). Hillsdale, NJ: Lawrence Erlbaum Associates.

Lown, B., Verrier, R. L., & Rabinowitz, S. H. (1977). Neural and psychologic mechanisms and the problem of sudden cardiac death. *American Journal of Cardiology, 39*, 890-902.

MacDougall, J. M., Dembroski, T. M., Dimsdale, J. E., & Hackett, T. P. (1985). Components of Type A, hostility, and anger-in: Further relationships to angiographic findings. *Health Psychology, 4*, 137-152.

Manuck, S. B., Kaplan, J. R., & Clarkson, T. B. (1983). Behaviorally induced heart rate reactivity and atherosclerosis in cynomolgus monkeys. *Psychosomatic Medicine, 45*, 95-108.

Matthews, K. A. (1982). Psychological perspectives on the Type A behavior pattern. *Psychological Bulletin, 91*, 293-323.

Matthews, K. A., & Haynes, S. G. (1986). Type A behavior pattern and coronary disease risk. *American Journal of Epidemiology, 123*, 923-960.

Matthews, K. A., & Krantz, D. S. (1976). Resemblances of twins and their parents in pattern A behavior. *Psychosomatic Medicine, 28*, 140-144.

Matthews, K. A., & Rakaczny, C. (in press). Familial aspects of the Type A behavior pattern and physiologic reactivity to stress. In T. Schmidt & T. Dembroski (Eds.), *Biobehavioral factors in coronary heart disease.* Basal: Karger.

Matthews, K. A., Rosenman, R. H., & Dembroski, T. M., Harris, E. L., & MacDougall, J. M. (1984). Familial resemblance in components of the Type A behavior pattern: A reanalysis of the California Type A twin study. *Psychosomatic Medicine, 46*, 484-497.

Miller, S. M., Lack, E. R., & Asroff, S. (1985). Preference for control and the coronary-prone behavior pattern: "I'd rather do it myself." *Journal of Personality and Social Psychology, 49*, 529-538.

Myers, A., & Dewar, H. A. (1975). Circumstances attending 100 sudden deaths from coronary artery disease with coroner's necropsies. *British Heart Journal, 37*, 1133-1143.

Ovcharchyn, C. A., Johnson, H. H., & Petzel, T. P. (1981). Type A behavior, academic aspirations, and academic success. *Journal of Personality, 49*, 248-256.

Perper, J. A., Kuller, L. H., & Cooper, M. (1975). Arteriosclerosis of coronary arteries in sudden, unexpected deaths. *Circulation, 51-52* (Suppl. III), 27-33.

Pickering, T. G. (1985). Should studies of patients undergoing coronary angiography be used to evaluate the role of behavioral risk factors for coronary heart disease? *Journal of Behavioral Medicine, 8*, 203-213.

Pickering, T. G., Harshfield, G. A., Kleinert, H. D., Blank, S., & Laragh, J. H. (1982). Blood pressure during normal daily activities, sleep, and exercise: Comparison of values in normal and hypertensive subjects. *Journal of the American Medical Association, 247*, 992-996.

Rhodewalt, F., Hays, R. B., Chemers, M. M., & Wysocki, J. (1984). Type A behavior, perceived stress, and illness: A person–situation analysis. *Personality and Social Psychology Bulletin, 10*, 149-159.

Rosenman, R. H., Brand, R. J., Jenkins, C. D., Friedman, M., Straus, R., & Wurm, M. (1975). Coronary heart disease in the Western Collaborative Group Study: Final follow-up experience of 8-½ years. *Journal of the American Medical Association, 233*, 872-877.

Rosenman, R. H., Rahe, R. H., Borhani, N. O., et al. (1974). Heritability of personality and behavior pattern. *Acta Genetic Medical Gemeloll, 23*, 37-42.

Rosenthal, R. (1984). *Meta-analytic procedures for social research.* Beverly Hills, CA: Sage.

Ross, R., & Glomset, J. A. (1976). The pathogenesis of atherosclerosis. *New England Journal of Medicine, 295*, 369-377.

Scherwitz, L., Berton, K., & Leventhal, H. (1978). Type A behavior self-involvement, and cardio-vascular response. *Psychosomatic Medicine, 40*, 593–609.

Scherwitz, L., McKelvain, R., Laman, C., Patterson, J., Dutton, L., Yusim, S., Lester, J., Kraft, I., Rochelle, D., & Leachman, R. (1983). Type A behavior, self-involvement, and coronary athero-sclerosis, *Psychosomatic Medicine, 45*, 47–57.

Schneiderman, N., & Pickering, T. G. (1986). Cardiovascular measures of physiologic reactivity. In K. A. Matthews, S. M. Weiss, T. M. Dembroski, B. Falkner, S. B. Manuck, & R. B. Williams (Eds.), *Handbook of stress, reactivity and cardiovascular disease* (pp. 145–186). New York: Wiley.

Shekelle, R. B., Gale, M., Ostfeld, A. M., & Paul, P. (1983). Hostility, risk of coronary disease and mortality. *Psychosomatic Medicine, 45*, 109–144.

Smith, T. W., & Brehm, S. S. (1981). Person perception and the Type A coronary-prone behavior pattern. *Journal of Personality and Social Psychology, 40*, 1137–1149.

Smith, T. W., & Frohm, K. (1985). What's so unhealthy about hostility? Construct validity and psy-chosocial correlates of the Cook and Medley hostility scale. *Health Psychology, 4*, 503–520.

Smith, T. W., & Rhodewalt, F. (1986). On states, traits and processes: A transactional alternative to the individual difference assumptions in Type A behavior and physiological reactivity. *Journal of Research in Personality, 20*, 229–251.

Spain, D. M. (1964). Anatomical basis for sudden cardiac death. In B. Surawicz & E. D. Pellegrino (Eds.), *Sudden cardiac death* (pp. 45–89). New York: Grune & Stratton.

Strube, M. J., Berry, J. M., Goza, B. K., & Fennimore, D. (1985). Type A behavior, age, and psychological well-being. *Journal of Personality and Social Psychology, 49*, 203–218.

Strube, M. J., Berry, J. M., & Moergen, S. (1985). Relinquishment of control and the Type A be-havior pattern: The role of performance evaluation. *Journal of Personality and Social Psycholo-gy, 49*, 831–842.

Suls, J., (1982). Social support, interpersonal relations, and heath: Benefits and liabilities. In. G. S. Sanders & J. Suls (Ed.), *Social psychology of health and illness* (pp. 255–278). Hillsdale, NJ: Lawrence Erlbaum Associates.

Suls, J., Becker, M. A., & Mullen B. (1981). Coronary-prone behavior, social insecurity and stress among college-aged adults. *Journal of Human Stress, 7*, 27–34.

Suls, J. Gastorf, J. W., & Witenberg, S. H. (1979). Life events, psychological distress and the Type A coronary-prone behavior pattern. *Journal of Psychosomatic Research, 23*, 315–319.

Troxler, R. G., Sprague, E. A., Albanese, R. A., Fuchs, R., & Thompson, A. J. (1977). The as-sociation of elevated plasma cortisol and early atherosclerosis as demonstrated by coronary an-giography. *Atherosclerosis, 26*, 151–162.

Verrier, R. L., DeSilva, R. A., & Lown, B. (1983). Psychological factors in cardiac arrhythmias and sudden death. In D. S. Krantz, A. Baum, & J. E. Singer (Eds.), *Handbook of psychology and health: Cardiovascular disorders and behavior* (pp. 125–154). Hillsdale, NJ: Lawrence Erl-baum Associates.

Weidner, G., & Matthews, K. A. (1978). Reported physical symptoms elicited by unpredictable events and the Type A coronary-prone behavior pattern. *Journal of Personality and Social Psychology, 36*, 1213–1220.

Wikland, B. (1968). Death from arteriosclerotic heart disease outside hospitals. *Acta Medica Scan-dinavica, 184*, 129–133.

Williams, R. B., Barefoot, J. C., & Shekelle, R. B. (1985). The health consequences of hostility. In M. A. Chesney, S. E. Goldston & R. M. Rosenman (Eds.), *Anger, hostility and behavioral medicine* (pp. 173–186). New York: Hemisphere.

Williams, R. B., Haney, T. L., Lee, K. L., Kong, Y., Blumenthal, J., & Whalen, R. Type A be-havior, hostility and coronary atherosclerosis. *Psychosomatic Medicine, 42*, 539–549.

Wortman, C. B., & Dunkel-Schetter, C. (1979). Interpersonal relationships and cancer: A theoreti-cal analysis. *Journal of Social Issues, 35*, 120–155.

Zajonc, R. B. (1984). On the primacy of affect. *American Psychologist, 39*, 117–123.

2

Historical and Current Developments in Coronary-Prone Behavior

Theodore M. Dembroski
Susan M. Czajkowski
University of Maryland Baltimore County

In most industrialized societies, including the United States, cardiovascular-related diseases are the chief cause of death. More than one half of all deaths in any given year in the United States is associated with heart and vascular diseases; in 1985, the mortality figure was approximately 1 million. The economic impact is staggering, estimated at $100 billion a year. The social costs and psychological suffering caused by both lethal and nonlethal manifestations of heart and blood vessel diseases are beyond comprehension. All the latter continues to occur despite the 20-year decline in death due to cardiovascular diseases (Havlek & Feinleib, 1979).

Clinical coronary heart disease (CHD) is complex and not fully understood. Genetic, physiological, chemical, nutritional, psychosocial, and environmental factors are all involved in the etiology and epidemiology of various facets of heart and vascular disease. The major goal of epidemiological research is to identify the risk factors for CHD to target interventions designed to reduce its incidence.

STANDARD RISK FACTORS

The international epidemiological community has identified elevations of blood pressure, serum cholesterol, and frequency of cigarette smoking as risk factors for the development of clinical manifestations of CHD (Aravanis, 1983; Blackburn, 1983; Keys, 1970; The Pooling Project Research Group, 1978). The latter risk factors are associated with behaviors including sedentary habits, excessive dietary ingestion of fats and cholesterol, habitual daily cigarette smoking, immoderate alcohol intake, abuse of certain drugs, exposure to environmental agents, and failure to diagnose high blood pressure and/or maintain hypotensive therapy. Such behaviors are thought to accelerate the atherosclerotic process and/or participate in precipitating a sudden coronary event or death. Enormous resources have been devoted to intervention programs designed to change risk-related behaviors to produce a clinically significant reduction in CHD events (Farquhar, 1978; MRFIT Research Group, 1982).

Epidemiologic evidence supporting the role of traditional risk factors in CHD is impressive. Nevertheless, the best combination of the classic risk factors does not predict most new cases of CHD in many instances (Jenkins, 1978; Keys, 1970; Rosenman, 1983). Although studies have demonstrated that individuals with all three risk factors have about six times the chance of developing clinical CHD relative to those with no risk factors, only a small minority of such individuals (between 5–15%) will show clinical manifestations of CHD over a 10-year period of observation (Marmot & Winkelstein, 1975; Syme, 1984). In fact, the dramatic pandemic of CHD that developed between 1910 and 1950 and the recent 20-year decline in CHD-related deaths cannot be satisfactorily explained by changes in standard risk factors or by any other apparently obvious considerations (Rosenman, 1986). In this regard, risk ratios uncovered in the famous Framingham study cannot be routinely applied in all other cultures or even to certain subgroups in the United States (Keys, 1970; Rosenman, 1983). Moreover, enormous efforts to alter behaviors thought to be closely linked to the traditional risk factors have not been encouraging in reducing risk (MRFIT Research Group, 1982). Nevertheless, the traditional risk factors remain extremely important in both primary and secondary prevention efforts, and, here, interventions on some behaviors such as cigarette smoking cessation and hypertension control offer promise of effective risk reduction (Kaplan, 1984). The discovery of new risk factors, however, can improve our efforts in the prevention and rehabilitation of CHD over and above attention to just the standard risk factors.

The Role of Nontraditional Risk Factors

The role of emotional and behavioral factors in the manifestation of CHD has been noted by physicians as far back as Celsus in 30 A.D. Observations on the importance of emotions in the etiology of CHD include those made by William Harvey (1628), the pioneer in the scientific study of the cardiovascular system, who stated that "every affection of the mind that is attended with either pain or pleasure, hope or fear, is the cause of an agitation whose influence extends to the heart." Heberden (1772), whose descriptions of the symptoms of angina pectoris broke new ground in the field, believed CHD was closely connected to strong emotion. And John Hunter, the 18th-century cardiovascular pathologist, asserted that "my life is in the hands of any rascal who chooses to annoy and tease me" (Dictionary of National Biography, 1975). Interestingly, Hunter believed his attacks of angina were precipitated by interpersonal conflict and apparently suffered cardiac arrest following a particularly heated argument with a colleague. Sir William Osler described it thus: "In silent rage and in the next room gave a deep groan and fell down dead" (cited in DeBakey & Gotto, 1977). Other 18th-

and 19th-century physicians describe similar incidents in which emotional states were linked to clinical manifestations of CHD (Fothergill, 1781; Trousseau, 1882; Wardrop, 1851).

In addition to this view of emotion as a predisposing factor in CHD, certain personality traits and behavioral patterns were also seen as contributing to the development and occurrence of CHD. The individual considered to be coronary prone was, according to Sir William Osler (1892), "not the delicate, neurotic person, but the robust, the vigorous in mind and body, the keen and ambitious man, the indicator of whose engine is always at full speed ahead." He considered CHD to arise from "the high pressure at which men live and the habit of working the machine to its maximum capacity." Similarly, the German physician Von Dusch (1868) considered working through the night and speaking loudly to be coronary-prone behaviors.

The Menningers (1936) were the first psychiatrists to emphasize aggressive qualities as predisposing factors in CHD (Rosenman, 1983). Other traits linked to CHD by psychiatrists in the 1940s include mastery, power and achievement motives, hard-driving tendencies, anger and hostility, and tough-mindedness (Arlow, 1945; Dunbar, 1943; Gildea, 1949; Kemple, 1945). But, in spite of the abundance of anecdotal material suggesting that such psychological/behavioral factors played a role in the pathogenesis of CHD, until recently the only scientific attempts to confirm such a role involved poorly designed prevalence studies using small samples. In addition, the specific personality traits or behaviors that typified coronary-prone individuals were not clearly defined or agreed on. Lacking a clear conceptual definition of coronary-prone behavior, the design of objective and replicable methods for assessing such a syndrome and correlating it with other personality traits and CHD endpoints was impossible. It was in response to this need for better definition and measurement of coronary-prone behavior that the concept of the Type A behavior pattern (TABP) first emerged.

Emergence of the Type A Patttern

Two pioneering cardiologists, Dr. Meyer Friedman and Dr. Ray Rosenman, were aware of the confusion regarding the role of behavioral factors in CHD. During the 1950s, they collaborated in the development of a conceptual definition of a behavior pattern they thought to be coronary prone. More importantly, they developed the first reliable method for its assessment (Friedman & Rosenman, 1959). For descriptive purposes, the behavior pattern was labeled Type A (Rosenman, 1986).

The evolution of the Type A Behavior Pattern (TABP) was based on observations of their own coronary patients, which suggested to them a variety of behaviors including: (1) a strong drive to accomplish many poorly defined things; (2) a love of competition; (3) an intense need for recognition and advancement; (4) habitual time-urgent behavior governed by the clock; (5) extraordinary acceleration of physical or mental activity; and (6) intense concentration and alertness (Rosenman, 1986). In their early studies, they used lay selectors to recruit acquaintances reflecting either the presence (Type A) or absence (Type B) of the preceding designated attributes. Results of the initial studies revealed significantly higher levels of serum cholesterol and evidence of CHD in the Type A relative to the Type B groups in both males and females (Friedman & Rosenman, 1959; Rosenman & Friedman, 1961). Eventually, the constellation of psychosocial and behavioral attributes was consolidated into a conceptual definition called the Type A coronary-prone behavior pattern (TABP). TABP was defined by Friedman and Rosenman (1974; also Rosenman & Friedman, 1974) as "an action-emotion complex that can be observed in any person who is aggressively involved in a chronic, incessant struggle to acheive more and more in less and less time, and if required to do so, against the opposing efforts of the other things or other persons" (p. 37).

Although results from the early prevalence studies supported the existence of a coronary-prone behavioral syndrome linked to CHD, establishing the TABP as a risk factor for CHD required a large-scale, prospective study. Such a study in turn required an assessment method that could be administered by others (Rosenman and Friedman themselves evaluated and classified the individuals used in the prevalence studies), and that would ensure accurate and reliable classification of the large numbers of subjects that would be necessary. A structured interview format was considered superior to self-report methods because the latter are subject to bias and influenced by the lack of self-insight thought to be typcial of Type A individuals. In addition, interviewers could observe the paralinguistic and motor activities of subjects in response to structured questions (Rosenman, 1978), behaviors thought by Rosenman and Friedman to reflect emotional overtones that were key elements of the behavior pattern. Finally, interviewers could challenge subjects in such a way that Type A responses would be elicited in susceptible individuals. This was important because Rosenman and Friedman believed the TABP was not a personality trait per se but was evoked by environmental challenges in those individuals prone to exhibit the behavior pattern (Rosenman, 1978).

Thus, in creating their assessment tool, Rosenman and Friedman relied more on the behaviors accompanying an individual's responses than on the actual content of those responses (Rosenman, 1978). Those attributes important in the conceptual definition of the TABP—self reports of hard-driving, competitive, time-urgent behavior—are actually of minor importance in assessment of the TABP using the Structured Interview (SI). It has since been established empirically that speech stylistics, particularly loud, explosive, and rapid-accelerated speech, are the primary criteria used in determining TABP categorization (Dembroski & MacDougall, 1985; Howland & Siegman, 1982; Glass, Ross, Isecke, & Rosenman, 1982; MacDougall, Dembroski, & Musante, 1979; Matthews, Krantz, Dembroski, & MacDougall, 1982; MacDougall, Dembroski, & Van Horn, 1983; Scherwitz, Berton, & Leventhal, 1977; Schucker & Jacobs, 1977).

The prospective study that established the TABP as a risk factor was the Western Collaborative Group Study (WCGS) (Rosenman et al., 1964). In this study, 3,154 men, aged 39 to 59 and free of CHD symptoms at intake, were followed for 8.5 years for evidence of CHD. Interviewers trained by Rosenman and Friedman tape recorded the Structured Interview with each participant; these were then audited and categorized under the direction of Rosenman. Other variables assessed at intake included education level, income, medical history, physical activity, smoking habits, systolic and diastolic blood pressure, serum total cholesterol, fasting serum triglycerides, and serum B/a-lipoprotein. Most of these measures were also repeated each year from 1961 to the end of the study. TABP was assessed at intake for all participants, and 12 to 20 months after intake for a significant subset of subjects. Agreement on SI classification of the A/B dichotomy between the two assessment sessions was 80% (Jenkins, Rosenman, & Friedman, 1968).

Approximately 50% of the participants in the WCGS were classified as Type A. At 8.5 years following the initial assessment, the results showed that Type A's were twice as likely as Type B's to manifest symptoms of CHD, even after multivariate adjustment for traditional risk factors (Brand, 1978; Rosenman et al., 1964; Rosenman, et al., 1975). Furthermore, the TABP predicted CHD incidence at all levels and for all combinations of the other risk factors, and the degree of risk it conferred was equal to that of any of the traditional risk factors (Brand, 1978). Such evidence considerably strengthened the argument that the TABP was an independent risk factor for CHD. Furthermore, SI-defined TABP was found to be related to severity of coronary artery disease (CAD) in the WCGS at autopsy and in a series of studies using coronary angiography (Blumenthal et al., 1978; Frank et al., 1978; Friedman et al., 1968; Williams et al., 1980).

Based on the evidence linking TABP to CHD both prospectively in the WCGS and in angiographic studies, a distinguished panel of scientists met in December of 1978 under the auspices of the National Heart, Lung, and Blood Institute and concluded that the TABP was a risk factor for CHD "over and above that imposed by age, systolic blood pressure, serum cholesterol, and smoking and appears to be of the same order of magnitude as the relative risk associated with any of these factors" (Cooper, Detre, & Weiss, 1981). Thus, for the first time, a psychosocial variable was accepted by the medical community as a risk factor for CHD.

Further Evidence Regarding the Epidemiological Validity of TABP

Since the Panel's findings, a number of studies, both prospective and retrospective, have called into question the status of TABP as an independent risk factor for CHD. Because this body of research has primarily involved two different measures of the TABP, the SI and the Jenkins Activity Survey (JAS), this more recent evidence is reviewed separately for each measure.

Structured Interview.   The Structured Interview is still considered the "gold standard,'' or best measure of the TABP, primarily because it is the assessment procedure that was first linked prospectively with CHD in the WCGS. However, recently a number of studies have failed to show a relationship between SI-assessed TABP and CHD. In a second major prospective study, the Multiple Risk Factor Intervention Trial (MRFIT), a subset of participants were administered the SI at intake and followed for approximately 7 years (Shekelle, Hulley, Neaton, et al. 1985). These men were initially free of coronary disease but considered at high risk for CHD due to the presence of one or more risk factors that placed them in the upper 10-15% at risk for CHD, such as smoking and elevated serum cholesterol (MRFIT Research Group, 1982). Rosenman trained and certified the interviewers who administered the SI as well as those who audited the interviews, and disagreements in classification between auditors were adjudicated by him (Shekelle et al., 1985). Stringent procedures were followed in both the assessment and follow-up phases, with an expert committee defining nonfatal myocardial infarction (MI) via EKG analysis, and all assessments were done blind to TABP status. Thus, many potential sources of bias were eliminated, though at some cost to the total number of events available for study. A 7-year follow-up revealed no relationship between Type A categorization and CHD mortality (Shekelle et al., 1985). Although this study differs from the WCGS in that MRFIT participants had one or more risk factors, recall that the TABP predicted CHD in WCGS at all levels of risk (Brand, 1978; Rosenman et al., 1975).

In addition to the negative findings for the TABP in the MRFIT study, at least seven angiographic studies have failed to find a relationship between SI-defined TABP and the extent and severity of coronary artery disease (see Dembroski & MacDougall, 1985, and Matthews & Haynes, 1986, for reviews). For example, Dimsdale et al. (1979) found no relationship between SI categorization and number of vessels occluded, even when comparing extreme Type A's and B's. Arrowood et al. (1982), Krantz et al. (1981), MacDougall, Dembroski, Dimsdale, and Hackett (1985), and Scherwitz et al. (1983) also found no association between SI-defined Type A and either number of vessels occluded or disease severity. And using a random sample of 131 patients from the total group of more than 2,000 patients at Duke University, Dembroski et al. (1985) found no relationship between SI-assessed Type A and CAD severity. The latter finding is particularly important because much of the angiographic evidence for a TABP–CAD relationship used by the 1978 Panel in their decision to assign risk-factor status involved the Duke University data base.

These negative angiographic findings should not, by themselves, be considered the most important evidence in evaluating the link between TABP and CHD because of interpretive and methodological problems associated with angiographic studies (Dembroski, MacDougall, & Williams, 1986; see Pickering, 1986, for a review). However, this evidence, combined with the prospective data available from the MRFIT study, severely weakens the argument for a global TABP–CHD relationship. Further research using the SI is necessary to establish whether specific components of the TABP, such as hostility, are more important than global TABP in the prediction of CHD.

Jenkins Activity Survey. The Jenkins Activity Survey (JAS) was created by Jenkins in collaboration with Rosenman and Friedman as an objectively scored, self-report measure of Type A behavior (Jenkins, 1978; Rosenman, 1978). A pool of items was created, which tapped the central conceptual features of the Type-A construct (e.g., hard-driving, impatient, competitive behaviors), and only those questions that best predicted SI categorization in the WCGS were retained in the final Type A scale. The JAS is scored for both a global Type A score, and for three factor scales indicative of Type A behavior: Speed and Impatience, Job Involvement, and Hard-Driving Behavior.

A positive feature of the JAS is the greater body of evidence concerning its construct validity than that available for the SI. In fact, the evidence showing the SI to measure the central features of the TABP is sparse and, where available, relatively weak. In studies correlating SI categorization with other psychological measures, the size of the relationships between SI and other measures of Type A-like behavior, though statistically significant, is often not very substantial (Matthews, 1982). On the other hand, a number of studies have shown that style of speech (e.g., speaking quickly, loudly, and explosively) is the aspect of the TABP most highly related to Type A categorization when the SI is used as the method of assessment (Dembroski & MacDougall, 1985; Glass et al., 1982; Howland & Siegman, 1982; Matthews et al., 1982).

In contrast to the paucity of evidence bearing on the construct validity of the SI and the weakness of the evidence that does exist, a wealth of information is available showing the JAS to be a good measure of the TABP's central features. For example, studies have found that JAS-defined Type A's differ from Type B's in the speed and persistence with which they perform tasks, and that the former show more hard-driving, time-urgent and achievement-oriented behaviors than the latter (see Mathews, 1982, for a review of the construct validity of the JAS).

In spite of its superiority to the SI in terms of construct validity, the epidemiological validity of the JAS (its ability to predict CHD endpoints) is much poorer than that of the SI. In Matthews and Haynes' (1986) extensive review of this area, the JAS predicted incidence of CHD endpoints in only two studies involving U.S. citizens, both using the WCGS population. These findings are questionable, however, because in both studies the JAS was used to predict disease using the same subject population on which it was validated (the subjects used in the WCGS). Furthermore, only univariate analyses were performed in the first study; more recent evidence shows that when multivariate analyses are used and other risk factors (e.g., age, blood pressure, cholesterol level) are taken into account, the significant relationship between JAS scores and CHD vanishes (Brand et al., 1978).

Both the prospective and retrospective evidence showing no relationship between the JAS and CHD far outweigh the evidence showing a positive relationship. Five additional prospective studies have found no relationship between the

JAS and incidence of CHD morbidity and mortality. In the Honolulu Heart Program study, 2,187 healthy men of Japanese descent (57–70 years of age) were administered the JAS and followed for 8 years for evidence of CHD. JAS-assessed Type A was not found to be related to MI incidence, angina, total CHD, or atherosclerosis, although it was related to prevalence of CHD (Cohen & Reed, 1985). In a study by Dimsdale et al. (1981), 189 men were followed for 1 year after cardiac catheterization. Stepwise discriminant function analyses revealed that, contrary to expectation, JAS-assessed *Type B behavior* was predictive of the occurrence of a new morbid event (e.g., hospitalization, MI, or death).

Case et al. (1985) administered the JAS within 2 weeks of discharge from the coronary care unit to 548 of 866 patients in the Multicenter Post-Infarction Program. The patients included in the group who were administered the JAS were generally healthier (in terms of less severe cardiac disease and lower mortality rates during the follow-up period) than those not included. JAS Type A scores were not predictive of mortality, left ventricular ejection fraction, time to death, or duration of stay in the coronary care unit over a 1 to 3 year follow-up period.

Shekelle, Gale, and Norusis (1985), in a study assessing the effects of aspirin use among patients who had a previous MI (the Aspirin Myocardial Infarction Study), followed 244 women and 2,071 men for 3 years. JAS-assessed Type A was not related to a recurrent event (fatal or nonfatal MI). Finally, in the MRFIT study mentioned previously, 12,772 initially coronary-disease free but high-risk men from 22 clinical centers were administered the JAS and followed for approximately 7 years. As with SI categorization, no relationship was found between JAS Type A and total morbidity or mortality from CHD (Shekelle, Hulley, et al., 1985).

In addition to these prospective studies, a majority of angiographic studies using the JAS has found no relationship between the JAS and CAD. An early study by Zyzanski et al. (1976) did find that overall JAS score and the three JAS subscales were related to occlusion in two or more vessels; however, further analyses using these and additional patients showed the overall JAS score not related to CAD but did find a relationship between CAD and the job involvement factor score for men only (Silver et al., 1980). Blumenthal et al. (1978) found that for 142 catheterization patients free of valve disease (80 men and 62 women with an average age of 47), the JAS and JAS subscales were not related to severity of disease. Similarly, Dimsdale et al. (1978), in a study involving 109 patients with evidence of CAD, found that the JAS was not predictive of number of diseased vessels. In another study, using 103 male patients, Dimsdale et al. (1979) again found no association between overall Type A score and number of vessels occluded. Finally, Krantz et al. (1979), in a study involving 67 male cardiac outpatients (average age 47), found the overall JAS score not related to the number of vessels occluded at the patients' first catheterization but did find a relationship between the JAS and occlusion at a repeated catheterization for patients who had progressed in CAD.

Based on the prospective and angiographic evidence available, it is clear that the JAS—ironically, the measure that appears to best represent the conceptual definition of the TABP—is not an adequate predictor of CHD endpoints. At this point, exclusive use of the JAS in research concerning the TAPB and heart disease must be discouraged, and use of the JAS even in conjunction with other paper-and-pencil measures of only globally defined Type A behavior is not recommended. On the other hand, the SI, which seems primarily to measure speech and paralinguistic aspects of the TABP and secondarily hostility rather than the central features of the construct, has been more consistently linked to CHD; recent evidence, however, has called its epidemiological validity into question, as well.

Because of the failure of global TABP, both JAS and SI assessed, to adequately predict CHD in a growing number of studies, the use of global TABP alone, however defined, is questionable as a strategy for identifying coronary-prone individuals. Instead, attention has turned to attempts to measure elements of global TABP that are its most potent or "toxic" components, with hostility being the component most often investigated. Interestingly, the fact that the JAS, which appears to better capture key elements of the TABP, has poorer epidemiological validity than the SI suggests, that it is not these components (e.g., hard-driving, achievement-oriented striving) that are most important in the development of clinical manifestations of CHD. In fact, the one component that is relatively neglected in the JAS is hostility (only 5 of 52 items in the JAS remotely assess some form of hostility). Because the SI does include hostility as an important element and its epidemiological validity is better established than that of the JAS, it appears likely that it is the hostility component that is responsible for SI's superiority in predicting CHD. In the following section, the role of hostility in the occurrence of CHD is reviewed.

Hostility and the Prediction of CHD

Studies investigating the role of hostility as the TABP component most predictive of CHD fall into two categories: (1) studies in which the measure of hostility used is derived from the SI itself; and (2) studies using questionnaire-based measures of hostility.

Studies using SI-derived Hostility. In the first study to attempt an examination of the relative importance of various components of SI-defined TABP, 62 new cases of WCGS participants under 50 years were compared with 124 participants free of symptoms matched for age and workplace on more than 40 different SI-derived attributes (Matthews, Glass, Rosenman, & Bortner, 1977). The attribute that best discriminated cases from controls (according to *p*-level values) was Potential for Hostility, followed by anger expressed outward, competitiveness, experiencing anger more than once a week, vigorousness of response, irritation at waiting in lines, and explosiveness of speech. The preponderance of attributes reflecting an anger/hostility dimension is evident. Similar results were found in a study by Hecker et al. (1985) in which Potential for Hostility was found to best discriminate cases (N = 250) from controls (N = 500) in a sample of WCGS participants, which included all available cases from the entire 8.5-year follow-up.

A component scoring system has been developed by Dembroski (1978) to routinely explore the importance of various elements of the SI. The elements that are scored include two representing the Hostility/Anger dimension (Potential for Hostility and Anger-In) and several capturing the speech stylistics that are important components in the SI-defined TABP (e.g., explosiveness, rapidity, and loudness of speech). The Potential for Hostility component (PoHo) is defined as the relatively stable tendency to react to a broad range of frustration-inducing events with responses indicative of anger, irritation, disgust, contempt, resentment, and the like, and/or actually to express antagonism, criticalness, uncooperativeness, and other disagreeable behaviors in similar situations (Dembroski & Costa, 1987; Dembroski et al., 1985; MacDougall et al., 1985). It is scored on a 5-point scale, as are the other elements of the component scoring system. Assignment of a score is based on three separate elements: (1) *response content*, which involves frequently reported experiences or displays of anger, irritation, annoyance, disgust, resentment, and other negative emotional reactions to everyday objectively mildly frustrating situations; (2) *response intensity*, which takes into account the use of emotion-laden words, profanity, and emphatic expressions; and (3) *style of interaction with the interviewer*, which includes rudeness, condescension, and contempt for and/or resentment of the interviewer during the SI session. Each of these categories receives a separate score on a 5-point scale, and each is used in assigning the overall PoHo score. Use of such an approach acknowledges the multidimensional nature of the hostility construct and allows an examination of those elements that may be its most "toxic" aspects. Interrater reliability for SI-defined Potential for Hostility ranges between .70 and .85, and test–retest reliability is approximately .55, about the same as that obtained for JAS scores and resting blood pressure (MacDougall, Musante, & Dembroski, 1986).

Another component of the hostility construct represented in the component scoring system is mode of anger expression, specifically the inability or unwillingness to express negative affect towards the source of frustration, called Anger In (AI) (Dembroski et al., 1985). Although AI and PoHo are ordinarily inversely related, this dimension is *conceptualized* as capable of being independent of the PoHo score, such that individuals could conceivably score high on hostility but low on anger expression (high on Anger-In). Examples would include individuals who suppress anger until it reaches a "boiling over" point, when it is displayed explosively, and those who report that their anger expression is situationally determined, and thus who do not express anger on the job, for example, but display it at home.

Two recent studies have demonstrated the utility of the component scoring system, especially use of Hostility/Anger-In components, in predicting angiographically documented CAD severity. In the first study, Dembroski et al.

(1985) reanalyzed 131 taped SIs randomly selected from the Duke sample and found both PoHo and Anger In significantly positively correlated with CAD severity. This was true even when age, sex, and the traditional risk factors were taken into account in multivariate analyses. In addition, a significant interaction occurred, such that among patients high on the Anger-In dimension, the higher the hostility score, the greater the CAD severity. Another interesting finding was that explosive speech—a component reflecting Type-A speech stylistics—became significantly *negatively* correlated with CAD when multivariate analyses were used to control for PoHo and Anger-In.

In the second study, MacDougall et al. (1985) reanalyzed SI data from a sample of patients from Massachusetts General Hospital, data originally used by Dimsdale et al. (1979). Similar to the Dembroski et al. study, both PoHo and AI were found to correlate positively with CAD severity; however, in contrast to Dembroski et al., there was no significant interaction between the two components. Also, there was a marginally significant negative correlation between explosive speech and CAD severity when PoHo and AI were statistically controlled for, and a significant correlation between time urgency and CAD.

It is important to note here that the role of Anger-In in the two angiographic studies just cited differs from that found in the study by Matthews et al. (1977), in which SI-based ratings of *Anger-Out* were predictive of CHD incidence in WCGS. At first glance, this is puzzling, especially because PoHo ratings reflect self-reported expressions of anger/irritation at everyday frustrating events and thus should be inversely related to Anger-In. Furthermore, in a random sample of more than 2,000 coronary angiography patients from the Duke University patient population, the correlation between PoHo and AI was zero (Dembroski et al., 1985). However, the correlation between the two components in a nonpatient sample was significantly negative ($r = -.47, p < .01$) (Musante, MacDougall, Dembroski, & Costa, 1987). An explanation for these findings is that self-reports of Anger-In may reflect a response to the disease process rather than to a predisposing factor. This explanation is supported by the fact that the correlation between PoHo and AI was significant and negative in the sample of Duke patients without severe disease or symptoms, whereas for patients with symptoms and disease the correlation was positive, though nonsignificant (Dembroski & Costa, 1987). Perhaps during the progression of the atherosclerotic process, the accompanying pain becomes associated with the tendency to express anger, so that the patient attempts to change from an Anger-Out to an Anger-In style of expression. This tendency would be exacerbated by physicians' and others' admonitions to the patient to "control" potentially damaging emotions, such as the expression of anger and hostility, that are believed to influence the disease process. A prospective study, in which the progression of disease, the emergence of symptoms, and changes in mode of anger expression are tracked is a fascinating necessity to clarify the relationship between anger expression and coronary disease.

Questionnaire Measures of Hostility.   Two early prospective studies that sought to investigate the hostility–CHD relationship used an MMPI derived measure of hostility—the Cook–Medley Hostility Scale (1954)—to predict both overall and CHD-related mortality. In the first study, Barefoot, Dahlstrom, and Williams, (1983) followed 255 physicians graduated from the University of North Carolina Medical School for 25 years postgraduation and found through multivariate analysis a significant, though nonlinear, relationship between hostility scores on the Cook–Medley scale and CHD endpoints. Similarly, Shekelle, Gale, Ostfeld, and Paul, (1983), in a study of 1877 middle-aged male employees of Western Electric Company, found that Cook–Medley defined hostility-predicted CHD and all forms of mortality in a 20-year follow-up. A more recent study also found a significant and linear relationship between hostility scores and all forms of mortality after 30 years among 118 law students (Barefoot, Dahlstrom, & Williams, 1986). However, McCranie, Watkins, Brandsma, and Sisson (1986) found no relationship between hostility scores and CHD endpoints using a sample of 278 physicians from the Medical College of Georgia. This sample differed from the UNC students, who took the MMPI as part of their regular curriculum, whereas the MCG students were administered the scale as part of the medical school application process. The lower MMPI scores in the MCG versus the UNC sample and the differences in findings between the two studies may thus be attributable to differences between the studies in terms of social desirability and evaluation apprehension biases.

Another line of research has linked MMPI-derived hostility scores with CAD severity at cardiac catheterization. Using 424 patients at Duke University referred for coronary angiography, Williams et al. (1980) found a significant relationship between their hostility scores and CAD severity using multivariate analyses. A relationship was also found between global TABP and CAD severity, but the effect size for hostility was larger than that for TABP: Type A's were 1.3 times more likely than non-A's to have clinically significant arterial occlusion, whereas those with higher hostility scores were 1.5 times more likely to have significant disease than those with lower hostility scores. In addition, in multivariate analyses controlling for sex and hostility, the significant correlation between SI-defined global TABP and CAD declined from $p < .01$ to $p < .05$, whereas controlling for sex and TABP increased the significance of the hostility–CAD relationship from $p < .02$ to $p < .008$.

Although the evidence for a relationship between Cook–Medley hostility and CHD is consistent, like cigarette smoking, it appears that the hostility scale measures a trait related to general survival, rather than one just specific to CHD incidence (Shekelle et al., 1983). Research has identified the construct captured by the Cook–Medley scale as cynicism, suspiciousness, distrust, and resentment of others rather than overtly aggressive behavior (Costa, Zonderman, McCrae, & Williams, 1986; Smith & Frohm, 1985). It may be that this type of hostility, which appears to differ from that represented by the Potential for Hostility component of the SI in its emphasis on a more general dissatisfaction with others and with life in general, is more generally associated with mortality from all causes, whereas a more antagonistic, expressive type of hostility may be specifically predictive of CHD morbidity and mortality.

The Multidimensional Nature of Hostility

It is clear that, just as the TABP itself is a multidimensional construct, so there are different facets of hostility. The correlation between SI-defined PoHo and Cook–Medley hostility is significant, but modest ($r = .37$), indicating that the two measures share only a minor amount of variance (Dembroski et al., 1985). Recent research on the construct validity of the Cook–Medley scale indicates that the type of hostility being captured is a cynical, suspicious, and distrustful attitude toward others, rather than overt anger or aggressiveness (Costa et al., 1986; Smith & Frohm, 1985). In addition, factor analyses have identified two dimensions comprising the Cook–Medley scale, one labeled *paranoid alienation*, the other *cyncial mistrust* (Costa et al., 1986; Smith & Frohm, 1985). As noted previously, cynicism and distrust represent a type of hostility distinct from the tendency to react with irritation and to display antagonistic behaviors to frustration-inducing events, which is the conceptual definition of the Potential for Hostility component of SI-assessed TABP. This latter conceptualization is, in turn, closer to current thought on the definition of hostility (Megargee, 1985), and it also differs from anger, which is considered a primary emotional state, labeled as such and associated with autonomic nervous system arousal.

The importance of viewing hostility as a multidimensional construct was demonstrated in a recent study in which the Buss–Durkee Hostility Inventory (BDHI; Buss & Durkee, 1957) was correlated with severity of CAD (Siegman, Dembroski, & Ringel, 1987). A factor analysis of the BDHI revealed two factors, one that reflected the experience of anger and one that reflected the expression of anger. The first was labeled neurotic hostility because it was significantly correlated with indices of anxiety; the latter, called expressive hostility, was unrelated to anxiety scores. Interestingly, these two dimensions of hostility differed in their relationship with CAD severity. Neurotic hostility correlated significantly negatively with severity of CAD, whereas reactive or expressive hostility correlated significantly positively with disease. The overall BDHI score was, of course, unrelated to CAD because the negative and positive relationships between the two subscales cancelled each other out.

The factor labeled neurotic hostility appears to capture at least some of the same underlying facets present in the Cook–Medley scale, that is, it represents a general tendency to distrust and be suspicious of others, and to feel resentful over mistreatment by others and by life in general. These attitudes are often associated with anxiety, depression, and somatic symptoms, which occur often in neurotic individuals (Costa, 1986).

Neuroticism has been found to be negatively related to CAD in a number of studies (see Costa, 1986, for a review). The relationship between CAD and neuroticism may be explained by the fact that neurotic individuals tend to complain about somatic symptoms, including chest pain. When the neurotic person reports symptoms suggesting angina to a physician, he/she is often referred for coronary angiography. However, because the angina symptoms are based on neuroticism rather than actual disease, there is a diminished likelihood of uncovering significant CAD through cardiac catheterization. The findings of Siegman et al. (1987), if viewed in this context, suggest that hostility measures that contain a significant neurotic component will be negatively correlated or unrelated to CAD severity. Similarly, other hostility/anger scales that correlated highly with neuroticism, such as the Spielberger Trait Anger Scale (Costa & McRae, 1987), have been found to be unrelated to CAD in two studies (Shocken et al., 1985; Smith, Follick, & Korr, 1984) and negatively related to CAD in a third study (Spielberger, personal communication). In addition, reanalysis of the Duke data confirms an inverse relationship between neuroticism and CAD with high MMPI H's scores being negatively correlated with CAD severity (Williams et al., 1986).

The expressive or reactive hostility dimension uncovered in Siegman et al. (1987), which is uncorrelated with neuroticism, is more reflective of the conceptualization of hostility that is considered a part of the TABP by Rosenman and Friedman. This factor includes items indicating that the individual frequently argues with others and has the capability of physically assaulting another if sufficiently provoked. This antagonistic and expressive hostility dimension is significantly related to SI-derived hostility ratings as are indices of neurotic hostility (Musante et al., in press).

Both indices of hostility discussed earlier—the Cook–Medley scale and SI-derived PoHo—reflect both neurotic and antagonistic hostility. Although the Cook–Medley scale does contain many items reflecting neurotic hostility (e.g., "No one cares much what happens to you"), it contains items reflecting the expressive hostility dimension as well (e.g., "I have at times had to be rough with people who were rude or annoying"). Perhaps its success in predicting coronary disease endpoints is due to the greater influence of the latter component in Cook–Medley scores (Dembroski & Costa, 1987). Similarly, PoHo contains a neurotic component although the primary emphasis is on antagonistic hostility; this neurotic element is reflected in PoHo's reliance on self-reports of dissatisfaction and frustration with everyday events and aspects of the subject's life (Dembroski & Costa, 1987). Research is currently underway to explore the extent to which the neurotic and antagonistic style aspects of each of these measures of hostility are related to CHD and CAD endpoints.

In an attempt to explicate the nature of the PoHo construct and further examine its components, Dembroski filled out an adjective checklist scale for samples of MRFIT (N = 111) and WCGS (N = 99) participants after rating these individuals using his component scoring system (Dembroski & Costa, 1987). The adjective checklist was an 80-item extension of Goldberg's (1983) 40-item scale. Previous studies have derived five factors from these adjective ratings (Costa & McCrae, 1985; 1987). In this study, PoHo was found significantly related to an Antagonism/Disagreeableness dimension and less strongly to a Neuroticism factor (Dembroski & Costa, 1987). Thus, the primary component of PoHo (as rated by TMD) appears to be a dimension very similar to that found in the Siegman et al. (1987) study, a reactive or expressive hostility dimension that involves a description of the individual as uncooperative, disagreeable, and callous. Thus, as mentioned, neurotic hostility is also involved in the ratings of PoHo, and in the future should be separated from the antagonistic hostility dimension. Similar research efforts should now focus on the relative contributions of neurotic hostility and hostile style of interaction in questionnaire measures such as the Cook-Medley scale, Buss-Durkee, and others.

Conclusions

With the utility of global TABP as a tool for identifying individuals at risk for CHD currently being called into question, investigation of the role of hostility in CHD development and occurrence represents the most promising strategy for clarifying the evolving concept of coronary-prone behavior. Future directions for research include further examination of the multidimensional nature of the hostility construct and the relationship of various types of hostility to CHD, as well as the development of more objective methods for assessing possible coronary-prone behaviors such as hostility. Research in these areas is of extreme importance in the attempt to understand and eventually prevent the development of coronary heart disease. To this end, these efforts can be expected to influence the development of intervention strategies; to further the study of the psychophysiological and pathophysiological mechanisms through which certain behaviors are translated into CHD and CAD; and finally, to aid in the exploration of genetic and environmental factors that are related to various coronary-prone behaviors.

ACKNOWLEDGMENT

Preparation of this chapter was supported by research grant HL-36027 from the National Heart, Lung, and Blood Institute, NIH, DHHS.

REFERENCES

Aravanis, C. (1983). The classic risk factors for coronary heart disease: Experience in Europe. *Preventive Medicine*, *12*, 16–19.

Arlow, J. A. (1945). Identification of mechanisms in coronary occlusion. *Psychosomatic Medicine*, *7*, 195–209.

Arrowood, M., Uhrich, K., Gomillion, C., Popio, K., & Raft, D. (1982). New markers of coronary-prone behavior in a rural population. *Psychosomatic Medicine*, *44*, 119. (Abstract)

Barefoot, J. C., Dahlstrom, W. G., & Williams, R. B. (1986). *HO scores as predictors of mortality: A follow-up study of 118 lawyers*. Submitted manuscript.

Barefoot, J. C., Dahlstrom, W. G., & Williams, R. B. (1983). Hostility, CHD incidence and total mortality: A 25-year follow-up study of 255 physicians. *Psychosomatic Medicine*, *45*, 59–63.

Blackburn, H. (1983). Diet and atherosclerosis: Epidemiologic evidence and public health implications. *Preventive Medicine, 12,* 2–10.

Blumenthal, J. A., Williams, R. B., Kong, Y., Schanberg, S. M., & Thompson, L. W. (1978). Type A behavior pattern and coronary atherosclerosis. *Circulation, 58,* 634–639.

Brand, R. (1978). Coronary-prone behavior as an independent risk factor for coronary heart disease. In T. M. Dembroski, S. M. Weiss, J. L. Shields, S. G. Haynes, & M. Feinleib (Eds.), *Coronary-prone behavior.* New York: Springer–Verlag.

Brand, R. J., Rosenman, R. H., Jenkins, C. D., Sholtz, R. I., & Zyzanski, S. J. (1978). Comparison of coronary heart disease prediction in the Western Collaborative Group Study using the structured interview and the Jenkins Activity survey assessments of the coronary-prone Type A behavior pattern. *American Heart Association CVD Epidemiology Newsletter, 24.*

Buss, A. H., & Durkee, A. (1957). An inventory for assessing different kinds of hostility. *Journal of Consulting Psychology, 21,* 343–348.

Case, R. B., Heller, S. S., Case, N. B., & Moss, A. J. (1985). Type A behavior and survival after acute myocardial infarction. *New England Journal of Medicine, 312,* 737–741.

Cohen, J. B., & Reed, D. (1985). Type A behavior and coronary heart disease among Japanese men in Hawaii. *Journal of Behavioral Medicine, 8,* 343–352.

Cook, W., & Medley, D. (1954). Proposed hostility and pharisaic-virtue scales for the MMPI. *Journal of Applied Psychology, 38,* 414–418.

Cooper, T., Detre, T., & Weiss, S. M. (Eds.). (1981). Coronary-prone behavior and coronary heart disease: A critical review. *Circulation, 63,* 1199–1215.

Costa, P. T. (1986). Is neuroticism a risk factor for CAD? Is Type A a measure of neuroticism? In T. Schmidt, T. M. Dembroski, & G. Blumchen (Eds.), *Biological and psychological factors in cardiovascular disease.* New York: Springer–Verlag.

Costa, P. T., & McCrae, R. R. (1985). *The NEO Personality Inventory manual.* Odessa, FL: Psychological Assessment Resources.

Costa, P. T., & McCrae, R. R. (1987). Personality assessment in psychosomatic medicine: The value of a trait taxonomy. In T. Wise & G. Fava (Eds.), *Advances in psychosomatic medicine.* Basel, Switzerland: Karger.

Costa, P. T., Zonderman, A. B., McCrae, R. R., & Williams, R. B. (1986). Cynicism and paranoid alienation in the Cook and Medley HO scale. *Psychosomatic Medicine, 48,* 283–285.

DeBakey, M., & Gotto, A. (1977). *The living heart.* New York: Charter Books.

Dembroski, T. M. (1978). Reliability and validity of procedures used to assess coronary-prone behavior. In T. Dembroski, S. Weiss, J. Shields, S. Haynes, & M. Feinleib (Eds.), *Coronary-prone behavior.* New York: Springer–Verlag.

Dembroski, T. M., & Costa, P. T. (1987). Coronary-prone behavior: Components of the Type A pattern and hostility. *Journal of Personality, 55,* 210–235.

Dembroski, T. M., & MacDougall, J. M. (1985). Beyond global Type A: Relationships of paralinguistic attributes, hostility, and Anger-In to coronary heart disease. In T. Field, P. McAbe, & N. Schneiderman (Eds.), *Stress and coping.* Hillsdale, NJ: Lawrence Erlbaum Associates.

Dembroski, T. M., MacDougall, J. M., & Williams, R. B. (1986). Reply to Professor Steptoe. *Psychosomatic Medicine, 48,* 371–373.

Dembroski, T. M., MacDougall, J. M., Williams, R. B., Haney, T. L., & Blumenthal, J. A. (1985). Components of Type A, hostility and anger-in: Relationship to angiographic findings. *Psychosomatic Medicine, 47,* 219–233.

Dictionary of National Biography (The compact edition) (1975). John Hunter. London: Oxford University Press.

Dimsdale, J. E., Gilbert, J., Hutter, A. M., & Block, P. C. (1981). Predicting cardiac morbidity based on risk factors and coronary angiographic findings. *American Journal of Cardiology, 47,* 73–76.

Dimsdale, J. E., Hackett, T. P., Hutter, A. M., Block, P. C., & Catanzano, D. M. (1979). Type A behavior and angiographic findings. *Journal of Psychosomantic Research, 23,* 273–276.

Dimsdale, J. E., Hackett, T. P., Hutter, A. M., Block, P. C., & Catanzano, D. M. (1978). Type

A personality and extent of coronary atherosclerosis. *American Journal of Cardiology, 43,* 583–586.

Dunbar, F. (1943). *Psychosomatic diagnosis.* New York: Paul B. Hoeber.

Farquhar, J. W. (1978). The community-based model of life-style intervention trials. *American Journal of Epidemiology, 108,* 103–111.

Fothergill, J. (1781). *Complete collection of the medical and philosophical works.* London.

Frank, K. A., Heller, S. S., Kornfeld, D. S., Sporn, A. A., & Weiss, M. B. (1978). Type A behavior pattern and coronary angiographic findings. *Journal of the American Medical Association, 240,* 761–763.

Friedman, M., & Rosenman, R. H. (1959). Association of a specific overt behavior pattern with increases in blood cholesterol, blood clotting time, incidence of arcus senilis and clinical coronary artery disease. *Journal of the American Medical Association, 169,* 1286–1296.

Friedman, M., & Rosenman, R. H. (1974). *Type A behavior and your heart.* New York: Knopf.

Friedman, M., Rosenman, R. H., Strauss, R., Wurm, M., & Kositchek, R. (1968). The relationship of behavior pattern to the state of the coronary vasculature. A study of 51 autopsy subjects. *American Journal of Medicine, 44,* 525–538.

Gildea, E. (1949). Special features of personality which are common to certain psychosomatic disorders. *Psychosomatic Medicine 11,* 273.

Glass, D. C., Ross, D. T., Isecke, W., & Rosenman, R. H. (1982). Relative importance of speech characteristics and content of answers in the assessment of behavior pattern A by the structured interview. *Basic and Applied Social Psychology, 3,* 161–168.

Goldberg, L. R. (1983). *The magical number five, plus or minus two: Some conjectures on the dimensionality of personality descriptions.* Paper presented at the Gerontology Research Center, Baltimore.

Harvey, W. (1628). *Exercitatio anatomica de mota cordis et sanguinis.* In Animabilus. Frankfurtan–Main.

Havlek, R. J., & Feinleib, M. (Eds.). (1979) *Proceedings of the conference on the decline in coronary heart disease mortality* (pp. 79–161), National Institutes of Health.

Heberden, W. (1772). Some account of a disorder of the breast. *Medical Transactions Royal College of Physicians, 2,* 59.

Hecker, M., Frautschi, N., Chesney, M., Black, G., & Rosenman, R. (1985, March). *Components of Type A behavior and coronary heart disease.* Paper presented at the meeting of the Society of Behavioral Medicine, New Orleans.

Howland, E. W., & Siegman, A. W. (1982). Toward the automated measurement of the Type A behavior pattern. *Journal of Behavioral Medicine, 5,* 37–53.

Jenkins, C. D. (1978). Behavioral risk factors in coronary artery disease. *Annual Review of Medicine, 29,* 543–562.

Jenkins, C. D., Rosenman, R., & Friedman, M. (1968). Replicability of rating the coronary-prone behavior pattern. *British Journal of Preventive and Social Medicine, 22,* 16–22.

Kaplan, R. (1984). The connection between clinical health promotion and health status: A critical review. *American Psychologist, 39,* 755–765.

Kemple, C. (1945). The Rorschach method and psychosomatic diagnosis. *Psychosomatic Medicine, 7,* 85.

Keys, A. (1970). Coronary heart disease in seven countries: XIII multiple variables. *Circulation, 41,* 138–144.

Krantz, D. S., Schaeffer, M. A., Davia, J. E., Dembroski, T. M., MacDougall, J. M., & Shaffer, R. T. (1981). Extent of coronary atherosclerosis, Type A behavior and cardiovascular response to social interaction. *Psychophysiology, 18,* 654–664.

Krantz, D. S., Sanmarco, M. E., Serlvester, R. H., & Matthews, K. A. (1979). Psychological correlates of progression of atherosclerosis in men. *Psychosomatic Medicine, 41,* 467–475.

MacDougall, J. M., Musante, L., & Dembroski, T. M. (1986). *Temporal stability of components of the Type A structured interview.* Unpublished manuscript.

MacDougall, J. M., Dembroski, T. M., Dimsdale, J. E., & Hackett, T. (1985). Components of Type A Hostility, and Anger-In: Further relationships to angiographic findings. *Health Psychology, 4,* 137–152.

MacDougall, J. M., Dembroski, T. M., & Musante, L. (1979). The structured interview and questionnaire methods of assessing coronary-prone behavior in male and female college students. *Journal of Behavioral Medicine, 2,* 71–83.

Marmot, M., & Winkelstein, W. (1975). Epidemiologic observations on intervention trials for prevention of coronary heart disease. *American Journal Epidemiology, 101,* 177–181.

Matthews, K., & Haynes, S. G. (1986). Type A behavior pattern and coronary risk: Update and critical evaluation. *American Journal of Epidemiology, 123,* 23–960.

Matthews, K. A. (1982). Psychological perspectives on the Type A behavior pattern. *Psychological Bulletin, 91,* 293–323.

Matthews, K. A., Krantz, D. S., Dembroski, T. M., & MacDougall, J. M. (1982). The unique and common variance in the structured interview and the Jenkins Activity Survey measures of the Type A behavior pattern. *Journal of Personality and Social Psychology, 42,* 303–313.

Matthews, K. A., Glass, D. C., Rosenman, R. H., & Bortner, R. W. (1977). Competitive drive, pattern A, and coronary heart disease: A further analysis of some data from the Western Collaborative Group. *Journal of Chronic Diseases, 30,* 489–498.

McCranie, E. W., Watkins, L., Brandsma, J., & Sisson, B. (1986). Hostility, coronary heart disease (CHD) incidence, and total mortality: Lack of association in a 25-year follow-up study of 478 physicians. *Journal of Behavioral Medicine, 9,* 119–125.

Megargee, E. I. (1985). The dynamics of aggression and their application to cardiovascular disorders. In M. Chesney & R. Rosenman (Eds.), *Anger and hostility in cardiovascular and behavioral disorders.* Washington, DC: Hemisphere.

Menninger, K. A., & Menninger, W. C. (1936). Psychoanalytic observations in cardiac disorders. *American Heart Journal, 11,* 10.

MRFIT Research Group (1982). Risk factor changes and mortality results. *Journal of the American Medical Association, 248,* 1465–1477.

Musante, L., MacDougall, J. W., Dembroski, T. M., & Costa, P. T. (in press). *Potential for hostility, and the dimensions of anger. Health Psychology.*

Musante, L., MacDougall, J. M., Dembroski, T. M., & Van Horn, A. E. (1983). Component analysis of the Type A coronary-prone behavior pattern in male and female college students. *Journal of Personality and Social Psychology, 45,* 1104–1117.

Osler, W. (1982). *Lectures on angina pectoris and allied states.* New York: Appleton.

Pickering, T. C. (1986). Should studies of patients undergoing coronary angiography be used to evaluate the role of behavioral risk factors for coronary heart disease. *Journal of Behavioral Medicine, 8,* 203–213.

The Pooling Project Research Group. (1978). Relationship of blood pressure, serum cholesterol, smoking habits, relative weight, and ECG abnormalities to incidence of major coronary events: Final report of the pooling project. *Journal of Chronic Diseases, 31,* 201–306.

Rosenman, R. (1986). Current and past history of Type A behavior pattern. In T. Schmidt, T. M. Dembroski, & G. Blumchen (Eds.), *Biological and psychological factors in cardiovascular disease.* New York: Springer–Verlag.

Rosenman, R. H. (1983). Current status of risk factors and Type A behavior pattern in the pathogenesis of ischemic heart disease. In T. M. Dembroski, T. H. Schmidt, & G. Blumchen (Eds.), *Biobehavioral bases of coronary heart disease.* New York: Karger.

Rosenman, R. H. (1978). The interview method of assessment of the coronary-prone behavior pattern. In T. M. Dembroski, S. M. Weiss, J. L. Shields, S. G. Haynes, & M. Feinleib (Eds.), *Coronary-prone behavior.* New York: Springer–Verlag.

Rosenman, R. H., Brand, R. J., Jenkins, C. D., Friedman, M., Straus, R., & Wurm, M. (1975). Coronary heart disease in the Western Collaborative Group study: Final follow-up experience of 8-½ years. *Journal of the American Medical Association, 233,* 872–877.

Rosenman, R. H., & Friedman, M. (1961). Association of a specific overt behavior pattern in females with blood and cardiovascular findings. *Circulation, 24,* 1173–1184.

Rosenman, R. H., & Friedman, M. (1974). Neurogenic factors in pathogenesis of coronary heart disease. *Medical Clinics of North America, 58,* 269–279.

Rosenman, R. H., Friedman, M., Straus, R., Wurm, M., Kositchek, R., Hahn, N., & Werthesson, N. T. (1964). A predictive study of coronary heart disease: The Western Collaborative Group study. *Journal of the American Medical Association, 189,* 15–22.

Scherwitz, L., Berton, K., & Leventhal, H. (1977). Type A assessment and interaction in the behavior pattern interview. *Psychosomatic Medicine, 39,* 229–240.

Scherwitz, L., McKelvain, R., Laman, C., Patterson, J., Dutton, L., Yusim, S., Rochelle, D., & Leachman, R. (1983). Type A behavior, self-involvement and coronary atherosclerosis. *Psychosomatic Medicine, 45,* 45–47.

Schucker, B., & Jacobs, D. R. (1977). Assessment of behavioral risk of coronary disease by voice characteristics. *Psychosomatic Medicine, 39,* 219–228.

Shekelle, R. B., Gale, M., Ostfeld, A. M., & Paul, O. (1983). Hostility, risk of coronary disease, and mortality. *Psychosomatic Medicine, 45,* 219–228.

Shekelle, R. B., Hulley, S., Neaton, J., Billings, J., Borhani, N., Gerace, T., Jacobs, D., Lasser, N., Mittlemark, M., Stamler, A., and the MRFIT Research Group. (1985). The MRFIT behavior pattern study: II. Type A behavior pattern and incidence of coronary heart disease. *American Journal of Epidemiology, 122,* 559–570.

Shekelle, R. B., Gale, M., & Norusis, M. (1985). Type A score (Jenkins Activity Survey) and risk of recurrent coronary heart disease in the Aspirin Myocardial Infarction Study. *American Journal of Cardiology, 56,* 221–230.

Shocken, D. D., Worden, T., Greene, A. F., Harrison, E. F., & Spielberger, C. (1985). Age differences in the relationship between coronary artery disease, anxiety, and anger. *The Gerontologist, 25,* 36.

Siegman, A. W., Dembroski, T. M., & Ringel, N. (1987). Components of hostility and the severity of coronary artery disease. *Psychosomatic Medicine, 49,* 127–135.

Silver, L., Jenkins, C. D., & Ryan, T. J. (1980). Sex differences in the psychological correlates of cardiovascular diagnosis and coronary angiographic findings. *Journal of Psychosomatic Research, 24,* 327–334.

Smith, T. W., & Frohm, K. D. (1985). What's so unhealthy about hostility? Construct validity and psychosocial correlates of the Cook and Medley HO scale. *Health Psychology, 4,* 503–520.

Smith, T. W., Follick, M. L., & Korr, K. S. (1984). Anger, neuroticism, Type A behavior and the experience of angina. *British Journal of Medical Psychology, 57,* 249–252.

Syme, S. L. (1984). Sociocultural factors and disease etiology. In W. D. Gentry (Ed.), *Handbook of behavioral medicine.* New York: Guilford Press.

Trousseau, A. (1882). *Clinical medicine.* Philadelphia.

Von Dusch, T. (1868). *Lehrbuch der Herzkrankheiten* [Leipzig: Verlag Von]. Wilhelm Engelman.

Wardrop, J. (1851). *Diseases of the heart.* London.

3

Agreeableness Versus Antagonism: Explication of a Potential Risk Factor for CHD

Paul T. Costa, Jr.
Robert R. McCrae
Gerontology Research Center
National Institute on Aging, NIH

Theodore M. Dembroski
Univ. of Maryland, Baltimore County

ABSTRACT

Recent studies have suggested that Potential for Hostility may be the toxic component in the Type A behavior pattern. This chapter provides conceptual and empirical evidence for the hypothesis that Potential for Hostility may best be viewed as an aspect of the larger personality domain of Agreeableness versus Antagonism. A number of different conceptualizations of Agreeableness and related constructs are reviewed, and data are presented showing correlates of the NEO Personality Inventory (NEO–PI) Agreeableness scale in the Baltimore Longitudinal Study of Aging. Data from college samples are used to show relations between reactive or antagonistic hostility, SI-derived Potential for Hostility ratings, and both self-reports and peer ratings of NEO–PI Agreeableness. It is suggested that future prospective studies of coronary prone behavior supplement SI ratings with measures of the broader domain of Agreeableness versus Antagonism.

Anger and hostility have been key concepts in the history of theory and research on psychosomatic medicine (e.g., Diamond, 1982), but the literature is rife with confusions and outright contradictions. Most obvious is the question of whether anger suppression or anger expression is pathological: Both anger-in (Dembroski, MacDougall, Williams, Haney, & Blumenthal, 1985; Harburg et al., 1973) and anger-out (Matthews, Glass, Rosenman, & Bortner, 1977) have been found to be associated with cardiovascular disease.

This chapter focuses on other, more subtle confusions about the nature of anger and hostility. Is anger a state or a trait? Is hostility an affect or an attitude? What about aggression? Are all forms of hostility equally toxic in the etiology of coronary heart disease (CHD)? We address these questions by reference to a taxono-my of personality traits that suggests a crucial distinction between hot-blooded and cold-blooded hostility and points to other personality traits that have been less often studied by psychosomaticists but show some potential as predictors of disease. Much of the chapter is devoted to a conceptual analysis of the personali-ty domain of Agreeableness versus Antagonism[1]; empirical data are also present-ed showing links between measures of Agreeableness and ratings of Potential for Hostility (Dembroski, McDougall, Williams et al., 1985), a known prospec-tive risk factor for CHD.

Most research on this topic has implicitly or explicitly emphasized anger as an emotion, sometimes a violent one. The image of an enraged, shouting, fist-pounding man felled by a heart attack or stroke is indelibly imprinted in all of us, and there are plausible reasons why the emotional experience of anger should be related to disease. Certainly there are transient changes in blood pressure, heart rate, and other physiological processes associated with extreme anger; in individu-als prone to the experience of these emotions, might not such physiological changes cumulatively insult the cardiovascular system and lead ultimately to disease and death?

Similar arguments have been made for other emotions associated with auto-nomic arousal—notably anxiety—and all negative affects, including depression, guilt, resentment, and self-consciousness, have been seen as potential causes of psychosomatic disease (Luborsky, Docherty, & Penick, 1973). Unfortunately, despite extraordinary research efforts, it has proved difficult or impossible to demonstrate that chronic negative emotions have any impact on morbidity or mortality—except when mediated through such behaviors as alcoholism, drug use, or suicide (Costa & McCrae, 1987; Keehn, Goldberg, & Beebe, 1974). The source of the confusion seems to have been that emotionally maladjusted individuals are likely to make unfounded somatic complaints and so appear to be in poor health when in fact they do not differ medically from their better adjusted peers (Costa & McCrae, 1985a).

Although anger may seem to be very different from anxiety and depression—in some respects their opposite—the fact is that the same people who are prone to anger are also prone to anxiety. Decades of research on the structure of per-sonality has repeatedly shown that the more fundamental distinction is between individuals who are emotionally stable and those who are high in Neuroticism (Costa & McCrae, 1980, 1985b). Hostility as the tendency to experience anger, frustration, or rage frequently, intensely, and in many situations is a facet of Neu-roticism and behaves very much like anxiety. Hostility in this sense is correlated with hypochondriasis, and, thanks to effects of self-selection, may even be in-versely related to objective signs of disease. For example, Spielberger (personal communication, October 10, 1986) reported a significant negative correlation be-

---

[1]Although psychosomatic researchers are perhaps more familiar with the negative concepts of Antagonism or disagreeableness, we will couch our discussion in terms of the positive pole of Agree-ableness, following conventions in the broader field of personality.

tween his State–Trait Anger Scale and the extent of stenosis revealed by coronary arteriography.

There is, however, an entirely different way to conceptualize hostility. Instead of viewing it in terms of intrapsychic affect, we can see it as an aspect of interpersonal behavior. Since the work of Leary (1957), a number of personality researchers have shown that interpersonal behaviors can be classified into a circumplex arrangement having two major dimensions. In the most recent version of the circumplex, Wiggins (1979; personal communication, August 11, 1986) proposes that the two axes of Assured-Dominant versus Unassured-Submissive and Cold-hearted versus Warm-Agreeable define the interpersonal plane. The second dimension, which corresponds to Leary's Hate versus Love, clearly points to a form of hostility, but one that is quite different from anger. The essence of this second kind of hostility appears to be an antagonistic orientation toward other people, and it may well be expressed in a very cool, unemotional style. (Note, however, that an apparently unemotional expression of antagonistic hostility does not necessarily imply a flat physiological reaction.)

There is one very good reason to intensify research on antagonistic hostility: Potential for Hostility as scored from the Rosenman (1978) Structured Interview (SI) has repeatedly been shown to be a prospective risk factor for CHD (Hecker, Frautschi, Chesney, Black & Rosenman, 1985; Matthews, Glass, Rosenman, & Bortner, 1977); and it has also been shown to be strongly related to ratings of Agreeableness versus Antagonism (Dembroski & Costa, 1987).

Both intrapsychic affects and interpersonal behavior can be subsumed by a taxonomy of personality traits developed over the past 25 years (Goldberg, 1981; McCrae & Costa, 1985b, 1987; Norman, 1963; Tupes & Christal, 1961). Five broad domains or dimensions of personality—Neuroticism, Extraversion, Openness, Agreeableness, and Conscientiousness—have been shown to encompass most traits in self-reports and ratings, in questionnaires and adjective checklists, and in English, German, and other languages. Hostility as the tendency to experience anger and frustration is a facet of Neuroticism; hostility as an interpersonal orientation is a facet of Agreeableness versus Antagonism (which, together with Extraversion, defines the interpersonal circumplex). Our intent in this chapter is to elaborate and articulate the domain of Agreeableness versus Antagonism by noting conceptual similarities to and empirical relations with other, perhaps more familiar, personality traits. We then present evidence on the link between Potential for Hostility and Agreeableness and discuss alternative assessments of this dimension for studies of CHD.

A CONCEPTUAL ELABORATION OF AGREEABLENESS

Potential for Hostility is seen in statements reflecting anger and irritation with others; in emotional emphasis, seen in the use of words like "hate" or in heightened voice; and in behavior toward the interviewer that is rude, condescending, and uncooperative (Dembroski & Costa, 1987). This latter aspect, in particular, shows a clear link to the personality domain of Agreeableness versus Antagonism. However, there is much more to this domain than uncooperative behavior, and by spelling out other aspects, we may be able to improve the assessment of the personality dimension that is relevant to the development of CHD. It is particularly notable that Potential for Hostility scoring attends only to the negative pole of this dimension—instances of uncooperativeness, which are relatively rare. Differentiation between individuals of average levels of cooperation and those who are conspicuously cooperative and considerate may also help in the prediction of disease, particularly if Agreeableness has protective effects, as suggested by some of the research of Williams et al. (1980). Defining the positive as well as the negative pole of Agreeableness should prove useful.

As one of the five major personality factors, Agreeableness has taken several different labels. Hogan (1983) calls it Likeability; Digman (1986) refers to Friendly Compliance; Lorr's (1986) version is Socialization. It appears from these labels that Agreeableness is a highly desirable quality (at least in others), but that it also shows elements of weakness and acquiescence. A better sense of the full dimension can be obtained from Tables 3.1 and 3.2, which give adjective and California Q-Set (CQS; Block, 1961) definers of Agreeableness factors found in our research on subjects in the Augmented Baltimore Longitudinal Study of Aging (McCrae & Costa, 1985b; McCrae, Costa, & Busch, 1986).

Note that the factors in Tables 3.1 and 3.2 are not merely conceptually similar; the correlation between them is $r = .60$, $N = 204$, $p < .001$. Both factors are also significantly correlated with the Agreeableness scale of the NEO Per-

TABLE 3.1
Adjective Definers of Agreeableness
In Self-Reports and Peer Ratings

Antagonistic Pole	Agreeable Pole
Irritable	Good-natured
Ruthless	Soft-hearted
Rude	Courteous
Selfish	Selfless
Uncooperative	Helpful
Callous	Sympathetic
Suspicious	Trusting
Stingy	Generous
Antagonistic	Acquiescent
Critical	Lenient
Vengeful	Forgiving
Narrow-minded	Open-minded
Disagreeable	Agreeable
Stubborn	Flexible
Cynical	Gullible
Manipulative	Straightforward
Proud	Humble

Note: Adapted from McCrae & Costa (1985b) and McCrae & Costa (1987).

sonality Inventory (NEO-PI; Costa & McCrae, 1985b), a measure that we describe in greater detail later in this chapter.

Any dimension of personality so fundamental as love versus hate is of course endowed with a long history of antecedents. Adler (1964/1938) developed the concept of *Gemeinschaftsgefühl*, or social interest, to explain his goal for personality adjustment. In addition to traits such as cooperation and empathy, social interest included selflessness or self-transcendance and identification with others and with the world in general. Crandall (1975, 1984) has developed an adjective scale to measure social interest; a comparison of its items with those in Table 3.1 shows the close relation of his operationalization of social interest to Agreeableness. For Adler and Crandall, this dimension is perhaps best defined in terms of the extension of the self. The low scorer is egocentric and selfish; the scorer is altruistic and self-transcending.

Horney (1945, 1950) provided a less glowing version of the domain in the neurotic tendency to move toward others. Here Agreeableness is seen in dependency and slavish compliance in response to feelings of personal inadequacy. Horney also made a valuable distinction at the antagonistic end of the dimension: She hypothesized that there are varieties of the neurotic style of moving against, including narcissistic, perfectionistic, and arrogant vindictive types. Individuals low in Agreeableness may actively seek out conflict with those around them, or they may simply be indifferent to others. They may express their Antagonism

TABLE 3.2
California Q-Set Definers of Agreeableness

Agreeableness Pole

17. Sympathetic, considerate
35. Warm, compassionate
28. Arouses liking
 5. Behaves in giving way
84. Cheerful
56. Responds to humor
21. Arouses nurturant feelings
88. Personally charming

Antagonism Pole

49. Basically distrustful
38. Has hostility
62. Rebellious, nonconforming
48. Avoids close relationships
91. Power oriented
94. Expresses hostility directly
65. Tries to push limits
27. Shows condescending behavior
52. Behaves assertively
 1. Critical, skeptical

Note: Adapted from McCrae, Costa, & Busch (1986).

in overt aggression or in subtle manipulation. The assessment of Agreeableness is complicated by the fact that disagreeable individuals may be skilled in presenting a facade of cooperation and courtesy, if this is useful in attaining their ulterior ends.

Cognitive, Affective, and Motivational Aspects

Most personality traits have cognitive, affective, and motivational aspects, and the distinction between these traditional categories is somewhat artificial. Conceptually, however, it is useful to consider how individuals high and low in Agreeableness may characteristically think and feel, and what their goals and interests are. The literature abounds in constructs theoretically related to Agreeableness that offer suggestions.

As the last CQS item in Table 3.2 points out, disagreeable individuals are "critical, skeptical, not easily impressed." These are desirable characteristics in a scientist, if not in a friend, and they point to a detached, rational approach to problems. Geis (1978) noted similar characteristics in individuals scoring high in Machiavellianism: They "stand off from others, maintaining psychological distance and keeping their minds on the situation as a whole in terms of their own private goals" (p. 338). By contrast, those scoring low in Machiavellianism concentrate on the people with whom they are interacting rather than on the task, and they are more easily manipulated.

The detached cognitive style of disagreeable individuals is probably related to a pervasive attitude of mistrust. Agreeable people are trusting individuals who believe that others are both trustworthy and altruistic (Stark, 1978), and they see no need to be on their guard. By contrast, disagreeable people are cynical, with a low opinion of human nature. This attitude perhaps reflects their self-knowledge and justifies their own lack of altruism. The term *cynicism* was used by both Johnson, Butcher, Null, and Johnson (1984) and Costa, Zonderman, McCrae, and Williams (1985) to designate one of the factors in MMPI item content; later studies showed that this factor was positively related to Neuroticism and negatively related to Agreeableness (Costa, Busch, Zonderman, & McCrae, 1986). MMPI Cynicism is, of course, also strongly related to the Cook and Medley HO scale (Costa, Zonderman, McCrae, & Williams, 1986), a prospective predictor of CHD (Barefoot, Dahlstrom, & Williams, 1983: Shekelle, Gale, Ostfeld, & Paul, 1983). The association of cynicism with Neuroticism in the MMPI may suggest to some readers that disagreeableness and mistrust are signs of emotional maladjustment. It is also possible, however, that the psychopathological cast of the MMPI items yields only a neurotic version of cynicism. There may well be a healthy skepticism, and even Machiavellianism may be seen as interpersonal competence or effective leadership when it achieves socially acceptable goals (Geis, 1978).

The hardheaded rationality of antagonistic people can be useful in situations where human emotion is disruptive. A surgeon cannot let empathy prevent the use of the knife; the general must make tactical decisions without pity for the enemy. William James distinguished between the tough and the tender minded, and the former, at least, often believe their decisions, although seemingly hard-hearted, result in the end in the greatest good for society. However, especially when combined with the closedness to experience, this attitude can also take on an authoritarian cast.

Agreeable individuals are more easily characterized by affective than by cognitive terms. They are warm, sympathetic, loving, with a quick and deep emotional attachment to others. Antagonistic people may be hostile and irritable, but they are just as likely to be characterized by a lack of emotional response: They are cool or cold, contemptuous, callous, unfeeling. The warmth that characterizes agreeable people often shades into the friendliness of Extraversion, as Wiggin's interpersonal circumplex shows, but it is possible to be both agreeable and introverted. Such a person would prefer to spend time alone, but when among others is kind and thoughtful. Because they are courteous, appreciative, and pleasant, agreeable people are well liked; they themselves may or may not enjoy the company of others.

In their studies of the interpersonal circle, Wiggins and Broughton (1985) have provided a wealth of correlates of the dimension of Agreeableness versus Antagonism. Among these are the needs defined by Henry Murray (1938) and operationalized by some researchers and instruments, including the Jackson (1976) Personality Research Form. Wiggins and Broughton showed that many of Murray's needs can be ordered by the interpersonal circumplex: The Agreeableness pole of the second dimension is defined primarily by Nurturance and secondarily by Affiliation (on the extraverted side) and Deference (on the introverted side); the antagonistic pole is defined primarily by Autonomy and secondarily by the more extraverted Aggression and the more introverted Rejection. Drawing on Murray's (1938) descriptions, we would say that the agreeable individual needs to give sympathy and support; needs to please others and win affection; needs to admire and support superiors. The antagonistic person needs to resist coercion and remain unattached; needs to oppose, attack, or punish others; needs to exclude, abandon, or snub those who are disliked or thought inferior.

Agreeableness also has an influence on vocational interests. Holland's (1985) hexagonal model classifies interests into six categories in a circumplex arrangement. Both Social and Enterprising interests are characteristic of extraverts (Costa, McCrae, & Holland, 1984); the distinction between them seems in part a function of Agreeableness. Among our longitudinal subjects, Agreeableness is positively associated with Social interests and occupations like Sociologist and High School Teacher; it is negatively related to Enterprising interests and occupations like Speculator, Advertising Executive, and Sales Manager. Presumably, occupations such as teaching give agreeable people the opportunity to help others; occupations such as sales give disagreeable people a chance to pursue their own ends aggressively.

Relations with Other Domains

All five of the major domains of personality are essentially independent, meaning that the standing of individuals on one dimension does not tell us anything about their standing on other dimensions. When we speak about the relations between domains, we are essentially referring to descriptions of individuals in terms of two (or more) dimensions simultaneously. With respect to Neuroticism, our chief interest has been to distinguish neurotic hostility, which is characterized by the frequent and intense experience of anger, from antagonistic hostility, which is characterized by cynicism, callousness, and uncooperativeness, These two forms are not mutually exclusive. A quarter of the population is above the median on Neuroticism and below the median on Agreeableness and is presumably characterized by both kinds of hostility.[2] By this same rough figuring, however, a quarter of the population is susceptible to neurotic hostility without being disagreeable, and an equal number of people should show antagonistic hostility without the frequent experience of anger.

We have also mentioned the joint effects of Agreeableness and Extraversion, which together define the plane of the interpersonal circle. For the sake of completeness, note that Agreeableness can also form meaningful planes with Openness and Conscientiousness. The various combinations of Agreeableness and Openness may prove particularly valuable in defining social and political attitudes. For example, Eysenck's (1954) two-dimensional model of attitudes appears to be related to the two dimensions of Agreeableness and Openness. Specifically, T, Tender-mindedness versus Tough-mindedness, seems to be related to Agreeableness versus Antagonism; R, Radicalism versus Conservativism, resembles Openness to Experience. Of course, we do not assume that political or social attitudes can be predicted solely on the basis of personality traits (cf. Brand, 1986); they are complexly determined by information, processes of persuasion, social circumstances, and so on. There does, however, seem to be a sense in which individuals may have an affinity for certain views. For example, disagreeable people might or might not believe that capital punishment is an effective deterrent to crime, but if they did, they would probably not flinch at imposing it. One of the items of the NEO-PI Agreeableness scale asks respondents if they are "hardheaded and tough-minded in their attitudes" (Costa & McCrae, 1985b).

Taken together, Agreeableness and Conscientiousness might be seen to define character, a venerable topic in personality psychology (e.g., Hartshorn & May, 1928), but one recently somewhat neglected. Agreeable people are well disposed, conscientious people are strong willed and dependable. Although both of these are desirable products of socialization, it is clear they do not necessarily covary. Some people are well intentioned but disorganized and ineffective; others are hardworking, thorough, and ambitious, but act only in pursuit of their own selfish goals.

---

[2]These numbers are illustrative only. Whether it is meaningful to use the median to divide antagonistic from agreeable persons is surely debatable; further, distinctions can be made among the facets of Neuroticism and Agreeableness. Some people score high in Neuroticism because they are anxious and depressed, even though they rarely experience anger.

Some Empirical Correlates of Agreeableness in the Augmented BLSA

In addition to conceptual analysis, understanding of a psychological construct must be based on empirical findings. In this section we present some data from the Augmented Baltimore Longitudinal Study of Aging (BLSA; Shock et al., 1984) on the correlates of an Agreeableness scale. The BLSA is an ongoing study; in the 27 years it has been in existence, a variety of measures have been administered to subjects and are available as criteria for examining other scales. Most of the personality data, and all the data from women, have been collected since 1978.

The Augmented BLSA is an extension of the BLSA in which husbands and wives of participants were invited to participate in questionnaire studies (McCrae, 1982). In general, the sample is well educated and healthy, but it does not differ markedly from national norms on the three personality dimensions of Neuroticism, Extraversion, or Openness to experience (Costa, McCrae et al., 1986).

The Agreeableness scale for which self-report data are available is a 10-item instrument that served as a preliminary form of the 18-item Agreeableness Scale of the NEO Personality Inventory (NEO–PI; Costa & McCrae, 1985b). The NEO–PI is a 181-item questionnaire designed to measure the five major domains of personality, with subscales, or facet scales, for important traits within each of the domains of Neuroticism, Extraversion, and Openness. In addition to the self-report form, there is a parallel observer rating form (Form R). Both forms have been extensively validated in a series of studies using other personality questionnaires, adjective checklists, observer ratings, and sentence completions. Due to the brevity of the preliminary Agreeableness scale, it seems likely that the correlations presented here underestimate the values that would be seen with the full scale. Peer ratings on the full, 18-item version of the Agreeableness scale are also available for a subset of subjects (McCrae & Costa, 1987). As with self-reports, peer rated NEO–PI Agreeableness is significantly correlated with the Agreeableness factors represented in Tables 3.1 and 3.2 (McCrae, Costa, & Busch, 1986).

Johnson, Butcher, Null and Johnson (1984) conducted a factor analysis of the items of the full MMPI and classified the resulting factors in terms of the five-factor model. They proposed that factors identified as Cynicism, Aggressive Hostility, Delinquency, and Family Attachment would fall within the domain of Agreeableness. Research on a subset of BLSA subjects who had completed the MMPI confirmed these expectations, with significant correlations ranging (in absolute value) from .30 to .48, $N = 131$, $p < .001$ (Costa, Busch, Zonderman, & McCrae, 1986). Aggressive Hostility and Delinquency were also significantly negatively related to peer rated Agreeableness. Of the standard MMPI scales, both self-reported and peer-rated Agreeableness are significantly inversely related to Psychopathic Deviate and Mania scales.

The association of disagreeableness with the MMPI Psychopathic Deviate scale was paralleled by results of a study using the Eysenck and Eysenck (1975) Psychoticism (P) scale, which has frequently been interpreted as a measure of psychopathic tendencies (McCrae & Costa, 1985a). Despite the restricted range in this sample and its consequent low internal consistency, the P scale was significantly correlated with both self-reported and peer-rated Agreeableness and loaded chiefly on the Agreeableness factor in a joint factor analysis.

The association with the MMPI Mania scale is also echoed in correlations with some aspects of Zuckerman's (1979) Sensation Seeking Scale (SSS-V). Although it is not correlated with Thrill and Adventure Seeking or Experience Seeking subscales, self-reported Agreeableness is inversely related to both Disinhibition and Boredom Susceptibility ($rs = -.18, -.12, N = 318, p < .05$); these relations are replicated in peer rating data ($rs = -.26, -.23, N = 193, p < .05$). Sensation seeking seems to include aspects of at least three domains of personality: Extraversion leads to an enjoyment of excitement, Openness leads to need for variety, and low Agreeableness leads to a disregard of others in favor of one's own amusement. The motorcyclist roaring through traffic at top speed does not show much *Gemeinschaftsgefühl.*

A somewhat different approach to personality assessment is offered by the Defense Mechanism Inventory (DMI; Ihilevich & Gleser, 1986). Based in psychoanalytic theories of defense, this instrument presents subjects with hypothetical situations and asks them to choose from among five defensive reactions how they would act, feel, think, and wish to act. Responses are scored for five categories of defense. In a subsample of BLSA participants who completed the DMI, Agreeableness was significantly related to Turning Against Object, $r = -.22$, Projection, $r = -.17$, Principalization, $r = .16$, and Reversal, $r = .16$, all $N = 156, p < .05$. Individuals who scored low on Turning Against Object and Projection and high on Reversal were also rated by peers as being significantly higher in Agreeableness, $rs = -.35, -.24$, and $.30$, respectively, $N = 88, p < .05$. Similar relations with DMI scales are reported by Lorr (1986) for Interpersonal Style Inventory scales measuring Socialization, Lorr's version of Agreeableness. As interpreted in the DMI manual, these correlations suggest that the antagonistic individual uses "direct or indirect aggression . . . to master perceived external threats or mask inner conflicts" (p. 18) and attributes "negative intent or characteristics to others" (p. 19); the agreeable individual, by contrast, "falsifies reality by reinterpreting it through . . . cliches, truisms, platitudes, and different forms of sophistry" (p. 20) and exhibits "Pollyanna-like attitudes, exaggeratedly cheerful emotions, and unduly positive behavioral responses to frustrating or threatening events" (p. 21). The hypothetical situations of the DMI bear some resemblance to the situations described in the SI, and it might be possible to score SI responses for these defenses. Would individuals who react to waiting in line with truisms about the virtues of patience be particularly protected from CHD?

Finally, the NEO-PI Agreeableness scale shows meaningful correlations with some of the Guilford-Zimmerman Temperament Scales (GZTS; Guilford, Zimmerman, & Guilford, 1976). The GZTS was administered to men in the BLSA almost from the beginning of the study, in 1959. Three scales are significantly related to both self-reports and peer ratings of Agreeableness: Restraint, Friendliness, and Personal Relations. The correlations range in magnitude from .18 to .33 and are of particular interest because they antedate the administration of the Agreeableness scale by from 4 to 24 years; the mean interval is 16.5 years. These findings suggest a substantial degree of longitudinal stability for Agreeableness scores—virtually a prerequisite for attributing causal status to Antagonism as a risk factor for CHD.

Summary

The purpose of reviewing these conceptions and correlates of Agreeableness has been to broaden and deepen understanding of the domain, and to alert researchers to the wealth of constructs that are candidates for the status of CHD risk factor. A summary seems in order, although it is the nature of the broadest level of personality traits that they defy simple definition. A description of extreme scorers is simplest, although few individuals will be aptly described by either characterization, as most people fall somewhere between. (In addition, of course, the same person will be more or less agreeable depending on the circumstances: Most people are more agreeable to members of their own family and social circle than to strangers.)

Agreeable people are genuinely concerned with others and are deeply touched by others' feelings. For them, cooperation is not a strategy but a natural response to common needs. They assume that other people share their generous feelings and gloss over contrary instances. To avoid offending others they may be annoyingly compliant, even to the point of dependency. In general, however, their transparent friendliness makes them particularly likeable.

Antagonistic people are fundamentally self-centered, concerned with their own gain, status, or amusement. They are willing to fight for their goals, and they regard others as either hostile competitors seeking the same selfish ends or as contemptible fools. Antagonistic people may be physically assaultive and verbally abusive, but they may also be skilled manipulators who never raise their voice, because they never need to. Because their emotional and motivational center of gravity is in themselves, the joys and sorrows of others do not concern them, and they can be coolly rational. Antagonistic people are not necessarily antisocial; indeed, their rationality and interpersonal skills may make them benefactors of society—but only when they regard service to society as enlightened self-interest.

EMPIRICAL LINKS BETWEEN POTENTIAL FOR HOSTILITY AND AGREEABLENESS

To examine empirical relations between measures of Agreeableness, hostility, and ratings based on the SI, we turn to two smaller samples. In the First College sample, 51 male and 65 female students participated in a study of smoking, personality, and cardiovascular reactivity, using an experimental protocol described elsewhere (Dembroski, MacDougall, Cardozo, Ireland, & Krug, 1985; MacDougall, Dembroski, Slaats, Herd, & Eliot, 1983). The SI was administered in two parts and scored by a trained rater. Subjects also completed a battery of self-report measures including the NEO Personality Inventory and several measures of anger and hostility.

In the Second College sample, 101 male students from a small college in the South were subjects. They completed a battery of tests including the NEO–PI and various anger measures, were given the SI, and were asked to nominate two male and two female friends or acquaintances who could provide data on the rating form of the NEO Personality Inventory. The SIs were scored by two trained psychologists;[3] Spearman–Brown corrected interrater reliability for the variables of interest here ranged from .86 to .91.

In previous research, only preliminary forms of the Agreeableness and Conscientiousness scales of the NEO Personality Inventory were available from self-reports, and adult rather than college-age samples were employed. It is necessary, therefore, first to consider the reliability and validity of these personality measures. In the Second College sample, internal consistency coefficients for the Agreeableness and Conscientiousness scales were .73 and .82, respectively, for self-reports, and .87 and .89, respectively, for peer ratings. As in adult samples (McCrae & Costa, 1987), external observers appear to provide somewhat more consistent ratings on these two dimensions. All the values, however, are acceptably high for 18-item scales.

Tables 3.3 and 3.4 give information on the convergent and discriminant validity of the NEO–PI domain scales. Table 3.3 shows intraclass correlations among pairs of peer raters computed by the double-entry method; the convergent correlations range from .30 for Agreeableness to .53 for Extraversion; none of the divergent correlations exceeds .15 in absolute magnitude. From these data and the fact that the average subject had 3.44 raters, it is possible to use the Spearman–Brown formula to calculate the interrater reliabilities of the mean peer ratings. These range from .59 to .79 and would generally be considered acceptable.[4]

Table 3.4 provides additional evidence of validity through strong correlations between self-reports and mean peer ratings. Particularly notable is the correlation of .51 for Agreeableness, which compares favorably with self/peer correlations for a wide range of personality characteristics (see McCrae, 1982, for a

---

[3]Our thanks to James MacDougall and Linda Musante for providing the SI ratings.

[4]Correlations among peer raters are noticeably lower than those between SI raters, in this as in most studies. This may be attributable to the training and expertise of SI-raters, but it may also reflect the fact that SI raters work with identical samples of behavior—the taped interview. Different peer raters are likely to have observed quite different aspects of the individual in very different settings. The greater breadth of behavior sampling in peer ratings may result in higher validity at the cost of lower interrater reliability.

TABLE 3.3
Intraclass Correlations Among Peer Raters
For NEO Personality Inventory Domain Scores

	1.	2.	3.	4.	5.
1. Neuroticism	.32	−.09	.07	−.11	−.15
2. Extraversion		.53	.08	−.02	.03
3. Openness			.42	.09	.00
4. Agreeableness				.30	.06
5. Consciousness					.44

Note: N = 884 pairs of 344 peer raters for 101 targets.

review). We can, therefore, employ these measures with some confidence that they are valid measures of the five factors.

Agreeableness, Neuroticism, and Hostility

Neuroticism is related to somatic complaints but not to objectively verifiable CHD; it is therefore likely to be a serious confound in psychosomatic research (Costa & McCrae, 1987). Much of the confusion surrounding the role of anger and hostility in cardiovascular disease is probably due to the fact that there are both neurotic and antagonistic forms of hostility. The former we have described as hot blooded, the latter as cold blooded.[5] Although this distinction is perhaps most easily seen from the perspective of the five-factor model, it is worth pointing out that a similar distinction has also been made repeatedly by researchers working within the area of hostility. As long ago as 1957, Buss and Durkee reported two factors in their Hostility Inventory (BDHI). The first was defined by the resentment and Suspicion subscales (with the addition of Guilt for women) and constituted an Experience or Awareness factor. The second factor, Expression, was primarily defined by Assault and Verbal Hostility. This two-factor structure has been widely replicated (Bendig, 1962; Edmunds & Kendrick, 1980; Sarason, 1961, and Zelin, Adler, and Myerson (1972) devised an instrument, the Anger Self Report (ASR), to provide explicit scales for the measurement of experience and expression of anger.

Our review suggests three clear hypotheses. First, the two factors of Experience and Expression should be related to Neuroticism and Agreeableness versus Antagonism, respectively; second, Potential for Hostility should be related primarily to the Expression factor; and third, the Expression, but not the Experience, of anger should be related to CHD.

Evidence in support of the first hypothesis is provided by the two studies of college students who were given the NEO Personality Inventory and a set of anger

[5]Recall that these distinctions apply only to experienced affect, not to physiological reactions. Studies of Neuroticism, Agreeableness, and cardiovascular reactivity (MacDougall, Dembroski, Slaats, Herd, & Eliot, 1983) are clearly needed.

TABLE 3.4
Correlations Between Self-Reports and Mean Peer Ratings
For NEO Personality Inventory Domain Scores

Peer Ratings	Self-Reports				
	1.	2.	3.	4.	5.
1. Neuroticism	.36***	−.08	.05	−.13	−.22*
2. Extraversion	−.11	.52***	.20*	−.02	−.02
3. Openness	.03	.17	.64***	.22*	−.11
4. Agreeableness	−.01	−.01	.13	.51***	−.01
5. Conscientiousness	.01	−.10	.04	.03	.51***

Note: $N = 100$.
*$p < .05$; ***$p < .001$.

and hostility items derived from the Buss Durkee Hostility Inventory (BDHI; Buss & Durkee, 1957), the State-Trait Anger Scales (Spielberger, Jacobs, Russell, & Crane, 1983), the Multidimensional Anger Inventory (Siegel, 1985), and the Anger Self-Report (Zelin, Alder & Myerson, 1972). Two factors were rotated from a pool of 77 items in both samples; items with loadings greater than .40 in both samples are given in Table 3.5. It is clear that these are the familiar Anger Experience and Anger Expression factors.

Correlations of the two-factor scores with NEO-PI domain scales are given in Table 3.6, and support the hypothesis that Anger Experience is related chiefly to Neuroticism and might equally well be called Neurotic Hostility; Anger Expression is related almost exclusively to low Agreeableness and might be called Antagonistic Hostility. As multimethod validity evidence, note the substantial correlation between the Anger Expression factor from self-reports and peer ratings of Agreeableness.

A different study addresses the hypothesis that Potential for Hostility is uniquely related to the Expression of anger. Musante, MacDougall, Dembroski, and Costa (in press) admistered a series of measures of anger and hostility to 82 male college students and 50 adult males and also obtained SI ratings of Potential for Hostility. A factor analysis of the scales confirmed the two-factor structure for hostility, with an Anger Experience factor best defined by the BDHI Irritability and Resentment scales, and an Anger Expression factor defined by the ASR General Expression of Anger and the BDHI Verbal Expression. Potential for Hostility was uncorrelated with the Experience factor but was significantly related to the Expression factor in both student, $r = .43$, and adult, $r = .49$, samples.

Finally, Siegman, Dembroski, and Ringel (1987) examined anger Experience and Expression factors in a group of patients who had been scheduled for coronary arteriography; they labeled these factors Neurotic Hostility and Reactive Hostility, respectively. The Reactive (or Antagonistic) Hostility factor, as hypothesized, was significantly positively related to severity of coronary artery disease, whereas the Neurotic Hostility factor was significantly negatively related. This study might be interpreted as providing support for the views that disagreeable-

TABLE 3.5
Items Defining Hostility Factors in Two Samples

Factor I: Anger Experience (Neurotic Hostility)

I am quick tempered.
It makes me furious when I am criticized in front of others.
When I get frustrated, I feel like hitting someone.
I tend to get angry more frequently than most people.
I am secretly quite critical of others.
I harbor grudges that I don't tell anyone about.
I often feel angrier than I think I should.
I feel guilty about expressing my anger.
When I am angry with someone, I take it out on whomever is around.
I am surprised at how often I feel angry.
At times, I feel angry for no specific reason.
I often make threats I don't mean to carry out.
When I get angry, I stay angry for hours.
I get so angry I feel like I might lose control.

Factor II: Anger Expression (Antagonistic Hostility)

When I disapprove of my friends' behavior, I let them know.
If I am mad, I really let people know it.
I will criticize someone to his face if he deserves it.
When I am angry with someone, I let that person know.
If someone annoys me, I am apt to tell him what I think of him.
If I don't like somebody, I will tell him so.
I find it easy to express anger at people.
Even when someone does something mean to me, I don't let him know I'm upset.
  (reversed)
It's difficult for me to let people know I'm angry. (reversed)

---

ness leads to CHD, whereas Neuroticism leads to false positive diagnoses.

Potential for Hostility and Agreeableness

Several lines of evidence thus suggest that Potential for Hostility as rated from the SI measures some aspect of the broader dimension of Agreeableness versus Antagonism. Both Potential for Hostility and Agreeableness are differentially related to the Expression of Anger factor. Instructions for scoring Potential for Hostility require the rater to consider instances of rudeness, criticality, and uncooperativeness as well as overt expressions of anger and aggressive reactions. Perhaps the most direct evidence of the conceptual similarity of Antagonism and Potential for Hostility, especially its Hostile Style scoring category, was given in a study that used adjective scales in conjunction with SI scoring. After listening to tapes and scoring for components of Type A including Potential for Hostility, Dembroski also rated subjects on the 80-item adjective checklist used to define the five factors (Dembroski & Costa, 1987). In both the Multiple Risk Factor Intervention Trials (MRFIT) and the Western Collaborative Group Study (WCSG)

TABLE 3.6
Correlations of Hostility Factors with NEO Personality Inventory
Domain Scales in two Samples

NEO–PI Domains	Factor I: Anger Experience	Factor II: Anger Expression
	First College Sample Self-Reports	
Neuroticism	.63***	.00
Extraversion	−.15	.16
Openness	−.21*	.08
Agreeableness	−.39***	−.36***
Conscientiousness	−.19*	−.12
	Second College Sample Self-Reports	
Neuroticism	.69***	.04
Extraversion	−.27**	.22*
Openness	−.22*	−.03
Agreeableness	−.27**	−.44***
Conscientiousness	.04	−.11
	Second College Sample Peer Ratings	
Neuroticism	.28**	.11
Extraversion	−.24*	.06
Openness	−.18	−.11
Agreeableness	−.20	−.42***
Conscientiousness	.08	−.15

Note: N = 108 for First College sample, 100 for Second.
*p < .05; **p < .01; ***p < .001

samples, Potential for Hostility was strongly correlated ($rs = -.66, -.71$) with the Agreeableness factor defined by the adjectives listed in Table 3.1. Total Potential for Hostility and two of its scoring categories, Hostile Content and Hostile Intensity, also had moderately large correlations with the Neuroticism factor; however, Hostile Style was virtually a pure measure of Antagonism.

This study shows that individuals who are rated as high in Potential for Hostility are seen by the same rater as being highly disagreeable. We do not know, however, if the raters would draw the same inferences from behavior outside the context of the interview, or whether these assessments correspond to Agreeableness as perceived by the subject, or by others who know the subject well. It would be extraordinarily useful to show that alternative assessments of Agreeableness versus Antagonism correspond to SI ratings of Potential for Hostility. Self-report scales in particular are a far more convenient form of gathering data, because they do not require the use of a trained interviewer or rater. It remains to be seen, however, whether self-assessments or lay rater assessments of Agreeableness are empirically related to ratings of Potential for Hostility; it is that question to which we now turn.

Table 3.7 presents correlations of the categories and total Potential for Hostility with NEO–PI scales in the two college samples described previously. The correlation of total Potential for Hostility with self-reported NEO–PI Agreeableness is significantly negative in both samples, as is that of Hostile Intensity. Hostile

TABLE 3.7
Correlations Between SI Ratings
And NEO Personality Inventory Domain Scores

NEO–PI Domains	SI Ratings			
	Hostile Content	Hostile Intensity	Hostile Style	Potential for Hostility
	First College Sample Self-Reports			
Neuroticism	.27**	.19*	.02	.27**
Extraversion	.02	−.07	−.18	−.05
Openness	.04	−.07	.11	.02
Agreeableness	−.24**	−.23**	−.12	−.33***
Conscientiousness	−.24**	−.18	−.15	−.27**
	Second College Sample Self-Reports			
Neuroticism	.15	.13	−.12	−.01
Extraversion	−.03	−.04	−.08	−.04
Openness	−.24*	−.22*	−.33***	−.36***
Agreeableness	−.17	−.33***	−.22*	−.30**
Conscientiousness	.00	−.09	.12	.09
	Second College Sample Peer Ratings			
Neuroticism	.07	−.01	.02	.03
Extraversion	−.13	−.08	−.09	−.11
Openness	−.19	−.14	−.27**	−.30**
Agreeableness	−.03	−.08	−.19	−.16
Conscientiousness	.07	−.06	.07	.04

Note: N = 116 for First College self-reports, 100 for Second College self-reports, and 101 for Second College peer ratings.
    *$p < .05$; **$p < .01$; ***$p < .001$.

Content shows the same pattern in the first sample but does not reach significance in the second; Hostile Style is significant in the second sample, but not the first.

The correlations of the Hostility scoring categories with Neuroticism is also of interest, given the dual nature of hostility. Hostile Content and Intensity are significantly positively related to Neuroticism in the first sample and show a similar trend in the second; this trend reaches significance when SI-derived Hostile Content and Intensity are correlated with the Hostility facet of Neuroticism, rs =.25, .31, N = 100, $p < .05$. By contrast, Hostile Style is unrelated to overall Neuroticism in both samples, and to NEO–PI Hostility, $r = −.06$, $n.s.$, in the second sample. As in Dembroski's MRFIT and WCGS ratings, Hostile Style appears to be related exclusively to the antagonistic form of hostility.

Correlations between SI ratings and peer-rated Agreeableness are in the same direction but fall short of statistical significance (although the correlation with Hostile Style, $r = −.19$, would be considered significant using a one-tailed test). Indeed, the only significant correlations in the bottom third of Table 3.7 are with Openness to Experience; they suggest that closed college males are perceived as higher in Potential for Hostility. The same correlations are also seen in self-reports in the Second College sample, but they are not theoretically expectable and are not replicated in the First College sample. Similarly, the correlations between Potential for Hostility and Conscientiousness seen in the First College sample are not replicated in the Second. Pending future findings, the associations of Potential for Hostility with Openness and Conscientiousness should probably be attributed to sampling error.

Recall that the data in Table 3.7 come from college samples, not groups at risk for CHD. In the First College sample in particular, there is considerable restriction in the range of Hostile Style, with only 4 out of 117 scoring above 3 on a 5-point scale. With a fuller range, stronger correlations might be seen.

Assessing Coronary-Prone Behavior

We have reviewed evidence that both Anger Expression factor scores from the BDHI and Potential for Hostility as rated from the SI are predictors of CHD and correlates of the broad personality dimension of Agreeableness versus Antagonism. Do measures of Agreeableness themselves predict CHD? Are they as good or better than measures of more limited traits in the same domain? At present we have no data on this question, but this is an extraordinarily attractive hypothesis.

It is possible that CHD is related only to the specific facet of Agreeableness versus Antagonism measured by Potential for Hostility, but it is also possible that other aspects of this broad dimension may be equally toxic. We have reason to believe that the individual who is rude, uncooperative, and argumentative is at risk for CHD, but what about individuals who are politely manipulative, or whose Antagonism is seen chiefly in stinginess or suspiciousness?

By focusing on the question "What is the toxic component of Type A?" researchers have limited themselves to the search for aspects of Type A—either as conceptualized or as actually assessed in SI scoring—that are related to CHD. If there are coronary-prone characteristics—that is, traits that in fact predict or causally contribute to CHD—that do not fall within the framework of TABP, they will not be found by pursuing this strategy. At some point the process of analyzing and refining the scoring of SIs is likely to reach a point of diminishing returns. Inferences made from a 10- to 15-minute sample of behavior channeled by a series of questions that may or may not be directly relevant to coronary-prone behavior form a tenuous basis for predicting future health status. In fact, given the limitations of the SI as a source of information about the individual, it is remarkable that correlations of the magnitude of .30 can be seen with self-report questionnaire measures of similar constructs.

It would certainly be premature to abandon the SI in research on coronary-prone behavior. Too much has been invested in it, and the alternatives are far from being well established as CHD risk factors. But it does seem necessary to begin to supplement the SI with additional predictors, and measures of Agreeableness should certainly be among them.

Historically, interviewer ratings have been the preferred method of assessing coronary-prone behavior. Many researchers, including Rosenman (1978), have a pervasive distrust of self-reports, feeling that subjects either lack insight into their own personality or deliberately distort their answers to present a more favorable impression. Undoubtedly it is the case that individuals can misrepresent themselves if they wish to, and, in some circumstances (such as employment screening) they probably do. For researchers who have faith only in the ratings of trained experts, an interview of some kind seems essential. One approach would be to conduct the standard SI and then add additional questions concerning hostility, cynicism, and interpersonal relations. Future results might show increased validity of such an extended interview.

A second approach is to utilize peer ratings. Friends and relatives may not be trained experts, but they do have the benefit of a much longer acquaintance under more representative circumstances. Data from previous studies (McCrae & Costa, 1987) and from Tables 3.3 and 3.4 of this chapter demonstrate that peer ratings of Agreeableness have acceptable degrees of reliability and validity, particularly when aggregated over several raters. The fact that the correlations between SI-derived Potential for Hostility and peer-rated Agreeableness do not achieve significance might be taken as evidence of the limited utility of peer ratings, but the criticism cuts both ways. SI raters may have been taken in by the self-presentational skills of the subject and may have failed to detect an underlying Antagonism with which longtime acquaintances were all too familiar. Peer ratings, hence, may be poor predictors of SI ratings, but very good measures of the characteristics that SI ratings are intended to uncover.

Data such as those in Table 3.4, however, also restore some confidence in self-reports. In many respects, individuals know themselves better than anyone else ever can, and for many purposes they are quite willing to describe what they know honestly and accurately. It might seem that Agreeableness would be particularly subject to distortion—hypocrisy is, after all, one of the cardinal features of Machiavellianism. But most disagreeable individuals are perfectly willing to let others know of their dispositions; indeed, they are often proud of being tough and cynical.

In judging the value of self-report questionnaires, we should be very careful to distinguish form and content. The Jenkins Activity Survey (JAS; Jenkins, Zyzanski, & Rosenman, 1979) and the Framingham Type A Scale (Haynes, Levine, Scotch, Feileib, & Kannel, 1978) have sometimes been criticized as being unable to predict objectively verifiable CHD (Costa, 1986), and it might be assumed that these failures are attributable to the questionnaire format. However, it is clear from a reading of the items and a review of their correlates that neither of these instruments is a clear measure of Agreeableness versus Antagonism. The JAS appears to measure aspects of Extraversion and Conscientiousness, whereas the Framingham scale is heavily saturated with Neuroticism (Chesney, Black, Chadwick, & Rosenman, 1981).

On the other hand, some scales do measure aspects of Agreeableness and have been shown to predict CHD outcomes. The Cook–Medley HO scale, for example, has been prospectively related to CHD mortality (Barefoot, Dahlstrom, & Williams, 1983; Shekelle, Gale, Ostfeld, & Paul, 1983), and Siegler (1985) reports that Scale L, Suspiciousness, of the Sixteen Personality Factor Questionnaire (Cattell, Eber, Tatsuoka, 1970) predicts coronary death in the Duke Longitudinal Study. Both these scales measure only limited aspects of the full domain of Agreeableness, and both are also related to Neuroticism. Despite these limitations, they have shown some value in the prediction of CHD, and they give additional grounds for supplementing interviews with self-report measures of Agreeableness in future studies of CHD.

REFERENCES

Adler, A. (1964). *Social interest: A challenge to mankind.* New York: Capricorn Books. (Original work published 1938)

Barefoot, J. C., Dahlstrom, W. G., & Williams, R. B., Jr. (1983). Hostility, CHD incidence and total mortality: A 25-year follow-up study of 255 physicians. *Psychosomatic Medicine, 45,* 59–63.

Bendig, A. W. (1962). Factor analytic scales of covert and overt hostility. *Journal of Consulting Psychology, 26,* 200.

Block, J. (1961). *The Q-sort method in personality assessment and psychiatric research.* Springfield, IL: Charles C. Thomas.

Brand, C. (1986). The psychological bases of political attitudes and interests. In S. Modgil & C. Modgil (Eds.), *Hans Eysenck: Consensus and controversy.* London: Falmer.

Buss, A. H., & Durkee, A. (1957). An inventory for assessing different kinds of hostility. *Journal of Consulting Psychology, 21,* 343–349.

Cattell, R. B., Eber, H. W., Tatsuoka, M. M. (1970). *The handbook for the Sixteen Personality Factor Questionnaire.* Champaign, IL: Institute for Personality and Ability Testing.

Chesney, M. A., Black, G. W., Chadwick, J. H., & Rosenman, R. H. (1981). Psychological correlates of the Type A behavior pattern. *Journal of Behavioral Medicine, 4,* 217–229.

Costa, P. T., Jr. (1986). Is Neuroticism a risk factor for CAD? Is Type A a measure of Neuroticism? In T. Schmidt, T. Dembroski, & G. Blümchen (Eds.), *Biological and psychological factors in cardiovascular disease* (pp. 85–95). New York: Springer–Verlag.

Costa, P. T., Jr., Busch, C. M., Zonderman, A. B., & McCrae, R. R. (1986). Correlations of MMPI factor scales with measures of the five factor model of personality. *Journal of Personality Assessment, 50,* 640–650.

Costa, P T., Jr., & McCrae, R. R. (1980). Still stable after all these years: Personality as a key to some issues in adulthood and old age. In P. B. Baltes & O. G. Brim, Jr. (Eds.), *Life span development and behavior* (Vol. 3, pp. 65–102). New York: Academic Press.

Costa, P. T., Jr., & McCrae, R. R. (1985a). Hypochondriasis, neuroticism, and aging: When are somatic complaints unfounded? *American Psychologist, 40,* 19–28.

Costa, P. T., Jr., & McCrae, R. R. (1985b). *The NEO Personality Inventory manual.* Odessa, FL: Psychological Assessment Resources.

Costa, P. T., Jr., & McCrae, R. R. (1987). Neuroticism, somatic complaints, and disease: Is the bark worse than the bite? *Journal of Personality, 55,* 301–316.

Costa, P. T., Jr., & McCrae, R. R., & Holland, J. L. (1984). Personality and vocational interests in an adult sample. *Journal of Applied Psychology, 69,* 390–400.

Costa, P. T., Jr., McCrae, R. R., Zonderman, A. B., Barbano, H. E., Lebowitz, B., & Larson, D. M. (1986). Cross sectional studies of personality in a national sample: II. Stability in neuroticism, extraversion, and openness. *Psychology and Aging, 1,* 144–149.

Costa, P. T., Jr., Zonderman, A. B., McCrae, R. R., & Williams, R. B., Jr. (1985). Content and comprehensiveness in the MMPI: An item factor analysis in a normal adult sample. *Journal of Personality and Social Psychology, 48,* 925–933.

Costa, P. T., Jr., Zonderman, A. B., McCrae, R. R., & Williams, R. B., Jr. (1986). Cynicism and paranoid alienation in the Cook and Medley HO scale. *Psychosomatic Medicine*, *48*, 283–285.

Crandall, J. E. (1975). A scale for social interest. *Journal of Individual Psychology*, *31*, 187–195.

Crandall, J. E. (1984). Social interest as a moderator of life stress. *Journal of Personality and Social Psychology*, *47*, 164–174.

Dembroski, T. M., & Costa, P. T., Jr. (1987). Coronary prone behavior: Components of the Type A pattern and hostility. *Journal of Personality*, *55*, 211–235.

Dembroski, T. M., MacDougall, J. M., Cordozo, J. R., Ireland, S. K., & Krug, J. (1985). Selective cardiovascular effects of stress and cigarette smoking in young women. *Health Psychology*, *4*, 153–167.

Dembroski, T. M., MacDougall, J. M., Williams, R. B., Jr., Haney, T. L., & Blumenthal, J. A. (1985). Components of Type A, hostility and anger-in: Relationship to angiographic findings. *Psychosomatic Medicine*, *47*, 219–233.

Diamond, E. L. (1982). The role of anger and hostility in essential hypertension and coronary heart disease. *Psychological Bulletin*, *92*, 410–433.

Digman, J. M. (1986, August). The Big Five factors of personality in developmental perspective. In W. T. Norman (Chair), *What are the basic dimensions of personality?* Symposium conducted at the annual meeting of the American Psychological Association, Washington, DC.

Edmunds, G., & Kendrick, D. C. (1980). *The measurement of human aggressiveness*. West Sussex, England: Ellis Horwood.

Eysenck, H. J. (1954). *The psychology of politics*. London: Routledge & Kegan Paul.

Eysenck, H. J., & Eysenck, S. B. G. (1975) *Manual of the Eysenck Personality Questionnaire*. San Diego, CA: EdITS.

Geis, F. (1978) Machiavellianism. In H. London & J. E. Exner, Jr. (Eds.), *Dimensions of personality* (pp. 305–364). New York: Wiley.

Goldberg, L. R. (1981). Language and individual differences: The search for universals in personality lexicons. In L. Wheeler (Ed.), *Review of personality and social psychology* (Vol. 2, pp. 141–165). Beverly Hills, CA: Sage.

Guilford, J. S., Zimmerman, W. S., & Guilford, J. P. (1976). *The Guilford–Zimmerman Temperament Survey Handbook: Twenty-five years of research and application*. San Diego, CA: EdITS.

Harburg, E., Erfurt, J. C., Hauenstein, L. S., Chape, C., Schull, W. J., & Schork, M. A. (1973). Socio-ecological stress, suppressed hostility, skin color, and black–white male blood pressure: Detroit. *Psychosomatic Medicine*, *35*, 276–296.

Hartshorn, H., & May, M. A. (1928). *Studies in the nature of character, Vol. I: Studies in deceit*. New York: Macmillan.

Haynes, S. G., Levine, S., Scotch, N. A., Feinleib, M., & Kannel, W. B. (1978). The relationship of psychosocial factors to coronary disease in the Framingham Study. I. Methods and risk factors. *American Journal of Epidemiology*, *107*, 362–383.

Hecker, M., Frautschi, N., Chesney, M., Black, G., & Roseman, R. H. (1985, March). *Components of the Type A behavior and coronary disease*. Paper presented at the meeting of the Society of Behavioral Medicine, New Orleans.

Hogan, R. T. (1983). Socioanalytic theory of personality. In M. M. Page (Ed.), *1982 Nebraska Symposium on Motivation: Personality—current theory and research* (pp. 58–89). Lincoln, NE: University of Nebraska Press.

Holland, J. L. (1985). *Self-Directed Search—1985 edition*. Odessa, FL: Psychological Assessment Resources.

Horney, K. (1945). *Our inner conflicts*. New York: Norton.

Horney, K. (1950). *Neurosis and human growth*. New York: Norton.

Ihilevich, D., & Gleser, G. C. (1986). *Defense mechanisms: Their classification, correlates, and measurement with the Defense Mechanism Inventory*. Owosso, MI: DMI Associates.

Jackson, D. N. (1976). *Jackson Personality Inventory manual*. Goshen, NY: Research Psychologists Press.

Jenkins, C. D., Zyzanski, S. J., & Rosenman, R. H. (1979). *Manual for the Jenkins Activity Survey*. New York: The Psychological Corporation.

Johnson, J. H., Butcher, J. N., Null, C., & Johnson, K. N. (1984). Replicated item level factor analysis of the full MMPI. *Journal of Personality and Social Psychology, 47,* 105–114.

Keehn, R. J., Goldberg, I. D., & Beebe, G. W. (1974). Twenty-four year mortality follow-up of army veterans with disability separations for psychoneurosis in 1944. *Psychosomatic Medicine, 36,* 27–46.

Leary, T. (1957). *Interpersonal diagnosis of personality.* New York: Ronald Press.

Lorr, M. (1986). *Interpersonal Style Inventory (ISI) manual.* Los Angeles: Western Psychological Services.

Luborsky, L., Docherty, J. P., & Penick, S. (1973). Onset conditions for psychosomatic symptoms: A comparative review of immediate observation with retrospective research. *Psychosomatic Medicine, 35,* 187–204.

MacDougall, J. M., Dembroski, T. M., Slaats, S., Herd, J. A., & Eliot, R. S. (1983). Selective cardiovascular effects of stress and cigarette smoking. *Journal of Human Stress, 9,* 13–21.

Matthews, K. A., Glass, D. C., Rosenman, R. H., & Bortner, R. W. (1977). Competitive drive, pattern A, and coronary heart disease: A further analysis of some data from the Western Collaborative Group Study. *Journal of Chronic Disease, 30,* 489–498.

McCrae, R. R. (1982). Consensual validation of personality traits: Evidence from self-reports and ratings. *Journal of Personality and Social Psychology, 43,* 293–303.

McCrae, R. R., & Costa, P. T., Jr. (1985a). Comparison of EPI and Psychoticism scales with measures of the five factor model of personality. *Personality and Individual Differences, 6,* 587–597.

McCrae, R. R., & Costa, P. T., Jr. (1985b). Updating Norman's "adequate taxonomy": Intelligence and personality dimensions in natural language and in questionnaires. *Journal of Personality and Social Psychology, 49,* 710–721.

McCrae, R. R., & Costa, P. T., Jr. (1987). Validation of the five factor model of personality across instruments and observers. *Journal of Personality and Social Psychology, 52,* 81–90.

McCrae, R. R., Costa, P. T., Jr., & Busch, C. M. (1986). Evaluating comprehensiveness in personality systems: The California Q-Set and the five factor model. *Journal of Personality, 54,* 430–446.

Murray, H. A. (1938). *Explorations in personality.* New York: Oxford University Press.

Musante, L., MacDougall, J. M., Dembroski, T. M., & Costa, P. T., Jr., (in press). *Potential for hostility, and the dimensions of anger. Health Psychology.*

Norman, W. T. (1963). Toward an adequate taxonomy of personality attributes: Replicated factor structure in peer nomination personality ratings. *Journal of Abnormal and Social Psychology, 66,* 574–583.

Rosenman, R. H. (1978). The interview method of assessment of the coronary-prone behavior pattern. In T. M. Dembroski, S. M. Weiss, J. L. Shields, S. G. Haynes, & M. Feinleib (Eds.), *Coronary-prone behavior* (pp. 55–69). New York: Springer-Verlag.

Sarason, I. (1961). Intercorrelations among measures of hostility. *Journal of Clinical Psychology, 17,* 192–195.

Shekelle, R. B., Gale, M., Ostfeld, A. M., & Paul, O. (1983). Hostility, risk of coronary heart disease and mortality. *Psychosomatic Medicine, 45,* 109–114.

Shock, N. W., Greulich, R. C., Andres, R., Arenberg, D., Costa, P. T., Jr., Lakatta, E. G., & Tobin, J. D. (1984). *Normal human aging: The Baltimore Longitudinal Study of Aging* (NIH Publication No. 84-2450). Bethesda, MD: National Institutes of Health.

Siegel, J. M. (1985). The Multidimensional Anger Inventory. In M. Chesney & R. H. Rosenman (Eds.), *Anger and hostility in cardiovascular and behavioral disorders.* Washington, DC: Hemisphere.

Siegler, I. C. (1985, August). *Invited Presidential Address, Division 20, Adult Development and Aging.* Paper presented at the annual convention of the American Psychological Association, Los Angeles.

Siegman, A. W., Dembroski, T. M., & Ringel, N. (1987). Components of hostility and the severity of coronary artery disease. *Psychosomatic Medicine, 49,* 127–135.

Spielberger, C. D., Jacobs, G. A., Russell, S. & Crane, R. S. (1983). Assessment of anger: The state–trait anger scales. In J. N. Butcher & C. D. Spielberger (Eds.), *Advances in personality assessment* (Vol. 2). Hillsdale, NJ: Lawrence Erlbaum Associates.

Stark, L. (1978). Trust. In H. London & J. E. Exner, Jr. (Eds.), *Dimensions of personality* (pp. 561–599). New York: Wiley.

Tupes, E. C., & Christal, R. E. (1961). Recurrent personality factors based on trait ratings. *USAF ASD Technical Report*, No. 61–97.

Wiggins, J. S. (1979). A psychological taxonomy of trait-descriptive terms: The interpersonal domain. *Journal of Personality and Social Psychology, 37*, 395–412.

Wiggins, J. S., & Broughton, R. (1985). The interpersonal circle: A structural model for the integration of personality research. In R. Hogan & W. H. Jones (Eds.), *Perspectives in personality* (Vol. 1, pp. 1–47). Greenwich, CT: JAI Press.

Williams, R., Haney, T., Lee, K., Kong, Y., Blumenthal, J., & Wahlen, R. (1980). Type A behavior, hostility and coronary heart disease. *Psychosomatic Medicine, 42*, 539–549.

Zelin, M. L., Alder, G., & Myerson, P. G. (1972). Anger self-report: An objective questionnaire for the measurement of aggression. *Journal of Consulting and Clinical Psychology, 39*, 340.

Zuckerman, M. (1979). *Sensation seeking: Beyond the optimal level of arousal.* New York: Lawrence Erlbaum Associates.

The Role of Hostility, Neuroticism, and Speech Style in Coronary-Artery Disease

4

Aron Wolfe Siegman

During the 1950s, two cardiologists, Dr. Meier Friedman and Dr. Ray Rosenman, identified a constellation of behaviors as risk factors for coronary heart disease (CHD). These putative coronary-prone behaviors are intense ambition, hard-driving job involvement, competitiveness, impatience, a chronic sense of time urgency, hostility, and aggression. For descriptive purposes, this behavior pattern was labeled Type A (Friedman & Rosenman, 1974). In a more general sense, the Type A individual has been described as someone who is in constant competition with his fellow men and with time; he or she has been contrasted with the Type B individual, who leads a much more relaxed life-style (Friedman & Rosenman, 1974; Rosenman & Friedman, 1974). Friedman and Rosenman also developed a structured interview (SI) for the assessment of the Type A behavior pattern (TABP). The questions in this interview focus on the respondent's hard-driving, competitive, time-urgent, impatient, and hostile behaviors (Rosenman, 1978) and are interspersed with occasional challenging remarks such as Why?, Why not?, Never?, and Always? Perhaps the most convincing evidence for the proposition that the Type A behavior pattern is a significant risk factor for CHD emerged from the Western Collaborative Group Study (WCGS). This was a large-scale prospective study involving 3,154 men, and in which Type A's, as assessed by the SI, were more than twice as much at risk for myocardial infarctions (MIs) and other clinical manifestations of CHD than Type B's, independent of the traditional risk factors such as smoking, overweight, cholesterol level, etc. (Brand, 1978; Rosenman et al., 1975). The amount of risk association with the TABP was approximately equal to that conferred by the other risk factors, and the TABP predicted incidence of CHD regardless of the presence or absence of any combination of the traditional risk factors (Brand, 1978). Supportive evidence also came from studies that found significant correlations between SI-derived TABP scores and the severity of angiographically documented coronary artery occlusion. These findings buttressed the link between the TABP and CHD (Blumenthal, Williams, & Kong, 1978; Frank, Heller, Kornfeld, Spoon, & Weiss, 1978; Friedman et al., 1968; Williams et al., 1980).

It is ironic that just about the time when general textbooks in abnormal and social psychology began to cite the link between the TABP and CHD as evidence of a causal relationship between psychosocial variables and disease, and just as the medical community appeared ready for the first time to accept a psychosocial variable as an independent risk factor for CHD (Cooper, Detre, & Weiss, 1981), evidence began to appear that challenged the validity of the presumed relationship between the TABP and CHD. Perhaps the most damaging evidence in this regard are the results of the Multiple Risk Factor Intervention Trial, or MRFIT study; this like the WCGS, was a large-scale prospective investigation, but it failed to replicate the relationship between SI-derived Type A designation and CHD (in a subset of 3,110 participants), despite great efforts on the part of the investigators to make the assessment of the TABP comparable to that of the WCGS (Shekelle et al., 1985). Although the MRFIT study differed from The WCGS in that subjects were selected on the basis of being at high risk for CHD, recall that in the WCGS the TABP predicted CHD at all levels of risk (Brand, 1978). Morever, MRFIT is not alone in its negative findings. A number of recent studies also failed to replicate the relationship between SI-derived Type A designation and severity of coronary occlusion (Arrowood et al., 1982; Dembroski et al., 1985; Dimsdale, Hackett, & Hutter, 1979; Krantz, Sanmarco, Selvester, & Matthews, 1979; Scherwitz, et al., 1983; Siegman, Feldstein, Tommaso, Ringel, & Lating, 1987). Also, a recent reanalysis of the WCGS data, based on additional CHD cases, failed to confirm claims of a significant relationship between TABP designation and CHD mortality when proper statistical controls were in effect (Ragland, Brand, & Rosenman, 1987). Nevertheless, not all the recent evidence is negative. Thus, Friedman and associates found a significant relationship between severity of SI-defined Type A behavior and the recurrence of MIs (Friedman et al., 1984), and Williams, Barefoot, Haney, and associates (1986) reported a significant relationship between SI-derived TABP and severity of CAD in those below the age of 50 among 2,289 Duke University patients. In the Duke study, however, the size of the effect was too small to be considered clinically significant. At best, then, SI-derived global Type A appears to account for only a small amount of the variance in CAD. Moreover, we need to address ourselves to the fact that preponderance of recent evidence regarding SI-defined TABP, CAD, and CHD is negative, and especially to the negative results of the large-scale, prospective MRFIT study. In what follows, I propose to offer possible explanations for the inconsistent findings, and to argue that, these negative findings notwithstanding, a strong case can still be made for the role of psychosocial variables, specifically for hostility, in CHD.

ON THE ASSESSMENT OF THE TABP

It may very well be that the inconsistent findings regarding SI-derived TABP and

CHD are, at least in part, related to a number of methodological problems that plague the SI as an assessment instrument. From the beginning, Rosenman (1978) has been quite clear that the SI be administered in a challenging manner. Thus, Chesney, Eagleston, and Rosenman (1980) recommend that the questions in the SI be asked in a crisp, abrupt, and staccato style, and the brief challenging remarks (Why?, Why not?) be presented in a rapid-fire manner. The rationale for conducting the interview in this confrontational manner is that it is designed to elicit a behavioral sample of the interviewee's response to challenge (Chesney, Eagleston, & Rosenman, 1980). However, it is by no means a simple matter to achieve a uniform level of challenge, and it is not at all obvious that different interviewers, even if they were trained by the same person, do in fact use comparable levels of challenge. In fact, there is evidence to the contrary. Thus, Scherwitz and associates (1987) noted systematic differences in the speech styles of the interviewers in the MRFIT project. These differences involve the very variables that define the level of interviewer challenge, and these differences obtained despite the great efforts that were made in that study to ensure that the interviews be administered in a uniform manner. More importantly, and of obvious relevance to the contradictory findings between the WCGS and MRFIT study, is the claim by Scherwitz, who had access to both the WCGS and the MRFIT interviews, that at least some of the interviewers in the MRFIT study were more challenging than the interviewers in the WCGS study. Of course, within the context of the present discussion, level of interviewer challenge is of interest only to the extent that is has a significant effect on the respondent's TABP scores. One study conducted in our laboratory with college students indicates that the level of interviewer challenge does indeed have a significant effect on the interviewees' TABP scores, with the direction of the effect depending on the relative weight assigned by the scorer to the interviewees' vocal style versus hostility (Siegman, Feldstein, Lating, & Barkley, 1987). Moreover, the participants gave significantly shorter responses in the highly challenging than in the nonchallenging interviews. When confronted with a highly challenging interviewer, some individuals apparently "clam up" and respond with very brief responses, sometimes with simple "yes" and "no" answers. Thus, some individuals were probably misclassified as X's or B's simply because their responses were too brief to reveal evidence of Type A behavior. Of course, this finding does not not tell us which of the two interviewer styles, challenging or nonchallenging, is more predictive of CHD. However, in a recent study (Siegman, Feldstein, Tommaso et al., 1987) we found that a number of SI-derived variables were more predictive of the severity of CAD when these variables were derived from a nonchallenging rather than from a challenging interview. If this finding can be confirmed, we may be able to achieve greater standardization in SI administration. Whereas it is exceedingly difficult to calibrate interviewers so they will administer the SI with identical levels of challenge and provocation, it is not difficult to train interviewers to simply avoid challenging behaviors.

Another problem with the SI as a measure of the TABP involves the scoring procedures. From the very beginning, Rosenman (1978) has stressed that the scoring of the SI be based not so much on the content of the interviewee's responses as it is on the interviewee's vocal and speech stylistics and other expressive nonverbal behaviors.[1] The vocal and speech stylistics include short response latencies, loud speech, rapid accelerated speech, and frequent interruptions of the interviewer. There is reason to suspect, however, that whereas some scorers ignore content completely, others give it at least some weight (Matthews, Krantz, Dembroski, & MacDougall, 1982; Scherwitz, Berton, & Leventhal, 1977). Moreover, there are no rules for how much weight should be assigned to each of the various stylistic components. Although it may be possible to train scorers to assign similar weights to the various stylistic and content components and thus achieve acceptable levels of interscorer reliability, there is no evidence that such high levels of agreements do in fact exist across studies, or that there is no slippage over time within studies.

In this connection it should be noted that the increasing reliance on speech stylistics in determining a person's SI-derived TABP designation has created a gap between the conceptual and the operational definitions of the TABP construct. Conceptually, the TABP is defined in terms of competitiveness, time urgency, hostility, and related behaviors, but operationally it is defined, to a large extent, in terms of speech stylistics, without much effort having been made to demonstrate what relationship if any there is between the two.

The need for a more objective measure of the TABP construct has led a number of investigators, including Rosenman and associates, to search for objective, questionnaire-type measures of the TABP. The most prominent among these is the Jenkins Activity Survey, or JAS (Jenkins, Zyzanski, & Rosenman, 1971). However, despite its psychometric soundness, and despite it being a valid predictor of many key components of the TABP construct, such as being achievement oriented, competitive, and time pressured (Glass, 1977; Matthews, 1982), even surpassing the SI in this respect (Matthews, 1982), the JAS did not predict incidence of CHD in the WCGS, when proper statistical controls were in effect (Brand, 1978); it did not do so in MRFIT, nor did it predict severity of CAD in prospective studies or numerous correlational angiographic studies (see Matthews & Haynes, 1986, for a comprehensive review). In this connection it should be noted that the correlation between SI-derived and JAS-derived TABP scores is only moderate (about .4, and sometimes less). It is clear that the two instruments share only a limited amount of variance, and that the two should not be viewed as interchangeable. Moreover, the questionable ability of the JAS to predict CHD (Matthews & Haynes, 1986) suggests that reference to the JAS as a measure of coronary-prone behavior is inappropriate. To the extent, then, that the SI has been successful in predicting CHD, it is probably not by virtue of it measuring the same components of the TABP construct that are being measured by the JAS,

---

[1]The other expressive behaviors involve gestures and movements presumably associated with competitiveness, anger, and other components of the TABP. However, because the SI is scored from audio recordings, these nonverbal indices have been ignored in most subsequent studies.

but rather by virtue of it tapping a dimension that is not being measured by JAS. A promising candidate for that position is hostility, given the fact that of all the components of the TABP construct hostility alone is not represented in the JAS. In fact, we now have a large body of evidence that suggests that hostility may indeed be the primary, and perhaps the only, "toxic" component of the TABP construct, as far as CHD is concerned.

THE ROLE OF HOSTILITY IN CHD

For some time now, a number of investigators (Dembroski et al., 1978; Dembroski & MacDougall, 1985; Dembroski et al., 1985; Matthews, 1982) have pointed out that the TABP construct, as originally defined by Friedman and Rosenman (1974), is a multidimensional construct consisting of many behavioral tendencies, not all of which are necessarily coronary prone. Some may be, others may not be, and some may even be protective. These considerations have led some investigators to advocate a component scoring approach to the SI, in which each behavioral component that contributes to the global Type A score is separately assessed for its relationship to CHD (Dembroski et al., 1978; Dembroski & MacDougall, 1983). Using this approach, Dembroski, MacDougall, and associates have repeatedly found a significant positive relationship between SI-derived potential for hostility ratings and severity of angiographically documented CAD, even in the absence of significant relationships between global Type A scores and severity of CAD. Further support for the hostility–CHD connection comes from the research by Williams and associates (e.g., 1980, 1984). Using the Cook–Medley Hostility (Ho) scale (1954)—an MMPI-derived questionnaire-type instrument—they have repeatedly obtained significant positive correlations between scores on this scale and CHD, severity of angiographically documented CAD, and incidence of CAD in prospective studies.[2]

But not all the studies on hostility and CHD are positive. For example, two recent studies failed to obtain a significant positive correlation between scores on Spielberger's Trait Anger Scale (TAS) (Spielberger, Jacobs, Russel, & Crane, 1983) and angiographically documented occlusion (Shocken, Worden, Greene, Harrison, & Spielberger, 1985; Smith, Follick, & Korr, 1984), and yet a third study found a significant *negative* correlation between TAS scores and severity

---

[2]It is not clear which aspect of hostility is being measured by the C–M Ho scale. Its correlation with the SI-derived potential for hostility measure is only .3, and sometimes less. Factor analyses of the C–M Ho scale have identified a "cynicism" and a "paranoia" factor, and evidence suggests that the items that make up the "cynicism" factor are related to the greater incidence of CAD (Dembroski & Williams, in press). These items suggest individuals who are mistrustful and alienated from their fellow men.

Recent findings (Seeman & Syme, 1987) suggest that individuals lacking in social support are more at risk for CHD than those who have such support. Perhaps cynical individuals are more vulnerable to CHD and other diseases because they lack the protection of social support systems. If so, the Ho scale may be more of a moderator variable than a causal factor in CHD.

of CAD (Spielberger, personal communication, October, 1986). Perhaps hostility is no less a multidimensional construct than the TABP, with only some dimensions related to coronary disease. We decided to explore this issue further, by comparing the relationship of the experience of anger and hostility versus overt-reactive hostility to coronary disease. A number of years ago, Buss and Durkee (1957) constructed several theoretically based hostility scales. A factor analysis of these scales yielded two factors, with the Resentment and Suspicion scales loading on one factor in both males and females, and the Assault, Verbal Hostility, Indirect Hostility, and Irritability scales loading on the second factor, also in both males and females. The first factor seems to be a measure of the *experience of anger and hostility*. Given that indices of the experience of anger and hostility correlate fairly highly—as much as .7—with neuroticism indices (e.g., Sarason, 1961; Siegman & Gjesdal, 1987), they could be viewed as measures of *neurotic hostility*. By way of contrast, the second factor seems to be a measure of frustration-induced reactive hostility and aggression, or *expressive hostility*. In a recent study, we investigated the relationship of these two dimensions of hostility—i.e., the experience of hostility and expressive hostility—with CAD (Siegman, Dembroski, & Ringel, 1987). The participants were 72 patients, 51 males and 21 females, scheduled for coronary angiography. In addition to the Buss–Durkee Hostility Inventory (BDHI), they were also administered Bendig's (1956) abbreviated form of the Taylor Manifest Anxiety Scale (MAS)—an index of neuroticism. In younger patients—up to the age of 60—the patients' expressive hostility scores correlated positively and significantly with the CAD endpoints. On the other hand, the patients' experience of hostility scores correlated negatively and significantly with the severity of coronary occlusion. It is of interest to note that in this group of younger patients ($N = 36$), not only the experience of hostility but neuroticism too, as indexed by the MAS, correlated negatively and significantly with severity of CAD (partial r, with gender partialled out, $= -.35, p < .05$) (Table 4.1). An item analysis was conducted to identify the specific BDHI items that correlated significantly with severity of occlusion in the below-age 60 group. The results show that patients with significant occlusion affirm items that suggest *impulsive, reactive hostility and anger and deny items that suggest neurotic concerns*, such as chronic resentment and suspiciousness (Table 4.2).

These results can help us understand why previous investigators failed to obtain significant positive correlations between scores on Spielberger's TAS and coronary disease. In an evaluation of this scale, Costa and McCrae (in press) conclude that "is perhaps two-thirds neuroticism and one-third antagonism." Given our findings, it is not likely that personality tests that also measure neuroticism and trait anxiety will correlate positively with severity of CHD. Depending on the level of confounding, the correlation can even be significantly negative.

The positive correlation between overt-expressive hostility and severity of CAD was, of course, expected. However, the significant negative correlation between the experience of hostility and severity of CAD was not expected and needs ex-

TABLE 4.1

Simple and Partial Correlations Between the Buss–Durkee
Factor Scores and CAD Endpoints in
Patients 60 and Younger (N = 36) than 60

Patient Group	Buss–Durkee Factor Scores	Simple r		Partial r (MAS partialed)		Partial r (Sex and MAS partialed)	
		NUMVES	Gensini	NUMVES	Gensini	NUMVES	Gensini
60 and younger	I-Neurotic hostility	−0.28	−0.38*	−0.22	−0.30	−0.20	−0.28
	II-Reactive hostility	0.38*	0.34*	0.40*	0.38*	0.32	0.34*
Older than 60	I-Neurotic hostility	−0.05	−0.09	−0.08	−0.12	−0.14	−0.19
	II-Reactive hostility	0.11	−0.17	0.11	−0.18	0.11	−0.19

*$p < 0.05$.
Note: From Siegman, Dembroski, & Ringel, 1987.

TABLE 4.2
Buss–Durkee Hostility Scale Items that Correlate
Significantly* with CAD Endpoints in Patients Age 60
and Less (N = 36)

Items Affirmed	Items Denied
Lose temper easily but get over it	Don't get what's coming to me
When people yell, I yell back	Feel resentful when I look back
I am capable of slapping someone	If made fun of, my blood boils
I have not had a temper tantrum	Being forgiven for my sins concerns me
I raise my voice when arguing	People have a hidden reason for doing something nice
People push me so far, we come to blows	I feel I get a raw deal out of life
	I would rather concede than argue

*$p < .05$.

planation, as does the significant negative correlation between neuroticism and CAD. One possibility is that these negative correlations are an artifact of how patients get selected for coronary angiography. Neurotic individuals may be prone to hypochondriacal angina-like pains, although they have perfectly clean arteries (Costa, 1986). When such individuals are selected for coronary angiography because of their repeated complaints about their chest pains, we are likely to obtain a wholly artificial inverse relationship between neuroticism and severity of CAD. Alternatively, it may be that neurotic individuals behave in ways that are protective against CHD in that they seek medical attention, engage in fitness programs, and watch their diets, more so than nonneurotic individuals. If correct, this explanation could also account for the otherwise puzzling inverse relationship between neuroticism and cancer reported by Eysenck (1985) and Grossarth-Maticek and associates (1985). The results of a study recently completed in our laboratory on cardiovascular reactivity, however, suggest that the protective effect of neuroticism on CAD is more direct than has been suggested thus far.

Components of Hostility, Cardiovascular Reactivity, and Testosterone Production

As yet there is not agreement about the mechanisms that translate behaviors such as the TABP or hostility into CHD. One leading hypothesis about how this occurs involves mechanisms associated with repeated, exaggerated episodes of cardiovascular reactivity (CVR) provoked by environmental challenge. According to some investigators, such cardiovascular hyperresponsivity to challenging or stressful situations may be a marker of the pathogenic process involved in the etiology of CHD and essential hypertension (EH) (Eliot, Buell, & Dembroski, 1982; Herd, 1978; Krantz & Manuck, 1984; Obrist, 1981; Schneiderman, 1983; Williams, see Chapter 9, this volume). Two sets of experimental findings provide support for the hypothesis that the link between hostility and CHD is mediated by heightened cardiovascular reactivity. First are the findings by Hokanson and associates (Hokanson, 1970) that frustration-induced anger is associated with increases in systolic blood pressure. Moreover, Siegman and Kruger (1988) have shown that just reminiscing about anger-arousing experiences is associated with significant increases in both systolic and diastolic blood pressure. Then there is the experimental evidence that links cardiovascular reactivity with the atherogenic process (see Chapter 10, this volume). Furthermore, a number of correlational studies have found significant positive associations between SI-derived potential for hostility scores and cardiovascular reactivity (Dembroski & MacDougall, 1983; Dembroski, MacDougall et al., 1978; Dembroski, MacDougall, Herd, & Shields, 1978; Dembroski, MacDougall, & Lushene, 1979). In this connection it should be noted that the SI-derived index for the potential for hostility is primarily a measure of overt-expressive hostility. Given our findings that only overt-expressive hostility correlates positively with CAD and that the experience of hostility correlates negatively with CAD, we asked whether an analogous divergence characterizes the relationship between these two dimensions of hostility and cardiovascular reactivity. In a study (Siegman, Dembroski, & Gjesdal, 1987; Siegman, Dohm, & Gjesdal, 1988; Siegman & Gjesdal, 1987) that was designed to answer this question, we ascertained the relationship between expressive hostility, the experience of hostility, and cardiovascular reactivity[3] during the administration of the SI and during a challenging arithmetic task (counting backwards by 7's) in a group of 53 male and 50 female college students.

In this study the two types of hostility, i.e., expressive (or overt) hostility and the experience of (or covert) hostility, were measured by two scales that differ slightly from those used in our CAD study. The two scales that were used in this study are based on a factor analysis of the individual BDHI items, rather than its subscales (Bendig, 1962). Participants in this study were also administered an anxiety scale (Bendig, 1956) and the Marlowe Crowne Social Desirability (S-D) scale (Crowne & Marlowe, 1964). The latter allowed us to partial out the social desirability response bias from the participants' hostility and anxiety scores. Finally, the participants were assigned Type-A/B score, based on their responses to the SI.

There was little support in this study for the expected positive correlation between expressive hostility and cardiovascular reactivity, despite the evidence for such a relationship in a number of other studies (Dembroski & MacDougall, 1985). On the other hand, the evidence clearly suggested a negative correlation between the experience of hostility and cardiovascular reactivity (systolic) during the SI

---

[3]Cardiovascular reactivity is usually measured by obtaining the difference between a person's systolic and diastolic blood pressure and heart rate in a challenging or stressful situation and that person's resting or baseline cardiovascular response. Given the statistical problems associated with difference scores, we partialled out baseline responses by means of multiple regression analyses and partial r's.

administration, even after partialling out the participants' social desirability response bias (partial r (83) $= -.30, p < .01$). There also was a significant negative correlation between the participants' anxiety and systolic reactivity scores during the SI administration (partial r (80) $= -.21, p < .05$). It would seem then, that overt hostility and the experience of hostility influence cardiovascular reactivity in different ways, as they did CAD. We do not believe that this inverse relationship between neuroticism, the experience of hostility and reactivity, can be attributed to a selection artifact. Perhaps, because of their chronic exposure to stress, neurotic individuals develop compensatory mechanisms to cope with stressful and challenging situations. A similar explanation has been offered by Eysenck (1985) for the divergent effects of acute versus chronic stress on cancer in both rats and humans.[4] Whatever the explanation may be, the inverse relationship between neuroticism and cardiovascular reactivity raises the possibility that neuroticism is yet another factor that *may* protect people from CHD. The next step is to prospectively investigate the relationship between neuroticism and CHD, with the expectation, based on our previous findings with CAD, of a negative relationship between the two.

Although, as noted earlier, there was little support in this study for the expected positive correlation between the expression of hostility and cardiovascular reactivity, significant positive correlations were obtained between the participants' SI-derived Type-A scores and their cardiovascular reactivity scores (systolic reactivity during the SI administration and diastolic reactivity during the arithmetic task). Thus, despite the waning support for the claim that the TABP plays a significant role in CHD, the evidence remains consistent that the TABP is related to cardiovascular reactivity. Of course, these data raise questions about the precise role of cardiovascular reactivity in CHD. In a more recent study on personality variables and cardiovascular responses during challenging tasks, we found that the expression of hostility was associated with fast recovery rates from blood pressure elevations and the experience of hostility with slow recovery rates. One may speculate that the "shear stress" and turbulence that is produced by the combination of high reactivity and a quick recovery is what is involved in the atherosclerotic process. Clearly, more research is needed to clarify the precise role of the hemodynamic mechanisms that are involved in atherogenesis.

Another hypothesis concerning how behavior gets translated into CHD involves the production of testosterone (Williams, see Chapter 2, this volume). There are a number of findings, which when taken together suggest that testosterone production may mediate the relationship between behavioral risk factors and CHD. First, there is the finding that the administration of testosterone accelerates atherogen-

---

[4]A similar reversal has been noted in relation to the expressive vocal correlates of anxiety. Experimentally induced anxiety, or state anxiety, is associated with an accelerated speech rate, whereas trait anxiety and neuroticism are associated with a slow speech rate (Siegman, 1987b). Here too the explanation has been offered that chronically anxious individuals have learned to overcompensate with a deliberate and slow speech rate (Siegman, 1987b).

esis in rats (Uzunova, Ramey, & Rumwell, 1978). Second, there is evidence to suggest that under challenging conditions Type-A men produce more testosterone than Type-B men. Thus, Williams and associates have shown that the administration of reaction-time tests in challenging circumstances increases plasma testosterone levels in Type-A but not in Type-B men (Williams et al., 1982). Finally, Zumoff, Rosenfeld, Friedman et al. (1984) found elevated daytime urinary excretion of testosterone glucuronide in Type-A but not Type-B men. There was no corresponding difference in the testosterone glucuronide levels of Type-A and Type-B men, during times of the day when people are less involved in competitive, time-pressured activities. A particularly attractive feature of the testosterone hypothesis is that it also accounts for the fact that men are significantly more at risk for CHD than women. However, if there is any validity to our contention that hostility, specifically overt-reactive hostility, is the "toxic" component in the TABP, we need to be able to demonstrate a relationship between reactive hostility and testosterone production. In fact, evidence to that effect appears in a study undertaken more than 17 years ago by Persky, Smith, and Basu (1971) on the role of testosterone in aggressive behavior in men; they were apparently unaware of the implications of their findings for the role of aggression in CHD. They found a significant positive correlation between overt-reactive hostility, as measured by the appropriate Buss–Durkee (B–D) hostility scales, and plasma testosterone levels (r (16) $= .52, p < .05$) and testosterone production rate (r (16) $= .69, p < .001$) in a group of 18 young males. By way of contrast, the experience of hostility, or neurotic hostility, as measured by the appropriate B–D scales, barely related to testosterone production rate at the 5% level. Furthermore, in a regression analysis in which these two measures of hostility plus two other indices of overt-reactive hostility were entered as independent variables and testosterone production rate as the dependent variable, both types of hostility contributed significantly to the variance in the participants' testosterone production rate, but in opposite directions: overt-reactive hostility positively, and the experience of hostility negatively. Between them they accounted for 82% of the variance in the participants' testosterone production rate. Similar findings were obtained more recently by Olweus and associates (1983, 1986) in a group of boys, ages 15–17. Two scales measuring reactive-expressive aggression correlated significantly with the boys' testosterone levels (r (56) $= .41$, $p < .01$). A detailed item analysis revealed that only items that involve a response to *provocation*, including threat or unfair treatment, showed a relationship with testosterone levels (Table 4.3). Note that both these items and the items that predicted severity of CAD in our angiographic study seem to measure reactive-expressive hostility. By way of contrast, a scale measuring aggressive attitudes, i.e., the experience of anger and hostility, showed no significant correlation with the boys' testosterone levels (Olweus, 1983).

It appears, then, that overt-reactive hostility and the experience of hostility relate differentially not only to the severity of CAD but also to cardiovascular reactivity and to the production of testosterone.

TABLE 4.3[a]
Correlation Between Testosterone Levels and Individual Items
from the Verbal and Physical Aggression Scales (N = 58)

Item	Correlation coefficient (r)
Verbal Aggression (5 items)	
1. When an adult is unfair to me, I get angry and protest.	.18
2. When an adult tries to take my place in a line, I firmly tell him it is my place.	.24
3. When a teacher criticizes me, I tend to answer back and protest.	.33
4. When a teacher has promised that we will have some fun but then changes his(her) mind, I protest.	.19
5. When an adult tries to boss me around, I resist strongly.	.33
Physical Aggression (5 items)	
6. When a boy starts fighting with me, I fight back.	.33
7. When a boy is nasty with me, I try to get even with him.	.37
8. When a boy teases me, I try to give him a good beating.	.15
9. I fight with other boys at school.[b]	.05
10. I really admire the fighters among the boys.[b]	.11

[a]From Olweus (1983).
[b]These items do not contain a clear element of provocative challenge.

To return to our main theme, it seems there is considerable evidence linking hostility and CHD, although the precise explanation of this relationship in terms of biological mechanisms still eludes us. Additionally, there is evidence that not all aspects of hostility are related to CHD in the same fashion. Whereas overt-expressive hostility correlates positively with CAD, the experience of hostility or neurotic hostility seems to be protective of CAD. A similar divergence seems to characterize the relationship between expressive hostility, the experience of hostility, and cardiovascular reactivity, as well as the production of testosterone.

It is also apparent that we need to improve our tools for the assessment of hostility. One problem with the SI-derived measure of the potential for hostility (Dembroski & MacDougall, 1983) is its subjectivity. Moreover, evidence obtained in our laboratory indicates that the SI-derived potential for hostility score is subject to the social desirability response bias, no less than the questionnaire measures of hostility. An alternative to subjective interpretations of interview responses and to paper-and-pencil questionnaires is, the use of objective, expressive correlates (vocal and nonverbal) of hostility. This, then, was the focus of our next study: to identify the objective, expressive correlates of coronary-prone behavior.

ON THE ROLE OF EXPRESSIVE BEHAVIOR
IN THE TABP AND CHD

From the very beginning, Friedman and Rosenman emphasized the role of expressive behavior in the assessment of the TABP. Thus, in describing the scoring of the SI, Friedman and associates (Friedman, Brown, & Rosenman, 1969) point out: "The assessment of the behavior pattern actually is determined far more by the stylistics in which the interviewee responds than by the content of his responses" (p. 829). Despite the recognition of the central role of expressive behavior in behavior typing, relatively few efforts were made to apply the rapidly emerging technology for the objective measurement of expressive behavior to the assessment of the TABP. That such objective indices of expressive behavior can be applied to the assessment of the TABP was demonstrated by Howland and Siegman (1982), who, using computerized indices of vocal behavior, correctly identified the Type A/B classification of 59 out of 66 individuals who had previously been typed by Rosenman. Beyond that, by focusing on the expressive correlates of coronary-prone behavior, we should gain a more precise understanding of the emotions and personality tendencies that are involved in such behavior. Over the past two decades, considerable progress has been made in identifying the expressive vocal correlates of fear and anxiety, sadness and depression, and anger and hostility (Siegman, 1985, 1987a, b; Siegman & Kruger, 1988). These and other expressive behaviors are viewed not as mere external correlates of emotions, but as integral parts and determinants of the emotional experience, on par with the physiological and cognitive dimensions of emotional experience (Epstein, 1984; Plutchik, 1984). To the extent, then, that the overt expression of anger is involved in CHD, as we have argued that it is, and that the experience of hostility, or neurotic hostility, is not, we should find evidence for these hypotheses in the expressive vocal correlates of CHD. In this connection note that although there is some overlap in the expressive vocal correlates of anger and fear (or hostility and anxiety), there are also differences, some of which emerge primarily in an *interactional context*. For example, although both expressive hostility and anxiety are associated with an acceleration of speech, only the former is associated with a struggle for "floor time" (simultaneous speech).

Objective Indices of Expressive Vocal Behavior and the Severity of CAD

In a study (Siegman, Feldstein, Tommaso, et al., 1987) that was designed to address these questions, the SI was administered to 90 patients who were referred for coronary angiography. To determine whether interviewer challenge is indeed essential for eliciting coronary-prone behavior, the first half of the SI was administered in a nonchallenging manner, the other half in a moderately challenging and provocative style. Each of the two subinterviews was computer scored for the following speech variables: average duration of response latencies, speech rate, average duration of silent pauses, productivity (sum duration of vocalizations throughout the interview), interruptive and noninterruptive simultaneous speech. Simultaneous speech, or overtalk, is considered interruptive if the speaker who initially had the floor loses it; if not, it is considered noninterruptive.

At the time of this study, we had no computer program for the scoring of speech intensity, or loudness. Lacking an objective measure of loudness, we relied on auditor judgments or ratings. The results of the previous research (Bond & Feldstein, 1982; Feldstein & Bond, 1981) showed that what reduced the validity of subjective loudness judgments is the confounding, on the part of the judges, of loudness with speech rate. In the present study, therefore, an objective index of speech rate was always used as a covariate for the subjective loudness ratings. In addition to the preceding vocal and stylistic variables, both interview segments were also assigned global TABP scores by a trained auditor.

Angiographic Endpoints.   One disease endpoint was the number of vessels showing greater than 75% occlusion (NUMVES). However, it is widely recognized that the anatomical location of a lesion is no less significant than the degree of vessel narrowing. Therefore, in the present study, we also used a scoring method developed by Gensini (1975) that takes into account both severity and location.

Results.   Significant interactions were obtained between the patients' age, speech measures, and the severity of CAD scores, which prompted us to conduct separate analyses in younger (60 and younger) and older (61 and older) patients.

In the younger patient group ($N = 46$), frequency of simultaneous speech accounted for about 18–20% of the variance in the patients' occlusion scores. When we added the patients' loudness scores (which were not computer scored in the present study, but can be so scored now) to their simultaneous speech scores, the two indices accounted for 38% of the variance in the patients' Gensini scores and 29% of the variance in the patients' NUMVES scores. These relationships were obtained when the two speech indices were derived from the nonchallenging segment of the SI. In the challenging interview segment, however, the two indices accounted for only 18% of the variance in the patients' occlusion scores. By and large, then, the two speech indices accounted for more of the variance in the patients' severity of occlusion when they were derived from the nonchallenging rather than from the challenging interview segment, and when severity of coronary occlusion was indexed by the Gensini method, in which the location of the occlusion is assigned differential weights rather than by the number of occluded vessels. Note that the two speech indices accounted for twice as much of the variance in the patients' occlusion scores than we were able to account for with the Buss–Durkee (1957) hostility measures. There was no significant correlations between the patients' SI-derived global Type A scores and their severity of occlusion scores.

Although we cannot conclude on the basis of our findings that a nonchallenging interview is superior to a challenging one, given that in this study the order of interviewer style was not counterbalanced, it is nevertheless reasonable to conclude that interviewer challenge is not *essential* for eliciting the relationship between the speech variables and severity of CAD. As pointed out earlier, this is encouraging news as far as introducing greater standardization in the administration of the SI is concerned, for it is much easier to standardize a nonchallenging interview than a challenging one. However we may resolve the problem of SI administration, the results of this study indicate that, in relatively younger patients, discrete, objective, and computer-scorable indices of expressive vocal behavior accounted for as much as 38% of the variance in the patients' severity of CAD scores, *even in the absence of a significant relationship between global Type A and CAD*. It should be pointed out that initially this study was conducted with a small group of 35 patients. We later added 55 patients from another hospital. Significant relationships between loudness, simultaneous speech, and severity of CAD were obtained in the first sample and among the male patients of the second sample (Siegman, in press). Our findings, then, should be viewed as replicated findings.

Of special interest to us is that loudness and simultaneous speech, the two vocal indices that correlated significantly with the severity of CAD, were also found in a previous investigation to be significant correlates of SI-derived potential for hostility ratings (Siegman, 1985). Thus, the results of this study are quite consistent with the hypothesis that expressive hostility mediates the relationship between behavior and CHD.

Let us now turn out attention to some of the vocal indices that were *not* significantly related to severity of CAD, specifically, response latency (RL) and speech rate. Recall that brief latencies and rapid accelerated speech are two stylistic components that contribute significantly to one's Type A designation, yet they did not bear a significant relationship with severity of CAD. One reason for this inconsistency may be that although these two speech indices may be correlates of hostility—there is clear evidence for this in the case of speech rate (Siegman & Kruger, 1988)—they are also related to anxiety arousal. There is considerable evidence that anxiety arousal (state anxiety) is associated with short latencies and rapid accelerated speech, provided the anxiety arousal is not too high and the speech task is not too difficult (Siegman, 1987a, b). Although trait anxiety or neuroticism is not associated with rapid accelerated speech, in fact the reverse may be the case, it is associated with short latencies (Siegman, 1987b). Murray (1971) cites six studies that investigated the relationship between trait anxiety and response latency. All six correlations were negative, three significantly so. Given the inverse relationship between neuroticism and CAD, it is not surprising that RL was not related to severity of CAD. This index may pick up some hostile individuals, but it is also likely to pick up neurotics. To the extent, then, that short latencies contribute to the SI-derived global Type A score, they are likely to undermine its ability to serve as an index of coronary-prone behavior. Similarly, rapid accelerated speech may very well be a measure of hostility but it is also a measure of anxiety arousal, which is not necessarily associated with CHD. It is not surprising, therefore, that a number of studies failed to find significant relationships between SI-derived global Type A scores and severity of CAD. The strength of this relationship is likely to depend on the number of neurotics in the study, with no significant relationship likely to emerge in studies with a substantial number of such patients.

Finally, the results of this study confirm the importance of considering the patients' age when looking at the role of psychological variables in CHD. Apparently, such variables are most salient in relatively younger patients. Older patients may represent "hardy" survivors in whom behavioral and psychosocial variables are only marginally relevant to disease status. This finding has obvious methodological implications. Nonsignificant findings obtained in populations that include older patients may become significant when the interaction with age is taken into consideration. In fact, inconsistencies between studies may be a result of differences in the age distributions in the respective studies. Clearly, more research is needed to understand the interaction of age with psychosocial risk factors in CHD.

SPEECH STYLE AND CHD, OR THE BIOPSYCHOLOGY OF HUMAN COMMUNICATION

In our discussion thus far of the relationship between a loud and interruptive speech style and severity of CAD, the emphasis has been on the mediating role of expressive hostility. An alternate hypothesis is that this speech style, by itself, puts one at risk for CHD. Some support for this hypothesis comes from a recently completed study in our laboratory, in which we monitored changes in BP and HR of 36 male undergraduates as they responded to an abbreviated SI. The results of regression analyses, in which measures of the participants' vocal behavior during the SI served as independent variables and their cardiovascular reactivity scores during the SI as dependent variables, showed significant relationships between the participants' productivity scores, loudness levels, and frequency of interruptive speech and their HR reactivity scores (the respective F values were 10.74, 4.99, and 3.28; the respective p values were $< .01$, $.05$, and $< .10$ in a two-tailed test). It is, of course, interesting to note that the same two speech variables that were related to the severity of CAD in angiographic patients (i.e., simultaneous speech and loudness) are also implicated in heightened cardiovascular reactivity in male college students. Perhaps, as suggested earlier, the chronic surges in cardiovascular activity that are associated with this speech style cause damage to the coronary arteries and lead to the development of arterial plaques and CHD (Herd, 1978).

The data presented thus far indicate that speech style affects autonomically mediated cardiovascular reactivity. However, the reverse is probably also the case. In the study summarized in the previous paragraph, the participants' diastolic blood pressure scores obtained during an initial resting period (for baseline purposes) correlated positively with their speech-rates and negatively with their pause durations and vocalization durations during the *subsequent* SI. This suggests that one's general arousal level may influence one's temporal pacing of speech. That there may be a relationship between one's autonomic activity and speech style is also supported by evidence that beta-blocking drugs attenuate a coronary-prone speech style (Krantz & Durel, 1983; Schmieder, Friedrich, Neus, & Ruddel, 1982). Traditionally, human communication has been viewed primarily as a social-psychological act. That it is, of course, but given the preceding findings it is becoming increasingly clear that we cannot ignore its biological context. Moreover, the evidence indicating a relationship between speech and illness provides additional support for the point of view that human communication must be approached from a biobehavioral or biopsychosocial perspective.

Of course, the two hypotheses, i.e., the hypothesis emphasizing reactive hostility and the hypothesis emphasizing an excessively empathic speech style in the genesis of CHD, are not mutually exclusive. To the contrary, the two reinforce each other, perhaps in a synergistic fashion. As people get angry they experience an increase in cardiovascular reactivity, raise their voices, accelerate their speech, and interrupt their partner, which in turn may further heighten their reactivity and their anger. Speaking with an "angry voice" about frustrating experiences is likely to exacerbate the emotional and cardiovascular reactions to that experience. Thus, Ekman, Levenson, and Frieson (1983) have shown that by simply "putting on" an angry face one can produce feelings of anger and the corresponding ANS arousal.[5] The same may occur when one speaks with an angry voice. In fact, Kearns (1987) found that just speaking loudly about a neutral topic raises one's anger level. A more detailed schematic illustration of this vicious cycle is represented in Fig. 4.1. This process needs to be complemented, however, by the listener's responses. There is considerable evidence for conversational congruence or synchrony in which participants in dyadic interactions match each other's speech style, including loudness level (Feldstein & Welkowitz, 1987). Thus, as an angry speaker raises his voice so will his partner. Furthermore, we now have preliminary evidence suggesting that angry speech also heightens the

---

[5]This phenomenon has been explained in terms of proprioceptive facial feedback (i.e., Buck, 1980). Another possible explanation is in terms of Bower's (1981) associative networks model. Bower (1981) invoked this model to explain why negative cognitions are more accessible than positive ones during depressed moods, and why positive cognitions are more accessible than negative ones during happy moods. However, in addition to moods triggering congruent cognitions, the reverse is also the case. Positive cognitions tend to trigger positive moods and negative cognitions tend to trigger negative moods (Teasdale, 1983). This too, of course, can be explained in terms of the associative networks model. Given the associative networks model and assuming that expressive behaviors are an integral part of emotional experiences, on par with their physiological and cognitive correlates, they too should be able to trigger associated cognitions and moods.

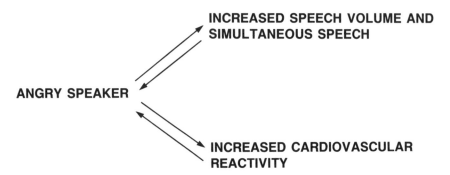

FIG. 4.1.   Schematic representation of the reciprocal interactions of anger, speech, and cardiovascular reactivity.

listener's cardiovascular reactivity. This, of course, is likely to increase the listener's anger, which in turn will affect the angry speaker, and so on. This model accounts nicely for the escalating and contagious nature of anger.

The Modification of Cardiovascular Reactivity

Given the findings reported thus far (whatever their explanation may be), we next addressed ourselves to the question whether it is possible to raise, and more importantly, to lower a person's cardiovascular reactivity in the SI by instructing the respondent to speak more loudly and quickly or more softly and slowly than usual. Should it be possible to reduce BP by speaking slowly and softly, such findings could have important implications for behavioral control of essential hypertension (EH) and perhaps even coronary-prone behavior. In a study designed to answer this question, 40 normotensive college students were administered an expanded version of the SI that was subdivided into three parts. Standard instructions preceded the first part of the interview. Before each of the other two parts, the participants were instructed either to speak more loudly and rapidly or more softly and slowly than usual. We used a within-subjects, or crossover, design, so that each subject participated in all three conditions: normal speech, loud-fast speech, and soft-slow speech. The participants' systolic and diastolic blood pressures, as well as their HRs, were monitored during a baseline period and throughout the SI. A comparison of the participants' cardiovascular reactivity scores in the three conditions revealed significant differences for SBP [F (2,76) = 19.57, $p < .001$] and HR [F (2,76) = 5.80, $p = .05$], but not for DBP. The participants evidenced significantly lower SBP scores [F (1,39) = 26.23, $p < .001$] and lower HRs [F (1,39) = 5.11, $p < .05$] in the "soft and slow" condition as compared to the standard interview condition (133 vs. 138 for SBP and 77.6 vs. 79.6 for HR). Analogous results were obtained when the analyses were based on the participants' delta (differences from baseline) scores. However, none of the "loud and fast" versus "standard speech" comparisons were significant. Information obtained from participants during the debriefing session suggest that, whereas most participants had little difficulty following the instructions that they speak softly and slowly, some found it difficult to speak more rapidly and loudly than usual.

In the preceding study loudness was confounded with speech rate. When subjects were instructed to speadk loudly, they were also instructed to speak rapidly. Conversely, when subjects were instructed to speak softly, they were also instructed to speak slowly. We cannot tell, therefore, whether it was slow speech or soft speech that was associated with reduced SBP and HR reactivity. In our next study (Siegman, Crump, Dembroski, & Gjesdal, 1987), therefore, we made an attempt to unconfound these two speech parameters. Furthermore, we took steps to ensure that the participants would indeed speak at the intended rate and volume level. In this study, instead of responding to an interview, the participants were asked to read a series of children's stories. Twenty-four females participated in the manipulation of rate condition, another 24 in the manipulation of volume condition. Each subject participated in three distinct conditions: soft, normal, and loud speech, or slow, normal and fast speech. When speech rate was manipulated, volume, or loudness, was held constant at a moderate level, and when loudness was manipulated, speech rate was held constant at a moderate level. To ensure that the participants would read the passages at the intended volume and rate, they were asked to "shadow" a trained actor. Manipulation checks indicated that the passages were indeed read at the intended rate and loudness levels. Participants who could not match the actor's rate or loudness were eliminated from the study. *Soft* speech was associated with significantly lower systolic blood pressure reactivity than either normal or loud speech (116 vs. 120 vs. 124), and *slow* speech was associated with significantly lower diastolic blood pressure than either normal or fast speech (79 vs. 83 vs. 84). Most importantly, from the perspective of modifying CVR by means of reducing speech rate and/or loudness level, is the finding that slow speech was associated with significantly lower systolic, diastolic, and HR reactivity than fast speech, and soft speech with significantly lower systolic and diastolic reactivity than loud speech. It appears, then, that both slow and soft speech are associated with reduced cardiovascular reactivity when compared to fast and loud speech.

Whatever the ultimate explanation may be, our findings suggest the feasibility of reducing cardiovascular reactivity by training people who speak fast or loud to speak more slowly and/or more softly. However, our studies thus far only involve short-term modifications of a speaker's speech style. We are now trying to establish the feasibility of long-term changes in coronary-prone speech styles, and the effects of such modifications on cardiovascular reactivity in both normotensive and hypertensive individuals.

CONCLUSIONS

The findings that have been presented and discussed in this chapter suggest that:

1. Conceptual problems with the TABP construct exist, insofar as its relation to CHD is concerned, and there are methodological problems with the SI as an assessment instrument. the TABP constuct is a multidimensional construct, not all of whose components are coronary prone. We need, therefore, to distinguish between the TABP and the coronary-prone behavior. The two are not identical. Moreover, there is a discrepancy between the conceptual definition of Type A, which focuses on competitiveness and related behaviors, and the operational definition, which focuses primarily on expressive speech characteristics. The methodological problems with the SI involve a lack of standardization in its administration and subjective scoring procedures.

2. Expressive hostility correlates positively and significantly with the severity of coronary occlusion, even in the absence of a significant relationship between SI-derived Type A and severity of CAD, and it (expressive hostility) may very well be the "toxic" component of the TABP construct.

3. We need to distinguish expressive hostility from the experience of hostility, or neurotic hostility. The latter correlates negatively with severity of coronary occlusion, as does general neuroticism. It is suggested that chronically anxious individuals become "immunized," or develop compensatory mechanisms to cope with the challenge and stress. We do need, however, prospective evidence to confirm the hypothesized negative relationship between neuroticism and CHD.

4. The same divergence that characterizes the relationship between the expression of hostility, the experience of hostility and the severity of CAD, also characterizes the relationship between the two types of hostility and cardiovascular reactivity and the relationship between the two types of hostility and testosterone production during challenging tasks. Although the evidence is not completely consistent, many studies show a positive correlation between expressive hostility and cardiovascular reactivity. By way of contrast, we obtained a significant negative correlation between the experience of, or neurotic, hostility and CVR. A similar divergence seems to characterize the relationship between the two kinds of hostility and testosterone production in challenging situations.

Also, despite the waning support for the TABP as a significant risk factor for CHD, the evidence remains consistent that the TABP is related to CVR. Clearly, more research is needed to identify the precise mechanism(s) that translate hostility into CHD.

5. Objective, computer-scorable indices of expressive vocal behavior, specifically loudness and simultaneous speech, have been shown in replicated findings to account for as much as 38% of the variance in patients' severity of occlusion scores. This augers well for the objective measurement of coronary-prone behavior. Future studies will need to look for additional objective, vocal, and nonverbal expressive correlates (e.g., facial expressions and body movements) of expressive anger and hostility and thus, hopefully, further improve the predictability of coronary events.

6. The evidence indicates that the coronary-prone speech style, i.e., loud and

interruptive speech, is associated with heightened cardiovascular reactivity. It is not unreasonable to speculate about a synergistic interaction between speech style and hostility during angry interactions. Expressive anger is likely to be associated with loud and interruptive speech, which in turn is likely to heighten the speaker's cardiovascular reactivity, which in turn is likely to increase the speaker's anger and "coronary-prone speech style," and so on.

7. The evidence suggests that by instructing people to speak softly and slowly, we can reduce their cardiovascular reactivity. Future research will need to look at the long-range effects of such modifications of people's risk for CHD and EH.

8. Finally, we need more research on the physiological (and brain activity) correlates of different speech styles, which is essential for developing a biology of human communication. There is reason to believe that the results of such research will provide us with preventive and therapeutic strategies for reducing people's risk for cardiovascular diseases.

REFERENCES

Arrowood, M., Uhrich, K., Gomillion, C., Popio, K., & Raft, D. (1982). New markers of coronary-prone behavior in a rural population. *Psychosomatic Medicine, 119*, 44.

Bendig, A. W. (1956). The development of a short form of the manifest anxiety scale. *Journal of Consulting Psychology, 29*, 384.

Bendig, A. W. (1962). Factor analytic scales of covert and overt hostility. *Journal of Consulting Psychology, 26*, 200.

Blumenthal, J. A., Williams, R. B., & Kong, Y. (1978). Type-A behavior pattern and coronary atherosclerosis. *Circulation, 58*, 634–639.

Bond, R. N., & Feldstein, S. (1982). Acoustical correlates of perception of speech rate: An experimental investigation. *Journal of Psychological Research, 11*, 385–392.

Bower, G. H. (1981). Mood and memory. *American Psychologist, 36*, 129–148.

Brand, R. (1978). Coronary-prone behavior as an independent risk factor for coronary heart disease. In T. M. Dembroski, S. M. Weiss, S. M. Shields, J. L. Haynes, & M. Feinlieb (Eds.), *Coronary-prone behavior*. New York: Springer–Verlag.

Buck, R. (1980). Nonverbal behavior and the theory of emotion: The facial feedback hypothesis. *Journal of Personality and Social Psychology, 38*, 811–824.

Buss, A. H., & Durkee, A. (1957). An inventory for assessing different kinds of hostility. *Journal of Consulting Psychology, 21*, 343–349.

Chesney, M. A., Eagleston, J. R., & Rosenman, R. H. (1980). The Type A structured interview: A behavioral assessment in the rough. *Journal of Behavioral Assessment, 2*, 255–272.

Cook, W., & Medley, D. (1954). Proposed hostility and pharasaic-virtue scales for the MMPI. *Journal of Applied Psychology, 238*, 414–418.

Cooper, T., Detre, T., & Weiss, S. M. (Eds.) (1981). Coronary-prone behavior and coronary heart disease: A critical review. *Circulation, 263*, 1199–1215.

Costa, P. T. (1986). Is neuroticism a risk factor for CAD? Is Type A a measure of neuroticism. In T. H. Schmidt, T. M. Dembroski, & G. Blumchen (Eds.), *Biological and psychological factors in cardiovascular disease*. New York: Springer–Verlag.

Costa, P. T., & McCrae, R. R. (in press). Neuroticism, somatic complaints and disease: Is the bark worse than the bite? *Journal of Personality.*

Dembroski, T. M., & MacDougall, J. M. (1983). Behavioral and psychophysiological perspectives on coronary-prone behavior. In T. M. Dembroski, T. H. Schmidt, & G. Blumchen (Eds.), *Biobehavioral bases of coronary heart disease.* New York: Karger.

Dembroski, T. M., & MacDougall, J. M. (1985). Beyond global Type A: Relationships of paralinguistic attributes, hostility, and anger-in to coronary heart disease. In T. Field, P. McCabe, & N. Schneiderman (Eds.), *Stress and coping* (pp. 223–241). Hillsdale, NJ: Lawrence Erlbaum Associates.

Dembroski, T. M., MacDougall, J. M., Herd, A. L., & Shields, J. L. (1978). Effect of level of challenge on pressor and heart rate responses in Type A and B subjects. *Journal of Applied Social Psychology, 9,* 209–228.

Dembroski, T. M., MacDougall, J. M., & Lushene, R. (1979). Interpersonal interaction and cardiovascular response in Type-A subjects and coronary patients. *Journal of Human Stress, 5,* 28–36.

Dembroski, T. M., MacDougall, J. M., Shields, J. L., Petitto, J., & Lushene, R. (1978). Components of the Type A coronary-prone behavior pattern and cardiovascular responses to psychomotor performance challenge. *Journal of Behavioral Medicine, 1,* 159–176.

Dembroski, T. M., MacDougall, J. M., Williams, R. B., Haney, T., & Blumenthal, J. (1985). Components of Type A, hostility and anger-in: Relationship to angiographic findings. *Psychosomatic Medicine.*

Dembroski, T. M., & Williams, R. B. (in press). In N. Schneiderman, P. Kaufman, & S. M. Weiss (Eds.), *Handbook of research methods in cardiovascular behavioral medicine.* New York: Plenum Press.

Dimsdale, J. F., Hackett, T. P., & Hutter, A. M. (1979). Type A behavior and angiographic findings. *Journal of Psychosomatic Research, 23,* 273–276.

Ekman, P., Levenson, R. W., & Frieson, W. V. (1983). Autonomic nervous system activity distinguishes between emotions. *Science, 221,* 1208–1210.

Eliot, R. S., Buell, J. C., & Dembroski, T. M. (1982). Biobehavioral perspectives on coronary heart disease, hypertension and sudden cardiac death. *Acta Medica Scandinavica, 13,* (Suppl. 606), 203–219.

Epstein, S. (1984). Controversial issues in emotion theory. *Review of Personality and Social Psychology, 5,* 64–86.

Eysenck, H. J. (1985). Personality, cancer, and cardiovascular disease: A causal analysis. *Journal of Personality and Individual Differences, 6,* 535–556.

Feldstein, S., & Bond, R. N. (1981). Perception of speech rate as a function of vocal frequency and intensity. *Language and Speech, 24,* 385–392.

Feldstein, S., & Welkowitz, J. (1987). A chronography of conversation: In defense of an objective approach. In A. W. Siegman & S. Feldstein (Eds.), *Nonverbal behavior and communication* (2nd ed.). Hillsdale, NJ: Lawrence Erlbaum Associates.

Frank, K. A., Heller, S. S., Kornfeld, D. S., Spoon, A. A., & Weiss, M. B. (1978). Type A behavior pattern and coronary angiographic findings. *Journal of the American Medical Association, 240,* 761–763.

Friedman, M., Brown, M. A., & Rosenman, R. H. (1969). Voice analysis test for detection of behavior pattern. *Journal of the American Medical Association, 2208,* 828–836.

Friedman, M., & Rosenman, R. (1974). *Type A behavior and your heart.* New York: Knopf.

Friedman, M., Rosenman, R. H., Straus, R. et al. (1968). The relationship of behavior pattern A to the state of the coronary vasculature: A study of 51 autopsied subjects. *American Journal of Medicine, 44,* 525–549.

Friedman, M., Thoresen, C. E., Gil, J. J., Powell, L. H., Ulmer, D., Thomson, L., Price, V. A., Rabin, D. D., Breal, W. S., Dixon, T., Levy, R., & Bourg, E. (1984). Alterations of Type A behavior and reduction in cardiac recurrences in postmyocardial infarction patients. *American Heart Journal, 108,* 237–248.

Gensini, G. G. (1975). *Coronary arteriography*. Mt. Kisco, NY: Future.

Glass, D. C. (1977). *Behavioral patterns, stress and coronary disease*. Hillsdale, NJ: Lawrence Erlbaum Associates.

Grosserth–Maticek, R., Kanazir, D. T., Schmidt, P., & Velter, H. (1985). Psychosocial and organic variables as predictors of lung cancer, cardiac infarct, and apoplexy: Some differential predictors. *Journal of Personality and Individual Differences*, 6, 313–321.

Herd, J. A. (1978). Physiological correlates of coronary-prone behavior. In T. M. Dembroski, S. Weiss, J. Shields, S. G. Haynes, & M. Feinleib (Eds.), *Coronary-prone behavior*. New York: Springer–Verlag.

Hokanson, J. E. (1970). Psychophysiological evaluation of the catharsis hypothesis. In E. I. Megargee & J. E. Hokanson (Eds.), *The dynamics of aggression*. New York: Harper & Row.

Howland, E. W., & Siegman, A. W. (1982). Toward the automated measurement of the Type-A behavior pattern. *Behavioral Medicine*, 5, 37–54.

Jenkins, C. D., Zyzanski, S. J., & Rosenman, R. H. (1971). Progress toward validation of a computer-scored test for the Type A coronary-prone behavior pattern. *Psychosomatic Medicine*, 33, 198–202.

Kearns, L. R. (1987). *The role of speech rate and loudness in cardiovascular responsivity*. Master's thesis, University of Maryland Baltimore County.

Krantz, D. S., & Durel, L. A. (1983). Psychological substrates of the Type-A behavior pattern. *Health Psychology*, 2, 393–411.

Krantz, D. S., & Manuck, S. B. (1984). Acute psychophysiologic reactivity and risk of cardiovascular disease: A review and methodologic critique. *Psychological Review*, 96, 435–464.

Krantz, D. S., Sanmarco, M. I., Selvester, R. H., & Matthews, K. A. (1979). Psychological correlates of progression of atherosclerosis in men. *Psychosomatic Medicine*, 41, 467–476.

Matthews, K. A. (1982). Psychological perspectives on the Type A behavior pattern. *Psychological Bulletin*, 92, 293–323.

Matthews, K. A., & Haynes, S. G. (1986). Type A behavior pattern and coronary risk: Update and critical evaluation. *American Journal of Epidemiology*, 123, 23–96.

Matthews, K. A., Krantz, D. S., Dembroski, T. M., & MacDougall, J. M. (1982). The unique and common variance in the structured interview and the Jenkins Activity Survey measures of the Type A behavior pattern. *Journal of Personality and Social Psychology*, 42, 303–313.

Murray, D. C. (1971). Talk, silence, and anxiety. *Psychological Bulletin*, 75, 244–260.

Obrist, P. A. (1981). *Cardiovascular psychophysiology*. New York: Plenum Press.

Olweus, D. (1983). Testosterone in the development of aggressive antisocial behavior in adolescents. In K. Van Dusen & S. A. Mednick (Eds.), *Prospective studies of crime and delinquency*. Boston: Klever–Nijhoff.

Olweus, D. (1986). Aggression and hormones. In D. Olweus & J. Block (Eds.), *Development of antisocial and prosocial behavior: Research, theories and issues*. New York: Academic Press.

Plutchik, R. (1984). Emotions: A general psychoevolutionary theory. In K. R. Scherer & P. Ekman (Eds.), *Approaches to emotion*. Hillsdale, NJ: Lawrence Erlbaum Associates.

Ragland, D. R., Brand, R. J., & Rosenman, R. H. (1987). *Type A/B behavior pattern: CHD and non-CHD outcomes in the Western Collaborative Study Group*. Paper presented at annual meetings of the Society for Behavioral Medicine, Washington, DC.

Persky, H., Smith, K. D., & Basu, G. K. (1971). Relation of psychological measures of aggression and hostility to testosterone production in men. *Psychosomatic Medicine*, 33, 265–277.

Rosenman, R. H. (1978). The interview method of assessment of the coronary-prone behavior pattern. In T. Dembroski, S. Weiss, J. Shields, S. Haynes, & M. Feinleib (Eds.), *Coronary prone behavior*. New York: Springer–Verlag.

Rosenman, R. H., Brand, R. J., Jenkins, C. D., Friedman, M., Straus, R., & Wurm, M. (1975). Coronary heart disease in the Western Collaborative Group Study: Final follow-up experience of 8½ years. *Journal of the American Medical Association*, 223, 872–877.

Rosenman, R. H., & Friedman, M. (1974). Neurogenic factors in pathogenesis of coronary heart disease. *Medical Clinics of North America*, 58, 269–279.

Sarason, I. G. (1961). Intercorrelations among measures of hostility. *Journal of Clinical Psychology, 17*, 192–195.

Scherwitz, L., Berton, K., & Leventhal, H. (1977). Type A assessment and interaction in the behavior pattern interview. *Psychosomatic Medicine, 39*, 229–240.

Scherwitz, L., Graham, L., Grandits, G., & Billings (1987). Speech characteristics and behavior type assessment in the Multiple Risk Factor Intervention Trial (MRFIT) structured interviews. *Journal of Behavioral Medicine, 10*, 173–195.

Scherwitz, L., McKelvain, R., Laman, C., Patterson, J., Dulton, L., Yusim, S., Lester, J., Kraft, I., Rochelle, D. & Leachman, R. (1983). Type A behavior, self-involvement, and coronary atherosclerosis. *Psychosomatic Medicine, 45*, 47–57.

Schmieder, R., Friedrich, G., Neus, H., & Ruddel, H. (March, 1982). *Effects of beta-blockers on Type A coronary-prone behavior*. Paper presented at annual meeting, American Psychosomatic Society, Denver.

Schneiderman, N. (1983). Pathophysiology in animals. In T. M. Dembroski, T. H. Schmidt, & G. Blumchen (Eds.), *Biobehavioral bases of coronary heart disease*. New York: Karger.

Shocken, D. D., Worden, T., Green, A. F., Harrison, E. F., & Spielberger, C. D. (1985). Age differences in the relationship between coronary artery disease, anxiety, and anger. *Gerontologist, 225*, 36.

Seeman, T. E., & Syme, S. L. (1987). Social networks and coronary artery disease: A comparison of the structure and function of social relations as predictors of disease. *Psychosomatic Medicine, 49*, 341–354.

Shekelle, R. B., Hulley, S., Neaton, J., Billings, J., Borhani, N., Gerace, T., Jacobs, D., Lasser, N., Mittlemark, M., & Stamler, J. (1985). The MRFIT behavior pattern study: II. Type A behavior pattern and incidence of coronary heart disease. *American Journal of Epidemiology, 122*, 559–570.

Siegman, A. W. (1985). Expressive correlates of affective states and traits. In A. W. Siegman & S. Feldstein (Eds.), *Nonverbal behavior: A multi-channel perspective*. Hillsdale, NJ: Lawrence Erlbaum Associates.

Siegman, A. W. (1987a). The pacing of speech in depression. In J. D. Maser (Ed.), *Depression and expressive behavior*. Hillsdale, NJ: Lawrence Erlbaum Associates.

Siegman, A. W. (1987b). The telltale voice. In A. W. Siegman & S. Feldstein (Eds.), *Nonverbal behavior and communication* (2nd ed.). Hillsdale, NJ: Lawrence Erlbaum Associates.

Siegman, A. W. (in press). Expressive vocal behavior and CHD: The psychobiology of human communication. In S. Feldstein, C. L. Crown, & M. Jasnow (Eds.), *Speech sounds and silences: A social-psychophysical approach to clinical concerns*. Hillsdale, NJ: Lawrence Erlbaum Associates.

Siegman, A. W., Crump, D., Dembroski, T. M., & Gjesdal, J. (March, 1987). *Speech and cardiovascular reactivity*. Paper presented at annual meetings of the Society for Behavioral Medicine, Washington, DC.

Siegman, A. W., Dembroski, T., & Gjesdal, J. (1987). *Hostility and cardiovascular reactivity*. Paper presented at annual meetings of the American Psychological Association, New York.

Siegman, A. W., Dembroski, T. M., & Ringel, N. (1987). Components of hostility and the severity of coronary artery disease. *Psychosomatic Medicine, 48*, 127–135.

Siegman, A. W., Feldstein, S., Lating, J., & Barkley, S. (March, 1987). *The effects of interviewer style in the structured interview of Type A behavior pattern scores*. Paper presented at the annual meetings of the Society for Behavioral Medicine, Washington, DC.

Siegman, A. W. & Kruger, H. P. (1988). *Effects of anger and speech style on cardiovascular reactivity*. Unpublished manuscript, University of Maryland Baltimore County.

Siegman, A. W., Feldstein, S., Tommaso, C. T., Ringel, N., & Lating, J. (1987). Expressive vocal behavior and the severity of coronary artery disease. Psychosomatic Medicine, *49*, 545–561.

Siegman, A. W., & Gjesdal, J. M. (April, 1987). *Neurotic hostility and cardiovascular reactivity*. Paper presented at annual meetings of the Eastern Psychological Association, Arlington, VA.

Smith, T. W., Follick, M. L., & Korr, K. S. (1984). Anger, neuroticism, Type A behavior and the experiences of angina. *British Journal of Medical Psychology, 257*, 249-252.

Spielberger, G., Jacobs, Russel, S., & Crane, R. S. (1983). Assessment of anger—The State-Trait Anger Scale. In J. N. Butcher & C. D. Spielberger (Eds.), *Advances in personality assessment* (Vol. 2). Hillsdale, NJ: Lawrence Erlbaum Associates.

Teasdale, J. D. (1983). Negative thinking in depression: Cause, effect or reciprocal relationship? *Advances in Behavior Therapy, 5*, 3-25.

Uzunova, A. D., Ramey, E. R., & Rumwell, P. W. (1978) Gonadal hormones and pathogenesis of occlusive arterial thrombosis. *American Journal of Physiology, 234*, 454-459.

Williams, R. B., Barefoot, J. C., Haney, T. L., Harrell, F. E., Blumenthal, J. A., Pryor, D., & Peterson, B. (1986). Type A behavior and angiographically documented coronary atherosclerosis in a sample of 2289 patients. *Psychosomatic Medicine, 48*, 302 (Abstract).

Williams, R. B., Jr., Barefoot, J. C., & Shekelle, R. B. (1984). In M. A. Chesney, S. E. Goldstein, & R. H. Rosenman (Eds.), *The health consequences of hostility, in anger, and behavioral medicine*. New York: Hemisphere/McGraw-Hill.

Williams, R. B., Haney, T. L., Lee, K. L., Kong, Y., Blumenthal, J. A., & Whalen, R. (1980). Type A behavior, hostility, and coronary atherosclerosis. *Psychosomatic Medicine, 42*, 539-542,

Williams, R. B., Jr., Lane, J. D., Kuhn, C. M., Melosh, W., White, A., & Schanberg, S. M. (1982). Type A behavior and elevated physiological and neuroendocrine responses to cognitive tasks. *Science, 218*, 483-485.

Zumoff, B., Rosenfeld, R. S., Friedman, M., Beyers, S. O., Rosenman, R. H., & Hellman, L. (1984). Elevated daytime urinary excretion of testosterone glucuronide in men with Type A behavior pattern. *Psychosomatic Medicine, 46*, 223-225.

5

Interactions, Transactions, and the Type A Pattern: Additional Avenues in the Search for Coronary-Prone Behavior

Timothy W. Smith
University of Utah

INTRODUCTION

The history of the Type A behavior pattern is one of cyclic acceptance. A 20-year stream of largely confirmatory findings led earlier reviews (e.g., Review Panel, 1981) to conclude that the Type A pattern was an established risk factor for coronary heart disease (CHD). This confidence has waned in recent years under the weight of several notable failures to replicate the relationship between Type A behavior and CHD (e.g., Case, Heller, Case, & Moss, 1985; Cohen & Reed, 1985; Shekelle, Gale, & Norusis, 1985; Shekelle et al., 1985). Recent evidence indicating that modification of the Type A pattern can produce clinically significant reductions in cardiac recurrences among CHD patients, however, has done much to renew attention to this area (Friedman, et al., 1984, 1986).

Throughout the last decade of Type A research, questions have become more focused and tentative answers have appeared. The search for the dangerous element within the broad band of Type A characteristics has produced a converging set of findings implicating hostility as the culprit (Dembroski et al., 1985; MacDougall, Dembroski, Dimsdale, & Hackett, 1985; Matthews, Glass, Rosenman, & Bortner, 1977; Williams et al., 1980). Attention to specific pathophysiological mechanisms linking pattern A to CHD has also produced tentative answers. A growing number of studies have indicated that the Type A pattern is associated with enhanced physiological reactivity to stressors, and that such responses may initiate and hasten the development of CHD (for reviews, see Contrada, Wright, & Glass, 1985; Krantz & Manuck, 1984; McKinney, Hofshire, Buell, & Eliot, 1984). The combination of these tentative but promising answers to more specific questions, coupled with evidence of the clinical utility of Type A research (Friedman et al., 1984, 1986), has led more recent reviewers to be cautious but optimistic in their appraisals of the status of the Type A pattern as a CHD risk factor (Manuck, Kaplan, & Matthews, 1986; Matthews & Haynes, 1986). Certainly, additional research is needed. If such undertakings incorporate the lessons learned in this area to date, the yield is likely to be valuable. This volume includes descriptions of several of the directions these efforts have taken in recent years.

This climate of renewed but critical interest and more focused investigations provides an important opportunity to examine the assumptions guiding research in this area. Basic assumptions obviously guide the development of empirical questions and shape the paradigms and methodologies chosen to answer them. More importantly, assumptions often exclude other questions. It is also true that operational questions often do not fit precisely the conceptual assumptions in which they are grounded. The search for the coronary proneness within the Type A pattern is currently conducted under a very bright light. The intensity of that illumination is the product of the valuable information produced to date. Current assumptions in the field, however, determine where this light shines. Some of the keys to coronary proneness may lie outside the current focus.

This chapter provides an examination of the assumptions guiding current Type A research from the viewpoint of evolving perspectives in the study of personality. Most conceptual approaches to Type A behavior are based in person-by-situation interaction models of personality. These interactional models maintain that overt Type A behavior and pathogenic physiological responses occur only when Type A's encounter certain kinds of situations. Much of the current Type A research, however, employs older "trait" approaches to the study of personality. Persons are classified as Type A or B without a concurrent assessment or classification of the situational or environmental variables cited in the conceptual approaches to the behavior pattern (cf. Matthews, 1983, 1985; Smith & Sanders, 1986; Thoresen & Ohman, 1985). Even more recent approaches to personality— *active interactional or transactional* approaches—hold promise for understanding Type A behavior and CHD risk, but they have not been studied empirically (Smith & Anderson, 1986; Smith & Rhodewalt, 1986). This transactional alternative holds that Type A persons do not simply react to stressors with enhanced physiological reactivity. Rather Type A's *create* such physiologically taxing situations through their actions and thoughts; that is, the Type A pattern may represent an ongoing process of challenge and demand-engendering behavior, with pathogenic physiological results.

After reviewing the existing models guiding Type A research, the chapter describes the transactional approach and reviews evidence of the Type A challenge and demand-engendering style. Finally, the implications of these contrasting models are discussed in terms of what kinds of empirical questions have been asked to date, and what kinds of questions have been excluded. The purpose of this chapter is not to suggest a less vigorous pursuit of the current central questions in Type A research. Rather, it is to point out additional avenues in the search for answers.

CONTRASTING MODELS OF TYPE A BEHAVIOR
AND CORONARY RISK

The Mechanistic or Statistical Interaction Model

Most conceptual approaches to the Type A pattern describe overt Type A behaviors (i.e., competitiveness, hostility, impatience, etc.) as a characteristic style of response to specific classes of situations; that is, Type A's are seen as displaying the behaviors that distinguish them from Type B's only when confronted with certain stimuli, such as challenges, demands, frustrations, interpersonal conflict, and threats to control or self-esteem. Further, the physiological arousal accompanying these behaviors is hypothesized to play a role in the initiation and progression of coronary atherosclerosis. For individuals with established coronary artery disease, this arousal may precipitate the occurrence of the clinical symptoms of CHD (Williams, Friedman, Glass, Herd, & Schneiderman, 1978). This model is depicted in Fig. 5.1.

Williams (1978), Glass (1977), and several others (e.g., Scherwitz, Berton, & Leventhal, 1978) have presented models of this type. They vary in the kinds of situational characteristics viewed as elicitors of Type A behavior. Glass (1977), for example, posits threats to perceived control as the relevant situational dimension, whereas Matthews and Siegel (1982, 1983) suggest that ambiguous stan-

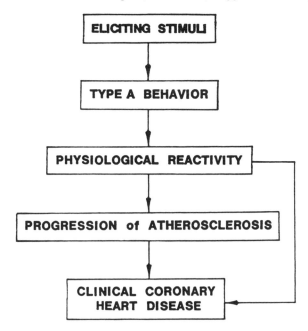

FIG. 5.1.   The mechanistic or statistical interaction model. (from Smith & Anderson, 1986)

dards for satisfactory performance activate the Type A's tendency toward aggressive striving. Models that have focused on hostility as the toxic element within the Type A pattern also posit situational activation of behavioral and physiological response tendencies as the link between the personality characteristic and disease (e.g., Williams Barefoot, & Shekelle, 1985).

These models are not formally presented as mechanistic or statistical person by situation interactional models, but they clearly are (cf. Magnusson & Endler, 1977; Thoresen & Ohman, 1985). Overt Type A behaviors and the critical physiological processes occur when Type A's are in the relevant situations, that is, when they are confronting potential stressors. In the analysis of variance framework, the Type A by situation *statistical* interaction accounts for overt behaviors, physiological responses, and presumably increased CHD risk. Such models are viewed as *mechanistic* because the person and situation variables are seen as static, independent, preexisting variables; that is, they are not seen as *dynamically* or *actively* interactional (Magnusson & Endler, 1977). The physiological or behavioral predispositions and situational characteristics are not seen as reciprocally related to each other, as they are in the active interactional or *transactional* approach to personality (Magnusson & Endler, 1977).

This framework implies that complete tests of the hypothesized relationships require assessment of the Type A pattern (i.e., the person), the relevant environmental elicitors (i.e. the situation), as well as the end point of interest (i.e., behavior, physiological response, or disease). Although many examples of this type of test of the model exist, such studies are the exception to the rule. Longitudinal and cross-sectional studies of Type A and CHD typically assess only the person dimension (Matthews, 1983, 1985; Smith & Sanders, 1986; Thoresen & Ohman, 1985). As a result, by default they operationally test simple trait approaches to personality. The added predictive power of the statistical interaction is lost, even though it is an integral part of the original model.

Several studies are consistent with a statistical interactional approach. Studies of physiological reactivity have indicated that Type A's are not more responsive than Type B's in all situations. Rather, Type A's are more reactive in situations characterized by difficult tasks, threats to self-esteem, threats to control, or negative interpersonal interactions but are not typically more reactive in situations involving minimal levels of psychological challenge or demand (Goldband, 1980; Pittner & Houston, 1980; Ward et al., 1986; for reviews see Contrada et al., 1985; Houston, 1983). Similarly two recent studies have demonstrated that Type A's have higher levels of physiologic risk factors (e.g., blood pressure, plasma lipids) than do Type B's, particularly if their work environment is characterized by relevant stressors (Chesney et al., 1981; Howard, Cunningham, & Rechnitzer, 1986). Finally, several studies of CHD endpoints have indicated that the risk associated with Type A behavior is dependent on situational variables including white-versus blue-collar employment (Haynes, Feinleib, & Kannel, 1980) and spouse characteristics (Carmelli, Swan, & Rosenman, 1985; Eaker, Haynes, &

Feinleib, 1983). In these studies, Type A's were at greater risk for CHD than were type B's , if they were employed in white-rather than blue-collar jobs, and if they were married to more highly educated, active, or dominant wives. Thus, the degree of risk associated with the trait of Type A behavior was dependent on what could be construed as an environmental or situational variable.

It is also interesting to note that a recent animal model of coronary artery disease (CAD) demonstrated this form of "trait-by-situation" interaction. Dominant cynomolgus monkeys developed more severe CAD than did subordinate animals, but only when exposed to recurrent social stress (Kaplan, et al., 1982). Thus, as others have indicated previously (Matthews, 1983, 1985; Smith & Sanders, 1986; Thoresen & Ohman, 1985), a variety of studies relevant to the Type A-CHD relationship suggest that one avenue to increasing the predictive utility of the Type A construct may be to adopt person-by-situation interactional methodologies more consistently.

The Biologic Interactional Model

A major variation of the mechanistic or statistical interactional approach to Type A posits a constitutional basis for the behavior pattern (Krantz & Durel, 1983; Krantz, et al., 1982). This variation is clearly a statistical or mechanistic interaction model, rather than a simple trait or more complex transactional model. The important pathogenic process is again seen as arising from the co-occurrence of an individual predisposition and situational characteristics. Unlike the more psychological models just described, however, the key individual difference or person variable is a biologic one. Overt Type A behaviors and situationally elicited physiological responses are seen as reflecting a constitutionally based predisposition toward autonomic nervous system reactivity. Thus, challenging or threatening situations interact *statistically* with a constitutionally based predisposition toward physiologic reactivity to produce the actual occurrence of pathogenic physiological arousal; that is, the *trait* of physiological reactivity is activated by relevant situational stimuli to produce the *state* of physiological reactivity. Further, this approach maintains that the overt Type A behavior pattern "in part reflects an excessive sympathetic response to environmental stressors" (Krantz, Arabian, Davia, & Parker, 1982). Some versions of this model suggest that constitutionally based reactivity may be enhanced by arousal produced by psychologically mediated Type A behaviors (Krantz & Durel, 1983). Thus, the relationship between reactivity and Type A behavior is bidirectional, as depicted in the illustration of this model in Fig. 5.2. One of the two pathways is emphasized in the figure, however, given that it is this assumption that distinguishes the biologic interactional model.

This model is based on the findings of several recent studies. Two studies (Kahn, Kornfeld, Frank, Heller, & Hoar, 1980; Krantz et al., 1980) found that Type A's had higher blood pressures than did Type B's while they were under

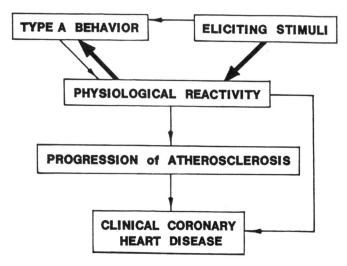

FIG. 5.2.   The biological interaction model. (from Smith & Anderson, 1986)

general anesthesia, suggesting that the Type A's exaggerated reactivity does not require psychological mediation. Further, two studies have demonstrated that pharmacological beta-adrenergic blockade produces lower levels of Type A speech stylistics, without a concurrent decrease in self-reported Type A behavior (Krantz, Durel et al., 1982; Schneider, Friedrich, Neus, & Ruddel, 1982). One interpretation of these findings is that there is an underlying, constitutional dimension of reactivity in Type A behavior.

This emphasis on biological traits as the key individual-difference variable has produced a great deal of research on reactivity itself (for a review see Krantz & Manuck, 1984; Matthews et al. 1986). Recent studies have produced evidence that the wide individual differences in reactivity (Krantz & Manuck 1984; Obrist, 1981) are stable (Giordiani, Manuck, & Farmer, 1981; Glass et al., 1983; Manuck & Garland, 1980; McKinney et al., 1985), generalize to settings outside of the laboratory where the trait is assessed (Dembroski & MacDougall, 1983; Manuck, Corse, & Winkelman, 1979; McKinney et al., 1985), and may have at least some genetic component (Carroll et al., 1985; Rose, Grim, & Miller, 1984; Smith et al., 1987). Further, there has been much progress in categorizing the types of task or situational variables that might serve to activate these individual predispositions (Krantz, Manuck, & Wing, 1986).

Given that physiological reactivity is the key individual-difference variable in the biologic interactional model and the "final common pathway" between Type A behavior and CHD in other models, it is not surprising that many authors have cited the need for large, prospective studies of reactivity as a risk factor for CHD. It is important to note that for such studies to accurately reflect the model on which they are based, assessments of the frequency with which subjects encounter situations hypothesized to elicit reactivity must be included. Only if situational factors are included can the biologic model be tested in full; that is, independent assessments of the *trait* of reactivity, situational characteristics, and the endpoint of interest (i.e., the *state* of reactivity, behavioral responses, degree of CAD, CHD occurrence, etc.) must be included. The highest risk individuals are those "hot reactors" who must also confront a high level of daily stress. Hot reactors fortunate enough to inhabit more peaceful environments would, presumably, be at less risk.

Little evidence is available to date that bear's on the relationship between reactivity and CHD, but the few available studies are consistent with the hypothesized link. Heart rate reactivity during capture has been found to be positively correlated with the degree of CAD on subsequent autopsy in monkeys (Manuck, Kaplan, & Clarkson, 1983, 1985). Diastolic blood pressure reactivity to the cold pressor task has been found to predict the development of CHD in a large-scale prospective study of humans (Keys et al., 1971). And finally, several case-control studies have demonstrated that CHD patients are more reactive than healthy controls (e.g., Corse et al., 1982; Dembroski, MacDougall, & Lushene, 1979; Krantz et al., 1981). Interestingly, in one of these studies (Krantz et al., 1981) reactivity was not related to the extent of CAD. Although largely consistent with the hypothesized link between reactivity and CHD, these studies have not included independent assessments of situational variables required for a more complete test of the biologic interactional model. They have, instead, been tests of a much more simple relationship between the trait of reactivity and disease. If the biologic interactional model is correct, presumably some predictive power was lost by the failure to include a consideration of situational stresses and their interaction with trait reactivity.

The Transactional or Biopsychosocial Interactional Model

The two models described previously contain potential limitations. These limitations are familiar to personality researchers. It is quite likely that the statistical interaction between traits (biologic or psychologic) and situations is embedded in an active psychosocial context; that is, rather than simply responding to challenges and demands, Type A persons seem likely to create them through their thoughts and actions. Further, challenging and demanding situations are likely to reinforce and maintain predispositions toward Type A behavior, rather than simply eliciting or activating them.

The transactional model spawned by these limitations is depicted in Fig. 5.3 (pathways of particular importance are emphasized). As in the previous models, physiological reactivity is the necessary final common pathway between Type A characteristics and CHD. Also as in previous models, specific stimuli in the proximal environment are hypothesized to elicit Type A behaviors from predisposed persons. Further, as in the biologic interactional model, challenging and

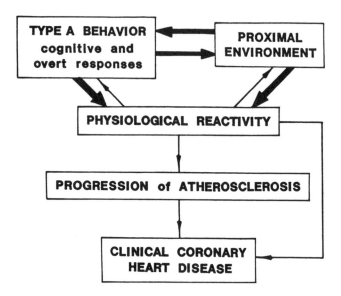

FIG. 5.3. The active interactional or transactional model. (from Smith & Anderson, 1986)

demanding stimuli in the proximal environment are likely to elicit increased physiological responses. Unlike these previous models, however, these potentially stressful aspects of the proximal environment are seen as reciprocally related (Bandura, 1977) to the cognitive and overt behavioral features of the Type A pattern. Through their thoughts and actions, Type A's are likely to increase the level of challenge and demand in their environment. Once created, such an environment is likely to maintain Type A behavior. As a result, Type A's, relative to Type B's, demonstrate increased physiological reactivity in two ways; through greater reactivity to a given challenge or demand, and through contact with the more frequent, severe, and enduring stressors they have created. Consistent with the biologic model, physiological reactivity may also augment the expression of some Type A behaviors. Also, to the extent that some correlates of reactivity may be overt (e.g., flushed face, increased muscle tension), physiological responsiveness may also influence social situations.

The assumptions underlying the transactional model are rooted in several recent approaches to the study of personality. These approaches are all, in some way, reactions to traditional trait and statistical trait-by-situation interaction models. Cognitive social learning theory (Bandura, 1977; Mischel, 1973), dynamic or active interactional approaches (e.g., Magnusson & Endler, 1977), and the emerging cognitive-social approach to personality (Cantor & Kihlstrom, 1981, 1982) all explicitly hold to a reciprocal view of the relationship between persons and situations. For example, Bandura (1977) has argued that ''behavior partly determines which of the many potential environmental influences will come into play and what forms they will take; environmental influences in turn, partly determine which behavioral repertoires are developed and activated'' (p. 195). In the present case, the overt behaviors of the Type A will determine, to some extent, the nature of the situational forces he or she will face, and such situational factors will, to some extent, influence the level of future Type A responses. Type A cognitive processes are an integral facet of this dynamic interaction or transaction. Mischel (1973), for example, suggests that "the person continuously influences the 'situations' of his life as well as being affected by them in a mutual, organic two-way interaction. These interactions reflect not only the person's reactions to conditions but also his active selection and modification of conditions through his cognitions and actions'' (p. 278). In addition to the increasing impact of this general perspective in personality research, the dynamic interactional or transactional approach has also been applied to the study of stress and coping and their relationship to health (Folkman & Lazarus, 1984; Lazarus & Launier, 1978).

The transactional model is also consistent with newer approaches to the interplay of genetic and environmental factors in the *development* of individual differences. Recent evidence suggests that at least some elements of the Type A pattern (i.e., speech loudness, hostility, competition for control) have a heritable component, although these genetic influences are small (Matthews, Rosenman, Dembroski, Harris, & MacDougall, 1984). Even if genetic factors explain some of the variance in Type A behavior, transactions with the environment may play a critical role in the development of the Type A pattern. Scarr and McCartney (1983), for example, describe two ways in which gene–environment transactions influence development. First, persons with different genotypes *evoke* different responses from the social environment. Second, persons with different genotypes actively *select or construct* distinct environments. As Scarr and McCartney (1983) describe this ''niche-buidling,'' ''we all select from the surrounding environment some aspects to which to respond, learn about, or ignore. Our selections are correlated with motivational, personality, and intellectual aspects of our genotype'' (p. 427). Once created, these environments contribute to further differentiation at the phenotypic or behavioral level. These processes may be reflected in the fact that Type A and B children elicit different responses from unfamiliar adults. Type A children seem to elicit more achievement-encouraging responses from unrelated adults than do Type B children (Matthews, 1977). Through the *transactional* processes described in the present model, Type A's are likely to construct an environment that facilitates the expression and further development of any inherited tendency toward hostile, controlling, and physiologically taxing responses. Further, these transactional relationships may be evident at a young age.

Described in a following section of this chapter is a variety of research findings that are relevant to the notion that Type A's are likely to create more frequent, severe, and enduring challenges and demands in their day to day environments, and that such challenges and demands are likely to be physiologically taxing. Direct tests of the transactional model have not appeared yet, except for a few psychophysiological studies (cf. VanEgeren, 1979a, 1979b). Implications of this model for research in the Type A area are discussed in the concluding section of this chapter. Before reviewing evidence concerning the Type A stress-engendering style, however, the three major models are compared further in an effort to clarify their differences regarding the nature of CHD risk in Type A's.

The Interactional and Transactional Views of the Expression of Risk

The two statistical interactional models differ from the transactional approach in their assumptions regarding the nature of the linking of Type A behavior, reactivity, and CHD risk. These differing assumptions can be depicted using recent models of the way laboratory-based assessments of reactivity might generalize to nonlaboratory settings. Manuck and Krantz (1984, 1986) have provided two very useful models. Note that these authors did not present these two models in the context of issues surrounding Type A and reactivity. Rather, their interests were with individual differences in reactivity alone. Nonetheless, these models serve nicely to clarify differences among models of Type A and reactivity.

The Prevailing State Model.   The simplest model of the relationship betwen reactivity assessed in the laboratory and cardiovascular responses outside the laboratory is the prevailing state model. Depicted in Fig. 5.4, this model suggests that task-related levels of arousal are typical of levels of arousal during the normal waking hours. Laboratory baselines may represent atypically relaxed or quiescent periods, never occurring during a usual day. Increases from such a baseline during laboratory task performance may be indicative of the individual's response to the steady flow of stimulation in the waking hours. Thus, if one assumes that the upper panel reflects the more laboratory-reactive Type A and the bottom panel reflects the Type B, this model would predict that the Type A displays tonically higher levels of arousal during typical daily events than does the Type A exposed to those same events.[1]

This model is quite close to a simple trait approach to the expression of risk in Type A's. Their greater reactivity to laboratory stressors reflects a cross-situational, steady, or prevailing state of increased arousal. Characteristics of *situations* outside the laboratory are not important; Type A's and B's are assumed to display differences in all situations during the day.

The Recurrent Activation Model.   The second model presented by Manuck and

---

[1]It is important to emphasize again that Manuck and Krantz (1984, 1986) did not link these models or the figures depicting them to the Type A pattern. The models are borrowed for the present discussion as explanatory devices.

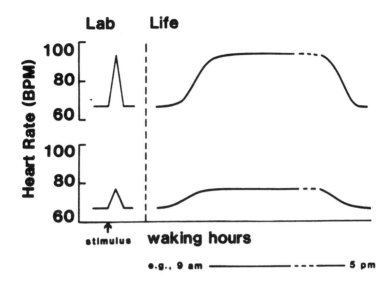

PREVAILING STATE MODEL

FIG. 5.4.   Stylized figure depicting the generalization to nonlaboratory settings of individual differences in laboratory-assessed heart rate reactivity, as predicted by the ''prevailing state model.'' (from Manuck & Krantz, 1984, p. 13) The reactive, Type A, is depicted in the top panel, whereas the less reactive, Type B, is portrayed in the bottom.

Krantz (1984, 1986) incorporates the situation specificity typical of statistical interaction models of personality. The recurrent activation model suggests that the reactive Type A depicted in the upper panel of Fig. 5.5 is not always more aroused than the Type B (lower panel). Type A's would respond to specific stressors—both within and outside the laboratory—with greater increases in arousal than those displayed by Type B's. In less stressful situations, such as laboratory baseline periods and outside situations relatively free of challenge and demand, Type A's and B's would display equivalent, low levels of arousal.

This model parallels person-by-situation models in that the behavior or response of interest (i.e., level of arousal outside the laboratory) cannot be accounted for by the person variable (i.e., ''trait reactivity'') alone. Rather the co-occurrence of high levels of trait reactivity and relevant situational stressors produces elevated arousal outside the lab.

The Transactional Approach.   The generalization of laboratory Type A/B differences in reactivity to the nonlaboratory environment is more complex from the transactional viewpoint, as depicted in Fig. 5.6. Again, the more reactive Type A is depicted in the upper panel, whereas the Type B is represented in the lower. As in the prevailing state and recurrent activation models, the Type A is more reactive to controlled laboratory stressors than is the Type B. Outside the laboratory, the Type A is characterized by *both* greater overall general arousal and great-

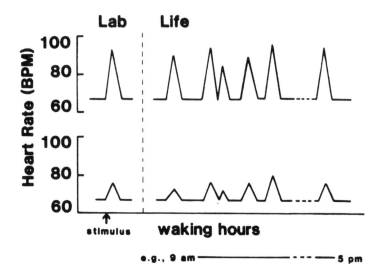

RECURRENT ACTIVATION MODEL

FIG. 5.5. Stylized figure depicting the generalization to nonlaboratory settings of individual differences in laboratory-assessed heart rate reactivity, as predicted by the "recurrent activation model." (from Manuck & Krantz, 1984) The reactive, Type A, is depicted in the top panel, whereas the less reactive, Type B, is portrayed in the bottom.

er reactivity. Examination of the nature of stressors reveals the explanation of this pattern. When confronted with equivalent stressors (e.g., the laboratory stressor and the first two stressors encountered outside the laboratory), the Type A is more reactive. This greater reactivity to equivalent stressors, however, is augmented by more frequent, more severe, and more enduring stressors in the nonlaboratory environment. These Type A/B differences in the "stressor topography" are the result of the Type A challenge and demand-engendering style described in the next section.

When the prevailing state, recurrent activation, and transactional models are compared, it is clear that the latter approach extends rather than contradicts the previous ones. As in the prevailing state approach, the transactional approach suggests that the Type A, relative to the Type B, has a higher overall level of arousal outside the laboratory. The explanation of this difference, however, involves a combination of a higher level of stressors and greater reactivity, rather than simply greater reactivity to an unchanging and equivalent level of stressors outside the laboratory. Further, the transactional approach assumes the increased reactivity to specific, equivalent stressors that is the core of the recurrent activation model, but goes on to suggest that the equivalence of stressors for Type A's and B's is artifical. Outside the laboratory, the Type A is likely to create a daily menu of more frequent, severe, and enduring challenges and demands.

THE TYPE A TRANSACTIONAL STYLE

Previous presentations of this model have included a detailed discussion of the ways in which Type A's might increase the level of challenge and demand in their proximal environment and have described the likely physiological cost of this style (Smith & Anderson, 1986; Smith & Rhodewalt, 1986). In this chapter, the relevant research is reviewed more briefly but focuses on the same theme; through their thoughts and actions, Type A's tend to increase their contact with physiologically taxing situations.

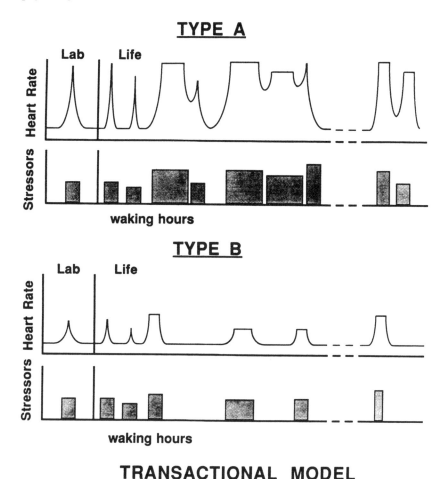

FIG. 5.6.   Stylized figure depicting the generalization to nonlaboratory settings of individual differences in laboratory-assessed heart rate reactivity, as predicted by the transactional model. (from Smith & Rhodewalt, 1986)

Choice of Situations

It is perhaps obvious that anticipating and performing difficult rather than easy cognitive tasks produces higher levels of cardiovascular reactivity (Contrada, Wright, & Glass, 1984; Solomon, Holmes, & McCaul, 1980). Several studies suggest that Type A's prefer greater levels of task difficulty than do Type B's. Type A college students carry a more demanding course load than do their Type B classmates (Ovcharchyn, Johnson, & Petzel, 1981), and demonstrate a preference for more difficult cognitive tasks (Holmes, McGilley, & Houston, 1984; Ortega & Pipal, 1984). These relatively higher levels of task difficulty have been found to elicit significantly greater levels of reactivity in Type A's as compared to Type B's (Contrada et al., 1984; Holmes et al., 1984).

Type A's, unlike Type B's, also tend to maintain control in laboratory task situations, even when the decision to delegate control to an available partner might increase their chances for success (Miller, Lack, & Asroff, 1985; Strube, Berry, & Moergen, 1985; Strube & Werner, 1985). Type A's, relative to Type B's, also report a generally increased desire to exert control over environmental events (Dembroski, MacDougall, & Musante, 1984; Smith & O'Keefe, 1985a). Such attempts to actively exert control are known to produce increased reactivity relative to passive coping conditions (Light & Obrist, 1980; Lovallo et al., 1985; Solomon et al., 1980; Smith, Houston, & Stukey, 1985). Further, tasks requiring active rather than passive coping are more likely to elicit the typical Type A/B differences in reactivity (Contrada et al., 1982; Pittner, Houston, & Spiridigliozzi, 1983). Thus, Type A's preference for difficult tasks and active coping are likely to place them in physiologically taxing situations more frequently than Type B's.

Cognitive Processes

Appraisal of Situations. Type A's, relative to Type B's, consistently appear to construe situations as being more challenging, difficult, or requiring more effort. They believe that more is expected of them by their parents (Ovcharchyn et al., 1981) and employers (Mettlin, 1976). They also set higher standards for themselves (Grimm & Yarnold, 1984; O'Keeffe & Smith, 1986; Ovcharchyn et al., 1981; Snow, 1978) and report that most events are more important (Rhodewalt, 1984). Type A's also view potential opponents as more competitive (Smith & Brehm, 1981a) and have a lower threshold for perceiving threats to their behavioral freedoms (Carver, 1980; Rhodewalt & Davison, 1983). As described earlier, to the extent that Type A's view tasks as more difficult, they are likely to respond whith greater levels of reactivity (Contrada et al., 1984; Homes et al., 1984). Some research suggests that the simple perception or appraisal of increased task difficulty, regardless of the actual or objective difficulty, is sufficient to elicit increased reactivity in Type A's relative to their Type B counterparts (Gastorf, 1981).

Cognitive Coping During Task Performance. Type A's tend to report the use of active rather than passive strategies in dealing with stressors (Smith & Brehm, 1981b; Vingerhoets & Flohr, 1984), perhaps because of their preference for control over environmental events (Dembroski et al., 1984; Glass, 1977; Smith & O'Keeffe, 1985a). This tendency may lead Type A's to persist in their efforts to cope actively with stressors they view as potentially controllable. As already noted, active coping attempts elicit increased reactivity in general and are likely to produce Type A/B difference in reactivity.

In addition to attempting to cope actively with stressors, Type A's tend to display denial or suppression when coping with their own negative affect and fatigue during task performance (Gentry, Oude-Weme, Musch, & Hall, 1981; Pittner & Houston, 1980; Pittner et al., 1983; Weidner & Matthews, 1978). It may be that the Type A's apparent denial of negative affect and fatigue during task performance actually reflects the fact that their attentional capacity is completely occupied by task demands (Stern, Harris, & Elverum, 1981; Humphries, Carver & Newman, 1983). Other authors have suggested that this inattention to, or denial or suppression of, fatigue and negative affect may prolong the Type A's contact with physiologically taxing stressors (Houston, 1981; Matthews & Brunson, 1979); that is, the Type A may not attend to the stress or fatigue that otherwise instigates the Type B to slow down, take a break, or just go home. As a result, the Type A is likely to persist longer in a demanding, physiologically taxing undertaking.

Self-evaluation. Type A self-evaluation tendencies may increase their contact with challenges and demands. As just noted, Type A's tend to set higher standards for performance than do Type B's. Type A's also tend to be more self-critical than do Type B's (Cooney & Zeichner, 1985; Manuck & Garland, 1979; O'Keeffe & Smith, 1986; Ovcharchyn et al., 1981; Smith & O'Keeffe, 1985b); that is, they tend to evaluate a given level of performance more negatively than do Type B's. Further, Type A's tend to attribute negative outcomes to internal factors, such as low effort (Furnham, Hillard & Brewin, 1985; Lueger & Brady, 1984; Rhodewalt, 1984). The combination of Type A's high standards, low self-evaluation of performance, and tendency to attribute failure internally may produce aggressive striving to reduce the perceived discrepancy between goals and current performance. Their self-regulatory pattern seems likely to place Type A's frequently in the position where they feel that they have fallen far short of a very high mark but also have the capability of reaching it with sufficient effort. The more persistent pursuit of these more subjectively difficult goals may produce greater physiological arousal in the Type A.

Interpersonal Behavior

Type A's may create challenge and demand in their interactions with others. As noted before, Type A's, relative to Type B's, expect future opponents to be more hard driving and competitive (Smith & Brehm, 1981a). Other social psychological research suggests that such expectations can channel interactions in such a way as to elicit confirming behaviors from the target of those expectations (cf. Snyder & Swann, 1978; for a review see Darley & Fazio, 1980). Thus, the Type A may create more frequent competitive interactions, which in turn may be physiologically taxing. The ability to Type A's to elicit competitive behaviors from others (especially other Type A's) has been well documented (VanEgeren, 1979a, 1979b; VanEgeren, Abelson, & Sniderman, 1983; VanEgeren, Sniderman, & Roggelin, 1982). Further, these competitive interactions appear to elicit increased cardiovascular arousal in Type A's (VanEgeren, 1979b).

Several studies indicate that Type A's, relative to Type B's, respond to interpersonal provocation (e.g., harrassment) with greater aggression (Carver & Glass, 1978; Holmes & Will; 1985; Strube, Turner, Cerro, Stevens, & Hinchey, 1984). Further, Type A's tend to be more dominant and aggressive during conversation than do Type B's (Yarnold & Grimm, 1986; in press; Yarnold, Mueser, & Grimm, 1985). If such aggressive interpersonal behavior is reciprocated, see how Type A's create and maintain ongoing hostile interactions with others. Previous research suggests that these hostile interactions elicit exaggerated physiological reactivity in Type A's (Friedman, Byers, Diamant, & Rosenman, 1975; Glass et al., 1980).

Interestingly, marital relationships may be one venue where Type A interpersonal behaviors are costly. Type A's and their spouses often report more marital strain and conflict than do Type B's and their spouses (Burke & Weir, 1980; Haynes, Scotch, Feinleib, & Kannel, 1978; Keegan, Sinha, Merriman, & Shipley, 1979; Kelly & Houston; 1985). Further, discordant marital interactions are characterized by greater physiological arousal than are more satisfactory interactions (Levenson & Gottman, 1985). When combined with previously noted findings of spouse characteristics as moderators of the degree of CHD risk associated with the Type A pattern, these studies suggest that the potentially stressful marital interactions of Type A's deserve further study (Smith & Sanders, 1986).

Summary of the Type A Transactional Style

This brief review indicates several ways in which Type A's appear to create a more challenging, demanding, and physiologically taxing environment. Through their characteristic ways of choosing situations, thinking, and behaving toward others, they seem likely to increase the frequency, severity, and duration of stressors in their daily lives. Further, it seems likely that this environment would tend to elicit and maintain additional Type A behavior. This physiologically taxing, reciprocal relationship between Type A's and their environment is likely to occur in relatively brief episodes, such as initially casual conversations with others that are transformed into heated arguments. This reciprocal pattern is also likely to be reflected in more longlasting, recurrent interaction patterns, much like those described in interactional approaches to personality (cf. Anchin & Kiesler, 1982;

Wachtel, 1977). As a result, the associated, "self-inflicted" physiological differences between Type A's and B's would accumulate over long periods of time.

CURRENT LIMITATIONS AND IMPLICATIONS
OF THE TRANSACTIONAL APPROACH

The transactional approach is admittedly speculative. Although based in important conceptual issues and consistent with many previous studies, it has not been subjected to direct tests. As already argued, its greatest value may be in pointing to additional avenues for future research. Before discussing these possibilities, it is important to note the potential limitations of the transactional model.

Is the Transactional Style a Benign Aspect of the Type A Pattern?

It is now clear that the most widely used measures of Type A behavior are at best modestly related to each other (e.g., Matthews, Krantz, Dembroski, & Mac-Dougall, 1982). Further, it is clear that the Type A Structured Interview (SI) is more consistently related to both CHD and physiological reactivity than is the Jenkins Activity Survey (JAS) (for reviews, see Manuck et al., 1986; Matthews & Haynes, 1986; Contrada et al., 1985). The majority of the research documenting the Type A challenge and demand-engendering style, however, has employed the JAS. This presents the distinct possibility that the transactional aspects of the behavior pattern are not dangerous. It is important to note, however, that the relevant studies on psychological and social correlates of the SI simply have not been undertaken, or at least are less frequent (Matthews, 1982). Thus, SI-defined Type A behavior may also be associated with challenge and demand-engendering tendencies, but this is presently not known.

Even if future research suggests that the SI is not associated with such tendencies, the Type A transactional style may not always be benign. The previous studies that have failed to find a relationship betwen the JAS and CHD have all used simple trait approaches. If the JAS is an index of the tendency to *create* challenges and demands but not necessarily to respond to them with exaggerated reactivity, then the combination—perhaps synergistic—between an independent assessment of reactivity and JAS scores may be useful in predicting disease. As others have suggested previously (Musante, MacDougall, Dembroski, & VanHorn, 1983), a combination of assessments of reactivity and the tendency to create or encounter relevant stressors may provide a useful index of CHD risk. Whether or not this stress-engendering style is dangerous may depend on individual differences in reactivity. It is important to note that this hypothesis requires an interactional approach to test of the relationship between the JAS and CHD, an approach that has not been used to date.

As noted earlier, several studies suggest that hostility may be the toxic element within the array of Type A characteristics. At first glance, this may seem to suggest that the transactional approach is not relevant to CHD risk. Many of the Type A challenge and demand-engendering tendencies do not appear to involve hostility. As in models of Type A and CHD, reactivity to environmental stressors is the link between hostility and disease in these models as well (cf. Williams et al., 1985). Further, similar tendencies to create physiologically taxing stressors may be associated with hostility (Smith & Frohm, 1985). Hostile persons, through their thoughts and actions, may increase the frequency, severity, and duration of interpersonal stresses, resulting in corresponding increases in pathogenic physiological arousal. Recent research has indicated that cynically hostile persons (Smith & Frohm, 1985) report more interpersonal stressors and conflicts in their families, marriages, and jobs (Smith, Pope, Sanders, Allred, & O'Keeffe, 1987). Further, cynically hostile persons, relative to more agreeable individuals, respond to interpersonal conflict with greater increases in diastolic blood pressure (Hardy & Smith, in press). As hostility becomes more clearly implicated as a CHD risk factor, interactional and transactional studies of this construct become more important.

Additional Questions in Future Research

This chapter has pointed to several possible additional avenues in Type A research. The first of these concerns the discrepency between conceptual models of the link between Type A and CHD on the one hand, and the operational tests of those models on the other. Clearly most Type A models are interactional; Type A's demonstrate pathophysiological responses in the presence of certain classes of stimuli. With few exceptions, however, studies of the prevalence and incidence of CHD or CAD severity have failed to include independent assessments of such situational factors. As a result, by default they are based in older, more simple trait approaches to personality. As others have argued (Matthews, 1983; 1985; Smith & Sanders, 1986; Thoresen & Ohman, 1985), some of the predictive utility of Type A concept may be lost in this oversight. Even if the Type A concept is replaced by other individual differences (i.e., hostility, reactivity), the relevant models are still interactional. The models would predict that highly hostile or physiologically reactive persons are at greater risk if they face a higher concentration of relevant environmental stressors than if they face a more relaxed environment.

But what research questions are implied as we move from interactional to transactional models? First, laboratory studies of Type A (or hostility) and reactivity could be expanded to include transactional issues. Are the typical Type A versus B differences in reactivity larger when subjects are allowed to alter the level of challenge and demand in the situation? The transactional approach would predict this outcome, given that Type A's would tend to create greater levels of challenge than would Type B's. This obviously requires a departure from the usual way laboratory studies of reactivity are conducted. Malleable stressors would have to be added to the controlled stressors that are typically employed.

Some authors would avoid the laboratory as a site for testing transactional approaches and instead advocate naturalistic studies (e.g., Lazarus & Folkman, 1984, p. 299). The technology for the ambulatory measurement of physiological reactivity has become increasingly accessible in recent years (cf. McKinney et al., 1985). Further, personality researchers have begun to develop methodologies for assessing the impact of an individual's situation choices in the natural environment (Emmons, Diener, & Larson, 1986). A combination of these methodologies may provide the opportunity to study the physiological consequences of the situation choices of Type A's and B's outside the confines of the psychophysiological laboratory.

These two types of studies suggest that transactional alternatives to traditional trait and trait-by-situation studies of reactivity exist. The question remains, however, whether or not one can imagine a transactional alternative to the trait and statistical interaction approaches to studies of CHD and CAD. How can an ongoing transactional process be assessed and used to predict disease? The nature of such designs is not immediately apparent. It may be that the value of the transactional approach lies in the explanation of trait and statistical interaction effects obtained in more traditional epidemiological studies. Stress-engendering behaviors documented in other research may be a useful account of how hostile persons, for example, come to be at greater risk. It is possible, however, that reliable and valid indicies of various challenge and demand-engendering tendencies could provide a useful addition of other trait and situation assessments used in prospective or cross-sectional studies of CHD and CAD.

Perhaps the most obvious benefit of transactional studies is the identification of targets for intervention. If studies identify challenge and demand-engendering behaviors that appear to elicit pathophysiological responses, therapy techniques could be focused to address them. Identification of specific traits and person-by-situation interactions as risk factors is useful in focusing interventions. Explication of the *process* by which such traits and combinations of people and situations contribute to disease, however, should allow an even more precise focus. The recent positive results of the Recurrent Coronary Prevention Project (Freidman et al., 1984, 1986) have increased the already substantial interest in treatments for Type A behavior (for a review, see Suinn, 1982). Transactional research could potentially provide a menu of targets for such intervention efforts. Indeed, others have noted the relevance of such reciprocal models for the design of Type A interventions (Thoresen, Telch, & Eagleston, 1981).

This chapter has clearly raised many questions while answering few. Hopefully, these questions and the alternative assumptions that guide them will prove useful. At the very least, it is important to clarify the prevailing assumptions in Type A research and the extent to which existing studies reflect their conceptual underpinnings. The transactional approach may serve as a useful counterpoint in this regard. The transactional model may also, however, explain an additional aspect of the way in which Type A's come to be at greater risk for CHD and how that risk might be reduced.

REFERENCES

Anchin, J. C., & Kiesler, D. J. (Eds.). (1982). *Handbook of interpersonal psychotherapy*. New York: Pergamon Press.

Bandura, A. (1977). *Social learning theory*. Englewood Cliffs, NJ: Prentice-Hall.

Burke, R. J., & Weir, T. (1980). The Type A experience: Occupational and life demands, satisfaction and well-being. *Journal of Human Stress. 6*(4), 28–38.

Cantor, N., & Kihlstrom, J. F. (Eds.). (1981). *Personality, cognition, and social interaction*. Hillsdale, NJ: Lawrence Erlbaum Associates.

Cantor, N., & Kihlstrom, J. F. (1982). Cognitive and social processes in personality. In G. T. Wilson & C. Franks (Eds.), *Contemporary behavior therapy: Conceptual and empirical foundations* (pp. 142–201). New York: Guilford Press.

Carmelli, D., Swan, G. E., & Rosenman, R. H. (1985). The relationship between wives' social and psychological status and their husbands' coronary heart disease: A case-control family study from the Western Collaborative Group Study. *American Journal of Epidemiology, 122*, 90–100.

Carroll, D., Hewitt, J. K., Last, K. A., Turner, J. R., & Sims, J. (1985). A twin study of cardiac reactivity and its relationship to parental blood pressure. *Physiology and Behavior, 34*, 103–106.

Carver, C. S. (1980). Perceived coercion, resistance to persuasion, and the Type A behavior pattern. *Journal of Research in Personality, 14*, 467–481.

Carver, C. S., & Glass, D. C. (1978). Coronary-prone behavior pattern and interpersonal aggression. *Journal of Personality and Social Psychology, 36*, 361–366.

Case, R. B., Heller, S. S., Case, N. B., & Moss, A. J. (1985).Type A behavior and survival after acute myocardial infarction. *New England Journal of Medicine, 312*, 737–741.

Chesney, M. A., Sevelius, G., Black, G. W., Ward, M. M., Swan, G. E., & Rosenman, R. H. (1981). Work environment, Type A behavior and coronary heart disease risk factors. *Journal of Occupational Medicine, 23*, 551–556.

Cohen, J. B., & Reed, D. (1985). The Type A behavior pattern and coronary heart disease among Japanese men in Hawaii. *Journal of Behavioral Medicine, 8*, 343–352.

Contrada, R. J., Glass, D. C. Krakoff, L. R., Krantz, D. S., Kehoe, K. Isecke, W., Collins, C., & Eltin, E. (1982). Effects of control over aversive stimulation and Type A behavior on cardiovascular and plasma catecholamine responses. *Psychophysiology, 19*, 408–419.

Contrada, R. J., Wright, R. A., & Glass, D. C. (1984). Task difficulty, Type A pattern, and cardiovascular response. *Psychophysiology, 21*, 638–646.

Contrada, R. J. Wright, R. A., & Glass, D. C. (1985). Psychophysiological correlates of Type A behavior: Comments on Houston (1983) and Holmes (1983). *Journal of Research in Personality, 19*, 12–30.

Cooney, J. L., & Zeichner, A. (1985). Selective attention to negative feedback in Type A and Type B individuals. *Journal of Abnormal Psychology, 91*, 110–112.

Corse, C. D., Manuck, S. B., Cantwell, J. D., Giordani, B., & Matthews, K. A. (1982). Coronary-prone behavior pattern and cardiovascular response in persons with and without coronary heart disease. *Psychosomatic Medicine, 44*, 449–459.

Darley, J. M., & Fazio, R. H. (1980) Expectancy confirmation processes arising in the social interaction sequence. *American Psychologist, 35*, 867–881.

Dembroski, T. M., & MacDougall, J. M. (1983). Behavioral and psychophysiological perspectives on coronary-prone behavior. In T. M. Dembroski, T. H. Schmidt, & G. Blumchen (Eds.), *Bio-*

behavioral bases of coronary heart disease (pp. 106–129). Basel, Switzerland: Karger.
Dembroski, T. M., MacDougall, J. M., & Lushene, R. (1979). Interpersonal interaction and cardio-
vascular response in Type A subjects and coronary patients. *Journal of Human Stress, 5*, 28–36.
Dembroski, T. M., MacDougall, J.M, & Musante, L. (1984). Desirability of control versus locus
of control: Relationship to paralinguistics in the Type A interview. *Health Psychology, 3*, 15–26.
Dembroski, T. M., MacDougall, J. M., Williams, R. B., Haney, T. L., & Blumenthal, J. A. (1985).
Components of Type A, hostility, and anger-in: Relationship to angiographic findings. *Psychoso-
matic Medicine, 47*, 219–233.
Eaker, E. D., Haynes, S. G., & Feinleib, M. (1983). Spouse behavior and coronary heart disease
in men: Prospective results from the Framingham Heart Study II. Modification of risk in Type
A husband according to the social and psychological status of their wives. *American Journal of
Epidemiology, 118*, 23–41.
Emmons, R. A., Diener, E., & Larson, R. J. (1986) Choice and avoidance of everyday situations
and affect congruence: Two models of reciprocal interactionism. *Journal of Personality and So-
cial Psychology, 51*, 815–826.
Friedman, M., Byers, S. O., Diamant, J., & Rosenman, R. H. (1975). Plasma catecholamine response
of coronary-prone subjects (Type A) to a specific challenge. *Metabolism, 24*, 205–210.
Friedman, M., Thoresen, C. E., Gill, J. J., Powell, L. H., Ulmer, D., Thompson, L., Price, V.
A., Rabin, D. D., Breall, W. S., Dixon, T., Levy, R., & Bourg. E. (1984). Alteration of Type
A behavior and reduction in cardiac recurrences in postmyocardial infarction patients. *American
Heart Journal, 108*, 237–248.
Friedman, M., Thoresen, C. E., Gill, J. J., Powell, L. H., Ulmer, D., Thompson, L., Price, V.
A., Rabin, D. D., Breall, W. S., Dixon, T., Levy, R., & Bourg, E. (1986). Alteration of type
A behavior and its effect on cardiac recurrences in post myocardial infarction patients: Summary
results of the recurrent coronary prevention project. *American Heart Journal, 112*, 653–665.
Furnham, A., Hillard, A., & Brewin, C. R. (1985). Type A behavior pattern and attributions of
responsibility. *Motivation and Emotion, 9*, 39–51.
Gastorf, J. W. (1981). Physiologic reaction of Type A's to objective and subjective challenge. *Jour-
nal of Human Stress, 7*(1), 16–20.
Gentry, W. D., Oude-Weme, J. D., Musch, F., & Hall, R. P. (1981). Differences in Type A and
B behavior in response to acute myocardial infarction. *Heart and Lung, 10*, 1101–1105.
Giordani, B., Manuck, S. B., & Farmer, J. F. (1981). Stability of behaviorally induced heart rate
changes in children after one week. *Child Development, 52*, 533–537.
Glass, D. C., (1977). *Behavior patterns, stress, and coronary disease.* Hillsdale, NJ: Lawrence Erl-
baum Associates.
Glass, D. C., Krakoff, L. R., Contrada, R., Hilton, W. F., Kehoe, K., Mannucci, E. G., Collins,
C., Snow, B., & Eltin, E. (1980). Effect of harassment and competition upon cardiovascular
and catecholamine responses in Type A and Type B individuals. *Psychophysiology, 17*, 453–463.
Glass, D. C., Lake, C. R., Contrada, R. J., Kehoe, K., & Granger, L. R. (1983). Stability of in-
dividual differences in physiologic responses to stress. *Health Psychology, 4*, 317–342.
Goldband, S. (1980). Stimulus specificity of physiological response to stress and the Type A behavior pattern. *Journal of Personality and Social Psychology, 39*, 670–679.
Grimm, L., & Yarnold, P. (1984). Performance standards and the Type A behavior pattern. *Cognitive Therapy and Research, 8*, 59–66.
Hardy, J. D., & Smith, T. W. (in press). Cynical hostility and vulnerability to disease: Social support, life stress, and physiological responses to conflict. *Health Psychology.*
Haynes, S. G., Feinleib, M., & Kannel, W. B. (1980). The relationship of psychosocial factors to
coronary heart disease in the Framingham Study: I. Methods and risk factors. *American Journal
of Epidemiology, 107*, 362–383.
Holmes, D., McGilley, B., & Houston, B. K. (1984). Task-related arousal of Type A and Type
B persons: Level of challenge and response specificity. *Journal of Personality and Social Psychology, 46*, 1322–1327.
Holmes, D., & Will, M. (1985). Expression of interpersonal aggression by angered and non-angered

persons with the Type A and Type B behavior patterns. *Journal of Personality and Social Psychology, 48*, 723–727.

Houston, B. K. (1981). *What links the Type A behavior pattern and coronary heart disease?* Paper presented at the meeting of the Midwestern Psychological Association, Detroit.

Houston, B. K. (1983). Psychophysiological responsivity and the Type A behavior pattern. *Journal of Research in Personality, 17*, 22–39.

Howard, J. H., Cunningham, D. A., & Rechnitzer, P. A. (1986). Role ambiguity, Type A behavior, and job satisfaction: Moderating effects on cardiovascular and biochemical responses associated with coronary risk. *Journal of Applied Psychology, 71*, 95–101.

Humphries, C., Carver, C. S., & Newman, P. G. (1983). Cognitive characteristics of the Type A coronary-prone behavior pattern. *Journal of Personality and Social Psychology, 44*, 177–187.

Kahn, J. P., Kornfeld, D. S., Frank, K. A., Heller, S. S., & Hoar, P. F. (1980). Type A behavior and blood pressure during coronary artery bypass surgery. *Psychosomatic Medicine, 42*, 407–414.

Kaplan, J. R., Manuck, S. B., Clarkson, T. B., Lusso, F. M., & Taub, D. B. (1982). Social status, environnment, and atherosclerosis in cynomolgus monkeys. *Arteriosclerosis, 2*, 359–368.

Keegan, D. L., Sinha, B. N., Merriman, J. E., & Shipley, C. (1979). Type A behavior pattern: Relationship to coronary heart disease, personality and life adjustment. *Canadian Journal of Psychiatry, 24*, 724–730.

Kelly K. E., & Houston, B. K. (1985). Type A behavior in employed women: Relation to work, marital and leisure variables, social support, stress, tension, and health. *Journal of Personality and Social Psychology, 48*, 1067–1079.

Keys, A., Taylor, H. L., Blackburn, H., Brozek, J., Anderson, J. T., & Somonson, E. (1971). Mortality and coronary heart disease among men studied for 23 years. *Archives of Internal Medicine, 128*, 201–214.

Krantz, D. S., Arabian, J. M., Davia, J. E., & Parker, J. S. (1982). Type A behavior and coronary artery bypass surgery: Intraoperative blood pressure and perioperative complicaitons. *Psychosomatic Medicine, 44*, 273–284.

Krantz, D. S., & Durel, L. A. (1983). Psychobiological substrates of the Type A behavior pattern. *Health Psychology, 2*, 393–411.

Krantz, D. S., & Durel, L. A., Davia, J. E., Shaffer, R. T., Arabian, J. M., Dembroski, T. M., & MacDougall, J. M. (1982). Propranolol medication among coronary patients: Relationship to Type A behavior and cardiovascular response. *Journal of Human Stress, 8*(3), 4–12.

Krantz, D. S., & Manuck, S. B. (1984). Acute psychophysiologic reactivity and risk of cardiovascular disease: A review and methodological critique. *Psychological Bulletin, 96*, 435–464.

Krantz, D. S., Manuck, S. B., & Wing, R. R. (1986). Psychological stressors and task variables as elicitors of reactivity. In K. A. Matthews, S. M. Weiss, T. Detre, T. M. Dembroski, B. Falkner, S. B. Manuck, & R. B. Williams, Jr. (Eds.), *Handbook of stress, reactivity, and cardiovascular disease* (pp. 85–107). New York: Wiley.

Krantz, D. S., Schaeffer, M. A., Davia, J. E., Dembroski, T. M., MacDougall, J. M., & Shaffer, R. T. (1981). Extent of coronary atherosclerosis, Type A behavior, and cardiovascular response to social interaction. *Psychophysiology, 18*, 654–664.

Lazarus, R. S., & Folkman, S. (1984). *Stress, appraisal, and coping*. New York: Springer-Verlag.

Lazarus, R. S., & Launier, R. (1978). Stress-related transactions between person and environment. In L. A. Pervin & M. Lewis (Eds.), *Perspectives in interactional psychology*. New York: Plenum.

Levenson, R. W., & Gottman, J. M. (1985). Physiological and affective predictors of change in relationship satisfaction. *Journal of Personality and Social Psychology, 49*, 85–94.

Light, K. C., & Obrist, P. A. (1980). Cardiovascular response to stress: Effects of opportunity to avoid, shock experience, and performance feedback. *Psychophysiology, 17*, 243–252.

Lovallo, W. R., Wilson, M. F., Pincomb, G. A., Edwards, G. L., Tompkins, P., & Brackett, D. J. (1985). Activitation patterns to aversive stimuation in man: Passive exposure versus effort to control. *Psychophysiology, 22*, 283–291.

Lueger, R. J., & Brady, K. R. (1984, August). *Attributions for stressful events and the Type A be-*

havior pattern. Paper presented at the meeting of the American Psychological Association, Toronto, Canada.

MacDougall, J. M., Dembroski, T. M., Dimsdale, J. E., & Hackett, T. P. (1985). Components of Type A hostility, and anger-in: Further relationships to angiographic findings. *Health Psychology, 4,* 137–152.

Magnusson, D., & Endler, N. S. (1977). Interactional psychology: Present status and future prospects. In D. Magnusson & N. S. Endler (Eds.), *Personality at the crossroads: Current issues in interactional psychology* (pp. 3–31). New York: Lawrence Erlbaum Associates.

Manuck, S. B., Corse, C. D., & Winkelman, P. A. (1979). Behavioral correlates of individual differences in blood pressure reactivity. *Journal of Psychosomatic Research, 23,* 281–288.

Manuck, S. B., & Garland, F. N. (1979). Coronary-prone behavior pattern, task incentive, and cardiovascular response. *Psychophysiology, 16,* 136–142.

Manuck, S. B., & Garland, F. N. (1980). Stability in individual differences in cardiovascular reactivity: A thirteen month follow-up. *Physiology and Behavior, 21,* 621–624.

Manuck, S. B., Kaplan, J. R., & Clarkson, T. B. (1983). Behaviorally induced heart rate reactivity and atherosclerosis in cynomolgus monkeys. *Psychosomatic Medicine, 45,* 95–108.

Manuck, S. B., Kaplan, J. R., & Clarkson, T. B. (1985). Stress-induced heart rate reactivity and atherosclerosis in female macaques. *Psychosomatic Medicine, 47,* 90.

Manuck, S. B., Kaplan, J. R., & Matthews, K. A. (1986). Behavioral antecedents of coronary heart disease and atherosclerosis. *Arteriosclerosis, 6,* 2–14.

Manuck, S. B., & Krantz, D. S. (1984). Psychophysiologic reactivity in coronary heart disease. *Behavioral Medicine Update, 6*(3), 11–15

Manuck, S. B., & Krantz, D. S. (1986). Psychophysiologic reactivity in coronary heart disease and essential hypertension. In K. A. Matthews, S. M. Weiss, T. Detre, T. M. Dembroski, B. Falkner, S. B. Manuck, & R. B. Williams, Jr. (Eds.), *Handbook of stress, reactivity and cardiovascular disease* (pp. 11–34). New York: Wiley.

Matthews, K. A. (1977). Caregiver–child interactions and the Type A coronary-prone behavior pattern. *Child Development, 48,* 1752–1756.

Matthews, K. A. (1982). Psychological perspectives on the Type A behavior pattern. *Psychological Bulletin, 91,* 293–323.

Matthews, K. A. (1983). Assessment issues in coronary-prone behavior. In T. M. Dembroski, T. H. Schmidt, & G. Blumchen, (Eds.), *Biobehavioral bases of coronary heart disease.* Basel, Switzerland: Karger.

Matthews, K. A. (1985). Assessment of Type A behavior, anger, and hostility in epidemiological studies of cardiovascular disease. In A. M. Ostfeld & E. D. Eaker (Eds.), *Measuring psychosocial variables in epidemiologic studies of cardiovascular disease* (NIH Publication No. 85–2270). Washington, DC: USDHHS.

Matthews, K. A., & Brunson, B. I. (1979). Allocation of attention and the Type A coronary-prone behavior pattern. *Journal of Personality and Social Psychology, 37,* 2081–2090.

Matthews, K. A., Glass, D. C., Rosenman, R. H., & Bortner, R. W. (1977). Competitive drive, Pattern A, and coronary heart disease: A further analysis of some data from the Western Collaborative Group Study. *Journal of Chronic Diseases, 30,* 489–498.

Matthews, K. A., & Haynes, S. G. (1986). Type A behavior pattern and coronary disease risk: Update and critical evaluation. *American Journal of Epidemiology, 123,* 923–960.

Matthews, K. A., Krantz, D. S., Dembroski, T. M., & McDougall, J. M. (1982). Unique and common variance in structured interview and Jenkins Activity Survey measures of the Type A behavior pattern. *Journal of Personality and Social Psychology, 42,* 303–313.

Matthews, K. A., Rosenman, R. H., Dembroski, T. M., Harris, E. L., & MacDougall, J. M. (1984). Familial resemblance in components of the Type A behavior pattern: A reanalysis of the California Type A twin study. *Psychosomatic Medicine, 46,* 512–522.

Matthews, K. A., & Siegel, J. M. (1982). The Type A behavior pattern in children and adolescents: Assessment, development, and associated risk. In A. Baum & J. E. Singer (Eds.), *Handbook*

of psychology and health (Vol. 2, pp. 99–118). New York: Lawrence Erlbaum Associates.
Matthews, K. A., & Siegel, J. M. (1983). Type A behaviors by children, social comparison, and standards for self-evaluation. *Developmental Psychology, 19,* 135–140.
Matthews, K. A., Weiss, S., Detre, T., Dembroski, T. M., Falkner, B., Manuck, S. B., & Williams, R. B. (1986). *Handbook of stress, reactivity, and cardiovascular disease.* New York: Wiley.
McKinney, M. E., Hofshire, P. J., Buell, J. C., & Eliot, R. S. (1984). Hemodynamic and biochemical responses to stress: The necessary link between Type A behavior and cardiovascular disease. *Behavioral Medicine Update, 6*(4), 16–21.
McKinney, M. E., Miner, M. H., Ruddel, H., McIlvain, H. E., Witte, H., Buell, J. C., Eliot, R. S., & Grant, L. B. (1985). The standardized mental stress test protocol: Test-retest reliability and comparison with ambulatory blood pressure monitoring. *Psychophysiology, 22,* 453–463.
Mettlin, C. (1976). Occupational careers and the prevention of coronary-prone behavior. *Social Science and Medicine, 10,* 367–372.
Miller, S. M., Lack, E. R., Asroff, S. (1985). Preference for control and the coronary-prone behavior pattern: "I'd rather do it myself." *Journal of Personality and Social Psychology, 49,* 492–499.
Mischel, W. (1973). Toward a cognitive social learning reconceptualization of personality. *Psychological Review, 80,* 252–283.
Musante, L., MacDougall, J. M., Dembroski, T. M., & Van Horen, A. E. (1983). Component analysis of the Type A coronary-prone behavior pattern in male and female college students. *Journal of Personality and Social Psychology, 45,* 1104–1117.
Obrist, P. A. (1981). *Cardiovascular psychophysiology.* New York: Plenum.
O'Keeffe, J., & Smith, T. W. (1986, March). *Self-regulation and Type A behavior.* Paper presented at Society of Behavioral Medicine annual meeting, San Francisco.
Ortega, D., & Pipal, J. (1984). Challenge seeking and the Type A coronary-prone behavior pattern. *Journal of Personality and Social Psychology, 46,* 1328–1334.
Ovcharchyn, C. A., Johnson, H. H., & Petzel, T. P. (1981). Type A behavior, academic aspirations, and academic success. *Journal of Personality, 49,* 248–256.
Pittner M. S., & Houston, B. K. (1980). Response to stress, cognitive coping strategies, and the Type A behavior pattern. *Journal of Personality and Social Psychology, 39,* 147–157.
Pittner, M. S., & Houston, B. K., & Spiridigliozzi, G. (1983). Control over stress, Type A behavior pattern, and response to stress. *Journal of Personality and Social Psychology, 44,* 627–637.
Review Panel on Coronary-Prone Behavior and Coronary Heart Disease. (1981). Coronary-prone behavior and coronary heart disease: A critical review. *Circulation, 63,* 1199–1215.
Rhodewalt, F. (1984). Self-involvement, self-attribution, and the Type A coronary-prone behavior pattern. *Journal of Personality and Social Psychology, 47,* 662–670.
Rose, J. R., Grim, C. E., & Miller, J. Z. (1984). Familial influences on cardiovascular stress reactivity: Studies of normotensive twins. *Behavioral Medicine Update, 6*(3), 21–24.
Scarr, S., & McCartney, K. (1983). How people make their own environments: A theory of genotype-environment effects. *Child Development,* 424–435.
Scherwitz, L., Berton, K., & Leventhal, H. (1978). Type A behavior, self-involvement, and cardiovascular response. *Psychosomatic Medicine, 40,* 593–609.
Schneider, R., Freidrich. G., Neus, J., & Ruddel, J. (1982). Effect of beta-blockers on Type A coronary-prone behavior. *Psychosomatic Medicine, 44,* 129–130.
Shekelle, R. B., Gale, M., & Norusis, M. (1985). For the Aspirin Myocardial Infarction Study Research Group: Type A score (Jenkins Activity Survey) and risk of recurrent coronary heart disease in the Aspirin Myocardial Infarction Study. *American Journal of Cardiology, 56,* 221–225.
Shekelle, R. B., Hulley, S. B., Neaton, J. D., Billings, J. H., Borhani, N. O., Gerace, T. A., Jacobs, D. R., Lasser, N. L., Mittlemark, M. B., & Stamler, J. (1985). The MRFIT behavior pattern study: II. Type A behavior and the incidence of coronary heart disease. *American Journal of Epidemiology, 122,* 559–570.
Smith, T. W., & Anderson, N. B. (1986). Models of personality and disease: An interactional ap-

proach to Type A behavior and cardiovascular risk. *Journal of Personality and Social Psychology, 50,* 1166–1173.

Smith, T. W., & Brehm, S. S. (1981a). Person perception and the Type A coronary-prone behavior pattern. *Journal of Personality and Social Psychology, 40,* 1137–1149.

Smith, T. W., & Brehm, S. S. (1981b). Cognitive correlates of the Type A coronary-prone behavior pattern. *Motivation and Emotion, 5,* 215–223.

Smith, T. W., & Frohm, K. (1985). What's so unhealthy about hostility? Construct validity and psychosocial correlates of the Cook and Medley Hostility Scale. *Health Psychology, 4,* 503–520.

Smith, T. W., Houston, B. K., & Stucky, R. J. (1985). Effects of threat of shock and control over shock on finger pulse volume, pulse rate, and systolic blood pressure. *Biological Psychology, 20,* 31–38.

Smith, T. W., & O'Keeffe, J. L. (1985a). The inequivalence of self-reports of Type A behavior: Differential relationships of the Jenkins Activity Survey and the Framingham Scale with affect, stress, and control. *Motivation and Emotion, 9,* 299–311.

Smith, T. W., & O'Keeffe, J. (1985b, August). *Self-control processes in Type A behavior and depression.* Paper presented at the American Psychological Association annual meeting, Los Angeles.

Smith, T. W., Pope, M. K., Sanders , J. D., Allred, K. D., & O'Keeffe, J. (1987). *Cynical hostility at home and work: Psychosocial vulnerability across domains.* Manuscript submitted for publication.

Smith, T. W., & Rhodewalt, F. (1986). On states, traits and processes: A transactional alternative to individual difference asuumptions in Type A behavior and physiological reactivity. *Journal of Research in Personality, 20,* 229–251.

Smith, T. W., & Sanders, J. D. (1986). Type A behavior, marriage, and the heart: Person-by-situation interactions and the risk of coronary disease. *Behavioral Medicine Abstracts, 7,* 59–62.

Smith, T. W., Turner, C. W., Ford, M. H., Hunt, S. C., Barlow, G. K., Stults, B. M., & Williams, R. R. (1987). Blood pressure reactivity in adult male twins. *Health Psychology, 6,* 209–220.

Snow, B. (1978). Level of aspiration in coronary prone and noncoronary prone adults. *Personality and Social Psychology Bulletin, 4,* 416–419.

Snyder, J., & Swann, W. B., Jr. (1978). Behavioral confirmation in social interaction: From Social perception to social reality. *Journal of Experimental Social Psychology, 14,* 148–162.

Solomon, S., Holmes, D., & McCaul, K. (1980). Behavioral control over aversive events: Does control that requires effort reduce anxiety and physiological arousal? *Journal of Personality and Social Psychology, 39,* 729–736.

Stern, G. S., Harris, J., & Elverum, J. (1981). Attention to important versus trivial tasks and salience of fatigue-related symptoms for coronary-prone individuals. *Journal of Research in Personality, 15,* 467–474.

Strube, M., Berry, J. M., & Moergen, S. (1985). Relinquishment of control and the Type A behavior pattern: The role of performance evaluation. *Journal of Personality and Social Psychology, 49,* 831–842.

Strube, M., Turner, C., Cerro, D., Stevens, J., & Hinchey, F. (1984). Interpersonal aggression and the Type A coronary-prone behavior pattern: A theoretical distinction and practical implications. *Journal of Personality and Social Psychology, 47,* 839–847.

Strube, M., & Werner, C. (1985). Relinquishment of control and the Type A behavior Pattern. *Journal of Personality and Social Psychology, 48,* 688–701.

Suinn, R. M. (1982). Intervention with Type A behaviors. *Journal of Consulting and Clinical Psychology, 50,* 933–949.

Thoresen, C. E., & Ohman, A. (1985). The Type A behavior pattern: A person–environment interaction perspective. In D. Magnusson & A. Ohman (Eds.), *Psychopathology: An interaction perspective,* New York: Academic Press.

Thoresen, C. E., Telch, M., & Eagleston, J. (1981). Approaches to altering the Type A behavior pattern. *Psychosomatics, 22,* 472–482.

Van Egeren, L. F. (1979a). Social interactions, communications, and the coronary-prone behavior pattern: A psychophysiological study. *Psychosomatic Medicine, 41,* 2–18.

Van Egeren, L. F. (1979b). Cardiovascular changes during social competition in a mixed-motive game. *Journal of Personality and Social Psychology, 37,* 858–864.

Van Egeren, L. F., Abelson, J. L., & Sniderman, L. D. (1983). Interpersonal and electrocardiographic responses of Type A's and Type B's in competitive socioeconomic games. *Journal of Psychosomatic Research, 27,* 53–59.

Van Egeren, L. F., Sniderman, L. D., & Roggelin, M. S. (1982). Competitive two-person interactions of Type A and Type B individuals. *Journal of Behavioral Medicine, 5,* 55–66.

Vingerhoets, A. J. J. M., & Flohr, P. J. M. (1984). Type A behavior and self-reports of coping preferences. *British Journal of Medical Psychology, 57,* 15–21.

Wachtel, P. L. (1977). *Psychoanalysis and behavior therapy: Toward an integration.* New York: Basic Books.

Ward, M. M., Chesney, M. A., Swan, G. E., Black, G. W., Parker, S. D., & Rosenman, R. H. (1986). Cardiovascular responses in Type A and Type B men to a series of stressors. *Journal of Behavioral Medicine, 9,* 43–49.

Weidner, G., & Matthews, K. A. (1978). Reported physical symptoms elicited by unpredictable events and the Type A coronary-prone behavior pattern. *Journal of Personality and Social Psychology, 36,* 1213–1220.

Williams, R. B., Jr. (1978). Psychophysiological processes, the coronary-prone behavior pattern, and coronary heart disease. In T. M. Dembroski, S. M. Weiss, J. L. Shields, S. G. Haynes, & M. Feinleib (Eds.), *Coronary-prone behavior* (pp. 141–146). New York: Springer-Verlag.

Williams, R. B., Jr., Barefoot, J. C., & Shekelle, R. B. (1985). The health consequences of hostility. In M. A. Chesney, S. E. Goldston, & R. H. Rosenman (Eds.), *Anger, hostility, and behavioral medicine* (pp. 173–186). New York: Hemisphere/McGraw-Hill.

Williams, R. B., Friedman, M., Glass, D. C., Herd, J. A., & Schneiderman, N. (1978). Section summary: Mechanisms linking behavioral and pathophysiological processes. In T. M. Dembroski, S. M. Weiss, J. L. Shields, S. G. Haynes, & M. Feinleib (Eds.), *Coronary-prone behavior* (pp. 119–128). New York: Springer-Verlag.

Williams, R. B., Haney, T., Lee, K., Kong, Y., Blumenthal, J., & Whalen, R. (1980). Type A behavior, hostility, and coronary heart disease. *Psychosomatic Medicine, 42,* 539–549.

Yarnold, P. R., & Grimm, L. G. (1986). Interpersonal dominance and coronary prone behavior. *Journal of Research in Personality, 20,* 420–433.

Yarnold, P. R., & Grimm, L. G. (in press). Interpersonal dominance of Type A's and B's during involved group discussions. *Journal of Applied Social Psychology.*

Yarnold, P. R., Mueser, K. T., & Grimm, L. G. (1985). Interpersonal dominance of Type A's in group discussions. *Journal of Abnormal Psychology, 94,* 233–236.

Type A Behavior Assessment in the Structured Interview: Review, Critique, and Recommendations

6

Larry Scherwitz, Ph.D.
University of California San Francisco

INTRODUCTION

The structured interview (SI) is widely considered the standard method for assessing Type A behavior (Chesney, Eagleston, & Rosenman, 1980). This is because the SI best fits the construct of Type A behavior as an observable set of behaviors and attributes that occur in a stimulating mileu. Research has repeatedly shown that *questionnaire measures* of global Type A are poorly correlated with global SI assessments (Chesney, Black, Chadwick, & Rosenman, 1981; Matthews, 1983; Matthews, Krantz, Dembroski, & MacDougall, 1982; Scherwitz, Berton, & Leventhal, 1977; Scherwitz, Graham, Grandits, & Billings, 1987). And both pioneers of the Type A concept maintain that questionnaires do not measure Type A behavior (Friedman, Hall, & Harris, 1985; Rosenman, Swan, & Carmelli, in press).

Thus, if we are to continue to progress in our assessment of Type A and coronary-prone behavior and ultimately develop a superior measure, we should proceed by *deepening our understanding and refinement of the interview method.* Although globally defined Type A/B assessment is regarded as the standard, it involves a set of implicit and empirically untested decisions about how an interviewer is to behave while conducting the interview. It remains unclear how interviewers or raters combine behaviors to arrive at global behavior-type judgments (A1, A2, X, B). Unfortunately, beyond the usual interrater reliability study and studies that simply correlate Type A components with global assessments, there has been little research that has directly focused on behavior-type assessment in the SI.

The purpose of this chapter is to critically examine the SI as an instrument for empirical research. As a preface to this analysis, I describe the interviewer training procedures used in the Western Collaborative Group Study (WCGS) and the Multiple Risk Factor Intervention Trial (MRFIT), as well as the current interviewing procedures. The WCGS was the first prospective epidemiological study to employ the interview, and the results indicated that Type A's were twice as likely as Type B's to incur CHD (Rosenman, Brand, Jenkins, Friedman, Straus, & Wurm, 1975). The MRFIT behavior pattern study was the second prospective attempt to link SI-defined Type A behavior with CHD incidence, but the MRFIT study did not find Type A behavior to be associated with CHD incidence (Shekelle et al., 1985). Whereas the WCGS did much to establish Type A behavior as a risk factor, the MRFIT did much to question its predictiveness, at least with U.S. males who were considered at risk based on high serum cholesterol, blood pressure levels, and cigarette smoking. Since these two epidemiological studies began, both Drs. Friedman and Rosenman have worked to refine their interviewing techniques, and their current procedures are also discussed in this chapter.

Following the description of interviewer training techniques, I review the methodological approaches and results of studies that have scored Type A components from the SI. The speech component research was spawned by the goal of improving SI assessment, primarily through identifying the pathogenic components of Type A behavior and through determining what interviewers/raters focus on to make the global behavior-type assessments. Given that a critical mass of research has been published now, it is an appropriate time to review the methods used to measure Type A components in the SI and summarize the findings of these studies.

Next, with the Type A component research as a tool, I examine potential biases in the SI with a special focus on our work with a large subset of the MRFIT SIs (Scherwitz et al., 1987). I address the major assessment issues including the consistency with which interviewers elicit Type A behavior, their reliability to focus on and weigh Type A components, and the interaction between the interviewer and subjects. Our findings indicate that in each area there are potential problems that need to be addressed if we are to confidently use global Type A assessments for research.

Because the root of assessment problems is conceptual, we must deepen our understanding of the coronary-risk process if we are to improve the predictive validity of the SI. A good place to begin is to reconsider the assumptions that guide Type A assessment. There is enough evidence to consider several of them untenable, including: Type A is a type, reliability assessments are accurate indicators of agreement, and the SI is a standard. I discuss each assumption in this section. Finally, I end the chapter with a set of methodological and theoretical recommendations for improving Type A assessment.

Before proceeding, it is important to acknowledge the scientific contribution of the concept of Type A behavior to behavioral medicine and the efforts of the pioneering researchers who worked against stiff resistance to develop the necessary empirical support for Type A as a risk factor. This critique and suggestions for refinement are a testament to the remarkable utility the concept has had as it is now defined. And the recommendations for improving SI assessment underscore the belief that there is a coronary-prone risk process that is best reflected in an interpersonal context.

DESCRIPTION OF THE STRUCTURED INTERVIEW

Overview

Since the collaboration between Friedman and Rosenman ended, the interview has evolved along two parallel lines: at the Harold Brunn Institute with Dr. Friedman and Ms. Fleishman and at SRI International with Drs. Rosenman, Chesney, and Hecker. Although there are more similarities than differences, it seems useful to consider the early and the recent SIs and to compare the current Friedman procedure with the current Rosenman procedure.

Friedman and Rosenman began Type A assessment by developing a set of questions based on their observations of patients' behaviors and their clinical experience in treating CHD. As Dr. Rosenman (Rosenman, Swan, & Carmelli, 1988) indicated:

> The SI evolved over a period of several years, during which the selected questions were distilled from a larger pool after being empirically found to be the most capable of eliciting the Type A behaviors in predisposed subjects. Specific questions were originally directed at assessment of the various component behaviors that comprise the global TABP (Type A behavior pattern), and multiple questions were developed in regard to each such behavior to reinforce the validity of the judgments. (p.4)

Based on questions asked in these earlier studies, the SI evolved as a systematic attempt to evaluate behavioral reactions to the question themes of ambitiousness, competitiveness, aggression and hostility, and sense of time urgency. The current interviews used by both Rosenman and Friedman still deal with these question themes.

Regarding the interviewers, in all cases they are asked to observe the subjects' behaviors. In observing these behaviors they are to maintain control of the question asking and to keep a certain pace of the interview; they are not to talk about themselves much or dawdle.

The WCGS Structured Interview

Whereas Friedman and Rosenman developed the SI with their early studies, it was the WCGS, the first large-scale study to employ their SI, that established it as a standard for interviewer training (Rosenman, et al., 1966.) The WCGS SI provided the basis for the question content and form and the interviewer techniques that researchers use today.

Dr. Friedman devised the original questions and trained the first of four interviewers in the WCGS (M. Friedman, personal communication, February 21, 1986). Dr. Rosenman added questions to the interview to further elicit hostility, and he monitored the SIs throughout the 18-month screening period. The questions asked about the subjects' background, their ambitiousness, competitiveness, impatience, and hostility, usually by referring to typical events in an ordinary day.

Drs. Friedman and Rosenman selected interiewers based on their being somewhat Type A, their intelligence, their presentableness, and their perceptiveness in recognizing Type A characteristics (M. Friedman, personal communication, February 21, 1986). All four WCGS interviewers were female, varying in age from 20 to 50. Both Drs. Friedman and Rosenman emphasized in the beginning, and continue to emphasize, the necessity of carefully selecting interviewers (Bortner & Rosenman, 1967; Friedman et al., 1985).

The WCGS interviewers were trained differently from interviewers today. Over a period of many weeks, they were trained with live subjects, many of whom had CHD. Both Drs. Friedman and Rosenman developed the interviewers' skills face to face as they sat in on the interviewers' SIs or listened to the tape recordings, pointing out the defining characteristics as well as giving feedback on their interviewing technique. In discussing the first WCGS interviewer training, Dr. Friedman said: "She would come in to my office on Saturdays after 5:00 and we would have volunteer 'A's and 'B's and coronaries come in and I would talk to them. I would point out to her what to look for when they came in. And after they left we'd have a discussion. And I think we saw 20 or 30" (M. Friedman, personal communication, February 21, 1986).

The subjects' Type A characteristics would be singled out and often mimicked. Interviewers were taught to look for "explosive or semiviolent accentuations in the rhythm of their speech" and a certain aggressive timbre, to look for physical signs, such as the vigorousness of the handshake, to look for an "enhanced eagerness to win at any competitive game or to perform any test in as superb a fashion as possible if the outcome was to be recognized by others," and to look for the "presence of a latent or usually covert, but often free-floating, hostility" (M. Friedman, personal communication, February 21, 1986).

Ms. Nancy Fleischmann was one of four WCGS interviewers and still conducts the SI at the Harold Brunn Institute. She received her training from Dr. Friedman and can still recall the first demonstration of free-floating hostility that she observed with Dr. Friedman in one of his patients:

> I can shut my eyes and still see that man's face, and I can remember his name, and I can remember some of the things he said. It was like being trapped in a telephone booth with a tiger. Oh, he was married to the most horrible woman. You know what she actually did? She would sometimes put his socks back in the drawer without seeing that they were all turned right side out, and would occasionally leave a cup on the drainboard at night. (N. Fleischmann, personal communication, March 10, 1986).

Ms. Fleischmann remembers Dr. Rosenman stressing the importance of hostility as a defining characteristic: "I do remember Dr. Rosenman cautioning me to pick up on the free-floating hostility when it was at a lower level than this tiger. I know you certainly didn't call anybody with free-floating hostility a B" (N. Fleischmann, personal communication, March 10, 1986).

After observing several interviews, the later WCGS inteviewers conducted interviews of their own after which Dr. Friedman commented on their technique. As Dr. Friedman recalls, "they were told to make a diagnosis, and don't worry about just answering your questions . . . don't worry that you're veering off" (M. Friedman, personal communication, February 21, 1986). When Dr. Friedman was asked about his original ideas of how interviewers should ask questions, he replied, "Ask them like detectives: gentle, not necessarily hostile, not to turn a patient off. Act as a human being, like a physician would act, interested in the individual at all times, as a person" (M. Friedman, personal communication, February 21, 1986).

Interviewers rated subjects' nonverbal characteristics immediately after the interviews and also made global ratings using four categories: A1, A2, B3, B4. After reviewing the nonverbal ratings and the interviewers' assessments, Dr. Rosenman made the final global assessments.

The MRFIT Structured Interview

In a major change from the WCGS and MRFIT interviewer training, the emphasis on provoking Type A behaviors was increased. Dr. Rosenman's belief is that "it is the ability of the SI to be presented in a way that the subject perceives as a challenge that is essential for the proper measurement of TABP" (Rosenman, Swan, & Carmelli, 1988, p. 14). Rosenman and his co-workers have emphasized varying the question-asking technique to challenge the subjects in order to elicit and pursue indications of Type A behavior. While varying the technique within an interview, the interviewers were also trained to be consistent across interviews. Rosenman interviewers are carefully trained to control: "(1) vocal style—intonation, inflection, speed, volume, and response latency; (2) interview length; (3) question and probe content; and (4) general demeanor" (Chesney et al., 1980; p. 266).

Dr. Rosenman's MRFIT questions contain "capitalized words which are to be emphasized with a crisp, abrupt, staccato style in a manner similar to the Type A's plosive words" (p. 263). The interviewers were trained to create "a sense of time urgency and hurry the subject" (p. 267), by speaking rapidly and interrupting, particularly in a five-question sequence toward the end of the interview. On the other hand, some questions were deliberately drawn out and faltering to provoke the subjects into interrupting the interviewer. The interviewers were trained to be "professional," and this style has been described as *aggressive, businesslike,* and *confrontive.* They were trained to interrupt as one technique to frustrate the subject, while watching for his response. "Interruptions were used purposely as part of the challenging nature of the interview and also to control its length" (p. 266).

The MRFIT interviewers were trained to get through the interviews fairly quickly. They moved on to the next question promptly, even on many occasions when they had gotten very short answers. Of the 540 interviews we have timed, the average is 8.7 minutes (S.D. = 2.8) with a median of 8.0. Often the MRFIT interviewers seemed satisfied with short answers, e.g., "yes" or "no," despite the fact that the Rosenman SI approach has depended primarily on verbal characteristics to make the behavior type assessments (Rosenman, 1978).

Current Friedman Videotaped Clinical Interview

After the WCGS, Dr. Friedman and his group began to focus on patients with a history of myocardial infarctions (MIs) as part of their major research project, the Recurrent Coronary Prevention Project (RCPP) (Friedman & Powell, 1984; Friedman, Thoresen, & Gill, 1981; Friedman et al., 1982). They added some deeply reflective questions to the WCGS interview question script: "Would your 20-year-old self have been proud or disappointed in what you have accomplished at this time?"; "Do you feel that most of the important parts of your life are now behind you?"; "Do you frequently just daydream?"; and "All of us have insecurities about certain things. What are your insecurities about?" (Friedman & Powell, 1984, p. 125). Two other questions added since the WCGS ask individuals how they would respond to acutely distressing situations, such as cigar smoke in a restaurant and a high-speed car ride to a hospital emergency. The questions on the Videotape Clinical Interview (VCI) script have four aims: One set of questions is aimed primarily at learning about the habits and beliefs of the respondent that are indicative of time urgency; a second set is asked to allow the interviewer time to scan the face, eyes, limb and body movements; a third set seeks to discover some of the habits of the respondent that suggest free-floating hostility; and a fourth set of questions are aimed at eliciting psychomotor signs of hostility (Friedman & Powell, 1984).

The current Friedman assessments rely more heavily on nonverbal behaviors than the WCGS did. For instance, the questions designed to assess time urgency and hostility provide both the stimulus and the opportunity for observations of the subject's face, body movement, and posture. According to Friedman: "10 new indicators of the presence of Type A behavior have been discovered since the WCGS structured interview was first formulated" (Friedman & Powell, 1984, p. 123). Friedman does not believe one can make valid assessments from audiotapes alone. He regards Type A behavior as a medical disorder, and the interviewer is to elicit symptoms and observe the signs of the subjects' struggle with time and with too many things to do. In addition to speech characteristics (SCs) such as the "disturbed vocal tones, the abnormal speech rhythms," the interviewer is to look for "respiratory dysfunctions, grimaces, tics, and body movements, facial perspiration and periorbital pigmentation" (M. Friedman, personal communication, February 21, 1986).

Friedman indicates that:

> A good interviewer should be intelligent and especially able to separate the style from the content of a response. For example, an interviewer should be observant of the facial and body movements of the persons with whom she/he communicates and quick to detect and interpret correctly sudden smiles and possible changes in the rhythm and timbre of the vocal response. The good interviewer also should possess the capacity to take interest in the activities and beliefs of every subject encountered. (Friedman & Powell, 1984, p. 124)

According to Nancy Fleischmann, "An interviewer should be friendly without being indulgent, convey competence and purposefulness without being controlling or hostile. Above all, an interviewer must be interested in the person being interviewed" (N. Fleischmann, personal communication, March 10, 1986). The VCI interviewers are not trained to interrupt or emphasize key words, and they are encouraged to probe within situations for certain signs of Type A behavior. This style may increase external validity of assessments if it allows individuals to reflect accurately about how they actually feel and behave in their environment.

In addition to expanding the focus to include visually obtained information, the Friedman group, particularly Dr. Powell, worked to increase the specificity of Type A assessment. Powell conducted a detailed analysis of over 49 Type A components from RCPP subjects who either incurred recurrent coronary heart disease (RCHD) or did not (Powell & Thoresen, 1985). Her findings led to a reworking of the interview score sheet so that now the interviewer evaluates the subject for the presence of 35 characteristics, each of which is rated on a 3-point scale. These 35 components rate the subjects' answer contents, motor behaviors, speech behaviors, hostile/competitive attitudes, and physiological indicators. Thus, the maximum score attainable is 105 (i.e., 35 items × 3).

Friedman and Powell (1984) found that the average score in 14 pure Type B men given the VCI was 5.5 (S.D. = 3.93). They consider that Type A behavior is present if a subject's score is more than 2 standard deviations above this mean of 5.5 (i.e., 13.41 or above). Unfortunately, with this very low cutoff score the large majority of subjects interviewed are classified as Type A, thus vastly reducing its specificity in identifying high-risk subjects. In a sample of 1,012 postinfarction subjects the average score was 28.0. There are 23 components grouped under time urgency and 12 grouped under hostility. And the total Type A score is the sum for all the characteristics, a continuous score that can be treated statistically as an interval scale. With its greater specificity and categorization, the current Friedman SI is a potentially useful tool in identifying the most pathogenic components of Type A behavior. However, the VCI has not been validated by other investigators as a predictor of CHD, and with the exception of one study by Powell, its interrater agreement and test–retest reliability remain to be demonstrated.

Current Rosenman Structured Interview

The current interviewer training by Drs. Rosenman, Chesney, and Hecker is designed to produce results very similar to the WCGS SIs in terms of the manner of eliciting answers to questions, question content, and order of topics. The CARDIA study, a prospective study of CHD risk fractors among 5,000 young adults, provides a good place to study the current SI technique taught by Drs. Chesney and Hecker. The SI has been modified to accommodate unemployed young adults. For unemployed subjects who are not in school, the script is designed to ask parallel questions about their major activity. And to get these young adults to talk about themselves, several questions, particularly probe or follow-up questions, were revised to encourage more speech. For example, after asking, "What IRRITATES you MOST about your work, or the PEOPLE you work with?," the interviewer would follow with, "WHY does this irritate you?" and "How do you HANDLE this irritation?"

CARDIA interviewers were prescreened before being sent to SRI, and in the screening interviews they practiced asking the SI questions. Out of the 37 candidates initially selected by the four CARDIA centers, 14 were chosen on the basis of their being somewhat Type A, alert, smart, not hostile, observant, able to think on their feet, and able to maintain eye contact. Of the 14 candidates, 11 were trained and approved by SRI after a 3-day workshop. Interviewers were trained first by reviewing audiotapes and videotapes that illustrated important features of a properly administered SI. They were taught to observe the following: behavioral dispositions including ambitiousness, aggressiveness, competitiveness, and impatience; specific behaviors including tense muscles, alert, rapid, emphatic speech, and rapid pace of most activities; emotional responses including irritation, potential for hostility, and anger held in or expressed; and the presence of excessive anxiety, depression, worry, fear, or other neurotic symptoms.

An important focus of the current training was on developing the interviewers' skill at gaining rapport with subjects by being a good listener, following the subjects' answers with open-ended probes, making eye contact, using the subjects' first name, and challenging the subjects by referring to their own answer content or expressions of feeling. Interviewers were carefully coached on the purpose and technique in asking each question. The interviewers were trained to make postinterview ratings on subject Type A characteristics, whereas behavior-type assessments were made by trained auditors at the Oakland CARDIA clinic. All CARDIA interviewers were carefully monitored throughout the screening period, and they were given feedback using a 20-point rating scheme developed by Dr. Hecker and a quantitative analysis of interviewers' SCs provided by Dr. Scherwitz.

SI Comparisons

Given that there has been a 30-year time span, cultural changes, and much experience since the original SI was developed, it would not be surprising if the
current SI procedures are different from the original. Indeed, one would hope
they have improved. In addition, it is not surprising that the current Friedman
interview is different from the current Rosenman interview. The current Friedman VCI focuses on at least 10 new components since the time of the WCGS,
and all assessments are made either live or using videotaped SIs. Although not
specifically advised by Dr. Rosenman, those who have been trained by Rosenman often rely primarily on verbal tape recordings for behavior-type assessment.
As a result, the Friedman VCI and the Rosenman SI could easily classify individuals differently if, as we suspect, the nonverbal and verbal indicators occur independently (Hughes, Jacobs, Schucker, Chapman, Murray, & Johnson, 1983).
Whether this affects the validity of assessments, and if so how much, is harder
to determine.

There are other potentially important differences between the MRFIT and
WCGS SIs (Scherwitz, Graham, Grandits, & Billings, 1985). The question content was mainly the same, but the manner of conducting the interview differed.
The WCGS SIs were generally slower and more relaxed than the MRFIT SIs.
WCGS interviewers elicited more speech from their subjects, they took an average of 5 minutes longer to administer the SI, and they interrupted only a third
as often as the MRFIT interviewers. We cannot be certain how this affected the
predictive validity, but if getting the subjects to recreate or to report their feelings as they experienced them in the past is central to the assessment process,
then the WCGS style may have had higher external validity.

In contrast to the WCGS, the MRFIT interviews seem to be more direct in
provoking responsiveness in a standard way. This could, if it worked, increase
interrater reliability. The interviewers were trained to be very similar in speech
stylistics and question form. The MRFIT SIs were much easier for our auditors
to score for SCs because of their uniformity. They are thus more scientific than
WCGS SIs in that they presented a standard stimulus. As a result, one would
expect to be able to compare behavior-type ratings across clinics.

Dr. Rosenman has maintained that his SI has remained essentially unchanged,
and he may be right, depending on how one defines change, and what aspects
one considers. The purpose, topic, question form, as well as some stylistics, have
not changed. Other characteristics, such as question order, speed of asking questions, frequency of interruptions, and total questions asked, did appear to change,
at least when comparing the WCGS with the MRFIT. But how great does a change
have to be to be regarded as important? According to Singer (1974), subtle interpersonal processes in interviews could substantially affect psychophysiological
reactivity, so it is conceivable that processes such as "engagement-involvement"
could affect the predictive validity of Type A assessments. Given the possible
importance of engaging subjects during the SI, the current Rosenman training

stresses the interviewers' skill in developing rapport, and it has refined the procedures for evaluating interviewer performance.

STUDYING TYPE A ASSESSMENT WITH BEHAVIORAL COMPONENTS

One way to study the assessment process in the SI empirically is with Type A
components. Many Type A components can be cearly defined and scored with
high reliability. And analytically, components can be used in several ways. Interviewee components can be correlated with global Type A assessments, as has
been done in the past, to see how interviewers or auditors have combined them
to make their behavior-type judgments. We can also assess whether individual
components are correlated with CHD incidence and morbidity (Hecker, Frautschi, Chesney, Black, & Rosenman, 1985; Scherwitz, Graham, Grandits, & Billings, 1988).

There are other useful ways to use Type A components that are no less interesting but are not studied as often. To search for an empirical type, one can
intercorrelate components within Type A, as has been attempted with factor analysis (Matthews, Glass, Rosenman, & Bortner, 1977; Matthews et al., 1982). The
hope here is that we could search for an expressed Type A cluster of factors and
therefore empirically define the ''type'' in Type A or Type B behavior.

The least researched use of components is to study the interpersonal process
between interviewer and subject, as we have begun to do (Scherwitz et al., 1977;
Scherwitz et al., 1987). A concern for Type A assessment is that interviewers'
behaviors differ according to respondents' behaviors. In a series of two-person
job and psychotherapy interview studies, Matarazzo and Wiens (1972) found good
evidence for what they call *synchrony*. Their findings indicated that subjects tend
to mimic an interviewer's speed of speech, length of utterances, and response
latency (time elapsed between the end of one person's speech and the beginning
of the other's next speech segment). This is relevant for Type A assessment because interviewers appear to use subjects' speed of speech and response latency
to make behavior-type judgments. Synchrony can affect the validity of behavior-
type assessments in at least two ways: first, it can bias assessments if the more
socially responsive individuals, who may be less coronary prone, respond more
synchronously than do less socially responsive, passive-aggressive, and hostile
individuals; second, it may undermine the predictive validity of assessments if
the interviewers rush through an interview so quickly that it shortcircuits the subjects' memory review connecting to feelings and also affects their reporting process
(Scherwitz, Graham et al., 1985). Conversely, synchrony can help discriminate
the more from the less coronary risk prone if the more coronary-prone individuals are more socially reactive. In a later section, I discuss synchrony in the SI
after presenting our own and Howland and Siegman's (1982) study findings.

Methods for Speech Analysis

Researchers have used three methods to actually score SCs in the SI. They involve (1) holistic, clinical judgments, either by the interviewer or by a rater, (2) electronic devices, and (3) trained auditors who time and count behaviors. Because there are differences in scope and accuracy, each method is reviewed separately.

Clinical Method

The clinical method of deriving ratings from the SI after listening to the entire interview was originally devised by Dr. Ray Rosenman, who maintained that interviewers should close their eyes after the interview and visualize the respondent. The first researcher to conduct a component analysis of the SI was Dr. Ray Bortner, who audited a subsample of 186 men from the WCGS for answer content to each of 37 SI questions, subjects' interruptions and sighs, as well as four clinical ratings: explosive voice modulation, vigorous answers, control and defenses, and potential for hostility. Unfortunately, Dr. Bortner died before he could finish this analysis; Matthews et al. (1977), however, using Bortner's data, found that potential for hostility, vigorous answers, explosive voice modulation, and admitted irritation at waiting in lines was significantly greater for the CHD cases than for CHD-free controls.

Dembroski and his co-workers revised the postexperimental ratings by interviewers originally developed by Friedman and Rosenman, and his clinical rating procedure has been most often employed for research on SI components (Dembroski, MacDougall, Herd, & Shields, 1979; Dembroski, MacDougall, Shields, Petitto, & Lushene, 1978). Using a 5-point scale, the Dembroski procedure scores four verbal stylistic dimensions (loudness of speech, explosiveness of speech, rapid-accelerated speech, and response latency), three attitudinal–behavioral dimensions (potential for hostility, anger-in, and verbal competitiveness), and five content dimensions (time pressure, hard-driving behavior, speed of activity, competitiveness, and anger–impatience). In a study of 84 male college students, Dembroski et al. (1979) showed that the preceding clinical ratings can be scored with satisfactory reliability, and each of the ratings is correlated with global, SI-defined Type A behavior.

But can we rely entirely on a clinical assessment of Type A components without further research to verify its accuracy? There may be problems with doing so. Leventhal, Berton, and Scherwitz addressed this question in 1974 when they compared the "clinical" method of scoring SCs with a "technical" method. In the clinical method well-trained auditors listened to the whole SI and then made judgments of combined characteristics, e.g., answer latency (subject's response latency), and voice emphasis ("voice volume" or "word emphasis"). In the technical method the same auditors scored only one SC separately for answers to individual questions. In addition, to control for the "halo effect" different auditors scored different SCs within each SI using procedures to ensure high reliability, e.g., stop watches and feedback for discrepancies. Using both methods, we scored 144 SIs of middle-aged, employed males from a sample provided by Dr. Rosenman. Both approaches had acceptable levels of interrater reliability, so we were very surprised to see the different results for the two methods. Intercorrelations among SCs were moderate to high for the clinical method, as other studies had found (Dembroski et al., 1979; Dembroski et al., 1978). But the intercorrelations of Type A components for the technical method were very low, as others who have used the technical auditor method have found (Hecker, Chesney, Black, & Rosenman, 1981; Hughes et al., 1983; Schucker & Jacobs, 1977).

Because both techniques were conducted on the same SIs, we suspected that the auditors' conceptual framework, interpreted as a clinical impression or "halo effect" had already biased the Type A component assessments. We know from other areas of psychology that "halo biases" exist, and they seem directly applicable to clinical assessment of Type A components. As Bem and Allen (1974) have indicated: "We hold 'implicit personality theories,' preconceived notions of what traits and behaviors go with what other traits and behaviors . . . This leads us not only to generalize beyond our observations and fill in the missing data with 'consistent' data of our own manufacture . . . but also to 'see' positive correlations which are, in fact, not there" (p. 508).

Unfortunately, with the components assessed clinically from the global SI, it is not possible to separate the interviewer's concept from the subjects' actual behaviors. So we probably cannot justifiably ignore the interviewers' descriptive framework any more than we can ignore the subjects' Type A behaviors. Thus, the clinical method has provided measures that have been predictive of CHD incidence, but exporting this method from those gifted clinicians to others and maintaining its quality control is yet to be demonstrated.

Electronic Method

The electronic method to assess Type A components was originally used by Friedman, Brown, and Rosenman (1969) to assess voice volume and speaking rate. They devised an instrument to measure the "loudness with which [the subject] modulated his speech and also the duration of this same loudness" (p. 829). The device consisted of a microphone, a preamplifier, a "rectifying detector," and a recording unit. They measured loudness and duration for 19 Type A's and 16 Type B's without clinical evidence of CHD, as well as 12 patients with angina and abnormal ECGs and 26 patients with healed MIs. When reading a passage in which "a military commanding officer exhorts his troops prior to their engagement in a battle" (p. 829), Type A's spoke louder and finished reading the passage quicker than Type B's. This was the first empirical support for voice emphasis as the key Type A SC.

Howland and Siegman (1982) developed a far more sophisticated electronic or computer speech analysis based on extensive prior work by Feldstein (1978). Although it requires considerable resources and expertise, it has the advantage of objectivity and is good for scoring total speech and temporal characteristics. Using this method Howland and Siegman scored speech productivity, average turn duration, average duration of vocalizations, reaction time, average pause duration, interruptions, volume, and volume variability for both the subjects and the interviewers. The sample was a subset of the original 100 Rosenman SI training tapes, including 66 employed middle-aged males in the San Francisco Bay Area. The answer latency, followed by voice volume, was found to be correlated most highly with the Rosenman behavior-type judgments ($r^2 = .47$); together all variables predicted 94% of the Type A's and 54% of the Type B's correctly.

Howland and Siegman's studies show that we can computer analyze certain SCs, particularly speed and quantity, with good reliability and that these measures are highly correlated with the behavior-type judgments of interviewers trained by Dr. Rosenman.

Auditor Method

The third method of scoring SCs is with trained auditors who count frequencies, time speed factors, and make scaled ratings (Hecker et al., 1985; Hughes et al., 1983; Scherwitz et al., 1977; Schucker & Jacobs, 1977). In one of the first studies (Schucker & Jacobs, 1977), auditors counted plosive and clipped words, uneven speed, repeated words and interruptions, and talkovers; they timed answer latency and made ratings for overall volume and speed of speech for the entire interview. In 98 interviews of the original 100 Rosenman SI training assessment tapes of middle-aged men, they found voice volume to correlate most strongly with behavior-type judgments ($r = .57$) followed by speed of speech, together correlating $r = .69$ with behavior-type judgments. Adding the other variables raised the multiple r to .71. Using the best cutoff value and the combined SCs, Schucker and Jacobs were able to correctly classify 95% of the Type A's and 76% of the Type B's.

In another of the first studies using trained auditors, Scherwitz et al. (1977) scored voice emphasis, speed of speech, answer latency, and answer content for 59 SIs of college males, with the author making the behavior-type judgments. Voice emphasis was most highly correlated with behavior-type judgments (36% of variance) followed by speed of speech (8%), answer latency (5%), and answer content (4%; total multiple $r = .72$).

Including nonverbal behavior in the analysis of Type A components, Hughes et al. (1983) scored (with trained auditors) 51 health professional students for promptness in arriving for the interview, and, while subjects waited for the interview, they also scored exploratory behavior, playing with objects, and postural tension. During the SI they scored head gestures, head nods, head shakes, and tense posture along with the SC analyses (voice volume, answer latency and speed of speech), which they had used in a previous study (Schucker & Jacobs, 1977). Dr. Beth Schucker provided the Type A judgments. Although individuals judged Type A while waiting for the interview did not arrive earlier or sit with a more tense posture, they were observed to spend more time moving about and exploring than Type B's. During the SI, Type A's gestured more significantly but tended to have fewer head nods and shakes than Type B's.

In a more recent study, Blumenthal, O'Toole, and Haney (1984) used a combination of whole-interview ratings, nonverbal behaviors, and SCs in scoring SIs of 60 middle-aged men who were reinterviewed 4 months later. They scored voice volume, interruptions, speed of speech, answer latency, plosive words, uneven speed, delay question latency (the delivery of some questions was purposefully delayed), and delay question interruptions. In addition, they scored potential for hostility using a procedure similar to Dembroski, as well as frequency of sighs and motoric activity from the videotaped SIs. Behavior-type ratings were provided by consensus between the interviewer, Dr. Blumenthal, and one of Dr. Blumenthal's trainees. In the first SI, potential for hostility, voice volume, speed of speech, uneven speed, and interruptions were significantly related to behavior-type judgments, with the first four factors accounting for 67% of the variance. Four months later, potential for hostility, speech volume, interruptions, delay question interruptions, and delay question latency were significantly related to judgments, with the first four factors accounting for 54% of the variance in assessments.

In the most comprehensive analysis of SCs, Hecker et al. (1981) developed and tested a method to measure "likely dimensions of Type A behavior." These were 20 dimensions including speech stylistics (hurrying, immediateness, strident inhalation, clicks, explosive starts, economy of words, sighs, forced laughter), SCs (loudness of voice, syllabic emphasis, speaking rate, acceleration, staccato delivery, hard voice), attitudes (competitiveness, hostility, self-aggrandizement, exactingness, despondency), and answer content. Each of these 20 characteristics have been scored for 20 epochs (about 30 seconds apiece) for 750 WCGS SIs, in an analysis correlating these 20 characteristics with CHD incidence. Results from this study have not yet been published. Whereas this method is tedious and requires specification of parameters and methods, as well as training and monitoring of auditors, it provides a very high level of specificity and detail.

Type A Components and Global Assessments Across Studies

In each of the preceding three methods, SCs have been correlated with the interviewer or auditor assessments to identify what behaviors distinguish Type A's from Type B's. The results for SCs alone indicated that voice emphasis, answer latency, and speed of speech have been most highly associated with interviewer/auditor judgments, with voice emphasis being the major SC in seven of eight studies (Anderson & Waldron, 1983; Blumenthal et al., 1984; Hecker et al., 1981; Howland & Siegman, 1982; Matthews et al., 1982; Scherwitz et al., 1977; Scherwitz et al., 1987; Schucker & Jacobs, 1977). Speed of speech was the second most correlated with global behavior-type assessments in four studies (Blumenthal et al., 1984; Hecker et al., 1981; Scherwitz et al., 1977; Schucker & Jacobs, 1977), the most strongly correlated in one study (Anderson & Waldron, 1983), and the third most correlated in another study (Matthews et al., 1982). Answer latency was the second most correlated in two studies (Howland & Siegman, 1982; Matthews et al., 1982) and the third most correlated in three others (Anderson & Waldron, 1983; Scherwitz et al., 1977; Scherwitz et al., 1987). The findings from these studies indicate the interviewers' or raters' focus on SCs as a primary source of information to make behavior-type judgments. This is not surprising given that most assessments were done from audio recordings.

Problems with Type A Assessment in the SI

The purpose of this section is to examine Type A assessment for potential methodological problems. The first issue to consider is whether one can depend on inter-rater reliability estimates to ensure accurate behavior-type assessments. The most often employed measure of interrater reliability is simply percentage of agreement, which usually varies from 65 to 85% using a gross A/B dichotomy. Percentages of agreement for subtypes separately are much lower, and often no longer acceptable. Agreement for Type B is not as good as for Type A, and agreement on Type "X" (those who cannot be classified as either an A or a B) is very poor. Whereas percentages of agreement in the 70–85 range are interpreted as acceptable or even good, they are misleading. First, these ranges are cited for the global A versus B categorization; agreement for the four-category assignments (A1, A2, X, B) is invariably much lower. Second, the percentage of agreement method for calculating reliability can largely be a function of chance. For example, if the prevalence of Type A is 75%, one could achieve a 75% agreement simply declaring that all subjects were Type A. When researchers use Cohen's Kappa to correct for chance, the reliability looks a lot lower. For example, the MRFIT percentage of agreement for the two-category A versus B assessment was 85.5%, varying from 83.3 to 92.1%. This is considered acceptable reliability and is representative of other studies. But the Cohen's Kappa for the two-category assignment was .59, varying from .16 to .77 for the six interviewer–auditor pairs, and the Cohen's Kappa for the four-category assignment was .42, varying from .16 to .60 (The MRFIT Group, 1979). Because most research uses the four-category global judgments in their statistical analyses, they should present the reliability for the four-category assignments taking chance into account. If this had been done, it is doubtful that most studies would have found their Type A assessments to reach acceptable levels of reliability.

How does one determine what is an acceptable interrater reliability of behavior-type assessments? We know that it is easier to distinguish subjects who are intermediate versus extreme in their Type A/B behaviors, yet the more extreme Type A's do not appear more prone to CHD (Rosenman et al., 1966), so being off by 25% still remains a problem as we could easily miss those who are most risk prone. We also know that for individuals under 65 only a small proportion incur CHD even within a decade. Yet 50% or more of the individuals are Type A, so the low specificity of Type A measures does not give us any comfort. In a prospective study, one could theoretically miscategorize the entire CHD sample within the 25% disagreement. Because of the lack of a dose-response relationship of Type A to CHD and because of its low specificity, one must maintain high standards for acceptable interrater reliability.

Now let us consider the procedure for assessing interrater reliability of behavior-type judgments and question whether this procedure accurately reflects reliability of Type A assessment across the field. There are at least three reasons for suspecting that the published interrater reliabilities overestimate the actual agreement that exists among SI-defined Type A measures. First, most studies of interrater reliability employ two or more raters; one of these raters usually trained the other rater(s). In training, the trainer and the rater(s) informally compare Type A ratings and discuss their observations and criteria for making Type A or Type B judgments. Then, raters usually do independent ratings and compare their judgments with some criterion (often the trainer's criterion). If the trainee more or less learns to apply the trainer's way of making judgments ("descriptive theory"), then they will agree to an acceptable level. In cases where behavior-type assessments do not have some other criterion, i.e., judgments provided by Dr. Friedman or Dr. Rosenman and co-workers, the trainer and rater may drift, and they may drift together, thus maintaining their reliability. It is quite possible, even likely with new populations, that trainer-rater pairs drift from the established training. This drift by trainer may come from being swayed by the trainee in the training or feedback process, by making adjustments according to the different populations and settings, or by the trainer's personality and skill.

A second reason that published reliability may be higher than agreement in the field is that many interviewers trained by Dr. Rosenman base their SI reliability assessments primarily only on audiotaped verbal characteristics. Two or more raters typically listen to the same batch of audiotaped SIs. This narrowed focus vastly restricts the range of features that are focused on and weighed by most interviewers who make their assessments during the SI. It was not the intent of the original Rosenman training to rely solely on audio characteristics. Dr. Rosenman has stressed from the beginning that interviewers should observe the subject's behaviors. Nevertheless, the cost and intrusiveness of video recording has unfortunately narrowed the scope of behaviors considered. The assessment issue this brings up is whether raters who focused primarily on nonverbal characteristics would agree with raters who focused on verbal characteristics. They would probably not agree very well, because according to one study nonverbal and verbal characteristics are, with few exceptions, not correlated (Hughes et al., 1983).

A third and perhaps the most important reason that published reliability may be higher than agreement in the field is that published studies employed raters who audited and assessed behavior type based on just one interviewer. If interviewers differ in the way they conduct the interview and there is a synchrony between interviewers' and subjects' Type A characteristics, the expression of subjects' Type A behaviors would differ for different interviewers. We have evidence in studying large numbers of SIs from both the MRFIT and WCGS that interviewers' behaviors do differ in the way they elicit subjects' Type A behaviors, and in the MRFIT we have good evidence of synchrony: at least five of the seven interviewers differed on at least one speech characteristic when interviewing Type A's versus Type B's (Scherwitz et al., 1987). Although this could contribute substantially to the variance in interrater reliability, no published studies have assessed reliability using different interviewers for the same subjects.

Unfortunately, little is known about the reliability across populations, about the effects of different SI training techniques, or about the drift of interviewer technique or criteria for judgment. Currently, Type A research has been conducted implicitly assuming that SI assessment is consistent with the standard and that the standard has not varied. This may be a naive assumption. The variability in the SI techniques could easily account for the inconsistent findings linking Type A behavior to CHD incidence or coronary artery disease severity.

To study the SI Type A assessment more deeply, the author conducted a detailed study of 577 SIs from the MRFIT, which was a prospective study of risk-factor change and CHD incidence (The MRFIT Group, 1982). A major aim of our research with the MRFIT SIs was to identify Type A components that were prospectively related to CHD incidence. Accordingly, the sample consisted of SIs from the 193 individuals who incurred a first CHD event during the 7-year follow-up and a control group of 386 individuals who remained free of CHD (Scherwitz, Graham, Grandits, Buehler, & Billings, 1986). All subjects were males, aged 35–57, from Chicago, Minneapolis, Newark, San Francisco, and Davis, California.

All 577 SIs were scored for the interviewers' voice emphasis, speed of speaking (syllables per second) and asking latency (interviewer's response latency) and the subjects' voice emphasis, speed of speaking, answer latency, and answer content. We scored these speech characteristics on a question-by-question basis using a well-established, highly reliable procedure (Scherwitz, Graham, Grandits, & Billings, 1988). One question we addressed with this data set was whether Type A raters employed similar characteristics to make their behavior-type judgments. The results for all interviewers combined indicated that all four SCs were significantly and independently related to behavior-type judgments. Voice emphasis was by far the most highly correlated with interviewers' judgments, followed by speed of speaking, answer latency, and answer content. But similar analyses for individual interviewers and auditors showed considerable variability in the relative weighing of the four SCs; no two interviewers weighed all the SCs similarly. The interviewer whose auditor agreement was poorest (Cohen's Kappa r = .16) appeared to weigh speed of speaking as a primary discriminative characteristic, whereas the auditor appeared to use voice emphasis (and these two SCs were poorly correlated with each other).

If interviewers varied in weighing certain speech characteristics, what about experienced auditors? Did they differ in the characteristics they weighed across *populations*? One of the experienced interviewer–auditors differed in weighing voice emphasis and speed of speaking across the two populations she audited, and the second interviewer–auditor, although more consistent, differed in weighing the asking latency across the five populations she audited (Scherwitz et al., 1987). Thus, the inconsistency between interviewers and auditors is to some extent evident within experienced auditors. How much inconsistency matters in terms of predictive validity of SI assessments is not clear, but it does appear to affect interrater reliability.

The inconsistency in weighing certain Type A speech characteristics would be a minor problem if these characteristics were highly intercorrelated, but our analyses show very low intercorrelations, as have other studies that have employed a technical method for scoring the speech characteristics (Hughes et al., 1983; Schucker & Jacobs, 1977). Thus, until there is a clearly defined formula for weighing the discriminative Type A and Type B characteristics, we can expect continued problems with interrater reliability in making subjective global assessments.

Whereas MRFIT raters differed in the way they weighed certain characteristics to make behavior-type assessments, an even more disturbing possibility is that raters may differ in their Type A/B thresholds. The threshold between Type A and Type B is very difficult to define. There is no absolute line, and it is in this "gray" region that interrater agreement is poorest. But what evidence is there that raters may have thresholds that differ? In the MRFIT study Type A prevalence varied across clinics (with one exception, there was one interviewer per clinic) from 55 to 89% (Shekelle, Neaton, Jacobs, Hulley, & Blackburn, 1973). To assess whether we could account for such large differences in prevalence, we compared our audited speech characteristics and the MRFIT JAS scores for these different populations. The results showed no systematic difference in the intensity of voice emphasis, answer latency, speed of speaking, Type A answer content, or JAS scores that could explain these differences in Type A prevalence. If these differences reflect a true prevalence of Type A behavior, then we would expect corresponding differences in the components we audited, because the MRFIT raters appeared to use them in making their behavior-type judgments (Scherwitz et al., 1987).

So what could determine an interviewer's threshold? Thresholds may vary based on the raters' scope of characteristics studied, their perceptiveness, and the degree to which they rigidly adopt the idea that "the presence of any Type A characteristic indicates a Type A.'' We know from previous research that even established experts vary considerably in what attributes they consider Type A (Herman, Blumenthal, Black, & Chesney, 1981). Similarly, interviewers or auditors differ in the scope of speech and other characteristics they consider Type A. The idea of ''any Type A characteristic means a Type A'' combined with a large scope of characteristics considered Type A can easily lead to very high Type A prevalence in assessment. Thus, any speculation about population differences of SI-defined Type A must deal with the issue of differences in threshold.

Interviewers' Behaviors and Subjects' Behavior Types

If interviewers or interviewer–auditors differed in the way they weighed Type A components, did they also differ in the way they conducted the interview? It is clear from our analyses of the MRFIT SIs that interviewers were significantly different from each other in their voice emphasis, number of follow-up questions, length of the interview, and interruptions of subject's speech (Scherwitz, Graham et al., 1985). To be sure, some of these differences, e.g., voice emphasis and speech stylistics, are small in magnitude and achieve statistical significance due to the large sample size, but other differences, i.e., interview length and number of interruptions, were more dramatic. Thus, we know that interviewers' styles of asking questions have differed across studies. It therefore behooves us to assess whether these differences affect the predictive validity of Type A assessments.

An important related question is whether interviewers conduct the interview differently with Type A versus Type B subjects. In a study of one interviewer (Scherwitz et al., 1977), the interviewer did not speak more emphatically or quickly with Type A's versus Type B's. However, in a later study Howland and Siegman (1982) found evidence that the interviewer behavior does differ. To address this question we analyzed the MRFIT interviewers' voice emphasis, speed of speaking, and answer latency according to behavior subtype. The results indicated that interviewers spoke more quickly and asked questions more quickly, but not more emphatically, with Type A than with Type B subjects. Separate analyses for the seven interviewers indicated that two spoke significantly more quickly, three began questions significantly sooner, and two spoke less emphatically with the more Type A than Type B subjects. Five of seven interviewers had at least one SC that varied according to the subjects' behavior types.

These differences in interviewer behavior raise the distinct possibility that subjects' Type A behaviors affected the interviewers' delivery of the questions and vice versa. This is to be expected for asking latency and answer latency, where two individuals' speaking styles and other behaviors adjust to one another, as Matarazzo and Wiens (1972) have documented in their research.

It is difficult to determine whether interviewer synchrony affects the validity or reliability of Type A assessment. One would need to know more precisely the nature of the psychosocial risk process. If one views the coronary-prone aspect of Type A behavior as something that resides solely in the subject and must be elicited by an appropriate stimulus, then differences in interviewer behavior introduces error into the assessment. The practical problem with this conceptual view is not knowing exactly how an interviewer should elicit Type A behavior and whether this behavior should be standardized across all subjects. What is it that should be standardized? Is it a certain stimulus intensity or pace of asking questions or a certain level of engagement with the subject? Given our inadequate conceptual understanding of the coronary-risk process, answers to these questions are not at all clear. From another viewpoint, if one assumes that the risk in Type A behavior is best assessed as a psychosocial process—that is, a transaction between the interviewer and subject, then the interviewer must adapt to the subject in some way to elicit the coronary-prone process. In other words, the discovery of the coronary-prone process may lie in the transaction of interviewer and subject, and the interviewer's own behavior would be a valid source of information in the assessment process.

Whatever conceptual model we may want to apply to the coronary-prone process, we must consider the interviewer as an integral aspect of SI Type A assessment. This should have been clear from the early concept of Type A behavior as an interaction between the individual and the environment. In the SI, the interviewer more than any other factor represents the challenge in the environment. And indeed, our in-depth analyses of the MRFIT point to tremendous interviewer specificity of assessments both from the standpoint of eliciting Type A behaviors as well as combining them to form behavior-type judgments.

Summary of Type A Assessment Problems

Although more research is needed to make firm conclusions, the differences in interviewer behavior in asking questions, the differences in what components are considered in making behavior-type judgments, and the differences in A/B threshold all strongly suggest that the SI is a seriously flawed instrument for epidemiological research.

Whereas our analyses of potential biases in SI assessment were focused on the MRFIT SIs, the MRFIT behavior-type study is not an anomaly. In fact, based on listening to interviewers from other labs across the country, I think the interview style was typical of many other studies done in the 1970s. In addition to being typical the MRFIT SIs were conducted with an intention to attain accurate assessments. Their well-documented efforts in selecting, training, and monitoring interviewers are exemplary (The MRFIT Group, 1979).

Assumptions of SI Assessment

Unfortunately, in our intent to identify the psychosocial risk mechanisms of Type A behavior, we as behavioral medicine researchers have ignored the fundamental issues of assessment. We have preferred to make blithe, untested, and implicit assumptions about the validity and reliability of Type A assessments. In this section, I discuss some of the assumptions we have made in pursuing the approach to SI assessment over the last 30 years.

Ecological Validity

In terms of validity we have assumed that Type A behavior is ubiquitous and consistent across situations, an assumption that is not supported by the considerable research on a host of related personality and behavioral characteristics (Bem & Allen, 1974; Mischel, 1969). There has been very little if any field research to assess whether those behaviors we use to make Type A assessments in the SI generalize to behaviors in the work and home environment. Consequently, we have yet to establish the ecological validity of the components interviewers use to make Type A assessments, and we are unnecessarily limited in our search for biobehavioral mechanisms.

The SI as Standard

In terms of reliability, we have assumed that the SI is a standard and remains so over time and from one population to another. This is evident in our attempts to summarize the findings across studies. More subtly, it is evident in the studies that correlate SI global assessments with other behavioral characteristics. For example, Type A's may be described as answering quickly, or emphatically. It is assumed that these are qualities of Type A's rather than simply characteristics that interviewers use to make judgments. It may be more accurate to say that interviewers weigh these characteristics to make their assessments; that is, we may be describing the interviewers' operational definition of Type A behavior rather than some true type.

Type A as a Type

It is clear that the trait/type assumption dominates our thinking about Type A and its assessment, and it is worthy of critical consideration (Matthews, 1983). First, let us discuss the term *Type A behavior pattern*. Dr. Friedman indicates that the term was suggested by Dr. C. J. Van Slyke at NIH to replace the term *emotional stress* hopefully to improve the chance for funding a resubmitted grant (Friedman & Ulmer, 1984). The term *Type A*, which is capitalized in most publications, has a direct analogue in biology of blood type. A blood type connotes a well-defined entity that is situated within the individual and consistent across situations. The term *behavior pattern* implicitly assumes that the risk is a set of behaviors and that these behaviors are interrelated. Thus, the term Type A behavior (whether intentional or not) denotes that Type A is a type. The trait assumption allowed investigators to believe that they had a scientific concept, one whose dependability was unalloyed by the circumstances of measurement and the passage of time, and one that could be considered on a par with serum cholesterol or blood pressure.

A second indication that Type A is regarded as a trait is that the focus of Type A research has been on the subject at the expense of the situation. For example, the use of questionnaire and factor-analytic formulations only considered the subject as did the bulk of Type A component research reviewed earlier. This is in violation of the repeatedly mentioned key construct that Type A is an interaction between the individual and the situation (Friedman, 1969; Rosenman & Friedman, 1974).

A third indication of Type A being regarded as a trait is the implicit assumption that the interview is a "standard" stimulus, where the interviewer is separate from the measure that is derived solely from the subject. Our research indicates that the SI is a standard neither in terms of eliciting nor in terms of combining the observed behaviors to make an assessment.

If Type A is a type or a pattern at the level of behaviors occurring in the SI, then we would expect there to be a strong intercorrelation among or at least between certain independently derived components. The results from the 577 MRFIT SIs show that, no matter what procedure we used to correlate the Type A speech characteristics, there was little intercorrelation (Scherwitz et al., 1987), and this is consistent with other research that employed the technical audit method to score objective components (Scherwitz et al., 1977; Schucker & Jacobs, 1977).

The independence of the SCs indicates why it is difficult to teach Type A assessment: The interviewer or auditor must attend to and weigh multiple, independent behaviors. To do this consistently with the Rosenman SI and get a high interrater reliability, one must simultaneously scan a variety of cues and make decisions about combining them without a clear formula for weighing different combinations. Past research strongly suggests that judges perform more poorly than simple calculators in integrating cues for prediction (Meehl, 1954).

Conceptually, the component, operational definition of Type A behavior does not indicate that there is a clearly defined "behavior type" on which all can agree, even with extensive training. This does not mean that a "type" does not exist, but among the factors that an interviewer or rater appears to use to make judgments, the "type" is not apparent.

What is really happening in the SI is probably much different than the trait notions imply. Type A or Type B behavior appears to be assessed by combining a unique set of characteristics that are based on the interviewer–auditors' conceptual framework, their experience, knowledge, practice, art, etc. This framework may vary or it may reflect the training given, but it is still a framework that contains personal hypotheses about how the characteristics fit together. Within this framework, the interviewer probably considers a restricted range of subjects' feeling expressions and verbal behaviors. Whereas it seems certain that interviewers match behaviors to Type A characterizations to make behavior-type judgments when such behaviors are salient, when the behaviors are not salient or not focused on, the interviewer's conceptual framework probably fills in; this filling in may be a constant source of error in interrater comparisons.

RECOMMENDATIONS

Methodological Recommendations

From a research perspective, we may be in deep trouble if we continue to regard Type A as a type and proceed with naive assumptions that the SI has been, is, and will continue to be a standard, and that all trained in the SI according to the standard were and remain consistent with one another across time. Rather than assume there is consistency in eliciting and weighing characteristics, we should, unless we know otherwise, assume there is inconsistency. Accordingly, we should tighten the standards for assessing and accepting reliability. Specifically, if 4-point global assessments are used in statistical analyses, then reliability must be acceptable for the 4-point assessments. Although it is difficult to specify an exact figure, I suggest the lowest acceptability should be .6, and any calculation of interrater agreement must take chance into account using statistical procedures such as Cohen's Kappa.

Further, we need to assess the interrater realibility of Type A assessments made by different interviewers with the same subjects, and these subjects should differ with regard to some of the important demographic characteristics such as age, sex, and geographical region. Unless this reliability is repeatedly found to be acceptable, we cannot safely assume that global SI behavior-type assessments can be compared across studies.

We need to compare the VCI and the SI. Currently, they differ in the way they elicit Type A behavior and the scope of characteristics they employ in making assessments. We need to know how differences in eliciting or provoking Type A behaviors change or do not change the expression of those behaviors. A major question to consider is whether to employ a reflective or a provocative strategy. Is it more important to have subjects reflect on life experiences in such a way that the original feelings are called up and connected to expressive behaviors, or is it more important to provide a challenging interpersonal stimulus and assess verbal responsiveness? The reflective strategy appears to be oriented to increasing external validity and the provocative strategy more oriented to increasing internal validity. We need to know which works better.

A second major issue in comparing the SI and VCI is whether raters who make behavior-type assessments from audiotapes differ from raters who make assessments from videotapes. Given the great differences in the scope of characteristics considered and the independence of verbal and nonverbal components (Hughes et al., 1983), I suspect that there may be considerable disagreement between the two methods. We need to compare the two interview methods using the same raters and we need to compare their ratings to some criterion, such as their sensitivity and specificity in discriminating CHD cases from controls.

A great number of interviewers have been trained over the last 15 years, particularly by Dr. Rosenman and his associates. With the exception of the MRFIT (Blumenthal et al., 1984) and an ongoing epidemiological project, CARDIA, there has been little if any follow-up on interviewers' interrater reliability with the original criterion interviews or with new populations interviewed. In addition, there has been little systematic effort to assess how interviewers' style in eliciting Type A behaviors changes over time and with different populations. The absence of quality control monitoring, without substantiating evidence of reliability, is a serious omission where measures are used in scientific research. The drift in interviewer technique, the favoring of specific characteristics (and omission of others) to make behavior-type judgments, and a shift in A/B thresholds is all too common. Although this issue is not high on anyone's research agenda, the results and the interpretation of the results rely heavily on accurate behavior-type assessments.

Related to reliability, we need to develop standards for interviewer behavior. Whether we want this to be or not, the interviewer is an independent variable in the subjects' response. The interviewer is a central figure affecting and being affected by the subject, both in the ways of eliciting subjects' behaviors and in the ways of combining perceptions of those behaviors. Accordingly, we need to develop clear standards for interviewer conduct. The first step is to conceptualize interview factors that might affect the predictive validity of Type A assessments, develop techniques to score these factors, and compare these factors for interviewers whose Type A assessments either do or do not predict CHD.

As a beginning, the author has developed a quantitative procedure for scoring interviewer behaviors. The interviewer behaviors are divided into those features that facilitate or inhibit the subjects' speech. Facilitative behaviors include question probes that are based on the content of the subjects' previous answer, acknowledgments of what the subjects previously said, and slow pace (speaking and response latency rates) of the interview; inhibitive behaviors include interruptions, fast pace of the interview, and a mechanical adherence to the script form for all questions. We have divided each of these behaviors according to whether they apply to standard script questions or nonstandard questions tailored to the content of subjects' answers. Interrater reliability studies indicate that we can score each of these behaviors with high reliability, and we are scoring these behaviors for large samples of the MRFIT and WCGS SIs. Given that the WCGS found Type A assessments to predict CHD incidence, it provides us an empirical standard to compare other interviewers.

Going further, we need to know how interviewers' behaviors affect subjects' behaviors. One issue to address is the synchrony between interviewers and subjects. Should interviewers strive to control their behaviors so that they are standard for all subjects, or should they be more spontaneous and thus stimulate further Type A behaviors? The answer to this question is not simple, yet it is important and we should think about it more deeply in continuing SI assessments.

A second issue is the extent to which interviewers use their own behaviors in making Type A assessments. There is a chance that the thus unaccounted-for variance in global assessments of Type A behavior (by scored components) are due to the fact that we have ignored the interviewers' characteristics. The results of Howland and Siegman point out the possibility that interviewers may use their own behaviors in making global Type A assessments. With 66 SIs, obtained from Rosenman (males aged 31–65 years), Howland and Siegman (1982) found significant correlations of interviewers' Type A assessments with their own speech behaviors. Negatively correlated with Type A were the interviewers' speech productivity ($-.23$), how long they spoke when it was their "turn" ($-.49$), and how many "turns" they took ($-.47$). The seven interviewer stylistics accounted for an astonishing 43% of variance in the global SI ratings.

If interviewers behaved differently when talking with Type A's than Type B's, it is reasonable that they may (whether consciously or not) look to their own behaviors when making behavior-type judgments. Maybe some of the unaccounted-for variance in global assessments is coming from the interviewers' focus on themselves. If interviewers observe their own feelings and behaviors, this could be responsible for some of the persistent 25% disagreement in interrater reliability studies. A good place to start research to address this question is with the WCGS SIs. If they show synchrony and the MRFIT interviewers do not, we may consider whether synchrony is a part of valid Type A assessments. This synchrony is reminiscent of Singer and her co-workers' concept of engagement-involvement (Singer, 1974). An engaged-involved dyad may elicit qualitatively different assessments of Type A behavior than a disengaged, more standardized format.

Another excellent approach would be to experimentally manipulate the interviewers' behaviors along dimensions that have both practical and clinical importance. One dimension to consider is how hard the interviewers should try to elicit Type A behavior in their subjects. Should they be quiet listeners or should they play verbal tennis with the subjects? Whether we want spontaneous or provoked Type A expressions seems a major issue. It is conceivable that the interviewers' eliciting techniques have varied sufficiently from study to study to affect the predictive validity of global SI assessments. Wherever possible, this issue should be addressed if we are to continue our successful search for the coronary-prone process.

If we are to continue to employ the Rosenman global SI assessments (i.e., AI, A2, X, B), interviewers need standards for SI assessment. Exactly what are interviewers supposed to focus on, and how heavily should they weigh each factor or combination of factors? What about the physical signs and symptoms that are available with videotapes? Can we ignore these and still get valid assessments?

This is a central question because the two major interviewer training centers use entirely different scopes for assessment. The procedure for SI assessment in the recent CARDIA study involves having one person conduct and audiorecord the SI and another person make assessments based on the taperecordings. The person making the A/B ratings has never seen the subjects. In contrast, the interviewer in the Friedman technique makes ratings in person, often at the time the interview is occurring. We need to know how a rater who is present with the subject compares with a rater who has never seen the subject.

In addition to standards for scope we need standards for weighing and threshold. Weighing is a relative comparison of two or more Type A characteristics. Interviewers weigh characteristics when they find conflict, e.g., emphatic but slow responses. They must decide whether voice emphasis is more diagnostic of Type A than the speed of subjects' answers. Interviewers may also weigh particular combinations of factors, e.g., in the assessment of hostility from voice tone and content. We should continue the component analyses in the search for a combination or pattern of characteristics that more clearly defines coronary proneness. An excellent resource is epidemiological samples with CHD endpoints. If we could find a subset of behaviors that is more predictive of CHD than global ratings, we should consider whether they can be quantitatively scored.

A major threat to interrater reliability may be an unstable A/B threshold. Threshold is subjective, even arbitrary, and it makes such a difference in the overall character of the statistical analyses and probably also in the results. And surely there are threshold differences among interviewers, so that research employing the SI should be sensitive to threshold problems. The problem of threshold differences is exacerbated by the lack of a dose-response relationship between the intensity of Type A behavior and CHD incidence. If the more extreme Type A's had more CHD than moderate Type A's, we could make the measure much more specific in our risk predictions. But as it is we must consider most carefully that area with the most ambiguity. Unfortunately, it is in this area of ambiguity that the majority of subjects' behaviors occur. Thus it appears that we need to revise the global SI assessment procedure, for the issue of threshold will remain a problem until we have a clearer standard for identifying and weighing Type A discriminative characteristics.

Friedman and his co-workers, particularly Dr. Powell, have worked to specify the components that go into the summary behavior-type score. Thus, the current Friedman interview does specify the components, but more work is needed to validate the current VCI. Its predictive validity has been assessed in only one large-scale study, the RCPP, and in that study the global summary score for Type A behavior did not correlate with recurrent CHD. We also need to determine the degree that VCI trainees agree in scoring the 35 components, as only one attempt, by Powell, has systematically assessed the interrater reliability. Another potential problem is that the threshold for Type A is so low that the vast majority of most populations interviewed with this technique would be Type A, and so assessments can have little hope in identifying those most at risk.

Conceptual Recommendations

I doubt if all the assessment problems can be resolved without a better conceptual understanding of pattern. As long as we view Type A behavior as simply the expression of explicit behaviors that occur in an interview, we will be plagued by questions of whether interviewer behaviors should be standardized or how valid a particular behavior may be in reflecting the risk process.

At the heart of the assessment problem is a conceptual problem. I agree with Matthews et al. (1982) and Price (1982) in the call for a better conceptual understanding of the psychological dimensions of Type A and Type B behavior. It is true that we need a theory that would help us differentiate the coronary-prone pattern from the myriad of features in its broad scope. How do we go about developing this theory?

We must get away from the trait idea and trait measure, which has blocked creative thinking, and continue the search for the nature of the Type A pattern. One path to the refinement of Type A assessment recommended by Matthews (1983) is the proposition that "Type A be assessed in a comprehensive manner and on a continuum, that environmental elicitors of Type A be measured, and that specific classifications of coronary heart disease be utilized" (p. 74).

As investigators in behavioral medicine, we are most deficient in how we conceptualize and measure context. There has not been one study that has attempted to test the ecological validity of the SI components in the subjects' work mileu or home life. This is unexplored territory and seems the most needed to help us identify and measure the coronary-risk pattern.

The Subjective Clinical Aspect

A further recommendation is that, in all our efforts to be quantitative and objective, we not let go of the subjective clinical nature of the interview where an individual can be considered as a whole person. As Dr. Friedman (Friedman & Ulmer, 1984) has maintained, the Type A individual is not just an "exemplar of medical statistics," but a "total human being" (p. 5). The risk process may be more related to the whole being than individual Type A components can ever be, and it may be critical to experience the sense of the subject to accurately assess the coronary-prone process. Until we know more about the nature of the risk process, we should not dispense with the subjective aspect of assessment just for the sake of scientific rigor.

Rather, we should combine the clinical and research approaches to develop further insights. For example, if the coronary-risk pattern is interactional, then we need to look at the nature of this interaction. A key ability that interviewers need is to understand and appreciate their impact on subjects and to sensitively interpret how interactional factors affect the SI process. Accordingly, it may be that much greater emphasis will need to be placed on developing interviewers' clinical skills in engaging respondents, in monitoring and modulating their own behaviors, in interpreting their own emotional reactions, and in integrating multiple characteristics within an implicit, clinically derived conceptual framework. We should combine the clinical and research approaches to deepening our knowledge of hostility. Among the components scored in the SI, hostility is most consistently and strongly related to CHD incidence. Thus, we should focus on hostility and develop a better interview to assess it than the SI. We need to discover how best to elicit it, how to weigh specific features, and how to train others to assess it reliably. The question content should extend to a wide range of social contacts. And we should appreciate that hostility, as a Type A component, shares many of the same problems as the global assessment, including the role of the interviewer, specification of its features, and ecological validity. Accordingly, these should be addressed in our attempts to refine its assessment.

ACKNOWLEDGMENTS

The author is grateful to Dr. Meyer Friedman, Dr. Ray Rosenman and Ms. Nancy Fleischmann for their SI interviewer training and for their help in describing the WCGS SI training methods and commenting on this draft. Thanks to Dr. Beth Schucker for describing the SI training and Type A assessment in the MRFIT, to the MRFIT principal researchers for their cooperation in providing tape-recorded SIs and other data, to Mr. Greg Grandits who conducted the MRFIT statistical analyses, and to Dr. Virginia Price who critiqued an earlier version of this chapter.

REFERENCES

Anderson, J. R., & Waldron, I. (1983). Behavioral and content components of the structured interview assessment of the Type A behavior pattern in women. *Journal of Behavioral Medicine, 6,* 123-134.

Bem, D. J., & Allen, A. (1974). On predicting some of the people some of the time: The search for cross-situational consistencies in behavior. *Psychological Review, 81,* 506-520.

Blumenthal, J. A., O'Toole, L. C., & Haney, T. L. (1984). Behavioral assessment of the Type A behavior pattern. *Psychosomatic Medicine, 46,* 415-423.

Bortner, R., & Rosenman, R. H. (1967). The measurement of pattern A behavior. *Journal of Chronic Diseases, 20,* 525-533.

Brand, R. J., Rosenman, R. H., & Jenkins, C. D. (1978). Comparison of coronary heart disease prediction in the Western Collaborative Group Study using the structured interview and the Jenkins Activity Survey assessments of the coronary-prone Type A Behavioral Pattern. *American Heart Association CVD Epidemiological Newsletter, 24.*

Chesney, M. A., Black, G. W., Chadwick, J. H., & Rosenman, R. H. (1981). Psychological correlates of the Type A behavior pattern. *Journal of Behavioral Medicine, 4,* 217-229.

Chesney, M. A., Eagleston, J. R., & Rosenman, R. (1980). The Type A structured interview: A behavioral assessment in the rough. *Journal of Behavioral Assessment, 2,* 255-272.

Dembroski, T. M., MacDougall, J. M., Herd, A., & Shields, J. L. (1979). Effects of level of challenge on pressor and heart rate responses in Type A and B subjects. *Journal of Applied and Social Psychology, 9,* 209-228.

Dembroski, T. M., MacDougall, J. M., Shields, J. L., Petitto, J., & Lushene, R. (1978). Components of the type A coronary behavior pattern and cardiovascular response to psychomotor performance challenge. *Journal of Behavioral Medicine, 1*, 159-176.

Feldstein, S. (1978). A chronography of conversation: In defense of an objective approach. In A. W. Siegman & S. Feldstein (Eds.), *Nonverbal behavior and communication*. Hillsdale, NJ: Lawrence Erlbaum Associates.

Friedman, H. S., Hall, J. A., & Harris, M. J. (1985). Type A behavior, nonverbal expressive style, and health. *Journal of Personality and Social Psychology, 48*, 1299-1315.

Friedman, M. (1969). *Pathogenesis of coronary artery disease*. New York: McGraw-Hill.

Friedman, M., Brown, M. A., & Rosenman, R. H. (1969). Voice analysis test for detection of behavior pattern. *Journal of the American Medical Association, 208*, 828-836.

Friedman, M., & Powell, L. H. (1984). The diagnosis and quantitative assessment of Type A behavior: Introduction and description of the videotaped structured interview. *Integrative Psychiatry, 2*, 123-129.

Friedman, M., & Rosenman, R. H. (1959). Association of specific overt behavior pattern with blood and cardiovascular findings: Blood cholesterol level, blood clotting time, incidence of arcus senilis, and clinical coronary artery disease. *Journal of the American Medical Association, 169*, 1286-1296.

Friedman, M., Thoresen, C. E., & Gill, J. J. (1981). Type A behavior: Its role, detection, and alteration in patients with ischemic heart disease. In J. W. Hurst (Ed.), *The heart update V*. New York: McGraw-Hill.

Friedman, M., Thoresen, C. E., Gill, J. J., Ulmer, D., Powell, L., Price, V., Brown, B., Thompson, L., Rabin, D. D., Breall, W. S., Bourg, E., Levy, R. A., & Dixon, T. (1986). Alteration of Type A behavior and its effect on cardiac recurrences in post myocardial infarction patients: Summary results of the Recurrent Coronary Prevention Project. *American Heart Journal, 112*, 653-665.

Friedman, M., Thoresen, C. E., Gill, J. J., Ulmer, D., Thompson, L., Powell, L., Price, V., Elek, S. R., Rabin, D. D., Breall, W. S., Piaget, G., Dixon, T., Bourg, E., Levy, R. A., & Tasto, D. L. (1982). Feasibility of altering Type A behavior pattern after myocardial infarction. Recurrent Coronary Prevention Project Study: Methods, baseline results and preliminary findings. *Circulation, 66*, 83-92.

Friedman, M., & Ulmer, D. (1984). *Treating Type A behavior and your heart*. New York: Knopf.

Hecker, M., Chesney, M., Black, G., & Rosenman, R. (1981). Speech analysis of Type A behavior. In J. K. Darby (Ed.), *Speech evaluation in medicine*. New York: Grune & Stratton.

Hecker, M., Frautschi, N., Chesney, M., Black, G., & Rosenman, R. (1985, March). *Components of the Type A behavior and coronary heart disease*. Paper presented at the meeting of the Society of Behavioral Medicine, New Orleans.

Herman, S., Blumenthal, J. A., Black, G. M., Chesney, M. A. (1981). Self-ratings of Type A (coronary-prone) adults: Do Type A's know they are Type A's? *Psychosomatic Medicine, 43*, 405-413.

Howland, E. W., & Siegmen, A. W. (1982). Toward the automated measurement of the Type-A behavior pattern. *Journal of Behavioral Medicine, 5*, 37-54.

Hughes, J. R., Jacobs, D. R., Schucker, B., Chapman, D. P., Murrary, D. M., & Johnson, C. A. (1983). Nonverbal behavior of the Type A individual. *Journal of Behavioral Medicine, 6*, 279-289.

MacDougall, J. M., Dembroski, T. M., & Krantz, D. S. (1981). Effects of types of challenge on pressor and heart rate responses in Type A and B women. *Psychophysiology, 18*, 1-9.

Manuck, S. B., Craft, S. A., & Gold, K. J. (1978). Coronary-prone behavior pattern and cardiovascular response. *Psychophysiology, 15*, 403-411.

Matarazzo, J. D., & Wiens, A. N. (1972). *The interview: Research on its anatomy and structure*. Chicago: Aldine-Atherton.

Matthews, K. A. (1983). Assessment issues in coronary-prone behavior. In T. M. Dembroski, T.

H. Schmidt, & G. Blumchen (Eds.), *Biobehavioral bases of coronary heart disease*. Basel, Switzerland: Karger.

Matthews, K. A., Glass, D. C., Rosenman, R. H., & Bortner, R. W. (1977). Competitive drive, pattern A, and coronary heart disease: A further analysis of some data from the Western Collaborative Group Study. *Journal of Chronic Diseases, 30*, 489–498.

Matthews, K. A., Krantz, D. S., Dembroski, T. M., & MacDougall, J. M. (1982). Unique and common variance in structured interview and Jenkins Activity Survey measures of the Type A behavior pattern. *Journal of Personality and Social Psychology, 42*, 303–313.

Meehl, P. (1954). *Clinical versus statistical prediction*. Minneapolis, MN: University of Minnesota Press.

Mischel, W. (1969). Continuity and change in personality. *American Psychologist, 24*, 1012–1018.

The MRFIT Group. (1979). The MRFIT behavior pattern study—I: Study design, procedures, and reproducibility of behavior pattern judgments. *Journal of Chronic Diseases, 32*, 293–305.

The MRFIT Group. (1982). The Multiple Risk Factor Intervention Trial: Risk factor changes and mortality results. *Journal of the American Medical Association, 248*, 1465–1477.

Powell, L., & Thoresen, C. (1985). Behavioral and physiologic determinants of long-term prognosis after myocardial infarction. *Journal of Chronic Diseases, 38*, 253–263.

Price, V. A. (1982). *Type A behavior pattern: A model for research and practice*. New York: Academic Press.

Rosenman, R. H. (1978). The interview method of assessment of the coronary-prone behavior pattern. In T. M. Dembroski, S. M. Weiss, J. L. Shields, S. G. Haynes, & M. Feinleib (Eds.), *Coronary-prone behavior*, New York: Springer-Verlag.

Rosenman, R. H., Brand, R. J., Jenkins, C. D., Friedman, M., Straus, R., & Wurm, M. (1975). Coronary heart disease in the Western Collaborative Group Study: Final follow-up experience of 8½ years. *Journal of the American Medical Association, 233*, 872–877.

Rosenman, R. H., & Friedman, M. (1961). Association of specific behavior pattern in women with blood and cardiovascular findings. *Circulation, 24*, 1173–1184.

Rosenman, R. H., & Friedman, M. (1974). Neurogenic factors in pathogenesis of coronary heart disease. *Medical Clinics of North America, 58*, 269–279.

Rosenman, R. H., Friedman, M., Straus, R., Wurm, M., Jenkins, C. D., & Messinger, H. B. (1966). Coronary heart disease in the Western Collaborative Group Study: A follow-up experience of two years. *Journal of the American Medical Association, 195*, 130–136.

Rosenman, R. H., Swan, G. E., & Carmelli, D. (1988). Definition, assessment and evolution of the Type A behavior pattern. In B. K. Houston & C. R. Snyder (Eds.), *Type A behavior pattern: Current trends and future directions*. New York: Wiley.

Scherwitz, L., Berton, K., & Leventhal, H. (1977). Type A assessment and interaction in the behavior pattern interview. *Psychosomatic Medicine, 39*, 229–240.

Scherwitz, L., Berton, K., & Leventhal, H. (1978). Type A behavior, self-involvement, and cardiovascular response. *Psychosomatic Medicine, 40*, 593–609.

Scherwitz, L., Graham, L., Grandits, G., & Billings, J. (1985, March). *Interviewer style and CHD predictiveness in the Multiple Risk Factor Intervention Trial*. Paper presented at the meeting of the Society of Behavioral Medicine, New Orleans.

Scherwitz, L., Graham, L., Grandits, G., & Billings, J. (1987). Speech characteristics and behavior type assessment in the MRFIT structured interviews. *Journal of Behavioral Medicine, 10*, 173–195.

Scherwitz, L., Graham, L., Grandits, G., & Billings, J. (1988). *Speech characteristics and coronary heart disease incidence in the MRFIT*. Manuscript submitted for publication.

Scherwitz, L., Graham, L., Grandits, G., Buehler, J., & Billings, J. (1986). Self-involvement and coronary heart disease incidence in the Multiple Risk Factor Intervention Trial. *Psychosomatic Medicine, 48*, 187–199.

Scherwitz, L., Hecker, M., & Chesney, M. (1985). *Protocol for Type A assessment in CARDIA*. Unpublished manuscript.

Schucker, B., & Jacobs, D. R. (1977). Assessment of behavioral risk for coronary disease by voice characteristics. *Psychosomatic Medicine, 39*, 219–228.

Shekelle, R., Hulley, S., Neaton, J., Billings, J. H., Borhani, N. O., Gerace, T. A., Jacobs, D. R., Lasser, N. L., Mittlemark, M. B., & Stamler, J., for the MRFIT Research Group. (1985). The MRFIT behavior pattern study II. Type A behavior and incidence of coronary heart disease. *American Journal of Epidemiology, 122*, 559–570.

Shekelle, R., Neaton, J. D., Jacobs, D., Hulley, S., & Blackburn, H. (1973). *MRFIT baseline monograph: Type A behavior pattern in MRFIT*. Unpublished manuscript.

Singer, M. T. (1974). Presidential address - Engagement-involvement: A central phenomenon in psychophysiological research. *Psychosomatic Medicine, 36*, 1–17.

Van Egeren, L. F. (1979). Cardiovascular changes during social competition in a mixed motive game. *Journal of Personality and Social Psychology, 37*, 858-864.

7

The Role of Emotional Expression in Coronary Heart Disease

Howard S. Friedman
University of California, Riverside

Understanding the relationship between psychological factors and heart disease has proven to be a chronic struggle against the weaknesses of vague constructs. After a century of speculation and three decades of intensive research, some even doubt that any reliable link at all exists between psychological factors and clogged arteries (Angell, 1985). The search for a "coronary-prone personality" has been seriously hindered by insufficient attention to construct validity, especially regarding the issues surrounding emotional expression.

Most attention has been directed toward the Type A behavior pattern (TABP), a collection of behaviors and emotional expressions that seems predictive of clinically apparent coronary heart disease (CHD) (Cooper, Detre, & Weiss, 1981; Dembroski, Weiss, Shields, Haynes, & Feinleib, 1978). There are, however, differing means of assessing the Type A pattern and different definitions of the key characteristics of a Type A person. Emotional expressions often are not adequately assessed or understood. Futhermore, the Type A construct is sometimes overextended: All unhealthy emotions are not necessarily part of the Type A pattern. It is important to recognize that "Type A behavior" is *not* synonymous with "coronary-prone behavior"; coronary-prone behavior leads to CHD by definition, but the effect of Type A behavior on health is an empirical matter.

Although commonly recognized, the Type A behavior pattern is ambiguously defined. A tense, driven, business executive who struggles for long hours at his desk, tappping his fingers and pencil, and talking rapidly into two telephones at once while grimacing hostilely at his dallying assistant would almost certainly be diagnosed "Type A." As defined by its discoverers (M. Friedman & Rosenman, 1974), the TABP refers broadly to "any person who is aggressively involved in a chronic incessant struggle to achieve more and more in less and less time . . . the most significant trait of the Type A man is his habitual sense of

149

time urgency or 'hurry sickness' '' (Ch. 6). However, the Type A person is most often diagnosed not in terms of hurrying but rather in terms of a certain expressive and emotional style. As M. Friedman and Rosenman (1974) said in looking back at their early efforts, "We could have done far more in those earlier years. We could have surveyed each patient in his entirety, as an individual. We could have studied his face, his gestures, listened intently to the quality of his voice and to the content of his informal speech" (p. 54). Nonverbal emotional expression is a key aspect of the Type A construct; it is considered in detail in this chapter.

The Type A person has been conceived of in a wide variety of ways, ranging from workaholism to aggression. Diagnosis of the Type A pattern often depends on unknown insights and behaviors made by an observer or interviewer (Scherwitz, Graham, Grandits, Buehler, & Billings, 1986). Long lists of expressive characteristics have been suggested (reviewed by H. S. Friedman, Harris, & Hall, 1984; Hall, Friedman, & Harris, 1986), but the analysis generally has not been guided by knowledge of emotional expression. Suggested expressive cues have included: walks briskly; exhibits an alert face; has very alive eyes; possibly displays a tense, teeth-clenching, jaw-grinding face; smile is a "lateral extension" not an oval; laugh is rarely a belly laugh; looks at others unflinchingly in the eye; sits on edge of chair; hands gesture with fist or pointed finger; may squirm or move about with impatience; uses explosive, accelerating speech; has few midsentence pauses; has short speech latency; interrupts; hurries speech; makes percussive sounds; sighs; manipulates objects with hand during speech; never whines; rarely whispers; often shows hostility around the eyes; uses terse speech; uses clipped words, has firm handshake; has loud and/or vigorous voice; displays general expression of vigor.

It should be obvious that such a list of cues is a hodgepodge of different classes of cues and different levels of conceptual analysis. Some of the important cues are highlighted in this chapter. Note that all nonlanguage cues of emotional expression are referred to here as "nonverbal" cues. This includes speech rate and tone of voice, which are sometimes termed *paralinguistic cues*. Also, note that although diagnosis of Type A in the prospective (and well-known) Western Collaborative Group study was based on audio cues, visual cues of expressive style are commonly used in current diagnosis. For example, an assessment course taught by M. Chesney and R. Rosenman explicitly teaches videotape analysis.

A heavily quoted passage of Sir William Osler (1910) says, "It is not the delicate neurotic person who is prone to angina, but the robust, the vigorous in mind and body, the keen and ambitious man, the indicator of whose engines is always at 'full speed ahead' '' (p. 839). This description of an active, ambitious, expressive person can be seen as evocative of the idea of "hurry sickness." In fact, it is often used in historical summaries of the Type A pattern. However, such a vigorous person does not necessarily share the impatience, hostility, tenseness, and other attributes also seen as characteristic of a coronary-prone person. Furthermore, there are presently no separate classifications for people of differing expressive styles who are not Type A. People could be slow, quiet, or unexpressive in various ways and for various reasons. However, all such people are generally classified, by default, as Type B. In this chapter, a more refined analysis of the role of emotional expression in coronary heart disease is presented.

The two primary methods of assessing Type A behavior have been the Structured Interview (SI) and the Jenkins Activity Survey (JAS). The SI format allows the interviewer to challenge the subject and to measure expressive style (nonverbal patterns of affective expression) as well as verbal responses. The JAS, on the other hand, is a paper-and-pencil, self-report questionnaire with three standard subscales (Speed & Impatience, Job Involvement, and Hard-Driving competitiveness). It tries to capture expressive style and activity level, but, as we see later, is in an important way unsuccessful. Various other measures, scales, and parts of scales have also been used to assess the Type A pattern or its components. In understanding coronary-prone behavior, it is useful to have multiple measures. If all the measures validly assess coronary-prone behavior, then there should be convergent validity and all should be related (though not identically) to CHD. If only one measure predicts CHD but other reliable, conceptually similar measures do not, then the construct itself must be called into question and possibly redefined. The various measures and components of the Type A pattern therefore need further examination and comparison.

CONCEPTUAL FRAMEWORK

What are the conceptual underpinnings of the Type A pattern as relevant to emotional expression? Type A behaviors such as talking fast and hurrying are generally seen as *indicative* of an underlying state that is unhealthy. The expressive cues themselves such as loud speech or vigorous gesturing are not believed to be the causal agents. Hence, complete understanding of the phenomenon depends on identification of the relevant underlying psychological states and/or traits. In particular, understanding of the coronary-prone behavior style can be improved if more attention is paid to the causes of individual differences in nonverbal emotional expressiveness and to emotional aspects of personality.

Of particular theoretical relevance to the discriminant validity of the Type A pattern is our research in the area of positive emotional expressiveness or "personal charisma." This research included the development of a short self-report scale of emotional expressiveness called the Affective Communication Test (ACT) (H. S. Friedman, Prince, Rigigo, & DiMatteo, 1980; H. S. Friedman & Riggio, 1981; Riggio & Friedman, 1982). It is clear that certain people are naturally nonverbally expressive or "charismatic." (Sample items of the ACT are: "People tell me that I would make a good actor or actress," "My laugh is soft and subdued" (reversed item), and "I often touch friends during conversations.") The ACT has been validated in terms of friends' ratings, social characteristics, personality variables, and nonverbal social skills. People who score high on the ACT are animated and easily noticed by others, are popular, and wind up in positions of leadership and social influence. Importantly, they seem emotionally healthy. This healthy expressiveness seems related to aspects of laughter and vocal expression, fast speech, head movements, fluid gestures, and ambition, dominance, and vigor. Thus, the people who are high on this expressiveness or personal charisma share certain characteristics with people who would be labeled Type A, but they do not appear to fit the overall description of a coronary-prone personality.

Several lines of research suggest that there are subgroups within the Type A/B categories, and that some "true" Type A (i.e., coronary-prone) individuals are characterized by a negative, hostile/competitive style. This view is consistent with schemes proposed by Dembroski (1979), Diamond (1982), Hansson, Hogan, Johnson, and Schroeder (1983), Heller (1980), and Totman (1979, Ch. 6), among others. Analogously , if an active "hurry sickness" is not the critical variable in poor health, then there may also be some unhurried but tense "Type B" individuals whose behavioral and emotional styles are unhealthy.

We therefore deduced the existence of four groups of people who might be relabeled as follows (H. S. Friedman, Harris, & Hall, 1984): (1) healthy charismatic people, who are expressive, dominant, and fast-moving but are in control, coping well, and sociable; (2) hostile, competitive people, who are also expressive and dominant but in a threatened, negative sense—they may be coronary prone; (3) tense overcontrolled people, who appear unexpressive and inhibited to casual observers but may explode under sufficient challenge—they may also be illness prone; and (4) relaxed, quiet people, who are unexpressive, somewhat submissive, and content. Our tests of this model are reported later in this chapter.

This four-group scheme is not exhaustive. There may be other relevant groups such as people who are unexpressive, relaxed, and quiet because they are depressed. Such groups are important though not directly relevant to the Type A construct. However, a more sophisticated understanding of different nonverbal expressive styles leads to new conceptions that more closely approximate the emerging relationships between psychological behavior patterns and disease.

Other Aspects of Personality and Emotion

To place the Type A pattern and its expressive components in an appropriate context, more attention must also be paid to other affective characteristics that may or may not be relevant to coronary proneness. Unfortunately, only several other psychological variables have been studied with much frequency in relation to heart disease. Fortunately, these are of great psychological interest: anger/hostility/aggression, anxiety, depression, and extroversion.

As already noted, evidence suggests that likely factors of relevance to CHD are hostility and/or repressed hostility, anger, and aggression (Chesney & Rosenman, 1985). Together, anger, hostility, and aggression have been termed the *AHA syndrome* (Spielberger et al., 1985). It is not yet clear whether the AHA syndrome should be considered an integral part of the Type A construct or a separate predictor of CHD. A study by Williams and his colleagues (1980) showed that both the TABP and hostility (as assessed by a scale derived from the MMPI) were independently related to the presence of coronary atherosclerosis.

Anxiety, depression, and introversion are not typically thought of as directly relevant to coronary proneness, but they have been studied fairly often over the years in relation to CHD and other disease. Attention to emotion-related personality disorders such as depression should facilitate our general understanding of the role of emotional expressive factors in CHD. Is general emotional distress a risk factor for CHD, or is there something special about the Type A pattern?

It has also been shown that although the overworked, overstressed business executive was the stereotypic image motivating research on Type A behavior, many hard-working executives have good health. They have an active personality variously termed *hardy, coherent,* or *competent* (Antonovsky, 1979; Cohen, 1979; Kobasa, 1979). This style of cognitive coping, taken in concert with a style of animation, vigor, and expressiveness may be related to people's abilities to cope with stress. Our research also addressed this issue.

Goals of This Chapter

This chapter takes the view that the construct of coronary-prone behavior cannot be adequately refined until the role and meaning of expressive behavior is more fully understood. It extensively reviews past evidence and presents new data about the nonverbal/expressive and the emotional/motivational predictors of coronary heart disease. In particular, this chapter first reviews what is known about Type A subcomponents and CHD, and what is known about the relationship of other releveant personality traits to CHD. It then presents the results of two studies that directly address the role of nonverbal emotional expressiveness in coronary proneness. Finally, the implications of this research for future approaches to finding the coronary-prone personality are discussed.

QUANTITATIVE LITERATURE REVIEWS

Our first efforts to refine the coronary-prone construct involved comprehensive reviews of the literature. Four areas of nonverbal expression and emotion are relevant. First, we need to know which nonverbal expressive cues are correlated with the diagnosis of the Type A pattern. Second, it is important to examine what is known about the nonverbal correlates of CHD. Third, we need to see which components of the broad Type A pattern seem most highly related to CHD. And fourth, we must assess discriminant validity by examining which other emotional elements of personality are or are not related to CHD. In undertaking these reviews, we performed quantitative summaries whenever possible.

The method of quantitative integration or *meta-analysis* (Light & Pillemer, 1984; Rosenthal, 1984) is a useful tool for combining the results of independent studies so they may be more easily viewed. Meta-analysis provides us with combined effect size estimates. It thus avoids reviewer bias in interpreting the results of each study and clearly reveals significant trends. Like any statistical technique, meta-analysis does not provide new information; it merely helps us understand the information we already have. And so like any technique, its value depends on the quality of data available.

Nonverbal Correlates of Type A Diagnosis

Led by Judith Hall, we first analyzed the relationships between nonverbal cues and the Type A pattern (Hall, Friedman, & Harris, 1986). Nonverbal behavior is explicitly a part of the SI Type A diagnosis, but which nonverbal cues are used? Our quantitative review and analysis showed that the cues most strongly related to Type A diagnosis are fast and accelerated speech, short speech latencies, uneven rate, loud and explosive voice, hard or staccato voice, restless body movements, cues of high energy, and cues of annoyance and hostility. Also related, but less strongly so, are number of interruptions, percussive sounds, gross body movments, alert look, and head nods. Other cues possibly related include laughs, sighs, hurrying cues, clenched jaw, and clenched fists. Of course, not all these cues are found to be relevant in every study.

Consistent with our conceptual scheme, this review indicates that cues of both an active, spontaneously expressive person and of a tense, competitive person are used in classifying someone as Type A. It thus seems reasonable to think that some active people are erroneously being classified as coronary prone. It also may be the case that some insightful clinicians are implicitly separating the active from the tense/competitive cues and so may be more likely to find a TABP–CHD relationship than are other clinicians.

Nonverbal Correlates of CHD

Another key question is of course whether knowledge of nonverbal behavior can be used by itself to predict heart disease. Until recently, there was little research in this area. Fidgeting, clenched jaw, and unpleasant grimaces distinguish heart patients from controls (M. Friedman & Rosenman, 1960), as does explosive speech (M. Friedman, Brown, & Rosenman, 1969). It has also been found that in prospective work heart disease victims differ from normals on explosive speech, hostility, and vigor of answers (Matthews, Glass, Rosenman, & Bortner, 1977; see also Matthews, 1982). Some more recent work is reported elsewhere in this volume (Siegman, ch. 4, this volume).

Although there has been relatively little work relating specific nonverbal cues to the development of disease, the existing evidence is consistent with notions of a negative emotional state involving tension, hostility, or competitiveness. However, it seems nonverbal predictors can be fully understood only in the context of a general knowledge of noverbal expressive style. It is a mistake to simply describe a Type A person as one who shows "explosive speech." We must relate the nonverbal cues to some underlying model. We do so later in this chapter.

Type A Component Correlates of CHD

Which components of the Type A pattern predict and which do not predict CHD? With Stephanie Booth-Kewley, extensive manual searches of the medical and psychological literature were performed to locate articles on the relationship between Type A behavior and atherosclerosis and CHD. (Then the relationship between personality and coronary heart disease was examined, summarized next). *Psychological Abstracts* and *Index Medicus* were searched. Second, articles were located via the bibliographies of the articles already located. Third, the *Journal of Behavioral Medicine*, *Journal of Chronic Diseases*, *Journal of Psychosomatic Research*, and *Psychosomatic Medicine* were manually searched from cover to cover (Booth-Kewley & Friedman, 1987).

These searches (which covered 1945 to 1984) yielded a preliminary data base of 150 studies. However, each study then had to be amenable to meta-analysis; that is, it had to include at least one of the components or traits of interest such as Type A, a component of the Type A construct (such as Job Involvement), anger, hostility, aggression, depression, extroversion, or anxiety; the study had to include a dependent variable consisting of some manifestation of coronary heart disease or arteriosclerosis; the study had to use quantifiable variables and could not have been purely descriptive or anecdotal in nature (such as a case study); it had to contain enough information to allow the estimation of effect size and significance level. Of the 150 studies yielded by the literature search, 79 studies met the preceding criteria.

Analyses were performed separately for a number of components, namely: (1) each of the components of the Type A construct (such as Job Involvement); (2) each of the primary methods of assessing Type A (the Structured Interview and the Jenkins Activity Survey); and (3) a number of other specific combinations of variables that appeared to be highly similar, such as anger and hostility. The categories (some overlapping) included: Type A—All Measures; JAS Type A; JAS Speed and Impatience; JAS Job Involvement; JAS Hard-Driving Competitiveness; SI Type A; SI Time Urgency; Speed and Impatience/Time Urgency—All Measures; Job Involvement—All Measures; Competitiveness/Hard-Driving Aggressiveness—All Measures (results obtained for all assessments of competitiveness, "hard-driving competitiveness," pressured drive, or aggressiveness); Competitiveness/Hard Driving—All Measures; Anger/Hostility/Aggression—of the 24 studies in this category, 8 assessed "anger," 10 assessed "hostility," 4 assessed "aggression," and 2 assessed two or more of these variables; Anger/Hostility; Anger (e.g., the items of the SI that pertain to anger, the Trait Scale of Spielberger's State–Trait Anger Scale, the anger-out and anger-discuss components of the Framingham Type A scale, the anger scale of the Profile of Mood States; and ratings made by the subject, the subject's spouse, or the interviewer on "gets angry easily," etc.); Hostility (e.g., the Hostility scale of the Profile of Mood States, the "potential for hostility" item of the SI, the MMPI Cook–Medley Hostility Scale, ratings of "hostility directed inward" and "ambivalent hostility" made by the interviewer, etc.); Aggression (e.g., the Indirect Aggression and the Verbal Aggression scales of the Buss Aggression Inventory, the Impunitiveness Scale of the Rosenzweig Picture Frustration Task, the Aggression scale of the Cesarec–Markes Personality Schedule, simple ratings on "aggression" made by the interviewer, etc.).

Various researchers have speculated about the possibility that psychological factors differentially impact the various CHD disease conditions. To provide greater specificity, we also analyzed results separately by disease outcome (such as MI or angina). In general, the results were similar for each disease outcome (see Booth-Kewley & Friedman, 1987, for detailed presentation). In the meta-analysis, the product-moment correlation (r) was used as the effect size estimate. Associated probability levels (p-values) for calculated standard normal deviates were also obtained.

Results.   The results for these meta-analyses showed that the combined effect size (combined correlation) between Type A behavior (all measures) and all coronary/artery disease outcomes was about .16. The associated probability is less than .0000001. Although this effect is small compared to many lab studies in psychology, it is highly reliable and very important from an epidemiological point of view (cf. Rosenthal & Rubin, 1982). Our analysis showed that it would take thousands of unpublished studies averaging an effect size of zero to bring the overall combined probability for the Type A–CHD relationship to a nonsignificant level.

A comparison of the results obtained for the two primary measures of the Type A behavior pattern revealed that the SI has a much stronger association with disease outcome than does the JAS. A contrast performed to test the difference between the results for these variables (Rosenthal, 1984) revealed it to be significant ($p < .05$).

Why is the JAS such a poor predictor? Which components of the JAS relate best to disease outcome? The Hard-Driving Competitiveness factor had the strongest association with disease outcome, being slightly greater than that found for Type A. In contrast, JAS Job Involvement is not significantly related to disease. The results suggest the portion of the JAS that does not measure Hard-Driving Competitiveness may actually reduce the overall validity of the JAS as a predictor of disease. This finding contradicts the idea of the "workaholic" who develops coronary heart disease. The Speed and Impatience factor of the JAS had a weak relationship with disease outcome. Taken together with Speed and Impatience measures sometimes available from the SI, our review found that Speed and Impatience may be a small part of the true coronary-prone pattern.

A relatively large combined effect size was obtained for the personality variable category of Competitiveness/Hard Driving/Aggressiveness (all measures). Similar results were obtained for a related, overlapping personality variable category called Competitiveness/Hard Driving. These results again suggest that an aggressive, competitive drive may be more central to the true coronary-prone behavior pattern.

The combined effect sizes obtained for anger/hostility/aggression and anger/ hostility as predictive of CHD were also substantial, comparable to that found for Type A. The results indicated that whereas anger, hostility, and aggression are all reliably related to coronary and artery disease, hostility exhibits the strongest relationship with disease of these three variables.

In sum, our review of the relationships between aspects of Type A behavior and CHD found: (1) The Structured Interview (SI) diagnosis is a much better predictor than is the self-report Jenkins Activity Survey (JAS), probably because one or two subscales of the JAS are invalid, and because only the SI assesses aspects of nonverbal expressive style; (2) the hard-driving and competitive aspects of the Type A personality may be somewhat related to CHD but the speed and job involvement aspects probably are not. Attempts to slow down the pace of activity or reduce job involvement are probably misguided; (3) anger and hostility are related to CHD.

Personality Correlates of CHD

The construct validation context for the TABP is provided in part by other aspects of personality. The "non-Type A" emotional traits reviewed were: Depression— results obtained for all measures of depression, such as the Depression scale of the MMPI, the Profile of Mood States, and the Welsh Depression Scale; Extroversion—all assessments of extroversion and sociability; and Anxiety—all assessments of anxiety, such as the Taylor Manifest Anxiety Scale, the State-Trait Anxiety Inventory, and simple ratings on the dimension "anxiety."

The results obtained for the personality variable categories of depression, extroversion, and anxiety are as important as the Type A components for understanding coronary proneness. Our review found that of all these attributes, *depression* appears to be the most strongly associated with disease outcome, having a combined effect size about .21, with an associated p value of less than .0000001. It is noteworthy that the combined correlation for depression is actually somewhat higher than that obtained for overall Type A behavior and is about the same size as the combined correlation obtained for SI-assessed Type A.

These results strongly suggest that depression is importantly related to artery disease and may play a role in its development. Yet previous writings and reviews have not concluded that depression is relevant. When one considers the vast amount of research performed on Type A behavior and the meager research attention given to depression (as each of these variables relates to coronary heart disease), the finding that depression appears to relate at least as strongly to disease outcomes as does Type A seems truly remarkable.

The results for anxiety indicate a positive association between anxiety and disease outcome; the combined effect size is about .12, which is small, yet reliable. This finding, although overlooked in previous reviews, is consistent with the conceptualization that hyperresponsiveness is a factor that may underlie some coronary-prone behavior and the corresponding predisposition to disease.

There was a very small but reliable relationship between extroversion and coronary/artery disease, suggesting a slight tendency for greater extroversion to be associated with an increased probability of disease.

In sum, our review of the relationship between emotional aspects of personality and CHD found: (1) Depression is related to cardiovascular disease, and this relationship is of comparable strength to that of the SI Type A variable. Much more attention should be directed toward this variable; (2) anxiety seems slightly related to cardiovascular disease; and (3) extroversion is not importantly related to CHD.

Summary of Literature Reviews.   This section of this chapter has presented a quantitative review of the relationships among nonverbal behaviors, personality patterns, Type A behavior, and coronary heart disease. Special attention was addressed to the different components of the Type A pattern and its discriminant validity. Overall, the picture of a coronary-prone personality that emerged from our quantitative reviews is not at all one of a hard-working person with "hurry-sickness," as is often claimed. Rather, the true picture seems to be one of a person with a number of negative emotions, perhaps someone aggressively competitive, easily frustrated, anxious, and often angry or depressed. Further clarification is provided by our own empirical studies, discussed next.

TWO EMPIRICAL STUDIES
OF EMOTIONAL EXPRESSION AND HEALTH

Empirical Study 1

Our first efforts to test our model of emotional expression and CHD involved 60 male participants who were coronary prone (Friedman, Hall, & Harris, 1985). They were part of the Harvard portion of the Multiple Risk Factor Intervention Trial (MRFIT). For these subjects, Type A/B classification using extreme scores on the Jenkins Activity Survey (JAS), nonverbal expressiveness using the ACT, some personality scores, archival health data, and 4-minute videotape of the subject in interpersonal interaction were obtained. From the videotapes, a wide range of expressiveness behaviors were analyzed in detail.

These middle-aged men were originally selected for the MRFIT study because of high values on the coronary disease risk factors, but none had diagnosed coronary heart disease at the time of the initial screening. Half our subjects were selected from among those scoring highest on the Jenkins Activity Survey and half from among those scoring lowest. Each of the 60 subjects was videotaped during a nonstressful interview, conducted routinely by MRFIT staff. Typical questions were: "What did you like most (and least) about participating in the MRFIT program?" and "What effect did MRFIT have on your life?" The interview was not as challenging as the Structured Interview (SI) but was more stressful than everyday casual conversation.

The videotapes were edited to maximally standardize content and to obtain as much continuous talking as possible (thus capturing "style"). Video clips were randomly ordered and were then coded and rated. Complete transcripts of the full-length clips (including "ahs" and stutters) were used in conjunction with original speech tapes to code speech disturbances and to measure speech rate. Coders were trained undergraduate assistants but raters were not trained; they were "naive" judges (students) whose mission was to record their impressions of the stimulus clips. All coders and raters were blind to the JAS and ACT scores of the subjects.

The coders were trained to code the following variables (adapted from Riggio & Friedman, 1983): (1) head shakes; (2) head nods; (3) head movements; (4) smiles; (5) other mouth movements (6) gaze at face/head of interviewer (eye contact); (7) posture shifts; (8) leg and feet movements; (9) leg cross; (10) hands and arms: (a) duration and number of times that the hand comes into contact with the head, neck, or hair—called hand-to-head contact; (b) hand-to-hand contact— any contact between the hands, fingers, or wrists; and (c) the total number of body-focused movements—movements of the hand against another part of the body, clothing, or chair; picking and scratching were recorded separately; (11) duration of hand clasps; (12) prop manipulators; (13) fists; (14) number of object-focused movements—movements of the arms, hands, or fingers away from the body. Coders classified object-focused gestures into one of two categories: emphatic (i.e., movements with an abrupt onset and a moderate amount of force and speed) and nonemphatic illustrators; (15) a special subcategory of object-focused movements—parallel gestures—movements where both hands move together outwardly, in symmetry.

Coders also coded the following from the transcripts in conjunction with the full-length original speech tapes: (1) loud words (spoken words judged as relatively loud): total number; (2) speech latency: average number of seconds elapsed between end of staff member's speech and start of subject's speech; (3) rate of speech: (a) the number of words divided by the length of the segment, and (b) the number of syllables divided by segment length; (4) paralinguistic cues: speech disturbances (Kasl & Mahl, 1965); (5) Hurrying—the insertion of brief vocalizations such as "uh-huh" while the interviewer is speaking (as a sign of impatience); (6) percentage of segment spoken—duration of subject's speaking time divided by total interview duration. All coded variables were corrected for segment length. All reliabilities were good.

Factor analyses were performed to reduce the number of variables for subsequent analyses. All cues were corrected for segment length and then standardized before performing the analysis. The analysis yielded six factors based on video cues with the following interpretation and composition: (1) repressed—leg cross, prop manipulators, body-focused contact, hand clasps and hand to hand contact; (2) defensive/hostile—posture shifts, leg movements, hand to head contact, fists, and emphatic object-focused gestures; (3) animated—nods, head shakes, frequency of eye contact, speech rate, and parallel gestures; (4) talkative—average length of utterance, percentage of segment length subject spoke, and duration of eye contact; (5) active face/head—movements, mouth movements, parallel gestures, and frequency of eye contact; (6) direct—smiles, duration of eye contact, nonemphatic object-focused gestures, and less picking and scratching. A seperate factor analysis performed on the coded audio cues, using the same method, revealed two additional factors: (7) impatient—"ah" speech disturbances, speech hurrying interruptions, number of speaking turns, and average speech latency; (8) disturbed speech—"ah" speech disturbances, non-ah speech disturbances, loud words, and speech hurrying.

Three self-report measures were: (1) Jenkins Activity Survey; (2) Affective Communication Test; (3) Internal–External Locus of Control. From the subjects' participation in the MRFIT project, a complete medical history and data from the most recent annual physical examination were available to us, including detailed information about subjects' health with respect to peripheral arterial occlusive disease. Although the TABP has been most often used to predict CHD, there is reason to believe that there is a relationship to atherosclerotic disease in general (e.,g., Cottier et al., 1983).

Creating the Four Conceptual Groups. As described earlier, our subjects were divided into four groups on the basis of their scores on the JAS (Type A/B) and the ACT (high/low as determined by the median split of the scores). People who scored highly on both scales (high-ACT Type A's) were predicted to be our healthy charismatic group. The hostile, competitive group consisted of low-ACT ("true") Type A's—that is, men who scored very high on the JAS but were not expressive in the charismatic sense. The high-ACT Type B's were predicted to be the tense, inhibited people. They scored very Type B on the JAS but seemed to express a motivation to be the center of attention (i.e., were high ACT). Low-ACT Type B's were expected to be the truly relaxed (and healthy) group.

Results of Study 1. Using observers' *ratings* of the videotapes, 2 by 2 analyses of variance (high or low ACT by Type A or B) were conducted. Exploratory regressions were also performed. A consistent pattern emerged. On the ratings of how "healthy" the men appeared, there were no main effects but a Type by ACT interaction. As predicted, the high ACT A's ("healthy expressives") and the low ACT B's ("true Type B's") were seen as healthier than the other two groups. On ratings of "tense" (rated by different observers), the expected reversal occurred: low ACT A's ("true Type A's") and high-ACT B's ("false B's) were rated as more tense than the other two groups. Other ratings generally fit this conception. For ratings of "alert," our two theoretically healthy groups scored higher than the other two groups. The high rating on "alert" for the high-ACT A's was expected; for the low-ACT Type B men, their perceived alertness seemed to come from an open, comfortable style. When rated on "expressiveness," the same interaction occured, with the "healthy" groups being rated as more expressive. On ratings of the "dominant," the pattern of results showed that the high-ACT Type B's appear submissive.

The clearest finding involving the *coded* nonverbal cues concerned the factor we named *"repressed."* People scoring high on this factor showed crossed legs, prop manipulators, body-focused gestures, and little hand clasping. These cues clearly distinguished the high-ACT A's from the low-ACT A's, with low-ACT A's appearing more repressed than the high-ACT A's. It was further the case that this cue factor distinguished the two "healthy" groups from the other two groups, as in the ANOVAs described earlier (with the "unhealthy" groups exhibiting more repressed cues than the "healthy" groups). Thus, previous observations that certain closed body positions are indicative of an unhealthy expressive style were supported in this study.

The "defensive/hostile" factor (e.g., fists) tended to distinguish Type A from Type B people as past reseachers had suggested. In addition, the low-ACT A's did score much higher on the defensive/hostile factor than (all) the B's. In terms of locus of control, high-ACT A's had a very internal locus of control, whereas low-ACT A's and low-ACT B's were more external, and high-ACT B's were especially external.

Consistent with our conception of the high-ACT A's being charismatic, this group scored much higher than low-ACT A's on the "talkative" factor (length and amount of talk, eye contact).

The peripheral *arteries* indices were also informative. Twenty-three patients had at least one missing pulse and/or intermittent claudication. A 2 by 2 (ACT by Type) ANOVA performed on these scores revealed the expected interaction: low-ACT A's and high-ACT B's had more peripheral artery problems. Because the analysis of variance on dichotomous items can be problematic, a chi-square was also computed for the interaction (using collasped groups) as a check, and the results were the same.

Correlations between the ratings and peripheral artery disease showed that better health with respect to peripheral artery disease was significantly correlated with the more positive ratings. Especially interesting is the fact that naive observers' ratings of emotional health were directly predictive of physical health. We also predicted that Type A's with poor health outcomes would exhibit greater hostility but not necessarily the vigor and activity that is traditionally believed to be part of the TABP. The findings on the nonverbal cue factors supported this prediction. Low-ACT Type A's with missing pulses (i.e., the true Type A's with disease) were characterized by very high scores on the defensive hostility cue factor (e.g., fists, posture shifts, and emphatic gestures). In addition, they scored very low on the animated factor (nods, head shakes, speech rate, and eye contact). The low-ACT A's with missing pulses also scored differently on the impatient audio cue factor: They had interruptions, speech hurrying, and short latencies.

The correlations between peripheral arterial health and the nonverbal cue factors showed that overall, the men with fewer missing pulses were higher on such variables as smiling, eye contact (frequency and duration), nonemphatic object-focused gestures, parallel gestures, nods, head shakes, and speech rate. We had also expected that those high-ACT Type B subjects with poor health outcomes would show repression. This tended to be the case: Those seven high-ACT Type B's with missing pulses scored very high on the repressed cue factor (involving crossed legs, body-focused contact, prop manipulators, and little hand clasping). Furthermore, another indication of repression appears when a person's verbal messages (words) are less negative than his voice tone (Weitz, 1972). For our high-ACT Type B's, this was the case: On ratings of "friendly," these men's words received high ratings but their filtered voices received low ratings.

Empirical Study 2

Our second empirical study of emotional factors in heart disease (Friedman & Booth-Kewley, 1987b) followed up the earlier findings in several important ways. First, to ascertain the effect of expressiveness style on diagnosis, we included the Structured Interview (SI) as well as the questionnaire JAS measure of Type A. Second, we studied a group of men who had already had a heart attack (and a control group) instead of coronary-prone men. Finally, we included other personality measures to help provide an understanding of the different types of healthy and illness-prone men that seemed to emerge from the first study. Simultaneous assessment on various relevant personality attributes also allows us to ascertain the inter-relationships among the various predictors, something that is not possible in the quantitative literature reviews described previously.

One hundred middle-aged men, 50 of whom had had a myocardial infarction and 50 healthy controls, were studied. Each person was administered the Structured Interview (SI), the Jenkins Activity Survey (JAS), the Affective Communication Test (ACT), the Cook–Medley hostility scale (HO), the Anxiety and Depression scales of the Hopkins Symptom checklist, and some scales of "hardiness'' (Kobasa, Maddi, & Kahn, 1982). Audiotapes of the SI were edited to remove references to health status and then were judged to determine A/B status. These predictors were then all analyzed in terms of their relationship to health status.

Results of Study 2. As expected, the SI measure of Type A distinguished between the healthy and unhealthy men. However, the JAS measure was not related to health, nor were any of the JAS subscales. The Structured Interview is tapping an aspect of coronary proneness that the JAS is missing.

To aid in our understanding of the differences between the JAS and the SI, individuals were divided, as in the previous research, into four groups, Type A versus Type B and high or low on expressiveness as measure by the ACT. A 2 by 2 (JAS by ACT) analysis of variance on health status revealed the predicted interaction, namely that high-ACT Type A's (healthy charismatics) and low-ACT Type B's (truly relaxed B's) were significantly healthier (i.e., less likely to have had a heart attack) than the men in the other two goups. Furthermore, the high-ACT A's were significantly more likely to be free of CHD than were the "true A's" (low-ACT high JAS); and the true B's (low-ACT low-JAS men) were significantly more likely to be free of CHD than were low-ACT A's. This study reproduced the results of Study 1, but this time heart attack status was used as the dependent variable.

Importantly, to examine whether emotional expressiveness (as measured by the ACT) distinguishes JAS Type A from SI Type A classification, two additional analyses were done. First, an analogous 2 by 2 ANOVA (ACT by SI) was done on health status; that is, the SI was substituted for the JAS. The interaction was nonsignificant. This lack of a finding suggests that the SI classification already takes emotional expressiveness into account. So, secondly a 2 by 2, JAS by ACT, ANOVA was performed using the SI classification as the dependent measure. A significant JAS by ACT interaction was found on SI classification, showing that the low-ACT low-JAS men ("true Type B's") were rated most Type B on the SI, the low-ACT high-JAS men ("unhealthy Type A's") were most Type A, and the other two groups were in between. Thus, the Structured Interview diagnosis of Type A behavior differs from JAS by including expressiveness assessment. It gains its predictive validity from its ability to take emotional expressiveness into account. SI Type A predicts coronary health status, but JAS Type A by itself is a very weak predictor.

What else characterizes the personalities of the men in these four groups? As might be expected, the healthy charismatics (high ACT, JAS Type A) were highest on hardiness: they were least alienated from self and work, least powerless, and highest on internal locus of control. The "true" Type B's (low ACT, low JAS) were least anxious, least depressed, and highest in SI-rated Type B. The high-ACT, low-JAS group (i.e., the JAS Type B people who reported being expressive/exhibitionistic) are especially interesting. They look and sound quiet and do not report "hurry-sickness" on the JAS, but their high scores on the ACT suggest an underlying motivation to be more popular. In our study, these high-ACT low-JAS individuals were the most depressed, most anxious, most powerless, most external, and most alienated. They are depressed but JAS Job-involved, perhaps suggesting a lack of accomplishing high goals.

Depression and Anxiety.   Regarding the Hopkins inventory, both the Anxiety scale and the Depression scale were significantly correlated with health status. (This finding is also consistent with the results of the meta-analytic review.) Also, Anxiety and Depression were highly correlated with each other and with the Powerlessness scale of hardiness. This suggests a general depression syndrome. However, Anxiety, Depression, and Powerlessness are all correlated .20 or less with SI Type A, indicating that they are assessing a different aspect of personality.

To find the best combination of predictors of health status, multiple regression analyses were performed. Consistently, only two variables—Anxiety and SI Type A, or Depression and SI Type A—were necessary to produce the maximum predictibility. Controlling for anxiety or depression, SI and health were reliably related. Controlling for SI Type A, the correlations between Anxiety or Depression and health were also reliable. These results suggest that both SI Type A and Depression/Anxiety have independent associations with health status, but that none of the other measures add significant predictive power.

In sum, these two empirical studies attempted to refine our understanding and our assessment of emotional factors in coronary-prone behavior by investigating the relationships among Type A/B classification by the JAS and SI, expressiveness (ACT), emotional aspects of personality, and health. It appears certain that healthy styles of emotional expression do exist.

DISCUSSION

It is clear that personality and expressive factors play some role in the development of coronary heart disease. Those reseachers who claim that such matters involve more "folklore" than fact (Angell, 1985) are simply wrong. We do not yet know, however, the precise nature of coronary-prone behavior nor the exact causal pathways.

Observation of expressive style (both visual and vocal) provides an important level of analysis for understanding personality-to-disease relationships. Emotional expressiveness patterns, although closely tied to biology, are clearly more "psychological" in nature than are their associated hormonal and neurological correlates. At the same time, emotional expressions are conceptually closer to likely disease pathways than are the more abstract and cognitive concepts of hurry-sickness, job-involvement, achievement motivation, hardiness, and so on. When healthy and unhealthy expressive styles are clearly delineated, it will be easier to find the cognitive and temperamental processes that produce them and the physiological dysfunctions associated with them.

This chapter, which summarizes two empirical studies and relevant literature reviews, has shown that the nonverbal expressions observed in the Structured Interview account for a substantial part, possibly even all, of the Type A variance relevant to the prediction of CHD. The SI is a much better predictor of CHD than is the JAS, and expressiveness (ACT) moderates the JAS to CHD link. This weakness of the JAS may explain some failures of prospective research to find a TABP-CHD link (reviewed by Matthews & Haynes, 1986). The JAS should no longer be used in its present form.

It appears that the hard-driving, competitive aspects of the Type A pattern predict CHD but the Job Involvement aspect does not. In addition, nonverbal cue analysis confirms, as many have suspected, that anger and hostility are key elements related to CHD and may be a central aspect of the Type A construct. However, depression, tenseness, and anxiety are also related to CHD without being a part of the Type A construct. All negative emotions cannot be considered part of the "Type A" pattern if the pattern is to have any clear meaning.

The bulk of the evidence analyzed and reviewed in this chapter indicates that emotional distress, whether expressed or inhibited, is related to coronary proneness, but vigor and activity is not. What types of underlying mechanisms might be at work? Two possibilities seem most likely. First, we might postulate a general stress model that involves a person's motivations and self-image on one hand, and abilities and successes on the other. A person who did not succeed as expected might first become frustrated and angry, and might later become anxious and depressed. The time that passed between "anger" and "giving up" would be a function of the individual's resources and the extent of the challenges. Depending on where in the process the person was studied, an investigator might find an association between anger and disease or between depression and disease. This model is similar to Selye's (1976) general "alarm/resistance/exhaustion" model and to Wortman and Brehm's (1975) notions of reactance and learned helplessness (see also Appels, Hoppener, & Mulder, 1987).

A second model would view either anger *or* depression as involved in disease proneness, without the necessity of one following from the other. In fact, the presence of one might be negatively correlated with the likelihood of the other. If this second model is valid, then coronary-prone angry people would generally not be or become depressed, and vice versa. With either model, the actual disease mechanisms could involve excessive catecholamine release with subsequent effects on metabolism and/or suppression of immune system functioning. Such general systemic effects should also be manifested in increased likelihood of other diseases as well (cf. H. S. Friedman & Booth-Kewley, 1987a).

What is the role if any of nonverbal expression itself in the disease process? Are the expressions merely manifestations of unhealthy personality traits such as hostility (cf. Matthews, 1982)? Are the expressions functioning as hostile communications that cut off the person's social support network (cf. Hall, Friedman, & Harris, 1986)? Are the expressions merely the observable evidence of a biological predisposition to disease? Or, are the nonverbal expressions intimately involved in the disease process itself through some feedback mechanism? The answers to these questions have implications for the types of treatment interventions that might prove successful.

A speculative answer to these questions, based on knowledge of expressive style, is as follows. Characteristic modes of emotional responding in the individual are likely biologically determined at birth or formed at a very early age. However, emotional expressive responses are also influenced by the social situation. Furthermore, most nonverbal emotional expressions are innately tied to underlying emotional states but can be somewhat controlled through effort and learning. It is also likely true that most nonverbal emotional expressions play some role in maintaining or modulating the underlying emotions. So, for example, a very shy and unexpressive child probably has a matching nervous system and personality; but this child will learn to "express" more or less as a function of his or her culture and family environment. For example, Protestant, American males learn to be less emotionally expressive. If the shy child grows up to achieve his modest goals or to be stoically resigned to his situation, then this child might become what we have termed a "healthy unexpressive" person. An inherently sociable, competent, and expressive child might grow up to success as a *healthy charismatic*. Trouble would arise if the unexpressive child wanted, for example, to be president, or if the expressive child became excessively competitve, never satisfied with his achievements.

This line of reasoning again points out the tremendous importance of the degree of congruence between a person's self-image and predispositions on the one hand, and the person's social situation—family, job, and culture—on the other. A hard-driving job and a fast-moving culture may be healthy for some people and unhealthy for others. It makes no sense to tell everyone to slow down, to talk more slowly, or to smile more. It may, however, matter a great deal whether people are fulfilled in their lives.

REFERENCES

Angell, M. (1985). Disease as a reflection of the psyche. *The New England Journal of Medicine, 312*, 1570–1572

Antonovsky, A. (1979). *Health, stress and coping.* San Francisco, CA: Jossey–Bass.

Appels, A., Hoppener, P., & Mulder, P. (1987). A questionnaire to assess premonitory symptoms of myocardial infarction. *International Journal of Cardiology, 17*, 15–24.

Booth-Kewley, S., & Friedman, H. S. (1987). Psychological predictors of heart disease: A quantitative review. *Psychological Bulletin, 101*, 343–362.

Chesney, M. A., & Rosenman, R. H. (Eds.) (1985). *Anger and hostility in cardiovascular and behavioral disorders.* New York: Hemisphere.

Cohen, F. (1979). Personality, stress, and the development of illness. In G. C. Stone, F. Cohen, & N. E. Adler (Eds.), *Health Psychology—A handbook* (pp. 77–111). San Francisco: Jossey-Bass.

Cooper, T., Detre, T., & Weiss, S. M. (1981). Coronary-prone behavior and coronary heart disease: A critical review. *Circulation, 63,* 1199–1215.

Cottier, C., Adler, R., Vorkauf, H., Gerber, R., Hefer, T., & Hurney, C. (1983). Pressured pattern or Type A behavior in patients with peripheral arteriovascular disease: Controlled retrospective exploratory study. *Psychosomatic Medicine, 45,* 187–193.

Dembroski, T. M. (1979). Cardiovascular reactivity in Type A coronary-prone subjects. In D. J. Osborne, M. M. Gruneberg, & J. R. Elser (Eds.), *Research in psychology and medicine* (Vol. 1, pp. 168–175) New York: Academic Press.

Dembroski, T. M., Weiss, S., Shields, J., Haynes, S. G., & Feinleib, M. (Eds.) (1978). *Coronary-prone behavior.* New York: Springer–Verlag.

Diamond, E. L. (1982). The role of anger and hostility in essential hypertension and coronary heart disease. *Psychological Bulletin, 92,* 41–433.

Friedman, H. S., & Booth-Kewley, S. (1987a). The "disease-prone personality": A meta-analytic view of the construct. *Amercian Psychologist, 42,* 539–555.

Friedman, H. S., & Booth-Kewley, S. (1987b). Personality, Type A behavior, and coronary heart disease: The role of emotional expression. *Journal of Personality and Social Psychology, 53,* 783–792.

Friedman, H. S., Hall, J. A., & Harris, M. J. (1985). Type A behavior, nonverbal expressive style, and health. *Journal of Personality and Social Psychology, 48,* 1299–1315.

Friedman, H. S., Harris, M. J., & Hall, J. A. (1984). Nonverbal expression of emotion: Healthy charisma or coronary-prone behavior? In C. Van Dyke, L. Temoshok, & L. S. Zegans (Eds.), *Emotions in health and illness: Applications to clinical practice* (pp. 151–165). San Diego, CA: Grune & Stratton.

Friedman, H. S., Prince, L. M., Riggio, R. E., & DiMatteo, M. R. (1980). Understanding and assessing nonverbal expressiveness: The Affective Communication Test. *Journal of Personality and Social Psychology, 39,* 33–351.

Friedman, H. S., & Riggio, R. E. (1981). The effect of individual differences in nonverbal expressiveness on the transmission of emotion. *Journal of Nonverbal Behavior, 6,* 96–104.

Friedman, M., Brown, A. E., & Rosenman, R. H. (1969). Voice analysis test for detection of behavior pattern: Responses of normal men and coronary patients. *Journal of the American Medical Association, 208,* 828–836.

Friedman, M., & Rosenman, R. H. (1960). Overt behavior pattern in coronary disease: Detection of overt behavior pattern A in patients with coronary disease by a new psychophysiological procedure. *Journal of the American Medical Association, 173,* 1320–1325.

Friedman, M., & Rosenman, R. H. (1974). *Type A behavior and your heart.* New York: Knopf.

Hall, J. A., Friedman, H. S., & Harris, M. J. (1986). Nonverbal cues and the Type A behavior pattern. In P. Blanck, R. Buck, & R. Rosenthal (Eds.), *Nonverbal communication in the clinical context.* University Park, PA: Penn State University Press.

Hansson, R. O., Hogan, R., Johnson, J., & Schroeder, D. (1983). Disentangling Type A behavior: The roles of ambition, insensitivity, and anxiety. *Journal of Research in Personality, 17,* 186–197.

Heller, B. W. (1980). *Nonverbal behavior and coronary-prone behavior: Hand movement and the Type A pattern.* Doctoral dissertation, University of California, Davis.

Kasl, S., & Mahl, G. (1965). The relationship of disturbances and hesitations in spontaneous speech to anxiety. *Journal Personality and Social Psychology, 1,* 425–533.

Kobasa, S. C. (1979). Stressful life events, personality, and health: An inquiry into hardiness. *Journal of Personality and Social Psychology, 37,* 1–11.

Kobasa, S. C., Maddi, S. R., & Kahn, S. (1982). Hardiness and health: A prospective study. *Journal of Personality and Social Psychology, 42,* 168–177.

Light, R. J., & Pillemer, D. B. (1984). *Summing up: The science of reviewing research.* Cambridge, MA: Harvard University Press.

Manuck, S. B., Corse, C. D., & Winkelman, P. A. (1979). Behavioral correlates of individual differences in blood pressure activity. *Journal of Psychosomatic Research, 23,* 281–288.

Matthews, K. A. (1982). Psychological perspectives on the Type A behavior pattern. *Psychological Bulletin, 81,* 293–323.

Matthews, K. A., Glass, D. C., Rosenman, R. H., & Bortner, R. W. (1977). Competitive drive, pattern A, and coronary heart disease: A further analysis of some data from the Western Collaborative Group Study. *Journal of Chronic Disease, 30,* 489–498.

Matthews, K. A., & Haynes, S. G. (1986). Type A behavior pattern and coronary disease risk: Update and critical evaluation. *American Journal of Epidemiology, 123,* 923–960.

Osler, W. (1910). The Lumleian lectures on angina pectoris. *Lancet, 2,* 696–700, 839–844, 974–977.

Riggio, R. E., & Friedman, H. S. (1982). The interrelationships of self-monitoring factors, personality traits, and nonverbal social skills. *Journal of Nonverbal Behavior, 7,* 33–45.

Riggio, R. E., & Friedman, H. S. (1983). Individual differences and cues to deception. *Journal of Personality and Social Psychology, 45,* 899–915.

Rosenthal, R. (1984). *Meta-analytic procedures for social research.* Beverly Hills, CA: Sage.

Rosenthal, R., & Rubin, D. B. (1982). A simple, general purpose display of magnitude of experimental effect. *Journal of Educational Psychology, 74,* 166–169.

Scherwitz, L., Graham, L., Grandits, G., Buehler, J., & Billings, J. (1986). Self-involvement and coronary heart disease incidence in the Multiple Risk Factor Intervention Trial. *Psychosomatic Medicine, 48,* 187–199.

Seyle, H. (1976). *The stress of life.* San Francisco: McGraw-Hill.

Spielberger, C. D., Johnson, E. H., Russell, S. F., Crane, R. J., Jacobs, G. A., & Worden, T. J. (1985). The experience and expression of anger: Construction and validation of an anger expression scale. In M. A. Chesney & Rosenman (Eds.), *Anger and hostility in cardiovascular and behavioral disorders* (pp. 5–30). New York: Hemisphere.

Totman, R. (1979). *Social causes of illness.* London: Souvenir Press.

Weitz, S. (1972). Attitude, voice, and behavior: A repressed affect model of interracial interaction. *Journal of Personality and Social Psychology, 24,* 14–21.

Williams, R. B., Haney, T., Lee, K., Kong, Y., Blumenthal, J., & Whalen, R. (1980). Type A behavior, hostility and coronary atherosclerosis. *Psychosomatic Medicine, 42,* 539–549.

Wortman, C. B., & Brehm, J. W. (1975). Responses to uncontrollable outcomes: An integration of reactance theory and the learned helplessness model. *Advances in Experimental Social Psychology, 8,* 277–336.

8

Type A Behavior in the Work Setting: A Review and Some New Data

Daniel C. Ganster
Department of Management
University of Nebraska

Wesley E. Sime
Stress Physiology Laboratory
University of Nebraska

Bronston T. Mayes
Department of Management
California State University—Fullerton

In this chapter our aim is to provide an overview of field research that has examined the Type A behavior pattern in the context of job stress. We have organized the review around a causal model that attempts to link the Type A pattern to sources of job stress. We conclude the review with a discussion of some of our own findings regarding the reactivity of Type A workers to job stress.

JOB STRESS AND CORONARY HEART DISEASE

There exists a considerable body of research suggesting a link between characteristics of the occupational experience and coronary heart disease (CHD) (Cooper & Marshall, 1976; House, 1974). However, we would be hard pressed to cite many empirical studies that demonstrate a convincing *causal* effect of specific work characteristics on disease outcomes. The lack of such hard evidence is in large part a function of practical constraints facing the researcher seeking to show the role of work in the etiology of CHD. One seldom has the opportunity to randomly assign workers to jobs that differ in characteristics that are suspected of causing ill health and to monitor their health for a long enough period for the work to take its toll. Such opportunity is sometimes available to organizational researchers who systematically redesign work environments and evaluate the impact of such interventions. At times, such experiments have been undertaken with some degree of experimental control. However, the outcomes of interest in such studies typically concern productivity, work attitudes, and various indicators of "quality of worklife," but not the development of CHD.

Despite the lack of long-term experimental studies, however, studies showing striking differences in morbidity across occupations (Kasl, 1978) and short-term experiments showing effects of certain job stressors on physiological and neuroendocrine responses (Frankenhaeuser, 1978) point toward a significant role for work in the development of various diseases. Experimental work such as that reported by Frankenhaeuser (1978) and Timio and Gentili (1976), in particular, show that work characterized by short-cycle time tasks, lack of control over pacing, high-attentional demands, and piecework payment leads to elevated levels of excretion of epinephrine, norepinephrine, and cortisol. Frankenhaeuser (1978) has also found that such elevated response levels can persist during off-work hours, which suggests that work experiences can lead to chronic elevations of physiological responsivity.

Type A and Physiological Reactivity

Just why individuals who display the Type A behavior pattern should be more susceptible to CHD is not entirely clear. The most likely mechanism appears to involve a heightened physiological reactivity in Type A's when they encounter situations that involve challenge, demands, and a loss of personal control. Chronic exposure to such evoking situations, and its concomitant chronic evaluation of physiological responsivity, is believed to cause some initial injury to the lining of coronary arteries, making them susceptible sites for atherosclerotic lesions and deposits. Also, chronic physiological arousal is believed to enhance the development of atherosclerotic lesions by increasing blood clotting and mobilizing circulating lipid substances (Williams, Friedman, Glass, Herd, & Schneiderman, 1978). Studies have demonstrated a relationship between Type A and heightened reactivity to certain environmental stimuli (challenge, frustration, demands, threats to control). This reactivity has been shown in cardiovascular variables (such as epinephrine and norepinephrine) (for reviews, see Houston, 1983; Krantz, Glass, Schaeffer, & Davis, 1982).

Type A and Work Stress

The dominant research paradigm for examining the physiological reactivity of Type A's has been the laboratory experiment in which the experimenter exposes Type A and Type B subjects to various eliciting stimuli in a controlled environment and observes their physiological and behavioral responses. It has been mainly in these, relatively short-term, exposures that the hyper-responsivity of Type A's has been observed. What makes the Type A construct potentially interesting to organizational researchers are the implications of this laboratory research when the findings are generalized to the work environment. Indeed, the primary environmental stimuli that have been implicated in eliciting the Type A response pattern—demands, competition, threats to internal control—are ubiquitous in occupational settings. One might hypothesize, then, that Type A's working in such environments are likely to suffer the consequences of a surfeit of chronic autonomic arousal. Moreover, to the extent that Type A behaviors might also lead to greater work accomplishments and career advancement, these behaviors may be reinforced by organizations. Work life, then, might not only provide physiologically arousing stimuli to which Type A's are particularly susceptible, but it might also create the contingencies that shape and reinforce the behavior pattern.

Figure 8.1 contains a structural model relating Type A behavior to disease outcomes. Embedded within this model is a general model of work stress similar to ones implicitly or explicitly invoked in most stress studies. This general model of work stress involves paths c, d, e, and h. In essence, there are presumed to be certain objective work-related stimuli (e.g., long hours, excessive mental and physical demands) that cause elevations in physiological responses such as serum cholesterol levels, epinephrine, and blood pressure. These stimuli are labeled "objective work stressors." Recognizing that one's cognitive appraisal of an environment might cause physiological responses independent of the nature of the objective environment (Lazarus, DeLongis, Folkman, & Gruen, 1985), a class of variables labeled "subjective work stressors" is also included in the model. Objective work environments, then, may have an impact on physiological response either directly (path d) or indirectly (via path c) through their effects on the individual's cognitive appraisal of their situation. Path h, depicting a causal relation between elevated physiological response and disease outcomes, is based on a growing corpus of research that attests to its plausibility (e.g., Williams et al., 1978) and thus is not discussed here. Similarly, the effects of work stressors (paths c, d, and e) are not reviewed in detail here.

The remaining paths in the model address three different causal processes and guide the discussion of the research in this chapter. The first causal process is depicted by paths f and g. These paths denote a moderating effect of Type A on the relationships between work stressors and physiological response. This moderating effect constitutes the hyper-responsivity hypothesis—that is, that Type A's show an exaggerated response (relative to Type B's) to work stressors. A second causal process concerns the eliciting potential of environmental stimuli on the Type A pattern itself. Paths a2 and b2 denote this effect, suggesting that certain stimuli evoke the characteristic behaviors and emotions of the Type A pattern, and that chronic exposure to these environments can actually abet the development of these behaviors into a long-term behavior pattern that generalizes to other work and nonwork situations. Finally, paths a1 and b1 reflect the final causal process—that the Type A pattern has a causal effect on the objective and subjective work environments themselves.

Type A and the Work Environment: Does One Cause the Other?

In Fig. 8.1 the a and b arrows indicate reciprocal causal relationships between

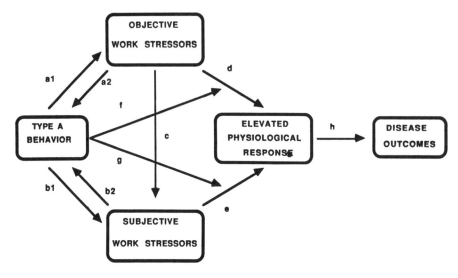

FIG. 8.1.   A causal model of Type A and work stress.

Type A and the objective and subjective work environment. Rosenman and Friedman (1959) originally conceived of Type A persons as having a predisposition
to respond in a characteristic way to certain environmental stimuli; that is, when
faced with demands they respond with a pattern of hostility, impatience, and aggressiveness. Of course, their response can be to stimuli of either an objective
or subjective nature. This model is represented by arrows a2 and b2 in Fig. 8.1.
Much of the laboratory research on Type A has explored the specific stimulus
conditions that activate the Type A pattern. Generalizing to the work setting, we
expect the Type A pattern to be elicited only in the situations that contained such
attributes as challenge, deadlines competition, or loss of control. Indeed, Friedman, St. George, Byers, and Rosenman (1960) noted that researchers studying
the biochemical responses of Type A workers should do so during exposure to
the milieu in which it is likely to be evoked, because it is not a fixed but a phasic
phenomenon. Howard, Cunningham, and Rechnitzer (1977) also proposed a model
in which such job conditions as supervisory responsibility, competitiveness, heavy
workloads, and conflicting demands would elicit Type A behaviors in individuals so disposed.

   In addition to providing the stimulus substrate necessary for evoking the Type
A pattern, work (and cultural) environments can also be instrumental in the long-
term development of the pattern. Margolis, McLeroy, Runyan, and Kaplan (1983),
for example, advocated an ecological approach to Type A, in which interpersonal, institutional, and cultural environments all elicit and strengthen Type A
behavior. From this view, we might hypothesize that individuals working in certain occupations, or under certain organizational conditions (such as reward systems that foster competition), will develop the Type A pattern with time.

Conversely, Type A behavior, itself, could be a factor in determining one's exposure to work stressors, as denoted by arrow a1. As Zyzanski and Jenkins (1970) suggested, Type A's may seek out "those vocational settings where intensive involvement in activity and the consequent rewards of high income, responsibility, and prestige are the pattern" (p. 790). Thus, we might hypothesize that Type A's will select themselves into more stressful occupations. Even within a given occupation, Type A's may redefine their job to increase stress. Laboratory studies, such as that by Burnam, Pennebaker, and Glass (1975), have demonstrated that Type A's, relative to B's, work at a higher capacity even in the absence of deadlines. Finally, Jenkins (1979) has described the Type A as egocentric, self-centered, abrasive, aggressive, and a poor listener. To the extent that such traits characterize Type A's, they may lead to poor interpersonal relationships with superiors, subordinates, and peers, and a reduction in social support.

Even if exposed to the same objective stressors as Type B's, Type A's may appraise their job demands as being more stressful (path b1). Again, support for this perceptual bias hypothesis is provided by laboratory experiments (e.g., Gastrof, 1981). Thus, Type A and work stressors may be causally related through both behavioral and perceptual processes. The research reviewed in the remainder of this section focuses on this causal linkage between the behavior pattern and the job environment.

A number of organizational studies provide relevant, but ambiguous, data regarding the reciprocal relationship between Type A and work stressors. One type of study has examined differences in the prevalence of Type A across occupations or job types. Haynes, Feinleib, and Kannel (1979) found that working women are more apt to display Type A behavior than are housewives. Lawler, Rixse, and Allen (1983), in comparing a sample of employed women and housewives, found that all the employed women were Type A whereas less than half of the housewives were. Furthermore, those unemployed women who wanted to work were more likely to be Type A. These studies suggest that Type A women are more apt to be employed, but whether this represents a higher exposure to stressors rests on the assumption that work outside the home is more stressful than housework.

Other researchers have made occupational comparisons. Caplan, Cobb, French, Harrison, and Pinneau (1975) compared the Type A scores of workers in 23 occupations, using the 9-item Sales questionnaire. High-Type A occupations included physicians, administrative professors, and tool and die workers, whereas low-Type A occupations included assemblers on machine-paced lines, continuous flow monitors, programmers, and accountants. From these data it is difficult to conclude either that Type A's select themselves into inherently stressful occupations or that exposure to stressful occupations leads to Type A behavior. It is extremely difficult, conceptually or empirically, to determine which of these occupations is objectively more stressful. On the one hand, administrative professors and physicians report more hours worked and higher quantitative workload than machine-paced assemblers, programmers, and accountants. On the other hand, the level of somatic health complaints is lower for administrative professors and physicians than it is for machine-paced assemblers, programmers, and accountants (Caplan et al., 1975). The report by Haynes et al. (1979) that Type A is more prevalent among white-collar workers than among blue-collar workers is similarly difficult to interpret in terms of the self-selection hypothesis.

Frost and Wilson (1983) evaluated nursing units as "high stress" or "low stress" based on "a subjective assessment of the physical and/or psychological demands placed on the nurse" (p. 404), and found no difference in the levels of Type A. Huang, Hewson, and Singer (1983) compared samples of university students, police officers, police recruits, and the general population on the basis of Type A scores. They found that both officers and recruits had lower Type A scores than did the general population. Similarly, policemen in the Caplan et al. (1975) survey were relatively low on Type A. Hurrell (1985), however, found that male postal workers on machine-paced jobs were more likely to be Type A than nonpaced workers. Because the level of Type A was uncorrelated with tenure on the job, Hurrell concluded that Type A's likely selected themselves into the more stressful machine-paced jobs. Hurrell's data directly conflict with those from the Caplan et al. (1975) study, in which machine-paced assemblers were less Type A than nonmachine-paced assemblers. In fact, in the Caplan et al. study machine-paced workers had the lowest Type A scores of the 23 occupations studied. Finally, Boyd (1984) examined the Type A scores of small business owners using the Jenkins Activity Survey. Boyd found that 82% of his 368 small business CEO's were classified as Type A's, and that this percentage exceeded those reported for managers in larger firms. Again, however, one must make some assumptions about the inherent stressfulness of being a small business owner if these data are to inform a self-selection hypothesis. In sum, data from occupational comparisons do not convincingly demonstrate that Type A's select themselves into inherently more stressful occupations, nor do they suggest that prolonged exposure to stressful occupations promotes the development of the Type A pattern.

Occupational comparisons of Type A prevalence are difficult to interpret both because of the aforementioned problem of objectively describing the stressfulness of different occupations and because there is likely great individual variability of working conditions within occupations. For these reasons, individual-level studies are apt to be more enlightening regarding the causal relationships between Type A and work stressors. In this vein many investigators have reported relationships between measures of the Type A pattern and various job stressors, although they heavily rely on self-reports. For example, Type A's generally report more workload than do Type B's (Burke & Weir, 1980; Caplan et al., 1975; French & Caplan, 1972; Howard et al., 1977; Ivancevich, Matteson, & Preston, 1982; Keenan & McBain, 1979; Kelly & Houston, 1985; Sales, 1969), although this is not always the case (Chesney & Rosenman, 1980; Orpen, 1982). In addition to workload, Type A's tend to report higher levels of other stressors as well, including supervisory responsibility (Howard et al., 1977), role conflict (Howard et al., 1977; Ivancevich et al., 1982; Kelly & Houston, 1985; Orpen, 1982), and employer expectations (Mettlin, 1976). Two studies found that Type A's reported more control or influence at work (Burke & Weir, 1980; Chesney & Rosenman, 1980), but one study of over 2,000 men (Kittel et al., 1983) found that Type A white-collar workers reported less control over work pacing than did Type B's.

In none of these studies is it possible to determine whether Type A's actually have greater exposure to various stressors (path a1), or whether they tend to cognitively appraise their jobs differently than do B's (path b1). Although some laboratory evidence suggests that Type A's will impose more demands on themselves (Burnam, Pennebaker, & Glass, 1975), and that they tend to prefer more challenging and demanding tasks (Holmes, McGilley, & Houston, 1984), there is no convincing evidence from organizational studies that the objective job demands facing Type A's are really higher than B's. The most nearly objective data, although still supplied by the respondents, indicates that Type A's work longer hours and more overtime hours (Caplan et al., 1975; Howard et al., 1977; Kelly & Houston, 1985) and travel more on the job (Howard et al., 1977). In concluding this section, one can only state that the reciprocal arrows (a and b) in Fig. 8.1 are supported by research in the lab but have little corroborating evidence from the field. Thus, a need clearly exists for field research that examines Type A–B differences in exposure to objective job stressors, particularly those most relevant to the construct (e.g., challenges, competition, etc.).

Are Type A's Hyper-reactive to Work Stressors?

Much of the experimental research comparing the reactivity of Type A's and B's suggests that Type A's have stronger physiological responses to certain stimuli (Houston, 1983; Krantz et al., 1982; Matthews, 1982). Generalizing from these studies, the hyper-responsivity of Type A's should be evident in the context of work stressors also. If A's and B's faced equal occupational demands, A's would show more pronounced physiological and emotional reactions. This general hypothesis is denoted by paths f and g in Fig. 8.1, which posit an interaction between stressors (real or imagined) and physiological response.

Investigators examining the moderating effects of Type A on the relationships between job stressors and outcome variables have almost all focused on the effects of subjective work stressors (path g in Fig. 8.1). Studies specifically testing Type A moderating effects are listed in Table 8.1, which also lists some of the study characteristics.

As noted in Table 8.1, almost all the 10 studies listed report some significant moderating effect of Type A on the relationships between stressors and some measure of psychological or physiological response. Several characteristics of these

TABLE 8.1
Type A Moderator Studies

Study	Sample	Type A Measure	Stressors	Outcomes
Caplan & Jones (1975)	122 Univ. computer users	4 items (Vickers)	Self-report	Psych, HR
Chesney & Rosenman (1980) (1)	145 male mgrs.	SI	Self-report	Psych
(2)	subsample of 76 from above		Self-report (Control)	Psych
Chesney et al. (1981)	384 mgrs.	SI	Self-report	BP
Howard et al. (1986)	217 mgrs.	SI	Self-report	BP, biochemical
Hurrell (1985)	5,518 postal workers	20 items (Thurstone)	Mach. pacing (Objective)	Psych
Kennen & McBain (1979)	90 mgrs.	10 items (Vickers)	Self-report	Job Sat.
Ivancevich et al. (1982) (1)	339 mgrs.	8 items	Self-report	Physio, biochemical
(2)	50 nurses	32 items & SI	Self-report	biochemical
Matteson & Ivancevich (1982)	315 med. techs.	32 items	Self-report	Psych, health
Orpen (1982)	91 mgrs.	12 items	Self-report	Psych, Physios. symptom
Rhodewalt et al. (1984)	49 Univ. Admins.	JAS	Self-report	Psych, Physios. symptom checklist

Note: SI = Structured Interview, JAS = Jenkins Activity Scale.
Physios refers to cardiovascular measures such as heart rate (HR) & blood pressure (PB).
Psych refers to various psychological outcomes, usually anxiety or depression.
Biochemical refers to serum tests (e.g., cholesterol, triglycerides).

studies are worth noting. First, every investigation, except Hurrell (1985), examined work variables that would be classified as "subjective work stressors" in Fig. 8.1; and most of these represent some type of role stress construct such as role conflict, ambiguity, or overload. The general design has been a field survey, and a moderator effect for Type A was inferred if correlations between stressors and outcomes were larger for Type A's than for B's.

Whereas one must be cautious when making inferences from a qualitative review of the literature, it nevertheless is somewhat striking that the only study to fail to find a moderating effect for Type A is that by Hurrell (1985), which is also the only study that examined a work stressor of an objective nature. Hurrell surveyed 5,518 postal workers, 2,803 working on machine-paced letter-sorting jobs, and 2,715 working on unpaced jobs. Reasoning that Type A's are particularly responsive to situations in which they lack personal control, in this case over pacing of their work, Hurrell hypothesized a pacing by Type A interaction, expecting Type A's to show more negative reactions to pacing than Type B's. Whereas pacing was, indeed, found to be stressful, as determined by responses on the Profile of Mood States, Type A's did not respond differently from B's. Although physiological or health outcome measures were not used, the anxiety and depression variables were similar to those employed by others (e.g., Caplan & Jones, 1975; Chesney & Rosenman, 1980). Moreover, the Type A measure used, the Thurstone Activity Scale, is reliable and has shown some convergence with the Structured Interview method (Mayes, Sime, & Ganster, 1984). And, finally, the failure to find an interaction between pacing and Type A in this study cannot be attributed to a lack of statistical power. Perhaps machine pacing is just not the kind of stimulus that evokes the hyper-responsivity of Type A's. However, it seems to have as many of the eliciting characteristics (demands, low personal control) as do the other more commonly assessed stressors (e.g., role conflict and ambiguity).

Many of these Type A moderator studies measured the behavior pattern with paper and pencil measures and not the Structured Interview (SI) method, which shows the strongest relationship with CHD. However, three studies did use the SI, and they all inferred Type A moderating effects (Chesney & Rosenman, 1980; Chesney et al., 1981; Howard, Cunningham, & Rechnitzer, 1986). Chesney and Rosenman (1980) observed the correlations between workload and anxiety and work pressure and anxiety for 145 male managers who were classified as A or B. They found significant correlations for Type A's (A1 on the SI) but not for B's. However, they did not report a test of the difference between the r's of the two samples (nor did they report the r's or the sample sizes of the subgroups). In a further analysis, they gave a measure of control in the workplace to a random subsample of 76 of these managers. Using this scale, the sample was divided into high-, medium-, and low-control groups. Chesney and Rosenman reported that A1s in the low-control group were more anxious than A1s in the high-control group. Type B's, however, reported less anxiety when they were not in control than when they were in control. In a later study by Chesney et al. (1981), 384 salaried workers were administered the Work Environment Scale (WES; Insel & Moos, 1974) and were assessed for Type A with the SI. A series of one-way ANOVAs were performed across groups formed on the basis of Type A and trichotomization of the WES subscales. The authors concluded that there were significant interactions between Type A and three of the WES scales (peer cohesion, physical comfort, and autonomy). Type A's had a lower blood pressure (systolic and diastolic) in the high-peer cohesion groups than in the low-cohesion groups, whereas Type B's showed just the opposite pattern. Similarly, Type A's showed lower blood pressure under conditions of high autonomy, whereas Type B's showed higher blood pressure under high autonomy. Finally, Type B's had a lower systolic blood pressure when they reported high physical comfort than when they did not, whereas Type A's showed no response to comfort.

A final study that used the SI was reported by Howard et al. (1986). Data were obtained from a panel of 217 managers over a 2-year period, including measures of role ambiguity at times 1 and 2, physiological measures at times 1 and 2 (blood pressure, cholesterol, triglycerides, uric acid), and job satisfaction and Type A (by the SI) at time 1. Their central thesis concerned the interaction between job satisfaction and changes in ambiguity (predicting changes in the risk factors); consequently, interactions between Type A and ambiguity were not directly tested. However, the regression coefficient relating change in ambiguity to change in systolic blood pressure was higher for A's than for B's. In fact, whereas more ambiguity was associated with significantly higher blood pressure for A's, it led to significantly lower pressure for B's, suggesting that Type B's are healthier with more role ambiguity.

As a whole these moderator studies support the notion that Type A's and B's respond differently to certain work factors, especially those involving role stresses and control. However, for several reasons it is difficult to conclude that these findings replicate the kinds of physiological hyper-responsivity results of laboratory research. First, all moderator effects reported in the work environment involve self-reported stressors, whereas objective manipulations were assessed in the lab. Second, there seem to be many disordinal interactions in the field studies, particularly among those using the SI; that is, A's differ from B's not only in responding more vigorously, but often their responses are in the opposite direction. The implication of this disordinal type of interaction is that A's and B's may actually thrive in different kinds of job environments. In fact, other writers such as Ivancevich and Matteson (1984) have proposed a person–environment fit model of Type A in the workplace. The difference between such a P–E fit model and the hyper-responsivity model is the proposition that there may be certain job conditions in which Type B's are hyper-responsive relative to Type A's. A fruitful avenue for future research would involve the delineation of the specific stimulus characteristics (e.g., personal control, competitiveness, time pressure, social support) that best fit Type A and B workers. Finally, even those researchers who measured Type A with the SI considered only the overall category scoring. No researchers have yet considered individual components of the construct in the work setting, even though recent evidence suggests that, at least with respect to cardiovascular disease, individual components such as anger-in and hostility are more predictive than overall Type A scores.

New Data from a Multiple Occupation Study

As noted in the review of Type A research in the work-stress domain, many occupational stress researchers have used measures of the Type A pattern other than the SI. Those who have used the SI have generally sampled individuals within a single occupational category (e.g., salaried workers, managers). Occupational comparisons of Type A prevalence have relied on questionnaire measures of the construct. Reviews of the various alternative measurement methodologies for the construct (Chesney & Rosenman, 1980; Matteson & Ivancevich, 1980; Mayes et al., 1984; Sparacino, 1979) have concluded that questionnaire measures of Type A do not converge well with SI-derived measures, and that the SI is the best predictor of CHD and physiological reactivity. Thus, we are reluctant to accord the same weight to findings from questionnaire measures of Type A than to findings produced by the SI, because it cannot be safely assumed that these various measures are all tapping the same construct. Moreover, the SI allows researchers to examine individual components of the Type A pattern. Given recent reports that suggest that certain components of the pattern, such as anger-in and hostility, are more predictive of disease states than the overall pattern (Dembroski, Mac-Dougall, Williams, Haney, & Blumenthal, 1985), it would seem of interest to examine these individual components in occupational research.

In this section we report on some of our data from a multioccupation study of stress and health. In all, data were gathered from almost 700 employees representing 26 occupations as defined by the Dictionary of Occupational Titles (DOT; U.S. Department of Labor, 1977). A variety of assessments were made regarding how these employees viewed various aspects of their jobs with respect to commonly studied work stressors, of various individual characteristics, and of psychological, behavioral, and physiological responses.

Of the total sample, 568 were administered the SI. The interview was conducted in a private room at or near the worksite by one of three interviewers. Two female assistants did most of the interviews under the supervision of one of us (WS) who was trained by Rosenman and Dembroski. All interviews were taperecorded and scored independently by two interviewers. Interscorer agreement was maintained at 90% and inconsistencies between raters were resolved using criteria outlined by Dembroski, MacDougall, and Lushene (1979). Each respondent was classified in a five-category scheme (A1, A2, X, B1, B2) and two-category scheme (A vs. B). From the two-category scheme, 45% of the sample was classified as Type A and 55% as Type B. A total of 156 individuals were classified as either extreme Type A (A1) or extreme Type B (B2). Of these 156 cases at the two extremes, 65% were extreme A's and 35% extreme B's. Analyses reported here that compare A and B categories use data only from these 156 extreme cases. In addition to the category schemes, each employee was rated on a 5-point scale for the speech stylistics of (a) loud and explosive, (b) rapid and accelerating, (c) response latency, (d) verbal competitiveness, and (e) potential for hostility. In addition, the content expressed by the employee was rated for intensity of response on 5-point scales for the categories of (a) competitive drive, (b) hostility, (c) speed, and (d) impatience.

A variety of measures were also taken regarding how employees responded to their job environment. Psychological strain responses were obtained by psychometric measures of anxiety, depression, and somatic complaints. Behavioral strains were indexed by self-reports of smoking and caffeine consumption. Finally, physiological reactivity was assessed by cardiovascular measures and catecholamine excretion measures. Cardiovascular measures included resting heart rate, and systolic and diastolic blood pressure taken during the workday. Values reported here are the average of two assessments. Urine samples were taken at the beginning of work shifts and after approximately 4 hours on the job. Values of epinephrine (EP) and Norepinephrine (NEP) reported here represent the levels excreted during the work shift.

Measures of perceived stress were made by surveying the employees. The survey focused on a number of psychological stressors that had been found to be important predictors of strain in prior occupational stress studies. These measures included the following: (a) workload—the amount of work output that the employee was expected to make; (b) variability—the extent to which the workload varied from low to high in generally unpredictable ways; (c) skill underutilization—the extent to which the employee's skills and abilities were underutilized on his job; (d) responsibility—the extent to which the employee was held responsible for work outcomes without being given an appropriate level of authority; (e) role conflict—the extent to which the employee received conflicting instructions from different individuals regarding how to fulfill his role in the organization; (f) role ambiguity—the extent to which the employee was uncertain of his role requirements and work priorities; and (g) control—the extent to which the employee felt he had control over various aspects of his job and work environment.

In addition to these perceived sources of work stress, the occupations represented in the sample were categorized as high or low stress using data from the DOT. The DOT is a functional occupational classification system. The designation of a job category depends primarily on differences in the nature or function of the work task relative to competing categories. A number of characteristics have been assigned to jobs in this system that were validated in actual job settings. We classified occupations in our sample based on the DOT "stress temperament" characteristic. Jobs classified as stressful under this designation are ones that the DOT asserts as requiring "an adaptability to performing under stress when confronted with emergency, critical, unusual, or dangerous situations; or situations in which working speed and sustained attention are make-or-break aspects of the job.'' The DOT has been shown to be a reliable classification system; however, this classification of occupations into high- or low-stress categories is far from perfect. For one, we are not sure as to the variety of specific job features that were observed by DOT job analysts for them to make the stressfulness classification. Second, any analyses made at the occupational level ignore the likely large variation of stressors across different workers within an occupation. Nevertheless, we made this classification here to provide some kind of objective assessment of the occupational stress faced by each of the employees in the sample. Approximately 56% of the employees in this sample are in the low-stress occupations, whereas 44% are in the high-stress ones. High-stress occupations in our data include the jobs of fire captain and fire fighter, senior estimator, police sergeants and officers, and detectives. Low-stress occupations include administrative secretary, clerk typist, police academy instructor, electronics inspector, welder, electrician, field engineer, and foreman.

Occupational Differences in Type A

The first issue we examined concerned the occupational distribution of Type A scores. Table 8.2 lists the mean Type A component scores in the occupations classified as high versus low stress by the DOT. As is evident in the listing, all mean Type A component scores differ significantly across occupations, except for impatience in interview content. However, component scores are higher in

TABLE 8.2
Mean Type A Component Scores by Occupation

	N = 303 Low Stress	N = 265 High Stress	
Stylistics:			
Loud and explosive speech	3.00	2.72	p < .01[a]
Rapid and accelerating speech	3.17	2.80	p < .01
Short response latency	3.32	2.80	p < .01
Potential for hostility	2.82	2.48	p < .01
Competitiveness	3.14	2.76	p < .01
Content:			
Competitiveness	3.36	3.14	p < .01
Hostility	2.83	2.38	p < .01
Speed	3.22	2.99	p < .01
Impatience	3.25	3.12	n.s.

[a]Significance of difference between occupations.

the *lower* stress occupations. When the distribution of individuals classified as extreme Type A and extreme Type B is examined, we reach the same conclusion. Of the extreme Type A's, 66% work in the low-stress occupations and 34% work in high-stress occupations. Of the extreme Type B's, 42% are in low-stress occupations and 58% are in high-stress occupations. From these data it appears that Type A's show no tendency to select themselves into high-stress occupations. We might add that our data replicate those of Huang et al. (1983) regarding the low Type A prevalence of police officers, even though they used a form of the Bortner scale rather than the SI.

Before dismissing the occupational selection hypothesis, however, one must consider the adequacy of the classification scheme provided by the DOT. At best, we have a very crude classification of high- and low-stress occupations. Tables 8.3 and 8.4 display the mean levels of self-reported work stressors and mean strains, respectively, by occupation. Table 8.3 shows that the convergence of the "objective" classification of the DOT and perceived stressors is somewhat mixed. Occupations classified as high stress by the DOT are higher in self-reported workload variability and lower in experienced control, as expected. However, respondents in the low-stress occupations report more responsibility without authority and more quantitive workload than do those in the high-stress occupations. Table 8.4 shows that there are few observed differences between high- and low-stress occupations on the strain variables. There is, however, a significant (and rather substantial) difference in the amount of caffeine consumed, and a small but significant difference in systolic blood pressure, both differences favoring the high-stress occupations. On the one hand, the mixed convergence of the individual-level data and the occupational classifications illustrates the lack of precision inherent in the occupational classifications. On the other hand, it is highly unlikely that the classifications are so wrong that they could lead to results in terms of Type A distributions that are the opposite of what are expected from the self-selection hypothesis. We can only conclude that the data argue against the hypothesis that Type A's select themselves into inherently high-stress occupations.

TABLE 8.3
Mean Self-Reported Stressors by Occupation

	$N = 293$ High Stress	$N = 371$[a] Low Stress	
Responsibility without authority	2.11	2.36	p < .01
Quantitative overload	3.16	3.38	p < .01
Workload variability	3.20	3.09	p < .05
Role conflict	3.56	3.59	n.s.
Role ambiguity	2.69	2.65	n.s.
Skill underutilization	2.75	2.67	n.s.
Experienced control	2.62	2.78	p < .01

[a]Average N's, sample size varies slightly throughout table from missing data.

TABLE 8.4
Mean Levels of Strains by Occupation

	N = 279 High Stress	N = 356[a] Low Stress	
Anxiety	1.78	1.78	n.s.
Depression	1.86	1.82	n.s.
Amount smoked per day	9.64	10.61	n.s.
Caffeine (cups/day)	7.47	4.85	p < .01
Somatic complaints	1.68	1.67	n.s.
Norepinephrine (μ gms/100 ml urine)	5.77	5.87	n.s.
Epinephrine (μ gms/100 ml urine)	.99	1.11	n.s.
Heart rate (BPM)	71.23	72.45	n.s.
Systolic BP	130.51	128.04	p < .05
Diastolic BP	80.69	80.20	n.s.

[a]Average N's, sample size varies slightly throughout table from missing data.

Effects of Type A Components on Perceived Stress and Strain

Though the evidence does not support the notion that Type A's select themselves into higher stress occupations than do Type B's, they, nevertheless, may experience more stress in their particular work situation. As noted earlier, differences in experienced stress between A's and B's may reflect either real or perceived differences in job demands. Table 8.5 lists correlations between perceived work stressors and components of the Type A pattern. Though more than a third of the relationships are statistically significant, none explain more than 2% of the variance in any perceived stressor. Some pattern to the relationships seems to exist, however, in that the components of a more interpersonal level (competition and hostility) tend to be related to the interpersonal stressors (role conflict, role ambiguity, and responsibility without authority). Those stressors more directly associated with work demands requiring effort and adjustment (workload, work variability) tend to be correlated with Type A components related to behavioral intensity (rapid and accelerating speech, response latency, speed, impatience). When the occupational stress rating from the DOT is used to control for "objective" stress, the partial correlations remain the same as those in Table 8.5. Bearing in mind the imperfect validity of the DOT stress rating, these findings do somewhat suggest that Type A's may be appraising their job demands differently than Type B's. Moreover, these differences in appraisals may depend on the specific components that characterize each of the Type A individuals.

To address the question of whether Type A's experience more strain on the job than do Type B's, correlations were computed between each of the component scores and the strain outcomes. Displayed in Table 8.6, this computation yields few significant correlations, and none of any appreciable size. However,

TABLE 8.5
Correlations Between Type A Components
and Perceived Work Stressors
N = 561

	Role Conflict	Role Ambig.	Skill Underut.	Work Overload	Work Variab.	Respons.	Control
Stylistics:							
Loud & expl.	.02	.02	−.10*	.07	.08*	.04	.07
Rapid & acc.	.04	.01	−.10*	.10*	.12**	−.01	.07
Response ltcy.	.06	.02	−.05	.13**	.11**	.02	.09*
Hostility	.11**	.12**	−.05	.06	.03	.03	.04
Compet.	.11**	.04	−.06	.08*	.11**	.06	.03
Content:							
Compet.	.12**	.02	−.06	.17**	.15**	.09*	.15**
Hostility	.19**	.14**	.01	.06	.00	.15**	−.01
Speed	.10*	.04	−.05	.15**	.15**	.05	.07
Impatience	.08*	.09*	−.05	.15**	.11**	.02	.10*

* p < .05 two-tailed.
** p < .01 two-tailed.

TABLE 8.6
Correlations Between Type A Components
and Strain Variables
N = 561[a]

	Anx.	Dep.	Som Comp.	Smoke	Caff.	EP	NEP	HR	SYS BP	DIAS BP
Stylistics:										
Loud & expl.	-.08	-.03	-.07	-.06	-.05	-.05	-.02	.07	.07	.08
Rapid & Acc.	-.02	.00	.01	-.08	-.09	-.01	.00	-.01	-.03	.05
Response ltcy.	-.03	.00	.00	.00	-.07	.00	.03	.07	.01	.09
Hostility	.00	.02	.01	.10	.05	-.07	.01	.08	.05	.08
Compet.	-.05	-.04	-.06	-.02	-.02	.01	.00	.02	.01	.06
Content:										
Compet.	-.05	-.06	.03	-.05	.01	.03	.01	-.08	-.02	.01
Hostility	.08	.07	.06	.07	.03	-.05	-.01	.01	.00	.05
Speed	.02	.04	.03	-.02	.00	.01	.00	.00	-.02	.01
Impatience	.02	.02	.07	.01	.02	-.04	.03	-.02	-.01	.04

[a]Critical value for r (p < .05 two-tailed) = .08.

the stylistic hostility component does correlate positively with smoking, heart rate, and diastolic blood pressure, although these correlations are very small. A conceptual weakness with this analysis, however, is that these correlations reflect the responsivity of Type A's across the whole range of job-stress conditions. Type A's may show increased strain (or reactivity) only under job conditions characterized by the presence of certain stressors.

Differential Reactivity of Type A's and B's to Work Stressors

A series of analyses was conducted to examine the question: "Do Type A's react more strongly to work stressors than Type B's?" The first analysis examined the potential interactions between each of the component scores and the objective stress rating of the occupation for each of the strain variables. From these 90 analyses (9 component scores by 10 dependent variables), only two significant interactions were detected. Given this less than chance frequency of interactions and the fact that nine multivariate tests yielded no significant results, we are reluctant to make any interpretation of the two interactions detected. Our next analysis consisted of testing the interactions between objective stress (defined by the DOT) and the Type A categorization, using only extreme Type A's and B's. From these nine tests for interactions (taking each strain as a dependent variable), two interactions were found, which involved diastolic blood pressure and EP excretion. These interactions are displayed in Fig. 8.2 and 8.3, and both show a reactivity of Type A's to stressful occupations that is not characteristic of Type

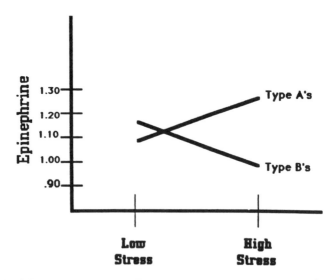

FIG. 8.2.   Interaction between Type A and occupational stress on epinephrine.

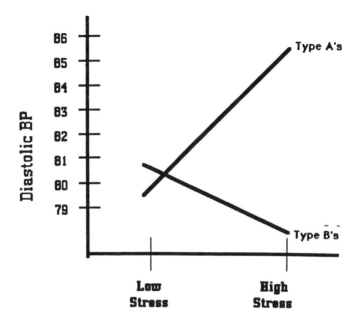

FIG. 8.3.   Interaction between Type A and occupational stress on diastolic blood pressure.

B's. In both interactions, Type A's do not differ from B's on low-stress jobs, but do on high-stress jobs. We again would caution the reader regarding the imprecision of the "objective stress" operationalization employed here. However, this is the first evidence we know of that shows some hyper-reactivity of Type A's to some objective measure of stressful work. In contrast, the only other study that examined the interaction of Type A with an objective stressor (Hurrell, 1985) failed to find evidence for hyper-reactivity. The difference in the findings may well be due to the fact that we compared extreme A's and B's as assessed by the SI, whereas Hurrell relied on the full range of Thurstone Activity scores.

Our final set of analyses focused on the differences in responsivity between A's and B's to perceived work stressors. This analysis consisted of computing correlations between perceived stressors and strains separately for extreme A's and B's. These correlations are reported in Tables 8.7, 8.8, and 8.9 in which only the correlations that were significant for at least one of the Type A groups are included. Note that although some correlations are statistically significant in one Type A group and not in the other, we infer a difference in reactivity only if the two correlations are significantly different from each other. Considering first the psychological strains (Table 8.7), extreme Type A's appear to react more strongly to workload than do extreme Type B's. This reactivity is evident in terms of anxiety and depression. Whereas Type B's are relatively unaffected by work-

TABLE 8.7
Correlations Between Stressors and Psychological
Strains by Type A and B

	Type A's N = 101	Type B's N = 55	
Strain = Anxiety			
Workload	−.24**	.05	$p < .10^a$
Role conflict	.24**	.16	
Role ambiguity	.26**	.28*	
Skill underutil.	.20*	.25	
Strain = Depression			
Workload	−.27**	.11	$p < .01$
Role Ambiguity	.21*	.21	
Skill Underutil.	.15	.26*	
Strain = Somatic Complaints			
Role conflict	.21*	.24*	
Responsibility	.20*	.26*	

[a]Significance of difference between *r*'s.
*p< .05.
**p < .01.

load, Type A's become anxious and depressed under conditions of *low* work-load, rather than high. In terms of physiological reactivity (Table 8.8), when A's and B's differ it is the B's who are more reactive. This difference is evident with respect to heart rate, which is associated with role conflict for B's but not for A's and is associated with skill underutilization only for B's. In the latter case, heart rate is *lower* for B's when they perceive their skills are underutilized. A's and B's also differ with respect to blood pressure responsivity to role conflict. In the case of both systolic and diastolic pressure, B's are more responsive than A's, although their blood pressure is *lower* when they perceive role conflict. B's are also more responsive to role ambiguity than are A's, in this case diastolic blood pressure being associated with high ambiguity. In terms of behavioral strain indicators (Table 8.9), A's tend to smoke more than B's under conditions of role conflict but tend to drink less coffee than B's when they are faced with responsibility without authority. Throughout these correlations there are other instances of apparent differences in reactivity between A's and B's. For example, A's show a rise in NEP secretion under conditions of role ambiguity, and B's show a rise in EP secretion when faced with workload variability. However, the corresponding correlations for A's and B's are not significantly different from each other in these cases.

TABLE 8.8
Correlations Between Stressors and Physiological
Strains by Type A and B

	Type A's N = 101	Type B's N = 55	
Strain = Heart Rate			
Role Conflict	.08	.27*	$p < .05^a$
Skill underutil.	−.02	−.35**	$p < .05$
Strain = Systolic BP			
Workload	.22*	.01	
Role conflict	.16	−.32*	$p < .01$
Responsibility	.11	.30*	
Strain = Diastolic BP			
Role conflict	.12	−.24*	$p < .05$
Role ambiguity	−.09	.30*	$p < .05$
Skill underutil.	.04	.25*	
Strain = Norepinephrine			
Role ambiguity	.25*	.19	
Strain = Epinephrine			
Work variability	.03	.25*	

[a]Significance of difference between *r*'s.
*$p < .05$.
**$p < .01$.

Though differences in reactivity seem to exist between A's and B's, these differences do not all fit neatly into a simple hyper-reactivity model. Type A's appear hyper-reactive on the parameters of epinephrine and diastolic blood pressure when in occupations classified as stressful. However, in a number of instances it is the Type B's who react more strongly to self-reported stressors. For example, in physiological responses B's tend to be more responsive than A's to role conflict and ambiguity. These data may be more consistent with a person–environment fit model of Type A that would hypothesize that a Type A will prefer one environment and a Type B another. At this point, however, it would be difficult to delineate exactly what job characteristics would best fit Type A's. On the one hand, Type A's show more anxiety and depression when they perceive they have little workload (i.e., work underload). On the other hand, Type A's tend to have higher systolic blood pressure when they perceive that their workload is high.

This apparent inconsistency in the psychological and physiological responses of Type A's appears to replicate laboratory findings of the responses of Type A's to challenge (Dembroski, MacDougall, Shields, Petitto, & Lushene, 1978).

Conclusions

Several summary statements can be made concerning what we know of the Type A behavior pattern. The model of Fig. 8.1 summarizes the evidence for each causal process:

1. Support for the moderator hypotheses (paths f and g) is relatively common especially with respect to responses to perceived stressors. Only two studies have examined the differential responsivity of A's and B's to some type of objective work stressor. Although we report some support for this hypothesis in this chapter, Hurrell's (1985) study of machine-paced workers failed to support the hypothesis. In terms of reactions to self-reported stressors, the data do not consistently support a simple hyper-reactivity model.

2. Empirical support for causal relationships between Type A and objective stressors (paths a1 and a2) is very weak. There is no supporting evidence for the hypothesis that Type A's select themselves into more stressful occupations. Furthermore, existing field studies yield little insight as to whether Type A's, through their behavior, partially determine their exposure to stressors (path a1) or whether prolonged exposure to such stressors encourages the development of the pattern (path a2).

3. The evidence is supportive of a relationship between Type A and perceived stressors (paths b1 and b2), although no research has addressed the magnitude of the causal path from Type A (b1, the perceptual bias hypothesis) relative to the path from subjective stressors (path b2).

TABLE 8.9
Correlations Between Stressors and Behavioral
Strains by Type A and B

	Type A's N = 101	Type B's N = 55	
Strain = Smoking			
Role conflict	.18*	−.15	$p < .10^a$
Strain = Caffeine			
Responsibility	−.01	.33**	$p < .05$

[a]Significance of difference between r's.
*$p < .05$.
**$p < .01$.

In addition, researchers have paid little attention to the individual components of the Type A construct in occupational settings. Some of our findings suggest that individual components may be differentially related to the cognitive appraisal of specific sources of work stress. Whether competitive and hostile types may actually create conditions of role conflict and ambiguity or are just more apt to perceive them, we do not know. In our view, researchers should focus their empirical efforts primarily on two objectives: (1) the need to develop measurement methods or experimental methods that allow us to more accurately assess objective sources of stress in the workplace; (2) the need to observe the specific behaviors of Type A's in the workplace—do they take on more tasks, do they exhibit more hostile behavior at work, do they set higher performance goals, do they seek out competitive performance situations, do they generate interpersonal conflict? By focusing on these two objectives we can begin to get a better sense of whether Type A's create or select less healthful environments, or whether they are simply more responsive, psychologically and physiologically, to stressful environments when they encounter them. To the extent that the former process is true, intervention efforts aimed at changing the operant behaviors of Type A's would be recommended. If the later process is true, intervention efforts designed to lower the responsivity of Type A's would be recommended.

To us, the work environment provides a rich setting for examining the ways in which the Type A behavior pattern might lead to disease outcomes. Whereas the laboratory environment offers much more experimental control than the work setting, the field does have its advantages. For practical and ethical reasons experimenters are constrained in creating stressful situations in the lab. In work settings, naturally occurring variance in exposure to stressors is very high. In addition, field studies allow the investigator to assess behavioral and physiological responses of people over a longer period of time than is possible in the lab. Following Matthews' (1982) call to take a more psychological perspective of Type A, work settings represent environments in which there are a wide range of eliciting stimuli for the pattern behaviors, and where differences in the behaviors of Type A's and B's might be more pronounced and easily observed. We see a need for researchers to focus more specifically on these behaviors as they are manifested in the work place.

ACKNOWLEDGMENT

The research reported in this chapter was supported by a grant from the National Institute of Mental Health (1 RO1 MH40368).

REFERENCES

Boyd, D. P. (1984). Type A behavior, financial performance, and organizational growth in small business firms. *Journal of Occupational Psychology, 57,* 137–140.

Burke, R. J., & Weir, T. (1980). The Type A experience: Occupational and life demands, satisfaction and well-being. *Journal of Human Stress*, December, 28–38.

Burnam, M. A., Pennebaker, J. W., & Glass, D. C. (1975). Time consciousness, achievement striving, and the Type A coronary-prone behavior pattern. *Journal of Abnormal Psychology, 84*, 76–79.

Caplan, R. D., Cobb, S., French, J. R. P., Jr., Van Harrison, R., & Pinneau, S. R., Jr. (1975). *Job demands and worker health.* HEW Publication No. (NIOSH) 75–160.

Caplan, R. D., & Jones, K. W. (1975). Effects of workload, role ambiguity, and Type A personality on anxiety, depression, and heart rate. *Journal of Applied Psychology, 60*, 713–719.

Chesney, M. A., & Rosenman, R. H. (1980). Type A behavior in the work setting. In C. L. Cooper & R. Payne (Eds.), *Current concerns in occupational stress* (pp. 187–212). New York: Wiley.

Chesney, M. A., Sevelius, G., Black, G., Ward, M., Swan, G., & Rosenman, R. (1981). Work environment, Type A Behavior, and coronary heart disease risks. *Journal of Occupational Medicine, 23*, 551–555.

Cooper, C. L., & Marshall, J. (1976). Occupational sources of stress: A review of the literature relating to coronary heart disease and mental health. *Journal of Occupational Psychology, 49*, 11–28.

Dembroski, T. M., MacDougall, J. M., & Lushene, R. (1979). Interpersonal interaction and cardiovascular response in Type A subjects and coronary patients. *Journal of Human Stress, 5*, 28–36.

Dembroski, T. M., MacDougall, J. M., Shields, J. L., Pettito, J., & Lushene, R. (1978). Components of the Type A coronary-prone behavior pattern and cardiovascular responses to psychomotor challenge. *Journal of Behavioral Medicine, 1*, 159–176.

Dembroski, T. M., MacDougall, J. M., Williams, R. B., Haney, T. L., & Blumenthal, J. A. (1985). Components of Type A, hostility, and anger-in: Relationship to angiographic findings. *Psychosomatic Medicine, 47*, 219–233.

Frankenhaeuser, M. (1978). Psychoneuroendocrine approaches to the study of emotion as related to stress and coping. In H. E. Howe & R. A. Dienstbier (Eds.), *Nebraska Symposium on Motivation 1978* (pp. 123–161). Lincoln, NE: University of Nebraska Press.

French, J. R. P., Jr., & Caplan, R. D. (1972). Organizational stress and individual strain, In A. J. Marrow (Ed.), *The failure of success.* New York: AMACOM.

Friedman, M., St. George, S., Byers, S. O., & Rosenman, R. H. (1960). Excretion of catecholamines, 17-ketosteroids, 17-hydroxycorticoids and 5-hydroxyindole in men exhibiting a particular behavior pattern (A) associated with high incidence of clinical coronary artery disease. *Journal of Clinical Investigations, 39*, 758–764.

Frost, T. F., & Wilson, H. G. (1983). Effects of locus of control and A–B personality type on job satisfaction within the health care field. *Psychological Reports, 53*, 399–405.

Gastorf, J. W. (1981). Physiologic reaction of Type As to objective and subjective challenge. *Journal of Human Stress, 7*, 16–20.

Haynes, S. G., Feinleib, M., & Kannel, W. B. (1979). *The relationship of psychosocial factors to coronary heart disease in the Framingham study: III. Eight year incidence of coronary heart disease.* Unpublished manuscript. Bethesda, MD: National Heart, Lung, and Blood Institute.

Holmes, D., McGilley, B., & Houston, B. K. (1984). Task-related arousal of Type A and Type B persons: Level of challenge and response specificity. *Journal of Personality and Social Psychology, 46*, 1322–1327.

House, J. (1974). Occupational stress and coronary heart disease: A review and theoretical integration. *Journal of Health and Social Behavior, 15*, 12–27.

Houston, B. K. (1983). Psychophysiological responsivity and the Type A behavior pattern. *Journal of Research in Personality, 17*, 22–39

Howard, J. H., Cunningham, D. A., & Rechnitzer, P. A. (1977). Work patterns associated with Type A behavior: A managerial population. *Human Relations, 30*, 825–836.

Howard, J. H., Cunningham, D. A., & Rechnitzer, P. A. (1986). Role ambiguity, Type A behavior, and job satisfaction: Moderating effects on cardiovascular and biochemical responses associated with coronary risk. *Journal of Applied Psychology, 71*, 95–101.

Huang, M. S., Hewson, V. A., & Singer, A. E. (1983). Type A behavior in the police and general population. *The Journal of Psychology, 115*, 171–175.

Hurrell, J. J., Jr. (1985). Machine-paced work and the Type A behavior pattern. *Journal of Occupational Psychology, 58,* 15–25.

Insel, P. M., & Moos, R. H. (1974). *Work Environment Scales.* Palo Alto, CA: Consulting Psychologists.

Ivancevich, J. M., & Matteson, M. T. (184). A Type A-B person–work environment interaction model for examining occupational stress and consequences. *Human Relations, 37,* 491–513.

Ivancevich, J. M., Matteson, M. T., & Preston, C. (1982). Occupational stress, Type A behavior, and physical well-being. *Academy of Management Journal, 25,* 373–391.

Jenkins, C. D. (1979). The coronary-prone personality. In W. D. Gentry & R. B. Williams (Eds.), *Psychological aspects of myocardial infarction and coronary care.* St. Louis: Mosby.

Kasl, S. V. (1978). Epidemiological contributions to the study of work stress. In C. Cooper & R. Payne (Eds.), *Stress at work* (pp. 1–48). London: Wiley.

Keenan, A., & McBain, G. D. M. (1979). Effects of Type A behavior, intolerance of ambiguity, and locus of control on the relationship between role stress and work-related outcomes. *Journal of Occupational Psychology, 52,* 277–285.

Kelly, K. E., & Houston, B. K. (1985). Type A behavior in employed women: Relation to work, marital, and leisure variables, social support, stress, tension, and health. *Journal of Personality and Social Psychology, 48,* 1067–1079.

Kittel, F., Kornitzer, M., DeBacker, G., Dramaix, M., Sobolski, J., Degré, S., & Denolin, H. (1983). Type A in relation to job stress, social and bioclinical variables: The Belgian physical fitness study. *Journal of Human Stress,* December, 37–45.

Krantz, D. S., Glass, D. C., Schaeffer, M. A., & Davia, J. E. (1982). Behavior patterns and coronary disease: A critical evaluation. In J. T. Cacioppo & R. E. Petty (Eds.), *Perspectives in cardiovascular psychophysiology* (pp. 315–346). New York: Guilford Press.

Lawler, K. A., Rixse, A., & Allen, M. T. (1983). Type A behavior and psychophysiological responses in adult women. *Psychophysiology, 20,* 343–350.

Lazarus, R. S., DeLongis, A., Folkman, S., & Gruen, R. (1985). Stress and adaptational outcomes: The problem of confounded measures. *American Psychologist, 40,* 780–785.

Margolis, L. H., McLeroy, K. R., Runyan, C. W., & Kaplan, B. H. (1983). Type A behavior: An ecological approach. *Journal of Behavioral Medicine, 6,* 245–258.

Matteson, M. T., & Ivancevich, J. M. (1980). The coronary-prone behavior pattern: A review and appraisal. *Social Science and Medicine, 14A,* 337–351.

Matteson, M. T., and Ivancevich, J. M. (1982). Type A and B behavior patterns and self-reported health symptoms and stress: Examining individual and organizational fit. *Journal of Occupational Medicine, 24,* 585–589.

Matthews, K.A. (1982). Psychological perspectives on the Type A behavior pattern. *Psychological Bulletin, 91,* 293–323.

Mayes, B. T., Sime, W. E., & Ganster, D. C. (1984). Convergent validity of Type A behavior pattern scales and their ability to predict physiological responsiveness in a sample of female public employees. *Journal of Behavioral Medicine, 7,* 83–108.

Mettlin, C. (1976). Occupational careers and the prevention of coronary-prone behavior. *Social Science and Medicine, 10,* 367–372.

Orpen, C. (1982). Type A personality as a moderator of the effects of role conflict, role ambiguity, and role overload on individual strain. *Journal of Human Stress,* June, 8–14.

Rhodewalt, F., Hays, R. B., Chemers, M. M., & Wysocki, J. (1984). Type A behavior, perceived stress, and illness: A person–situation analysis. *Personality and Social Psychology Bulletin, 10,* 149–159.

Rosenman, R. H., & Friedman, M. (1959). The possible relationship of the emotions to clinical coronary heart disease. In G. Pincus (Ed.), *Hormones and atherosclerosis.* New York: Academic Press.

Sales, S. M. (169) Differences among individuals in affective, behavioral, biochemical, and physiological responses to variations in work load (Doctoral Dissertation, University of Michigan). *Dissertation Abstracts International, 30,* 2407-B (University Microfilms No. 69-18098).

Shekelle, R. B., Shoenberger, J. A., & Stamler, J. (1976). Correlates of the JAS Type A behavior pattern score. *Journal of Chronic Diseases, 29,* 381–394.

Sparacino, J. (1979). The Type A behavior pattern: A critical assessment. *Journal of Human Stress, 5,* 37–51.

Timio, M., & Gentili, S. (1976). Adrenosympathetic overactivity under conditions of work stress. *British Journal of Preventive Social Medicine, 30,* 262–265.

U.S. Department of Labor, (1977). *Dictionary of Occupational Titles (4th Ed.).* Washington, DC: U.S. Government Printing Office.

Williams, R. B., Friedman, M., Glass, D. C., Herd, J. A., & Schneiderman, N. (1978). Section summary: Mechanisms linking behavioral and pathophysiological processes. In T. M. Dembroski, S. M. Weiss, J. L. Shields, S. J. Haynes, & M. Feinleib (Eds.), *Coronary-prone behavior* (pp. 119–128). New York: Springer–Verlag.

Zyzanski, S. J., & Jenkins, C. D. (1970). Basic dimensions within the coronary-prone behavior pattern. *Journal of Chronic Diseases, 22,* 781–795.

Biological Mechanisms Mediating the Relationship Between Behavior and Coronary Heart Disease

9

Redford B. Williams, Jr., M.D.
Professor of Psychiatry
Associate Professor of Medicine
Director, Behavioral Medicine Research Center
Duke University Medical Center

INTRODUCTION

As indicated by the title of this book and by the content of the other chapters, there is at the present time considerable ferment in the field of research concerned with coronary-prone behavior. As detailed in Dembroski's chapter, in several recent studies globally defined Type A behavior pattern (TABP) failed to predict or correlate with various manifestations of coronary heart disease (CHD). Recent research suggesting that components of the TABP related to hostility, anger, and modes of anger expression are the only aspects that are coronary prone (see chapter by Costa, McCrae, & Dembroski, this volume) has brought some order to the confusion.

Whatever the outcome of the research efforts currently under way to define more precisely the nature of coronary-prone behavior, it appears self-evident that the major, if not the only, final common pathway whereby such behavior is translated into coronary atherosclerosis (CAD) and its various clinical sequellae, must involve relationships between such behavior and the biological processes that underly atherogenesis and/or the precipitation of acute coronary events.

The choice of the term *relationships* in the preceding sentence is made with some care. Whereas most theorizing in this area assumes that coronary-prone behavior *causes* biological alterations that lead to pathogenesis, it is equally possible that certain biological traits that predispose to accelerated atherogenesis (e.g., sympathetic nervous system hyperreactivity) could also exert primary effects on behavior, resulting in behavioral patterns that appear coronary prone.

Although new research efforts are now exploring the biological correlates of various measures of hostility and anger, the recentness of the realization that hostility and anger form the toxic core of the TABP means that most of the extant research on the biological correlates of coronary-prone behavior has focused on the TABP. Therefore, most of the evidence reviewed in this chapter deals with the biological correlates of the TABP. This research remains relevant to the present topic, however, because there is evidence that, albeit weaker than measures of hostility, the TABP does correlate with more severe CAD in younger patients evaluated by coronary angiography (Williams, Barefoot, Haney, Harrell, Blumenthat, Pryor, & Peterson, 1988). Where there are data on biological correlates of hostility measures, these are also described in the following review. As this field evolves, such data will undoubtedly expand.

In general, the research on the biological mechanisms of coronary-prone behavior can be grouped into two general areas. The first deals with studies of biological responses of Type A and B individuals to various behavioral challenges where cognitive interpretation of the situation by the subjects is presumed to play a key role in the observed biological response differences. The second deals with studies of biological responses to physical or pharmacologic stimuli where more basic biological characteristics, presumably not cognitively mediated, appear to be more prominent. The remainder of this chapter reviews these two research areas and the implications of the findings for pathogenic mechanisms. It concludes with a consideration of how knowledge of biologic mechanisms of coronary-prone behavior might be used to develop more effective prevention and treatment approaches.

Note at the outset that this review is not intended to be an exhaustive consideration of the literature on TABP "reactivity" studies. Rather, it focuses primarily on the programmatic research on biobehavioral mechanisms of coronary-prone behavior that has been conducted in my laboratory at Duke over the past 15 years. For a more comprehensive review, the interested reader is referred to excellent surveys recently published by Krantz and Manuck (1984) and Houston (1986).

Cognitively Mediated Biological Responses

Following the original report documenting that TABP is a risk factor for CHD in healthy, middle-aged men (Rosenman et al., 1975), myriad studies have been conducted to evaluate Type A and B subjects' responses to a wide variety of behavioral challenges, often with harassment or incentives to perform at a high rate of speed. For the most part, these studies have found Type A's have larger responses than their Type B counterparts. Of 37 studies reviewed by Krantz and Manuck (1984), increased cardiovascular (usually blood pressure and heart rate, but also including greater EKG T-wave attenuation) and neuroendocrine (mainly catecholamines) responses were found among the Type A subjects in 26 instances. With respect to hostility, Dembroski and his co-workers have reported positive associations between the potential for hostility component assessed during the structured interview (SI) and cardiovascular responses to both cognitive and physical stressors (Dembroski, 1978; Dembroski, MacDougall, Herd & Shields, 1979). In general, these findings have been interpreted as evidence of more pronounced activation of the sympathetic nervous system among Type A's.

Based on the hypothesis (see Williams, 1985) that mental work and sensory intake lead to qualitatively different patterns of cardiovascular and neuroendocrine response, Williams et al. (1982) extended the research on cognitively mediated biologic responses to include measures of skeletal muscle hemodynamics and a broader range of neuroendocrine responses than had previously been studied. The findings confirmed earlier reports of increased catecholamine responses among Type A's and extended them to include other neuroendocrine response parameters as well.

During performance of a mental arithmetic task, young Type A males exhibited a larger skeletal muscle vasodilation and larger increases in plasma norepinephrine, epinephrine, and cortisol than their Type B counterparts. Plasma testosterone response to the mental arithmetic task was not significant, nor were the A's and B's different on this measure. In contrast, during performance of a sensory intake (reaction time) task, there were no A/B differences in plasma catecholamine or cortisol responses, but type A's showed a significantly larger increase in plasma testosterone levels. Suggesting that the plasma testosterone hyperresponsivity of Type A's extends to more naturalistic settings, Zumoff et al. (1984) reported significantly higher levels of urinary testosterone glucuronide excretion among Type A's during the working hours but not during the nocturnal period.

A subsequent (unpublished) study has replicated the finding of significantly larger plasma testosterone responses among Type A's during a different sensory intake (word identification) task. In both the original Williams et al. (1982) study and this latter study, addition of scores on the Cook and Medley (1954) Hostility (Ho) scale from the MMPI resulted in improved discrimination of subjects with large versus small testosterone responses, above that obtained with TABP alone.

If we accept for the moment that certain individuals reliably exhibit increased neuroendocrine responses and sympathetically mediated cardiovascular responses to certain kinds of behavioral challenge, as the research just reviewed suggests for hostile Type A's, then how might such enhanced biologic responses to cognitively mediated challenges play a role in the development of CAD or the precipitation of acute coronary events?

First of all, it is necessary to acknowledge that complete understanding of the etiology and pathogenesis of CAD and the various resulting clinical manifestations of CHD is still not available. Although new developments in molecular biology may eventually modify this view, the most widely held current hypothesis is that the initiation and progression of the atherosclerotic plaque are determined by various factors that contribute to "injury" of the arterial endothelium (Ross & Glomset, 1973). Thus, to the extent that the TABP, hostility, and anger, or other psychological traits are playing a role in atherogenesis, it should be possible to identify biological response characteristics associated with such traits that are at least plausible candidates to contribute to processes associated with endothelial injury.

Returning now to the findings just summarized, it appears eminently plausible that increased sympathetic nervous system responses to cognitive stressors could play an important role in both endothelial injury and the subsequent deposition of lipids in the arterial wall. Well-known effects of catecholamines to mediate both increased cardiovascular activation and lipid mobilization from fat depots could be critical pathways to increased CAD among individuals with high levels of coronary-prone behavior, whatever our ultimate understanding of such behavior turns out to be.

Another biologic system that has received less attention in theorizing about biologic mechanisms of coronary-prone behavior, but one that could be of equal or greater importance than sympathetic nervous system responsivity, is the pituitary–adrenal axis. Chronic corticosteroid excess has been cited by Henry (1983) as having a number of effects that could be important in atherogenesis: (1) increases in serum lipids; (2) increased atherosclerosis in animal models; and (3) increased proportions of dead or injured endothelial cells. Directly implicating corticosteroid excess in human atherogenesis, Kalbak (1972) reported accelerated arteriosclerosis in arthritic patients treated with systemic steroids. In addition, pilots with increased plasma cortisol levels during an oral glucose tolerance test were found to have more severe CAD on coronary angiography (Troxler, Sprague, Albanese, Fuchs, & Thompson, 1977).

Corticosteroid excess could achieve the effects just cited via known actions (reviewed in Williams, 1985) that amplify sympathetic neurotransmitter bioavailability by stimulating activity of catecholamine-synthesizing enzymes and by inhibiting the activity of degradative enzymes that act to terminate the biologic activity of catecholamines. Moreover, once sympathetic nervous system neurotransmitters are released from either the adrenal medulla or sympathetic nerve endings, corticosteroids in humans potentiate alpha adrenergically mediated vascular responses and increase beta adrenergic receptor density on leukocytes.

There is ample reason, therefore, to postulate that the combination of catecholamine and cortisol hyperresponsivity during mental work, as found in the Williams et al. (1982) study, could, if repeated day in and day out among individuals with certain psychological and behavioral characteristics, play a key role in the development of atherosclerosis among those individuals. At the present time, however, the only available direct evidence for such a sequence of events comes from research using animal models. For example, Sprague, Troxler, Peterson, Schmidt, and Young (1980) found increased atherosclerosis in monkeys fed an atherogenic diet when exogenous cortisol was administered.

Although the evidence just reviewed for a causal role for excessive corticosteroid responses in the pathogenesis of CAD is quite plausible, ultimate support for such a role will come only from prospective studies of humans in which subsequent risk of CHD is linked to cortisol responses to laboratory and naturalistic stressors. In the meanwhile, it will be important to continue research using animal models to document the etiologic involvement of corticosteroids in atherogenesis.

Another good candidate for involvement in atherogenesis, and one that has received even less attention than corticosteroids, is the testosterone hyperresponsivity that appears to be present during both the working environment (Zumoff et al., 1984) and performance of laboratory tasks involving vigilance or sensory intake behavior in Type A men (Williams et al., 1982), particularly those with high Ho scores.

It has long been known that prior to puberty males and females have similar levels of HDL cholesterol, the so-called "good" cholesterol, that appears to protect against development of atherosclerosis. At puberty, however, and coinciding with the increased testosterone levels in males, there is a divergence in HDL levels, with females continuing at the same levels and males showing a decline. More direct evidence for the involvement of testosterone excess in atherogenic processes comes from research using the model of endothelial injury artifically induced by catheter stress in the rat aorta. When exogenous testosterone is administered, there is significant acceleration of atherosclerotic plaque development (Uzunova, Ramey, & Ramwell, 1978).

In summary, then, a wide array of experimental evidence suggests that the coronary proneness of the TABP, as well as that of hostility and anger, could be mediated by enhanced neuroendocrine and sympathetic responses during certain cognitively mediated responses to behavioral challenges. If increased levels of cynical mistrust, anger, and antagonistic responding to irritations are key aspects of coronary-prone behavior (see chapters by Dembroski and by Costa, McCrae, & Dembroski, this volume), the following pathophysiologic scenario is easy to visualize.

The cynical mistrusting person is one who feels that others are selfish, mean, and always out to achieve their own ends, no matter what the cost or harm done to others (Cook & Medley, 1954). It would not be surprising, therefore, if such persons spent considerable amounts of their waking hours in a state of vigilant observation of those about them. As suggested by their increased testosterone responses to vigilance tasks in the laboratory (Williams et al., 1982) and in "real life" (Zumoff et al., 1984) such behavior among hostile, Type A persons might be expected to result in chronic elevations of plasma testosterone, which could in turn lead to increased atherogenesis via the mechanisms postulated previously.

As a result of their expectations of bad behavior on the part of others, as well as their being constantly and vigilantly "on guard" to detect such behavior, persons with high levels of cynical mistrust, anger, and antagonistic resonding will be more likely to become angry, thus activating defense or "fight–flight" responses day in and day out. The resulting excessive responses of the sympathetic nervous and pituitary–adrenal systems that appear to occur in Type A persons (e.g., Williams et al., 1982) could also, if repeated chronically, lead to increased rates of atherogenesis via the mechanisms reviewed earlier.

The mechanisms reviewed thus far do not exhaust the possibilities with respect to pathogenic mechanisms of coronary-prone behavior. It is also possible that, rather than contributing to pathogenesis via predisposing to increased cognitively mediated biologic responsses, coronary-prone behavior may itself be a result of more fundmental biologic differences among individuals.

Reponses Mediated by Basic Biologic Characteristics

Several lines of evidence suggest the existence of noncognitively mediated biologic differences between groups with and without certain coronary-prone characteristics; e.g., TABP and hostility. For example, even during general anesthesia, where conscious mediation is unlikely, Type A's are reported to exhibit increased levels of cardiovascular arousal (Krantz & Durel, 1983). A direct role for increased sympathetic nervous system responding in determining at least some Type A characteristics is suggested by observations that administration of beta-blocking drugs results in a diminution of some Type A speech stylistics, as well as potential for hostility (Krantz & Durel, 1983: Schmeider, Friedrich, Neus, & Ruddel, 1982).

In addition to the somewhat more intuitively obvious behavioral effects of sympathetic nervous system activity, the other neuroendocrine response excesses that have been found associated with the TABP and high hostility levels could also contribute to (as well as result from) behavioral characteristics. As noted earlier, the prediction of plasma testosterone responses to vigilance tasks is stronger when a combination of TABP and Ho scores is used than when either measure is used alone. In addition to TABP and high hostility levels causing larger testosterone responses during vigilance tasks, it is possible also to consider the opposite causal sequence: A "hard-wired" (i.e., biologically determined) tendency toward increased testosterone secretion might be the cause of at least some aspects of the TABP and high hostility levels. At the basic behavioral level, Thompson and Wright (1978) report increased persistence and narrowing of attentional focus in rats and chicks to whom exogenous testosterone is administered. Also, increased testosterone levels have been found associated with increased dominance and aggressive behaviors in man (Ehrenkranz, Bliss, & Sheard, 1974; Rose, 1980). Thus, rather than being a result of hostility and the TABP, testosterone excess could be a determinant of increased vigilance and hostility, as well as a mediator of the increased CHD risk that appears associated with high levels of hostility and TABP.

There is also evidence that chronic cortisol excess can affect behavioral states. Central nervous system adrenergic neurones are involved in many aspects of responses to stress (Kopin, 1980). Because corticosteroids are known to modulate the function of brain adrenergic systems (Maas & Mednieks, 1971; Mobley & Sulser, 1980), it is easy to postulate that a hard-wired adrenocortical hyperresponsivity to certain behavioral challenges could also enhance, via effects on brain adrenergic systems, behavioral tendencies associated with TABP and hostility. Clinical observations that found paranoid elements often present in patients suffering from steroid psychosis might be relevant in this regard.

A recent series of studies conducted at Duke provides further evidence for the existence of more basic—i.e., noncognitively mediated—biologic correlates of hostility and the TABP. Rather than expose subjects to behavioral challenges where cognitive mediation could be inferred to play a prominent role in determining biological responses, these studies have used pharmacologic and physical stimuli to evaluate biologic responses in which cognitive factors can be presumed to play a much less central role.

In the first study, Muranaka, Williams, Lane, Anderson, and McCown (1986) evaluated cardiovascular and electrophysiologic responses of young Type A and B men to equipotent (on a ug/kg/min basis) intravenous infusions of the beta-adrenergic agonist isoproterenol (ISO). The key finding in this study was a more prolonged attenuation in EKG T-wave amplitude (TWA) among the Type A men in response to the ISO infusion. As with the testosterone response to vigilance tasks, addition of Ho scores to TABP status resulted in improved discrimination of subjects with good versus poor TWA recovery during ISO infusion.

Other beta-adrenergically mediated responses—i.e., heart rate, forearm blood flow, and plasma cyclic–AMP levels—did not differ between the Type A and B subjects. Therefore, the A/B difference in TWA response to ISO infusion does not appear to result from any A/B differences in beta receptor functions. Another possible mechanism for the more rapid recovery of TWA during ISO infusion among the nonhostile Type B subjects could be a more robust parasympathetic antagonism (Levy, 1977) of sympathetically mediated electrophysiologic effects on the myocardium among Type B's. Supporting this mechanissm, better TWA recovery was significantly correlated with a smaller heart rate increase during ISO infusion in the subjects of this study.

A second study (Muranaka et al. 1987) was undertaken to evaluate further the possibility that Type B subjects are characterized by a more robust parasympathetic response than their Type A counterparts. In this study, application to the forehead of a bag containing water and ice was used to induce a sympathetically mediated vasoconstriction in skeletal muscle and a vagally mediated decrease in heart rate. Both effects, but especially the heart rate slowing, were significantly greater and more prolonged in the Type B subjects.

In addition to their increased cardiovascular and neuroendocrine responses to cognitive tasks, it appears, therefore, that hostile Type A subjects are also characterized by a less robust parasympathetic antagonism of sympathetically mediated cardiac effects than their nonhostile Type B counterparts. It will be important in future research—e.g., using atropine to remove parasympathetic antagonism and acetylcholinesterase inhibitors to increase it—to document more directly the presence of parasympathetic nervous system correlates of TABP and hostility levels.

If confirmed in future research, the findings just reviewed will have important implications for both coronary-prone behavior and biological mechanisms leading to disease. With respect to how a hard-wired tendency toward more robust parsympathetic nervous system activity could play a role in determining behavioral characteristics that we presently describe as coronary-prone, we may need to look no further than Gellhorn's (1967) characterization of the effects on behavior of activation of the brain's "trophotropic" system: decreased arousal and decreased reactivity to environmental stimuli.

With respect to how increased parasympathetic activity could protect nonhostile Type B's against the development of CAD and the precipitation of acute coronary events, there is evidence that monkeys with smaller heart rate responses to threat of capture (which could be mediated by increased parasympathetic activity as well as by increased sympathetic reactivity) develop less severe CAD when fed an atherogenic diet (Manuck, Kaplan & Matthews, 1986). Suggesting a protective role for parasympathetic activity against acute coronary events, vagal nerve stimulation has been found to protect against ventricular fibrillation in dogs in whom the coronary arteries have been ligated (Verrier and Lown, 1981). Finally, from the epidemiologic perspective, a lower casual heart rate, which could be due to increased vagal tone, was among the best predictors of CHD risk in the Seven Countries Study (Keys, 1970).

To summarize, although final answers are not possible regarding the specific biological pathways leading from coronary-prone behavior to atherogenesis and acute coronary events, there are numerous quite plausible candidates for such a role, as reviewed in this chapter. It now appears likely that increased sympathetic and other neuroendocrine responses to behavioral challenges will eventually be shown to be important mediators of increased risk. It is unclear at present, however, whether such responses result from or are themselves the cause of psychological and behavioral characteristics that at present are described as coronary prone.

In addition to increased cognitively mediated biologic responses to behavioral stressors, another qualitatively different kind of biological mediator involves the *inhibitory* action of the parasympathetic nervous system. These two biologic mechanisms of coronary-prone behavior are not mutually exclusive. It is plausible that both excessive sympathetic/neuroendocrine activation and deficient parasympathetic inhibition will ultimately be shown to play complementary roles in the etiology and pathogenesiss of CAD and CHD.

I conclude with a brief consideration of how knowledge of biologic mediators of coronary-prone behavior might help to guide efforts to devise more effective and efficient means of preventing CHD.

Biologic Mediators: Implications for Prevention

First, a disclaimer: As already noted, final knowledge as to the specific biological mediators of CAD and CHD events is not yet firm. Thus, what follows must be considered as a speculative and hopefully heuristic attempt to apply the preliminary findings that have been reviewed in this chapter.

Focus first on those interventions that are already in use, and how they might be working via effects on biobehavioral mechanisms of coronary-prone behavior. Aerobic exercise training is widely used in both primary and secondary prevention programs. One known consequence of increased aerobic fitness is slowing of heart rate that is felt to be mediated by increased vagal tone. This could have a protective effect, especially in hostile Type A's, by virtue of the effects of increased parasympathetic tone to antagonize sympathetic nervous system effects in various organs, including the heart. Direct evidence for such a potentially protective effect of exercise training is provided by the observation of diminished cardiovascular responses to mental arithmetic stress following a program of exercise training (Blumenthal et al., 1987).

A reduction in risk of recurrent CHD events in post-MI patients treated with beta blockers is now accepted by most clinicians, to the extent that virtually all MI patients are treated with beta blockers for a year following their MI. Although prevention of potentially fatal arrhythmias is certainly one means whereby beta blockade can be beneficial in the post-MI period, it is also possible that other benefits may derive from effects of beta blockade to interfere with biologic mechanisms of coronary-prone behavior. Illustrative of such an effect is a recent study (Williams et al. 1984) in which the following effects of pretreatment with propranolol on biologic responses to mental arithmetic in Type A men were observed: decreased heart rate and plasma norepinephrine responses, but *increased* plasma cortisol response. Whereas the former might be beneficial in protecting coronary-prone individuals against biologic consequences of behavioral challenge, the increased cortisol responding could be counterproductive.

Another recent study (Williams, Schanberg, Kuhn, & Lane, 1986) suggests that another pharmacologic agent might be more effective in preventing cortisol responses to stress in coronary-prone individuals. In this study of young Type A men, pretreatment with alprazolam (Xanax, Upjohn) was found to block completely the significant cortisol respone observed when pretreatment was with placebo.

It might be premature to use a combination of propranolol and alprazolam to achieve a more effective preventive approach in post-MI patients, but it is certainly possible at the present time to begin preclinical investigations of the effectiveness of such a combination in preventing CAD, using the animal models described earlier in this chapter. If the results of such investigations are encouraging, it would then be justified to begin clinical trials in specific high-risk patient groups—e.g., CHD patients treated with coronary angioplasty, the goal being to reduce the 30% incidence of restenosis that is presently observed at 6 months following the angioplasty.

Whatever the specific biologic mechanisms of coronary-prone behavior turn out to be, it can scarcely be doubted that a better understanding of such mechanisms will result ultimately in better means of prevention and treatment.

ACKNOWLEDGEMENTS

Preparation of this chapter was supported in part by grants from the National Heart, Lung, and Blood Institute (HL-18589, HL-22740, and HL-36587), the National Institute of Mental Health (MH-70482), and the John D. and Catherine T. MacArthur Foundation.

REFERENCES

Blumenthal, J. A., Emery, C. F., Walsh, M. A., Cox, D. R., Kuhn, C. M., Williams, R. B., & Williams, R. S. (1987 March). *Effects of exercise on the Type A behavior pattern.* Paper presented at annual meeting, American Psychosomatic Society, Philadelphia.

Cook, W., & Medley, D. (1954). Proposed hostility and pharisaic-virtue scales for the MMPI. *Journal of Applied Psychology, 238,* 414–418.

Dembroski, T. M. (1978). Reliability and validity of procedures used to assess coronary-prone behavior. In T. Dembroski, S. Weiss, J. Shields, S. Haynes, & M. Feinleib (Eds.), *Coronary-prone behavior.* New York: Springer–Verlag.

Dembroski, T. M., MacDougall, J. M., Herd, J. A., & Shields, J. L. (1979). Effect of level of challenge on pressor and heart rate responses in Type A and Type B subjects. *Journal of Applied Psychology, 9,* 209–225.

Ehrenkranz, J., Bliss, E., & Sheard, M. H. (1974). Plasma testosterone: Correlation with aggressive behavior and social dominance in man. *Psychosomatic Medicine, 36* (6), 469–475.

Gellhorn, E. (1967). *Principles of autonomic-somatic integrations.* Minneapolis MN: University of Minnesota Press.

Henry, J. P. (1983). Coronary heart disease and arousal of the adrenal cortical axis. In T. M. Dembroski & T. Schmidt (Eds.), *Biobehavioral bases of coronary heart disease.* Basel, Switzerland: Karger.

Houston, B. K. (1986). Psychological variables and cardiovascular and neuro-endocrine reactivity. In K. A. Matthews, S. M. Weiss, T. Detre, T. M. Dembroski, B. Fakner, S. B. Manuck, & R. B. Williams. (Eds), *Handbook of stress, reactivity, and cardiovascular disease,* New York: Wiley.

Kalbak, K. (1972). Incidence of arteriosclerosis in patients with rheumatoid arthritis receiving long-term corticosteroid therapy. *Annals of Rheumatic Disease, 31,* 196–200.

Keys, A. (1970). Coronary heart disease is seven countries: XIII. Multiple variables. *Circulation, 251,* 138–144.

Kopin, I. J. (1980). Catecholamines, adrenal hormones, and stress. In D. J. Krieger & J. C. Hughes (Eds.), *Neuroendocrinology.* New York: Hospital Practice Publishing Co.

Krantz, D. & Durel, L. A. (1983). Psychobiological substrates of the Type A behavior pattern. *Health Psychology, 2,* 393–411.

Krantz, D. S., & Manuck, S. B. (1984). Acute psychophysiologic reactivity and risk of cardiovascular disease: A review and methodologic critique. *Psychological Bulletin, 96,* 435–444.

Levy, M. N. (1977). Parasympathetic control of the heart. In W. C. Randall (Ed.), *Neural regulation of the heart.* New York: Oxford University Press.

Maas, J. W., & Mednieks, M. (1971). Hydrocortisone-mediated increase of norepinephrine uptake by brain slices. *Science, 171,* 178–179.

Manuck, S. B., Kaplan, J. R., & Matthews, K. A. (1986). Behavioral antecedents of coronary heart disease and atherosclerosis. *Atherosclerosis, 6,* 2–14.

Mobley, P. L., & Sulser, F. (1980). Adrenal steroids affect the norepinephrine-sensitive adenylate cyclase system in the rat limbic forebrain. *European Journal of Pharmacology, 65,* 321–323.

Muranaka, M., Lane, J. D., Suarez, E. C., Anderson, N. B., Suzuki, J., & Williams, R. B. (1987, March). *Autonomic balance in Type A and Type B persons: Larger forearm vasoconstriction and vagal reflex in Type B's during cold face stimulus.* Paper presented at annual meeting, American Psychosomatic Society, Philadelphia.

Muranaka, M., Williams, R. B., Lane, J. D., Anderson, N. B., & McCown, N. (1986, March). *T-wave amplitude during catecholamine infusion study: A new approach to biological mechanisms of coronary-prone behavior.* Paper presented at annual meeting, Society of Behavioral Medicine, San Francisco.

Rose, R. M. (1980). Endocrine responses to stressful psychological events. In E. J. Sachar (Ed.), *Advances in psychoneuroendocrinology.* Philadelphia: Saunders.

Rosenman, R. H., Brand, R. J., Jenkins, C. D., Friedman, M., Straus, R., & Wurm, M. (1975). Coronary heart disease in the Western Collaborative Group Study: Final follow-up experience of 8½ years. *Journal of the American Medical Association, 233,* 872–877.

Ross, R., & Glomset, J. (1973). Atherosclerosis and the arterial smooth muscle cell. *Science, 180,* 1332–1339.

Schmeider, R., Friedrich, G., Neus, H., & Ruddel, H. (1982, March). *Effects of beta-blockers on Type A coronary-prone behavior.* Paper presented at annual meeting, American Psychosomatic Society, Denver.

Sprague, E. A., Troxler, R. G., Peterson, D. F., Schmidt, R. E., & Young, J. T. (1980). Effect of cortisol on the development of atherosclerosis in cynomolgus monkeys. In S. S. Kalter (Ed.), *The use of non-human primates in cardiovascular diseses.* Austin, Texas: University of Texas Press.

Thompson, W. R., & Wright, J. S. (1978). ''Persistence'' in rats: Effects of testosterone. *Physiological Psychology, 7,* 291–294.

Troxler, R. G., Sprague, E. A., Albanese, R. A., Fuchs, R., & Thompson, A. J. (1977). The association of elevated plasma cortisol and early atherosclerosis as demonstrated by coronary angiography. *Atherosclerosis, 26,* 151–162.

Uzunova, A. D., Ramey, E. R., & Ramwell, P. W. (1978). Gonadal hormones and pathogenesis of occlusive arterial thrombosis. *American Journal of Physiology, 234,* 454–459.

Verrier, R. L., & Lown, B. (1981). Autonomic nervous system and malignant cardiac arrhythmias. In H. Weiner, M. A. Hofer, & A. J. Stunkard (Eds.), *Brain, behavior, and bodily disease.* New York: Raven Press.

Williams, R. B. (1985). Neuroendocrine response patterns and stress: Biobehavioral mechanisms of disease. In R. B. Williams (Ed.), *Perspectives on behavioral medicine: Neuroendocrine control and behavior.* Orlando, FL: Academic Press.

Williams, R. B., Barefoot J. C., Haney, T. L. & Harrell, F. E., Blumenthal, J. A., Pryor, D. B., & Peterson, B. (1988). *Type A behavior and angiographically documented coronary atherosclerosis in a sample of 2,289 patients. Psychosomatic Medicine,* 50: 139–152.

Williams, R. B., Schanberg, S. M., Kuhn, C. M., & Lane, J. D. (1986, December). *Influence of alprazolam on neuroendocrine and cardiovascular responses to stress in Type A men.* Paper presented at annual meeting, American College of Neuropsychopharmacology, Washington, DC.

Williams, R. B., Schanberg, S. M., Kuhn, C. M., Lane, J. D., Knopes, K., & Shand, D. (1984, December). *Effects of propranolol on cardiovascular and neuroendocrine responses to mental arithmetic in Type A men.* Paper presented at the annual meeting, American College of Neuropsychopharmacology, San Juan.

Williams, R. B., Lane, J. D., Kuhn, C. M., Melosh, W., White, A. D., & Schanberg, S. M. (1982). Type A behavior and elevated physiological and neuroendocrine responses to cognitive tasks. *Science, 218,* 483–485.

Zumoff, B., Rosenfeld, R. S., Friedman, M., Byers, S. O., Rosenman, R. H., & Hellman, L. (1984). Elevated daytime excretion of urinary testosterone glucuronide in men with The Type A behavior pattern. *Psychosomatic Medicine, 46,* 223–225.

10 Coronary Artery Atherosclerosis and Cardiac Response to Stress in Cynomolgus Monkeys

Stephen B. Manuck and Matthew F. Muldoon
University of Pittsburgh

Jay R. Kaplan and Michael R. Adams
Wake Forest University

Joanna M. Polefrone
University of Pittsburgh

A growing literature, much of which is reviewed in this volume, demonstrates that behavioral attributes of individuals contribute to the development and clinical expression of coronary heart disease (CHD) (Manuck, Kaplan, & Matthews, 1986). Associated prominently with an increased risk for CHD in prospective studies of initially healthy individuals is the well-known Type A behavior pattern. Moreover, of the several dispositional characteristics that define Type A behavior, it now appears that a high "potential for hostility" and related aspects of anger and its expression most strongly predict subsequent coronary disease. These epidemiologic associations have also been found, on multivariate analysis, to be independent of concomitant variability in such standard CHD risk factors as hyperlipoproteinemia, hypertension, cigarette smoking, and age. In turn, the latter findings have generated much speculation regarding physiologic mechanisms that may mediate psychosocial influences on coronary disease (Manuck & Krantz, 1986). In this respect, it is widely hypothesized that pronounced or recurrent hemodynamic reactions to behavioral stimuli heighten CHD risk, perhaps by precipitation of acute clinical events or by an exacerbation of coronary artery atherosclerosis. This possibility, as well as potential pathogenic effects associated with patterns of neuroendocrine response to stress (such as an increased release of the catecholamines and corticosteroids) are discussed at length by Dr. Williams in Chapter 9. Our objective in this chapter is to consider, more specifically, individual differences in cardiac responsivity to stress, as these are related to both coronary artery atherosclerosis and social behavior in a nonhuman primate model of atherogenesis. The research summarized here is based on recent studies conducted at the Arteriosclerosis Research Center of Bowman Gray School of Medicine, Wake Forest University. Because we have observed that patterns of association among the variables studied differ as a function of animals' sex, results of investigations involving male and female monkeys are described separately here. Finally, we conclude the chapter with a brief discussion of hemodynamic parameters in atherogenesis; here we propose, as a working hypothesis, that arterial flow disturbances evoked by behavioral stimuli serve to promote endothelial injury, an early stage in the development of atherosclerosis.

HEART RATE REACTIVITY AND ATHEROSCLEROSIS IN MALE CYNOMOLGUS MONKEYS

Our interest in the potential atherogenicity of stress-related cardiovascular reactions stems, in part, from the predominant findings of two current literatures. First, it is frequently observed that Type A individuals respond to diverse psychomotor, cognitive and interpersonal challenges with larger hemodynamic and catecholamine reactions than do their more placid Type B counterparts. (Principal results of these studies are summarized elsewhere in this volume, as well as in several recent reviews [e.g., Houston, 1986; Wright, Contrada, & Glass, 1985].) Secondly, there is preliminary evidence that persons who develop CHD exhibit heightened blood pressure responsivity to laboratory stressors. Most frequently cited in this regard is a 23-year prospective study conducted by Keys and colleagues (Keys, Taylor, Blackburn, Brozek, Anderson, & Somonson, 1971); in this investigation, CHD-free males exhibiting diastolic blood pressure elevations of more than 20 mm Hg during cold immersion (the so-called cold pressor test) were found to be at increased risk for later coronary disease (relative risk = 2.4), including such "hard" endpoints as CHD death and myocardial infarction. The psychophysiologic reactions of persons with and without CHD have also been contrasted in a number of small clinical studies (Corse, Manuck, Cantwell, Giordani, & Matthews, 1982; Dembroski, MacDougall, & Lushene, 1979; Nestel, Verghese, & Lovell, 1967; Shiffer, Hartley, Shulman, & Abelmann, 1976; Sime, Buell, & Eliot, 1980). In most of these investigations, patients with histories of angina pectoris or previous infarction showed larger blood pressure responses to common experimental stressors (e.g., mental arithmetic, Raven's progressive matrices) than patients without CHD or nonpatient controls. Unfortunately, a number of these studies can be faulted on methodological grounds, including failure to control for medications or the presence of other chronic disorders (e.g., essential hypertension) that are known to affect vascular responses. One study seeking to correlate behaviorally induced cardiovascular reactivity with extent of coronary atherosclerosis among patients undergoing diagnostic angiography also failed to demonstrate a significant association (Krantz, Schaeffer, Davia, Dembroski, MacDougall, & Shaffer, 1981). In sum, then, cardiovascular reactions to stress tend to be elevated in persons who have a behavioral predisposition to coronary disease (i.e., Type A individuals) and, in a single prospective investigation, predicted the subsequent development of CHD. While retrospective observations offer suggestive evidence as well, available case-control studies are of mixed quality and report somewhat inconsistent results.

The foregoing findings (particularly the well-replicated Type A-reactivity association) encouraged us to examine, in an animal model, relationships between coronary artery atherosclerosis and individual differences in cardiovascular responsivity to stress. Animal models play an important role in atherosclerosis research, as they afford opportunities for careful control of relevant environmental variables and allow a more exact measurement of lesion extent than is feasible in patient populations. Animal studies also permit the evaluation of atherosclerosis prior to its clinical manifestation, an assessment that for ethical reasons is not possible when studying asymptomatic human beings.

While many mammals develop atherosclerosis of the coronary arteries, only some species exhibit lesions of similar location and morphologic characteristics to those observed in man (Kaplan, Manuck, Clarkson, & Pritchard, 1985). In our own research we have employed the cynomolgus macaque *(Macaca fascicularis)*, an Old World monkey that develops extensive atherosclerosis at proximal portions of the main branch coronary arteries and does so readily when maintained on diets inducing a moderate hyperlipoproteinemia. Cynomolgus monkeys also develop atherosclerosis at other sites having clinical importance for man, as in the carotid arteries, and similarly experience both myocardial infarction and stroke. Perhaps as important as the macaque's susceptibility to atherosclerosis is its rich behavioral repertoire. The social organizations of Old World monkeys, in general, subsume a variety of inter-individual relationships based on patterns of affiliative and competitive interaction (Lancaster, 1975). When living in groups, macaques form stable hierarchies of social dominance based on the abilities of each monkey to defeat other group members in antagonistic encounters: "dominant" monkeys are those animals most likely to succeed and "subordinates" are those most likely to submit to competitors in such interactions. Many prominent features of primate behavior—social status, competition, aggression, affiliation—therefore reflect significant dimensions of human social behavior as well. Moreover, certain behavioral attributes of monkeys (e.g., competitiveness, aggression) are descriptively analogous to those which appear to heighten risk for coronary artery disease in man.

Our observations regarding individual differences in physiologic responsivity to stress were made on two sets of experimental animals, one consisting of 26 adult male monkeys and the other 21 adult females (Manuck, Kaplan, & Clarkson, 1983, 1985). These animals were derived from two ongoing investigations examining effects of a disrupted social environment and animals' social status on coronary artery atherosclerosis. Our interest in cardiovascular reactivity developed near the completion of these studies and, hence, the "reactivity" assessments described below were made on only a single occasion shortly before sacrifice of the animals. For this reason the findings presented here are essentially retrospective.

First, it should be noted that as part of the experiments from which these monkeys were drawn, all animals were housed under one of two social "conditions." In one condition (designated "unstable"), monkeys lived in small, generally five-animal social groups, the memberships of which were reorganized on a regular basis. Redistribution of animals among the affected social groups occurred at 1- to 3-month intervals and in a manner ensuring that each monkey would be placed with either three or four new animals on every reorganization. Monkeys assigned to the alternate (or control) condition lived in comparably sized groups that retained their original memberships over the course of the investigation; these groups were designated the "stable" social condition. Our use of periodic group reorganization as a "naturalistic" social challenge was based on the observation that, in macaques, status relationships among members of an established social grouping are perturbed by the appearance of unfamiliar monkeys. Abrupt changes in group membership tend to intensify antagonistic interactions between monkeys (as seen, for instance, in increased rates of aggressive behavior) as animals seek to reestablish generalized hierarchical associations and affiliative coalitions (Bernstein, Gordon, & Rose, 1974). It was our general hypothesis that monkeys housed in the unstable social groups would develop exacerbated coronary atherosclerosis relative to animals assigned to the stable social condition.

Our experiment involving male cynomolgus monkeys was of 22 months' duration, and that involving females, 30 months. Throughout these investigations, all animals were fed a moderately atherogenic diet having a cholesterol and fat composition similar to that consumed by urban, North American men. Routine measurements were made of animals' serum lipid concentrations (total serum cholesterol; HDL cholesterol), blood pressure, fasting glucose concentration, ponderosity and behavior. The latter measurements involved frequent evaluations of the aggressive, submissive, affiliative and nonsocial behaviors of each monkey. Also assessed was the social status, or dominance ranking, of the individual animals, as determined from the observed outcomes of each monkey's aggressive interactions with all other members of the same social group. Monkeys ranked either first or second in their respective groups across the majority of evaluations made over the course of the study (i.e., animals of consistently high rank) are designated "dominant" monkeys; the remaining, lower ranked animals are identified as "subordinates."

At the time of necropsy, the animals' coronary arteries were dissected from the heart. Five tissue blocks each were cut perpendicularly to the long axis of the left anterior descending, left circumflex and right coronary arteries, and sections from each block were stained for subsequent evaluation. Atherosclerosis was assessed by a standard morphometric technique, in which the area of each arterial cross-section occupied by intima and/or intimal lesion (i.e., the area between the internal elastic lamina and lumen of the artery) is measured. The mean intimal area of all arterial sections was taken as an index of the animal's coronary artery atherosclerosis.

Before describing the procedures used to assess animals' psychophysiologic reactivity, it will be helpful to summarize effects of our psychosocial manipulation and of social dominance on coronary artery atherosclerosis. We defer discussion of the experiment employing females until later and present here only those findings that derive from our study of males. In this investigation (Kaplan, Manuck, Clarkson, Lusso, & Taub, 1982), neither the social condition to which monkeys had been assigned (unstable, stable) nor animals' social status (dominant, subordinate) independently influenced lesion development. However, there was a signficant interaction between these two variables ($p < 0.04$); in particular, dominant monkeys exhibited greater atherosclerosis than did subordinates, but only if they were housed in unstable social groups. The "unstable" dominants also had significantly more atherosclerosis than dominant monkeys assigned to the stable social condition, and again, there was no effect of social status on atherosclerosis in the stable groups. Importantly, this interaction could not be attributed to corresponding group differences in serum lipids, blood pressure, ponderosity or fasting glucose concentration. Thus, animals that successfully maintained positions of social dominance exhibited exacerbated atherosclerosis when fed a cholesterol-containing diet, but did so only if also subjected to a periodically disrupted social environment.

Next we summarize the relationship between atherosclerosis and individual differences in cardiac responsivity to stress in the same experimental animals. Due to the commercial availability of instrumentation for EKG radiotelemetry, we selected heart rate as our parameter of interest for this evaluation. While the study would be more informative had we collected other cardiovascular variables (e.g., blood pressure) as well as blood samples for concomitant neuroendocrine assessments, we are yet unable to obtain such data without recourse to obtrusive procedures (e.g., tethering) that arouse the animal and preclude detection of meaningful baseline values (Adams, Kaplan, Manuck, Uberseder, & Larkin, in press). Following attachment of portable EKG telemetry units, however, we are able to secure good measurements of heart rate under both resting and stressed conditions.

Animals' baseline heart rates in this study were recorded during an interval of relative quiet, when no personnel were present or visible to the monkeys. Heart rate measurements under stress were obtained at the same time on a subsequent day and involved the presentation of a standardized challenge, during which a large "monkey glove" was displayed by the experimenter prominently and threateningly before the target animals. This maneuver was conducted in a stylized manner mimicking encounters typically preceding the capture and physical handling of animals. The stimulus evoked a mean heart rate acceleration, across all monkeys, of 91 beats per minute (bpm). That this response was largely attributable to the threatening qualities of the experimenter's display, rather than to his presence alone, is indicated by a much smaller increase in heart rate (16 bpm) in recordings taken on a third occasion, at which time the experimenter simply paraded, without glove, before the animals.

We wished to address three questions with these data. First, do cynomolgus monkeys exhibit individual differences in the magnitude of their heart rate responsivity to our behavioral stimulus? If so, we wanted next to determine whether severity of atherosclerosis, as seen on necropsy, would be greatest among those animals that had shown the largest cardiac reactivity. Our final question concerned the possible covariation of individual differences in heart rate reactivity with the behavioral attributes of these animals. With respect to our first question, the monkeys did show great variability of heart rate response. In reaction to the behavioral challenge, a fourth of these animals exhibited heart rate elevations that were more than 100% above baseline values; in contrast, the stress-period heart rates of roughly another quarter of the monkeys rose less than 50% over baseline measurements. Subsequent observations involving other groups of cynomolgus monkeys indicate that, as in man, differences in the heart rate responses of cynomolgus monkeys are reproducible on retesting and generalize to other conditions of measurement.

In regard to atherosclerosis, we compared the intimal area measurements of monkeys representing clearly differentiated groups of ''high'' and ''low'' heart rate reactive animals. These two groups were comprised of monkeys falling within the upper and lower 30% of the overall distribution of heart rate reactions, when expressed as baseline-adjusted (or residualized) change scores. The stress-period heart rates of ''high'' and ''low'' reactors differed by about 35 bpm ($\bar{X}$s = 236 and 199 bpm, respectively; $p < 0.001$), whereas corresponding baseline values for the two groups were nearly the same ($\bar{X}$s = 126 and 123 bpm; N.S.). Interestingly, the heart rates of ''high'' and ''low'' reactors differed significantly not only in response to deliberate challenge (threatened capture), but also on exposure to the more benign manipulation involving the experimenter's mere appearance in the area where monkeys were housed ($\bar{X}$s = 170 and 118 bpm; $p < 0.01$). Note, too, that heart rates rose above baseline under the latter conditions among the high reactors alone, suggesting that for these animals the ''threshold'' of behavioral stimulation required to evoke a significant cardiac response may be lower as well, relative to low heart rate reactive monkeys.

Supporting our hypothesis that the more reactive animals would show a greater severity of coronary artery atherosclerosis, ''high'' heart rate reactors had twice the intimal lesion seen among their ''low'' reactive counterparts ($p < 0.04$). This difference in the atherosclerosis of ''high'' and ''low'' heart rate reactors could not be accounted for by concomitant group differences in animals' systolic and diastolic blood pressures, or in their total serum cholesterol or HDL cholesterol concentrations. While in comparison to the ''low'' heart rate reactors, ''high'' reactive animals did have a slightly higher ratio of total-to-HDL cholesterol, this difference only approached statistical significance ($p = 0.10$). ''High'' heart rate reactors were of somewhat greater ponderosity, however, and had significantly greater heart weights (both in absolute weight and when calculated in proportion to body weight) than did the ''low'' heart rate reactive animals (p's < 0.05). The latter finding suggests that a greater heart rate reactivity may be associated with alterations in cardiac morphology, as well as coronary artery atherosclerosis.

Of the various social behaviors recorded over the 22-month experimental period, rates of contact aggression (e.g., slapping, grabbing) of the "high" reactive animals were found to be significantly greater than among "low" heart rate reactors ($p < 0.02$). Milder forms of aggression (e.g., stare threats, passive displacement) were unrelated to heart rate reactivity, as were indexes of affiliative behavior. Recall that in the experiment from which these animals were drawn, the socially dominant animals housed in unstable social groups developed more extensive atherosclerosis than either subordinate animals or dominants assigned to the stable social condition (Kaplan et al., 1982). Interestingly, "unstable" dominants were *not* disproportionately represented among our "high" heart rate reactive animals, and social dominance *per se* (i.e., irrespective of conditions of housing) covaried only weakly (and nonsignificantly) with heart rate reactivity. Coincidentally, social status in this experiment was not well predicted by an animal's propensity to initiate aggressive enounters—socially dominant monkeys tended simply to be those animals which, aggressive or not, were least likely to submit to other group members when engaged in an antagonistic interaction.

Hence, aggressiveness was associated with a heightened cardiac responsivity to our laboratory stressor, and this reactivity was, in turn, related to the atherosclerosis seen in these experimental animals. That aggressiveness was not also related to animals' social status suggests that the interactive influences of dominance and social instability on atherosclerosis (as described above) may have been mediated by factors other than those associated with an elevated heart rate reactivity. It is our hypothesis, however, that cardiovascular reactions to stress and/or their various autonomic and neuroendocrine correlates underlie each of these behavior-atherosclerosis relationships, but that in the two instances such responses may have been variably influenced by intrinsic and extrinsic (e.g., environmental) factors. Some animals (e.g., "high" heart rate reactors), for instance, may possess an intrinsic hyperresponsivity, the expression of which is independent of the nature of eliciting stimuli. Recall in this regard that the "high" reactors responded more strongly than their "low" heart rate reactive counterparts to both the experimental challenge (threatened capture) and a more trivial stimulus involving only the experimenter's presence near the animals. It is conceivable, too, that this highly generalized, intrinsic hyperresponsivity has a significant behavioral correlate, which in this model may be related to the animal's aggressive potential.

The second possibility (relating to extrinsic factors) is that animals having a less generalized propensity to experience large heart rate reactions may still exhibit pronounced or repeated cardiac responses if faced with sufficiently stressful events in their social environments. The likelihood that a particular type of social challenge will evoke such responses may vary, in turn, with differences in animals' behavioral characteristics. We have noted previously, for example, that the heart rates of freely-moving cynomolgus monkeys fluctuate greatly as a function of varying proximity and physical contact with other animals, and that during the initial formation of new social groupings the magnitude of these fluctuations is substantially larger in dominant than in subordinate monkeys (Manuck, Kaplan, & Clarkson, 1986). While interpretation of this status-dependent influence of proximity and affiliation on heart rate is still unclear, it is arguable that behavioral demands experienced during periods of group formation are greatest among the more dominant monkeys; after all, it is the social preeminence of these animals that must be defended against newcomers in competitive interactions. The potential impact of such environmentally-elicited cardiac responses would vary, of course, with the frequency of an animal's exposure to new social groupings. In our experiment, periodic reorganization of group memberships *defined* the unstable social condition and our principal finding, that dominant monkeys in this condition developed the most extensive coronary artery atherosclerosis, is consistent with the foregoing argument. Hence, some monkeys (e.g., "high" heart rate reactors) may be susceptible to development of atherosclerosis due to an intrinsic hyperresponsivity to behavioral stimuli, whereas others may be at increased risk owing to frequent cardiovascular responses evoked by an exceptionally stressful social environment.[1]

HEART RATE REACTIVITY AND ATHEROSCLEROSIS IN FEMALE CYNOMOLGUS MONKEYS

The findings described above are all derived from data collections involving male cynomolgus monkeys. Of growing interest in the study of coronary disease, however, is the relative protection against CHD accorded women during their reproductive years. Overall, the development of clinically manifest coronary disease in Western societies is delayed by roughly 10–15 years in women, relative to men (e.g., Hazzard, 1986; Lerner & Kannel, 1985; Stout, 1982). Because the established risk factors for CHD, such as hyperlipoproteinemia, hypertension, and cigarette smoking, appear to be similar in males and females (Eaker & Castelli, 1987; Lerner & Kannel, 1985; Johansson, Vedin, & Wilhelmson, 1983), it is conceivable that the prevalence of these factors simply differs between men and women in a manner commensurate with the observed sex differential in coronary disease. In their premenopausal years, women do tend to have more favorable

---

[1]The notion that social dominance in an unstable environment heightens risk for atherosclerosis through consequent hemodynamic adjustments (or associated aspects of sympathetic nervous system arousal) is supported by findings of a second experiment, again involving male cynomolgus monkeys (Kaplan, Manuck, Adams, Weingand, & Clarkson, 1987). In this study, we observed that the chronic administration of a beta-adrenoreceptor blocking agent, propranalol HC1, to animals that were fed a cholesterol-containing diet and housed in unstable social groups inhibited coronary artery atherogenesis, but did so only among socially dominant monkeys. Notably, propranolol did not differentially influence the resting (or casual) heart rates or blood pressures of treated dominant and subordinate monkeys. In the absence of such differences, we believe it reasonable to hypothesize that the status-selective antiatherogenic effects of beta-blockade were due, in part, to a dampening of animals' cardiovascular reactions to the behavioral challenges evoked by a disrupted social environment—responses that are seen in greatest magnitude (as previously noted) among the more highly competitive, dominant monkeys.

risk profiles, at least with respect to blood pressure and hypertension (McGill & Stern, 1979; Rowland & Roberts, 1982), serum lipid concentrations (Hazzard, 1986), and cigarette smoking (Lerner & Kannel, 1985; Wingard, Suarez, & Bartett-Connor, 1983). Yet despite these associations, several studies indicate that the varying prevalence of such risk factors among men and women cannot account adequately for sex differences in the incidence of CHD (Kuller, Mei-lhan, & Costello, 1984). Results of one population-based study demonstrate, for instance, that age, plasma cholesterol, blood pressure, smoking, education, marital status, fasting plasma glucose, and obesity accounted for only one-half of the relative risk for CHD seen in men, compared to women (Wingard et al., 1983). These findings, and results of other similar studies (Friedman, Dales, & Ury, 1979; Johnson, 1977; Wingard, 1982), suggest that "female protection" against coronary disease remains largely unexplained by the most commonly examined risk factors.

It is therefore probable that the delayed expression of coronary disease in women arises from other, as yet inadequately studied, risk variables. Not surprisingly, many investigators have proposed that the presence of ovarian hormones, especially estrogen, contribute in some measure to female protection. There is indirect support for the hypothesis that ovarian function underlies gender differences in coronary disease, and that among women, quality of ovarian function may contribute to risk for CHD. Some, though not all, investigations demonstrate an increase in coronary risk with either natural or surgical menopause, for instance, and particularly when menopause or bilateral oophorectomy is experienced at an early age (Bengtsson, 1973; Colditz, Willett, Stampfer, Roksner, Speizer, & Hennekens, 1987; Gordon, Kannel, Hjortland, & McNamara, 1978; Kannel, Hjortland, McNamara, & Gordon, 1976; Oliver, 1974; Parrish, Carr, Hall, & King, 1967; Ritterband, Jaffe, Densen, Magagna, & Reed, 1963; Rosenberg, Hennekens, Rosner, Belanger, Rothman, & Speizer, 1981; Sznaj-derman & Oliver, 1963; Talbott, Kuller, Perper, & Murphy, 1981; Wuest, Dry, & Edward, 1953).

Because coronary artery atherosclerosis arises over the course of decades (rather than months or years), it is unlikely that the coronary artery disease that develops postmenopausally, even if accelerated, is fully responsible for the clinical events seen among older women. Rather, if ovarian function is responsible, in part, for female protection against coronary disease, the delayed incidence of CHD in women is likely to be attributable to the protracted influence of ovarian function (presumably, of the reproductive hormones) prior to menopause. If so, chronic differences in premenopausal ovarian function might, in turn, contribute to variability among women in the early progression of coronary artery disease. Such modulation of female protection would be expected to vary with the quality of reproductive function—for instance, with persistent deficiencies of reproductive hormone concentrations due to chronic ovarian dysfunction or, conversely, with recurrently elevated levels of these same hormones due to multiple pregnancies. While studies of parity as a coronary risk factor yield inconsistent results (e.g.,

Beard, Fuster, & Annegers, 1984; Bengtsson, 1973; Winkelstein & Rekate, 1964; Kannel et al., 1976; Mann, Doll, Thorogood, Vessey, & Waters, 1976; Mann, Vessey, Thorogood, & Doll, 1975; Restreppo, Guzman, Eggen, & Strong, 1972; Oliver, 1974; Talbott, Kuller, Detre, & Perper, 1977), data indicating a heightened incidence of spontaneous abortions or stillbirths among women with CHD (Bengtsson, 1973; Winkelstein & Rekate, 1964; Winkelstein, Stenchever, & Lilienfeld, 1965) suggest the probable need for more sensitive indicators of ovarian function in epidemiologic investigations. Interestingly, in one recent study of females under 55 years of age (LaVecchia, Decarli, Franceschi, Gentile, Negri, & Parazzini, 1987), women with lifelong histories of menstrual irregularity were found to have a twofold increased risk for acute myocardial infarction, even after multivariate adjustment for the concomitant influences of such factors as hypertension, hyperlipoproteinemia, smoking, diabetes, and family history of CHD.

Of more direct relevance to the present topic, there is evidence that females exhibit less appreciable cardiovascular and catecholamine responses to stress then do males (Frankenhaeuser, 1983; Manuck & Polefrone, 1987; Stoney, Davis, & Matthews, 1987). The extent to which gender differences in psychophysiologic reactivity are attributable to biological sex, or alternatively, to psychological factors such as sex-role orientation, remains unclear. However, insofar as behaviorally elicited cardiovascular and neuroendocrine reactions may contribute to coronary risk, it is reasonable to speculate that an attenuated responsivity to stress in women (of whatever origin) accounts for some portion of female protection against coronary disease. There is some evidence, too, that cardiovascular reactivity is itself influenced by ovarian function. The small (and admittedly somewhat contradictory) literature addressing this question suggests that elevated concentrations of the reproductive hormones inhibit stress-related cardiovascular reactions, while impairment of ovarian function (e.g., by oophorectomy or natural menopause) is associated with an enhanced responsivity to behavioral stimuli. For a more detailed discussion of these studies, the reader is referred to recently published reviews by ourselves and others (Manuck & Polefrone, 1987; Stoney et al., 1987). Finally, the apparent influences of gender and ovarian function on psychophysiologic reactivity prompted us to examine how individual differences in heart rate responsivity might be related to coronary artery atherosclerosis and social behavior among female cynomolgus monkeys.

First, it should be noted that the coronary atherosclerosis of females of this species is less extensive than that seen among comparably treated males (Hamm, Kaplan, Clarkson, & Bullock, 1983), as it is in human populations, when these animals are fed cholesterol-containing diets. In addition, loss of ovarian function by surgical ovariectomy abolishes this relative protection (Adams, Kaplan, Clarkson, & Koritnik, 1985), while serial pregnancy—a persistent hyperestrogenic state—further retards coronary atherogenesis relative to reproductively intact females that do not become pregnant (Adams, Kaplan, Clarkson, & Koritnik, in press). As noted previously, the female monkeys on whom we have collected heart rate observations were drawn from an experimental study in which animals were housed, like the males previously described, in either periodically reorganized or stable social groups (Kaplan, Adams, Clarkson, & Koritnik, 1984). Regarding behavioral influences on atherogenesis, females assigned to the unstable and stable social conditions did not differ in extent of intimal lesion, nor was there an interaction between the conditions of housing and animals' social status. Irrespective of social condition, however, socially subordinate females developed significantly greater coronary artery atherosclerosis than did dominants. Indeed, lesions seen among subordinate females were of equal severity to those of male controls. Of potential importance, subordinate monkeys also evidenced some degree of ovarian dysfunction, as indicated by luteal phase progesterone deficiencies and a high frequency of anovulatory menstrual cycles over the course of the experiment. It appears, then, that impairment of ovarian function in this species, whether experimentally produced (i.e., by ovariectomy) or occurring as a correlate of social subordination among reproductively intact individuals, compromises the female monkey's ordinary protection against coronary artery atherosclerosis.

With respect to heart rate measurements, we recorded telemetered EKGs under both baseline and stressed conditions, as in males. Here, our laboratory challenge elicited an average heart rate acceleration of somewhat lesser magnitude than in males. However, it is noteworthy that among females having a high percentage of anovulatory menstrual cycles ($>30\%$) heart rate changes between the baseline and stress periods were quite similar to those of males ($\bar{X}\Delta = 86$ and 91 bpm, respectively; N.S.). The attenuated heart rate reactivity of females in general, then, was largely attributable to animals having normal ovarian function ($\bar{X}\Delta = 68$ bpm; $p < .01$, relative to males.

To examine the relationship between heart rate reactivity and atherosclerosis, we again calculated baseline-adjusted change scores and selected the ends of the resulting distribution of values (here, the upper and lower 33%) for comparison. Replicating our previous finding in males, "high" heart rate reactive females were found to have nearly twice the coronary artery atherosclerosis of their less responsive counterparts ($p < 0.03$). The findings in females were similar to those for males in a number of other respects as well, though some interesting differences also emerged. Again, for instance, "high" and "low" heart rate reactors did not differ in systolic and diastolic blood pressure or in their total serum cholesterol or HDL cholesterol concentrations. Among males, there was a weak and nonsignificant difference in the ratio of total-to-HDL cholesterol between "high" and "low" reactors; this difference was apparent in females as well, and here more closely approached statistical significance ($p < 0.07$). The heart weights of "high" heart rate reactive females (calculated in ratio to animals' body weights) were also significantly greater than among "low" reactors, as in males. This finding is especially noteworthy as the "high" reactive females were less ponderous and of lower body weight than "low" heart rate reactors, a pattern exactly opposite that observed in male monkeys.

From preceding comments, it is not surprising that the "high" heart rate reactors showed some evidence of ovarian dysfunction, including lower luteal phase peak progesterone concentrations ($p < 0.05$) and somewhat fewer ovulatory menstrual cycles ($p < 0.09$), compared to "low" reactive animals. In behavioral observations, "high" heart rate reactors were found to be less aggressive than their "low" reactive counterparts ($p < 0.05$)—a reversal of the association observed in males, but consistent with overall relationships between behavior and atherosclerosis seen here and in other experiments involving female cynomolgus monkeys (Hamm et al., 1983; Kaplan et al., 1984). Social dominance *per se*, however, did not differ significantly between groups. Finally, like males, observations relating to animals' affiliative behaviors (e.g., grooming) also failed to discriminate "high" and "low" heart rate reactive monkeys.

ENDOTHELIAL INJURY, HEMODYNAMIC FACTORS AND ATHEROSCLEROSIS

The findings described here offer preliminary evidence that a heightened cardiac responsivity to stress may be implicated in atherogenesis and potentially mediate associations between psychosocial factors and the development of coronary artery disease. To recapitulate, we have observed that among monkeys consuming moderately atherogenic diets, those animals that show the largest heart rate reactions to a standarized behavioral challenge also exhibit, on necropsy, the most extensive coronary artery atherosclerosis. Additionally, we have found this association in studies of both male and female cynomolgus monkeys. The relationship between heart rate reactivity and atherosclerosis appears to be independent of concomitant variablility in animals' blood pressures and serum lipid concentrations, with one exception: the ratio of total-to-HDL cholesterol is somewhat greater in high, relative to low, heart rate reactive monkeys. In females, too, chronic ovarian endocrine deficiencies tend to be associated with an increased heart rate reactivity and more severe coronary artery atherosclerosis. Finally, animals' social behavior, and in particular aggression, is correlated with heart rate responsivity in both males and females. The directionality of this relationship varies as a function of gender, though, as heart rate reactions to our laboratory challenge covary positively with aggressiveness in males and negatively in females.

We noted earlier that our findings in relation to atherosclerosis are basically retrospective, in as much as heart rate evaluations were made only near the completion of the experiments from which study animals were drawn. However, we do not believe that differences in the stress-related heart rates of "high" and "low" reactive monkeys were themselves a consequence of the different amounts of intimal lesion observed in these animals. In recordings made on other groups of cynomolgus monkeys fed either an atherogenic or prudent diet, for instance, we found no differences in the magnitude of heart rate response to our laboratory stressor; these groups also differed greatly in extent of atherosclerosis, but due only to dietary manipulation (Manuck et al., 1983).

If an elevated heart rate responsivity to behavioral stimuli is related to the development of coronary artery atherosclerosis, what is the nature of this association? Conceivably, heart rate is only a marker or correlate of other pathogenic processes which more directly influence lesion development. For instance, impairment of ovarian function results in a loss of female protection against coronary atherosclerosis in cynomolgus monkeys, and in our data ovarian endocrine deficiencies among reproductively intact females were associated with both exacerbated atherosclerosis and increased heart rate reactivity. While the elevated heart rates seen under stress in these animals may be a consequence of their ovarian dysfunction, that dysfunction nonetheless may potentiate atherogenesis for reasons unrelated to an accelerated heart rate. Of course, this explanation would not account for the similar relationship between heart rate reactivity and atherosclerosis seen in male cynomolgus monkeys.

A second possibility is that aspects of a more general elevation in sympathetic-adrenomedullary activity (e.g., increased levels of circulating catecholamines) promote atherogenesis, either directly or via influences on other pathogenic factors, such as platelet aggregation and lipid metabolism (Herd, 1983; Schneiderman, 1987). The latter mechanism might be especially relevant here, as the ratio of total-to-HDL cholesterol tended to be greatest among "high" heart rate reactive monkeys. Indeed, there is much evidence that emotional arousal, or stress, elevates levels of free fatty acids, triglycerides and cholesterol (Dimsdale & Herd, 1982). Dimsdale, Herd, and Hartley (1983) have demonstrated, as well, that a persistent pharmacologic elevation of epinephrine at physiologic levels in cynomolgus monkeys produces a significant increase in plasma cholesterol concentrations. In our own data, we have employed covariance techniques to examine whether variability in the ratio of total-to-HDL cholesterol among female monkeys (where this ratio differed most strongly between "high" and "low" reactors) could account for the overall relationship observed between heart rate responsivity and coronary artery atherosclerosis. This analysis revealed that, after adjustment for differences in the total-to-HDL ratio, there still existed a significant reactivity-atherosclerosis association. Parenthetically, serum lipids have also failed to explain behavioral influences on atherogenesis in all other investigations we have conducted using cynomolgus monkeys (Hamm et al., 1983; Kaplan et al., 1982; Kaplan, Manuck, Clarkson, Lusso, Taub, & Miller, 1983; Kaplan et al., 1987).

One other, perhaps obvious pathogenetic hypothesis is that arterial lesions result from the acute hemodynamic disturbances accompanying sympathetic nervous system responses to stress. When in the natural history of atherosclerosis such perturbations might influence lesion development most appreciably is unclear, but it is likely that hemodynamic factors, if important, contribute in some measure to initial endothelial damage (Clarkson, Manuck, & Kaplan, 1986). In this regard, there is much agreement that the beginnings of the atherosclerotic process occur when some form of "injury" is sustained by the arterial endothelium (Ross, 1981; Schwartz, Gajdusek, & Shelden, 1981). Resulting disruption of the normal functioning of the endothelium as a thromboresistant barrier with limited permeability to macromolecules, such as lipoproteins, is the initial step in athero-genesis, leading to subsequent lipid accumulation, platelet aggregation, and smooth muscle cell replication (potentiated by platelet derived growth factor) (Davies, 1986; Schwartz, Campbell, & Campbell, 1986). Evidence that naturally occur-ring injury may be capable of initiating such a sequence of events is provided, in part, by the observations that mechanical damage to the endothelium induces alterations in cellular morphology, increased proliferation and turnover rates of endothelial cells, increased permeability of the endothelium to macromolecules, secretion of smooth muscle mitogens, and increased adhesion of platelets (Hauden-schild, Prescott, & Chobanian, 1980; Chobanian, Prescott, & Haudenschild, 1980; Crane & Dutta, 1963; Schwartz & Benditt, 1977; Still & Dennison, 1974; Dewey, Bussolari, Gimbrone, & Davies, 1981; Duncan, Cornfield, & Buck, 1962; Chien et al. 1981).

Moreover, evidence that behavioral factors may promote endothelial injury, at least in the aorta, has been provided in studies of laboratory rats. Gordon, Guyton, and Karnovsky (1981) observed that physical restraint and electric tail shock caused structural changes in the arterial intima, accompanied by suben-dothelial accumulation of mononuclear leukocytes. In a second study, reported by Hirsch, Maksem, and Gagen (1984), experimental animals were subjected to physical restraint and, together with unstressed controls, infused with tritiated thymidine (a label that is taken up preferentially by the nuclei of actively replicating cells). Subsequent autoradiographic evaluation showed endothelial cell replica-tion rates in the aortic intimas of experimental rats to be five times greater than among control animals. It is noteworthy that the restraint manipulation also elicited a signficant hemodynamic response, reflected in elevations in heart rate and blood pressure. Treatment of similarly stressed rats with propranolol both attenuated animals' cardiovascular reactions to the behavioral stimulus and resulted in cell replication rates comparable to those of autonomically intact, unstressed controls. These results demonstrate a quite rapid turn over of endothelial cells in response to stress and suggest that this effect may be due to the cardiovascular adjustments associated with sympathetic nervous system activation.

Hemodynamic parameters are often invoked as contributing factors in athero-genesis (including the induction of endothelial injury), in part, because ather-osclerosis tends to be distributed focally, occurring primarily within large arteries and in close proximity to bifurcations or bends in vessels. Blood flow at such sites is more turbulent than along straight, unbranching vessels, where laminar flow generally predominates; the latter is characterized by high velocity flow at the center of the lumen and very low velocity near the endothelial surface. Depar-tures from laminar flow are accentuated at birfurcations or bends, but also occur with alterations in vessel caliber and with dynamic changes in blood velocity (Bur-ton, 1972; Friedman, O'Brien, & Ehrich, 1975). With the disruption of laminar flow, a variety of flow disturbances are observed, including areas of high and low shear stress, boundary layer separation, and axial stream impingement (Spence, 1987). One notable effect of nonlaminar flow is the increased conversion of potential, or pressure, energy to kinetic energy, which is transferred (as heat and vibration) to the vessel wall (Burton, 1972). Although there is some controversy regarding the specific aspects of turbulent flow that contribute most significantly to atherogenesis, it is nonetheless widely hypothesized that such disturbances—which again, are especially prominent at branch points or turns in the artery—promote endothelial damage and help to explain the regional distribution of subsequent atherosclerotic lesions. It follows, then, that any factor potentiating disruption of laminar flow might, in turn, predispose to atherosclerosis.[2]

Turbulence can be roughly predicted by calculation of the "Reynolds number":

$$\mathrm{Re} \ = \ \frac{V \, D \, d}{u} \,,$$

where V represents blood velocity, D the diameter of the vessel, d the density and u the viscosity of the blood. For any given system, there exists a value defining the limits of laminar flow, above which turbulence develops. From this equation, it can be seen that large arteries are prone to turbulence both because of high velocity flow and due to their large diameter. It is important to note that numerous factors characterizing mammalian circulation, such as the rheological properties of blood, elasticity of the vessels and the pulsatile nature of blood flow, make the investigation of hemodynamics considerably more complex than usual studies of fluid dynamics—where model systems typically employ straight, rigid tubes and are predicated on a constant flow. For example, pulsatile flow promotes turbulence, and the more rapid the oscillatory flow the greater the turbulence produced (Yellin, 1966). The rapidly alternating acceleration and deceleration of blood velocity associated with an elevated heart rate, then, might be expected to foster flow disturbances.

That accelerated heart rate may represent an important predisposing hemodynamic factor in atherogenesis, particularly at arterial sites subject to abrupt changes in the direction and strength of pulsatile blood flow (e.g., carotid bifurcation, proximal portions of the coronary arteries) was recently proposed by Beere, Glagov, and Zarins (1984). In testing this hypothesis, these investigators contrasted the coronary artery atherosclerosis of groups of cholesterol-fed cynomolgus monkeys that differed significantly in heart rate. Relatively lower heart rates in this experiment were either naturally occurring or induced by sino-atrial node ablation; all non-ablated animals were sham-operated to control for surgical procedure. Monkeys having the lower postoperative heart rates developed less than half the coronary atherosclerosis of animals with more elevated heart rates. In

---

[2]Areas of low shear stress are characterized by stagnant flow, which may promote platelet adherence and thereby potentiate thrombogenesis (Jorgensen, Packham, Rowsell, & Mustard, 1972; Hugh & Fox, 1970). Note also that the expanding athersclerotic plaque itself, as it protudes increasingly into the lumen of the artery, provides a further stimulus for disruption of laminar flow and development of turbulence.

addition, the "high" and "low" heart rate groups did not differ in blood pressure, serum cholesterol, triglycerides, or body weight.

We have also examined the relationship of differences in heart rate to coronary artery atherosclerosis (Kaplan, Manuck, & Clarkson, 1987). Here, "high" and "low" heart rates were defined by "casual" measurements obtained over 22 months in a subset ($n = 15$) of the male cynomolgus monkeys described earlier in this chapter. These heart rate evaluations were derived from a variety of sources, including radiotelemetry and calculations made from EKG tracings recorded periodically under anesthesia. The mean heart rates of the "high" and "low" groups were 159 and 133 bpm, respectively ($p < 0.005$). As in the study of Beere et al. (1984), our "high" heart rate animals were found, on necropsy, to have developed more than twice the coronary atherosclerosis of monkeys exhibiting lower casual heart rates ($p = 0.01$). In our study, though, animals with "high" and "low" heart rates differed in their HDL cholesterol concentrations and there was some association between casual heart rate measurements and heart rate responsivity to our laboratory stressor. The difference in coronary artery atherosclerosis between "high" and "low" heart rate animals, however, retained statistical significance ($p < 0.05$) after covariance adjustment for the concomitant variability in both HDL cholesterol and heart rate reactivity.

An interesting observation derived from the equation for calculation of the Reynold's number is that blood pressure is not directly related to turbulence, but only indirectly so through its influence on blood velocity. This relationship has led Spence (1987) to hypothesize that the atherogenicity of hypertension is attributable to elevations in blood velocity and associated flow disturbances, and not to blood pressure *per se*. Both in experimental observations on rhesus monkeys and in clinical studies of patients with carotid stenosis, Spence and colleagues (Spence, Pesout, & Melmon, 1977; Spence, 1983) demonstrated that different antihypertensive agents have varying effects on arterial flow disturbances. For instance, abnormal high velocity flow patterns (turbulence, vortex formation) were reduced with propranolol, but increased with the peripheral vasodilator, hydralazine, when compared to baseline measurements. Moreover, in a study of cholesterol-fed, hypertensive rabbits, Spence, Perkins, Kline, Adams, & Haust (1984) found that propranolol more effectively retarded aortic atherogenesis than did hydralazine—despite the fact that cholesterol concentrations were higher among propranolol-treated animals and blood pressure was more effectively lowered by hydralazine. While unknown metabolic differences between drugs might account for these findings, the greater protection against atherosclerosis accorded animals treated with a beta-antagonist that reduces blood velocity and ameliorates flow disturbances is at least consistent with a hemodynamic hypothesis.

The foregoing observations lead us to propose, as a working hypothesis, that behaviorally elicited cardiac responses of large magnitude and frequent occurrence promote coronary artery atherogenesis. The mechanism implicated may be of a hemodynamic nature and involve the generation of arterial flow disturbances. Such disturbances, in turn, may cause injury to the arterial endothelium at sites of predilection for lesion development. That behavioral stressors (and associated arousal of the sympathetic nervous system) can cause endothelial damage is demonstrated in the experimental studies of Gordon et al. (1983) and Hirsch et al. (1984). The sequelae of endothelial injury may include an intimal accumulation of lipoproteins, release of mitogenic substances from the damaged endothelium or by activated platelets, and intimal smooth muscle cell proliferation (Davies, 1986; Schwartz et al., 1986).

In the work described in this chapter, we have focused on heart rate responsivity to stress, in part, because heart rate can be measured both noninvasively and unobtrusively. However, the recent findings of Beere et al. (1984) and ourselves (Kaplan et al., 1987) regarding associations between casual heart rate and atherosclerosis suggest that this parameter of cardiovascular function has special relevance for atherosclerosis and that an increased heart rate alone may promote lesion development. From this perspective, exacerbated atherosclerosis due to behaviorally evoked elevations in heart rate—either among intrinsically "hyperresponsive" individuals or when occurring on exposure to excessive environmental challenges—may be conceived as an aspect of a wider association existing between heart rate and atherogenesis. More general considerations, and in particular the work by Spence previously cited, suggest that other hemodynamic factors (e.g., increased velocity) that cause departures from laminar flow and promote arterial flow disturbances may also potentiate lesion development; if elicited by behavioral stimuli, such disturbances might similarly mediate associations between psychosocial variables and atherosclerosis.

ACKNOWLEDGMENTS

Research summarized in this chapter and preparation of the manuscript were supported, in part, by grants from the National Institutes of Health (HL 14164, HL 26561, HL 35221) and a grant from R. J. Reynolds Industries, Inc.

REFERENCES

Adams, M. R., Kaplan, J. R., Clarkson, T. B., & Koritnik, D. R. (1985). Ovariectomy, social status, and atherosclerosis in cynomolgus monkeys. *Arteriosclerosis, 5*, 192–200.

Adams, M. R., Kaplan, J. R., Clarkson, T. B., & Koritnik, D. R. (in press). Pregnancy associated protection against coronary artery atherosclerosis in cynomolgus macaques. *Circulation.*

Adams, M. R., Kaplan, J. R., Manuck, S. B., Uberseder, B., & Larkin, K. T. (in press). Persistent sympathetic nervous system arousal associated with tethering in cynomolgus macaques. *Laboratory Animal Science.*

Beard, M. C., Fuster, V., & Annegers, F. (1984). Reproductive history in women with coronary heart disease. *American Journal of Epidemiology, 120*, 108–114.

Beere, P. A., Glagov, S., & Zarins, C. K. (1984). Retarding effect of lowered heart rate on coronary atherosclerosis. *Science, 226*, 180–182.

Bengtsson, C. (1973). Ischemic heart disease in women. *Acta Medica Scandinavica, 549,* 1–128.

Bernstein, I. S., Gordon, T. P., & Rose, R. M. (1974). Aggression and social controls in rhesus monkey *(Macaca mulatta)* groups revealed in group formation studies. *Folia Primatologica, 21,* 81–107.

Burton, A. C. (1972). *Physiology and biophysics of the circulation.* Chicago: Year Book Medical Publishers.

Chien, S., Lee, M. M., Laufer, L. S., Handley, D. A., Weinbaum, S., Caro, C. G., & Usami, S. (1981). Effects of oscillatory mechanical disturbances on macromolecular uptake by arterial wall. *Arteriosclerosis, 1,* 321–336.

Chobanian, A. V., Prescott, M. F., & Haudenschild, C. C. (1980). Aortic endothelial changes during the development and reversal of experimental hypertension. In A. M. Gotto, L. C. Smith, & B. Allen (Eds.), *Atherosclerosis* (Vol. 5, pp. 699–702). New York: Springer-Verlag.

Clarkson, T. B., Manuck, S. B., & Kaplan, J. R. (1986). Potential role of cardiovascular reactivity in atherogenesis. In K. A. Matthews, S. M. Weiss, T. Detre, T. Dembroski, B. Falkner, S. M. Manuck, & R. B. Williams (Eds.), *Handbook of stress, reactivity and cardiovascular disease* (pp. 35–47). New York: Wiley-Interscience.

Colditz, G. A., Willett, W. C., Stampfer, M. J., Roksner, B., Speizer, J. E., & Hennekens, C. H. (1987). Menopause and the risk of coronary heart disease in women. *New England Journal of Medicine, 316,* 1106–1110.

Corse, C. D., Manuck, S. B., Cantwell, J. D., Giordani, B., & Matthews, K. A. (1982). Coronary-prone behavior pattern and cardiovascular response in persons with and without coronary heart disease. *Psychosomatic Medicine, 44,* 449–459.

Crane, W. A., & Dutta, L. P. (1963). The utilization of tritiated thymidine for deoxyribonucleic acid synthesis by the lesions of experimental hypertension in rats. *Journal of Pathology and Bacteriology, 86,* 83–97.

Davies, P. F. (1986). Vascular cell interactions with special reference to the pathogenesis of atherosclerosis. *Laboratory Investigation, 55,* 5–24.

Dembroski, T. M., MacDougall, J. M., & Lushene, R. (1979). Interpersonal interaction and cardiovascular response in type A subjects and coronary patients. *Journal of Human Stress, 5,* 28–36.

Dewey, C. F., Bussolari, S. R., Gimbrone, M. A., & Davies, P. F. (1981). The dynamic response of vascular endothelial cells to fluid shear stress. *Journal of Biomechanical Engineering, 103,* 177–185.

Dimsdale, J. E., & Herd, J. A. (1982). Variability in plasma lipids in response to emotional arousal. *Psychosomatic Medicine, 44,* 413–430.

Dimsdale, J. E., Herd, J. A., & Hartley, L. (1983). Epinephrine mediated increases in plasma cholesterol. *Psychosomatic Medicine, 45,* 227–232.

Duncan, L. E., Cornfield, J., & Buck, K. (1962). The effect of blood pressure on the passage of labeled plasma albumin into canine aortic wall. *Journal of Clinical Investigation, 41,* 1537–1545.

Eaker, E. D., & Castelli, W. P. (1987). Coronary heart disease and its risk factors among women in the Framingham Study. In E. D. Eaker, B. Packard, N. K. Wenger, T. B. Clarkson, (H. A. Tyroler (Eds.), *Coronary heart disease in women* (pp. 122–130). New York: Haymarket-Doyma.

Frankenhaeuser, M. (1983). The sympathetic-adrenal and pituitary-adrenal response to challenge: Comparison between the sexes. In T. M. Dembroski, T. H. Schmidt, & G. Blumchen (Eds.), *Biobehavioral bases of coronary artery disease* (pp. 91–100). New York: Karger.

Friedman, G. D., Dales, L. G., & Ury, H. K. (1979). Mortality in middle-aged smokers and nonsmokers. *New England Journal of Medicine, 300,* 213–217.

Friedman, M. H., O'Brien, V., & Ehrich, L. W. (1975). Calculations of pulsatile flow through a branch. *Circulation Research, 36,* 277–284.

Gordon, D., Guyton, J. R., & Karnovsky, M. J. (1981). Intimal alterations in rat aorta induced by stressful stimuli. *Laboratory Investigation, 45,* 14–27.

Gordon, T., Kannel, W. B., Hjortland, M. C. & McNamara, P. M. (1978). Menopause and coronary heart disease. *Annals of Internal Medicine, 89,* 157–161.

Hamm, T. E., Kaplan, J. R., Clarkson, T. B., & Bullock, B. C. (1983). Effects of gender and social behavior on the development of coronary artery atherosclerosis in cynomolgus macaques. *Atherosclerosis, 48,* 221–233.

Haudenschild, C. C., Prescott, M. F., & Chobanian, A. V. (1980). Effects of hypertension and its reversal on aortic intima lesions of the rat. *Hypertension, 2,* 33–44.

Hazzard, W. R. (1986). Biological basis of the sex differential in longevity. *Journal of the American Geriatrics Society, 34,* 455–471.

Herd, J. A. (1983). Physiological basis for behavioral influences in atherosclerosis. In T. M. Dembroski, T. H. Schmidt, & G. Blumchen, (Eds.), *Biobehavioral bases of coronary heart disease* (pp. 248–256) Basel: Switzerland.

Hirsch, E. Z., Maksem, J. A. & Gagen, D. (1984). Effects of stress and propanolol on the aortic intima of rats [abstract]. *Arteriosclerosis, 4,* 526.

Houston, B. K. (1986). Psychological variables and cardiovascular and neuroendocrine reactivity. In K. A. Matthews, S. M. Weiss, T. Detre, T. M. Dembroski, B. Falkner, S. B. Manuck, R. B. Williams (Eds.) *Handbook of stress, reactivity, and cardiovascular disease* (pp. 207–230). New York: Wiley.

Hugh, A. E., & Fox, J. A. (1970). The precise localization of atheroma and its association with stasis at the origin of the internal carotid artery—a radiographic investigation. *British Journal of Radiology, 43,* 377–383.

Johansson, S., Vedin, A. & Wilhelmson, C. (1983). Myocardial infarction in women. *Epidemiology Reviews, 5,* 67–95.

Johnson, A. (1977). Sex differentials in coronary heart disease: The explanatory role of primary risk factors. *Journal of Health & Social Behavior, 18,* 46–54.

Jorgensen, L., Packham, M. A., Rowswell, H. C., & Mustad, J. F. (1972). Deposition of formed elements of blood on the intima and signs of intimial injury in the aorta of rabbit, pig, and man. *Laboratory Investigation, 27,* 341–350.

Kannel, W. B., Hjortland, M. C., McNamara, P. M., & Gordon T. (1976). Menopause and risk of cardiovascular disease. *Annals of Internal Medicine, 85,* 447–452.

Kaplan, J. R., Adams, M. R., Clarkson, T. B., & Koritnik, D. R. (1984). Psychosocial influences on female "protection" among cynomolgus macaques. *Atherosclerosis, 53,* 283–295.

Kaplan, J. R., Manuck, S. B., Adams, M. R., Weingand, K. W., & Clarkson, T. B. (1987). Propranolol inhibits coronary atherosclerosis in behaviorally predisposed monkeys fed an atherogenic diet. *Circulation, 76,* 1364–1372.

Kaplan, J. R., Manuck, S. B., & Clarkson, T. B. (1987). The influence of heart rate on coronary artery atherosclerosis. *Journal of Cardiovascular Pharmacology. 10*(Suppl. 2), 112–115.

Kaplan, J. R., Manuck, S. B., Clarkson, T. B., Lusso, F. M., & Taub, D. B. (1982). Social status, environment, atherosclerosis in cynomolgus monkeys. *Arteriosclerosis, 2,* 359–368.

Kaplan, J. R., Manuck, S. B., Clarkson, T. B., Lusso, F. B., Taub, D. B., & Miller, E. W. (1983). Social stress and atherosclerosis in normocholesterolemic monkeys. *Science, 220,* 733–735.

Kaplan, J. R., Manuck, S. B., Clarkson, T. B., & Pritchard, R. W. (1985). Animal models of behavioral influences on atherogenesis. In E. S. Katkin & S. B. Manuck (Eds.), *Advances in behavioral medicine* (Vol. 1, pp. 115–163) Greenwich, CT: JAI.

Keys, A., Taylor, H. L., Blackburn, J., Brozek, J., Anderson, J. T., & Somonson, E. (1971). Mortality and coronary heart disease among men studied for 23 years. *Archives of Internal Medicine, 128,* 201–214.

Krantz, D. S., Schaeffer, M. A., Davia, J. E., Dembroski, T. M., MacDougall, J. M., & Shaffer, R. T. (1981). Extent of coronary atherosclerosis, Type A behavior, and cardiovascular response to social interaction. *Psychophysiology, 18,* 654–664.

Kuller, L. H., Meilhan, E. N., & Costello, E. J. (1984). Relationship of menopause to cardiovascular disease. *Behavioral Medicine Update, 5*(4), 35–49.

Lancaster, J. (1975). *Primate behavior and emergence of human culture.* New York: Holt, Rinehart & Winston.

LaVecchia, C., Decarli, A., Franceschi, S., Gentile, A., Negri, E., & Parazzini, F. (1987). Menstrual and reproductive factors and the risk of myocardial infarction in women under fifty-five years of age. *American Journal of Obstetrics and Gynecology, 157*, 1108–1112.

Lerner, D. J. & Kannel, W. B. (1985). Patterns of coronary heart disease morbidity and mortality in the sexes: A 26-year follow-up of the Framingham population. *American Heart Journal, 111*, 383–390.

Mann, J. I., Doll, R., Thorogood, M., Vessey, M. P., & Waters, W. E. (1976). Risk factors for myocardial infarction in young women. *British Journal of Preventive & Social Medicine, 30*, 94–100.

Mann, J. I., Vessey, M. P., Thorogood, M., & Doll, R. (1975). Myocardial infarction young women with special reference to oral contraceptive practice. *British Medical Journal, 2*, 241–245.

Manuck., S. B., Kaplan, J. R., & Clarkson, T. B. (1983). Social instability and coronary artery atherosclerosis in cynomolgus monkeys. *Neuroscience & Behavioral Reviews, 7*, 485–491.

Manuck, S. B., Kaplan, J. R., & Clarkson, T. B. (1985). Stress-induced heart rate reactivity and atherosclerosis in female macaques. *Psychosomatic Medicine, 47*, 90 (Abstract).

Manuck, S. B., Kaplan, J. R., & Clarkson, T. B. (1986). Atherosclerosis, social dominance and cardiovascular reactivity. In T. H. Schmidt, T. D. Dembroski, & G. Blumchen, (Eds.), *Biological and psychological factors in cardiovascular disease* (pp. 459–475). Berlin: Springer-Verlag.

Manuck, S. B., Kaplan, J. R., & Matthews, K. A. (1986). Behavioral antecedents of coronary heart disease and atherosclerosis. *Arteriosclerosis, 6*, 2–14.

Manuck, S. B., & Krantz, D. S. (1986). Psychophysiologic reactivity in coronary heart disease and essential hypertension. In K. A. Matthews, S. B. Weiss, T. Detre, T. M. Dembroski, B. Falkner, S. B. Manuck, & R. B. Williams (Eds.), *Handbook of stress, reactivity and cardiovascular disease* (pp. 11–34). New York: Wiley-Interscience.

Manuck, S. B., & Polefrone, J. M. (1987). Psychophysiologic reactivity in women. In E. D. Eaker, B. Packard, N. K. Wenger, T. B. Clarkson, & H. A. Tyroler (Eds.), *Coronary heart disease in women* (pp. 164–171) New York: Haymarket-Doyma.

McGill, H. C., & Stern, M. P. (1979). Sex and atherosclerosis. In R. Paoletti & A. M. Gotto (Eds.), *Atherosclerosis Review* (Vol 4, pp. 157–242). New York: Raven Press.

Nestel, P. J., Verghese, A., & Lovell, R. R. (1967). Catecholamine secretion and sympathetic nervous responses to emotion in men with angina pectoris. *American Heart Journal, 73*, 227–234.

Oliver, M. F. (1974). Ischemic heart disease in young women. *British Medical Journal, 4* 253–259.

Parrish, H. M., Carr, C. A., Hall, D. G., & King, T. M. (1967). Time interval from castration in premenopausal women to development of excessive coronary atherosclerosis. *American Journal of Obstetrics & Gynecology, 99*, 155–162.

Restreppo, C., Guzman, M. A., Eggen, D. A., & Strong, J. P. (1972). Pregnancy and atherosclerosis. *Atherosclerosis, 15*, 371–382

Ritterband, A. B., Jaffe, I. A., Densen, P. M., Magagna, J. F., & Reed, E. (1963). Gonadal function and the development of coronary heart disease. *Circulation, 27*, 237–251.

Rosenberg, L., Hennekens, C. H., Rosner, B., Belanger, C., Rothman, K. J., & Speizer, J. E. (1981). Early menopause and the risk of myocardial infarction. *Gynecology, 139*, 47–51

Ross, R. (1981). Atherosclerosis: a problem of the biology of arterial wall cells and their interactions with blood components. *Arteriosclerosis, 1*, 293–311.

Rowland, M., & Roberts, J. (1982). Blood pressure levels and hypertension in persons 6–74 years: United States, 1976–1980. *(Vital and Health Statistics report #84)*. Washington, DC: National Center for Health Statistics.

Schneiderman, N. (1987). Psychophysiologic factors in atherogenesis and coronary artery disease. *Circulation* (Suppl.), *76*, 41–47.

Schwartz, S. M., & Benditt, E. P. (1977). Aortic endothelial cell replication. II. Effects of age and hypertension in the rat. *Circulation Research, 41*, 248–255.

Schwartz, S. M., Cambell, G. R., Campbell, J. H. (1986). Replication of smooth muscle cells in vascular disease. *Circulation Research, 58* 427–444.

Schwartz, S., Gajdusek, C., Shelden, S. (1981). Vascular wall growth control: the role of endothelium. *Arteriosclerosis, 1,* 107–126.

Shiffer, F., Hartley, L. H., Schulman, C. L., Abelmann, W. H. (1976). The quiz electrocardiogram: A new diagnostic and research technique for evaluating the relation between emotional stress and ischemic heart disease. *American Journal of Cardiology, 37,* 41–47.

Sime, W. E., Buell, J. C., Eliot, R. S. (1980). Electrocardiogram and blood pressure responses to emotional stress (quiz interview) in post-infarct cardiac patients and matched control subjects. *Journal of Human Stress, 6,* 39–46.

Spence, J. D. (1983). Effects of hydralazine versus propranolol on blood velocity patterns in patients with carotid stenosis. *Clinical Science, 65,* 91–93.

Spence, J. D. (1987). Hypertension and atherosclerosis: Effects of antihypertensive drugs on arterial flow patterns. *Journal of Cardiovascular Pharmacology, 10* (Suppl. 2), 112–115.

Spence, J. D., Perkins, D. G., Kline, R. L., Adams, M., & Haust, M. D. (1984). Hemodynamic modification of aortic atherosclerosis: Effects of propranolol vs. hydralazine in hypertensive hyperlipidemic rabbits. *Atherosclerosis, 50,* 325–333.

Spence, J. D., Pesout, A. B., & Melmon, K. L. (1977). Effects of antihypertensive drugs on blood velocity in rhesus monkeys. *Stroke, 8,* 589–594.

Still, W. J., & Dennison, S. (1974). The arterial endothelium of the hypertensive rat. *Archives of Pathology, 97,* 337–342.

Stoney, C. M., Davis, M. C., & Matthews, K. A. (1987) Sex differences in physiological responses to stress and in coronary heart disease; A causal link? *Psychophysiology 24,* 127–131.

Stout, R. W. (1982). *Hormones and atherosclerosis.* Boston: MTP Press.

Sznajderman, M., & Oliver, M. F. (1963). Spontaneous premature menopause, ischemic heart disease, and serum lipids. *Lancet, 1,* 962–965.

Talbott, E., Kuller, L. H., Detre, K., & Perper, J. (1977). Biologic and psychosocial risk factors of sudden death from coronary disease in white women. *American Journal of Cardiology, 39,* 858–864.

Talbott, E., Kuller, L. H., Perper, J., & Murphy, P. A. (1981). Sudden unexpected death in women: Biologic and psychosocial origins. *American Journal of Epidemiology, 114,* 671–682.

Wingard, D. L. (1982). The sex differential in mortality rates: Demographic and behavioral factors. *American Journal of Epidemiology, 115,* 205–216.

Wingard, D. L., Suarez, L., & Barrett-Connor, E. (1983). The sex differential in mortality factors. *American Journal of Epidemiology, 117,* 165–172.

Winkelstein, W., & Rekate, A. (1964). Age trend of mortality from coronary artery disease in women and observations on the reproductive patterns of those affected. *American Heart Journal, 67,* 481–488.

Winkelstein, W., Stenchever, M. A., & Lilienfeld, A. M. (1965). Occurrence of pregnancy, abortion, and artificial menoapuse among women with coronary artery disease: A preliminary study. *Journal of Chronic Disease, 4,* 273–286.

Wright, R. A., Contrada, R. J., & Glass, D. C. (1985). Psychophysiologic correlates of Type A behavior. In E. D. Katkin, & S. B. Manuck (Eds.), *Advances in behavioral medicine* (Vol. 1, pp. 39–88). Greenwich, CT: JAI.

Wuest, J. H., Dry, T. J., & Edward, J. E. (1953). The degree of coronary atherosclerosis in bilaterally oophorectomized women. *Circulation, 7,* 801–809.

Yellin, E. L. (1966). Laminar-turbulent transition process in pulsatile flow. *Circulation Research, 19,* 791–804.

Author Index

Numbers in *italics* indicate pages with complete bibliographic information.

229

Levenson, R. W., 81, *86*, 106, *112*
Leventhal, H., 1, 4, 19, *20*, 24, *39*, 68, 88, 93, 114, 117, 126, 127, 129, 131, 135, 138, *146*
Levine, S., 59, *61*
Levy, M. N., 201, *204*
Levy, R. A., 66, *86*, 91, 109, *111*, 122, *145*
Light, K. C., 104, *112*
Light, R. J., 154, *167*
Lilienfeld, A. M., 216, *227*
Lorr, M., 44, 50, *62*
Lovallo, W. R., 104, *112*
Lovell, R. R., 208, *226*
Lown, B., 4, 14, *19*, *20*, 202, *205*
Luborsky, L., 42, *62*
Lueger, R. J., 105, *112*
Lushene, R., 69, 73, *86*, 97, *111*, 127, 128, *145*, 179, 190, *192*, 208, *224*
Lusso, F. B., *225*
Lusso, F. M., 95, *112*, 211, 213, 219, *225*

M

Maas, J. W., 200, *204*
Maddi, S. R., 163, *167*
MacDougall, J. M., 1, 2, 6, 9, 12, *18*, *19*, 24, 26, 27, 29, 30, 33, *36*, *37*, *38*, 41, 42, 52, 53, 54, *61*, *62*, 66, 68, 69, 73, 76, *86*, *87*, 91, 95, 96, 97, 99, 105, 107, *110*, *111*, *112*, *113*, *114*, 117, 126, 127, 128, 131, 143, *144*, *145*, *146*, 179, 190, *192*, *204*, 208, *224*, *225*
Magagna, J. F., 215, *226*
Magnusson, D., 94, 98, *113*
Mahl, G., 160, *167*
Maksem, J. A., 220, *225*
Mann, J. I., 216, *226*
Mannucci, E. G., 106, *111*
Manuck, S. B., 6, 11, *19*, 72, *87*, 91, 92, 95, 96, 97, 100, 101, 102, 105, 107, *110*, *111*, *112*, *113*, *114*, *145*, *167*, 196, 197, 202, *204*, 207, 208, 209, 211, 213, 214, 216, 218, 222, *223*, *224*, *225*, *226*
Margolis, L. H., 172, *193*
Marmot, M., 22, *38*
Marshall, J., 169, *192*
Matarazzo, J. D., 126, 135, *145*
Matteson, M. T., 174, 175, 178, 179, *193*

Matthews, K. A., 3, 6, 10, 12, 13, 16, *19*, *20*, 24, 26, 27, 28, 30, 32, *37*, *38*, 41, 43, *62*, 66, 68, *87*, 91, 92, 93, 94, 95, 96, 97, 99, 105, 107, 108, *110*, *113*, *114*, *116*, 117, 126, 127, 131, 137, 143, *145*, *146*, 154, 165, *168*, 175, *193*, 202, *204*, 207, 208, 216, *224*, *226*, *227*
May, M. A., 48, *61*
Mayes, B. T., 169, 177, 179, *193*
McBain, G. D. M., 174, *193*
McCartney, K., 99, *114*
McCaul, K., 104, *115*
McCown, N., 201, *205*
McCrae, R. R., 14, *18*, 31, 33, 34, *36*, 41, 42, 43, 44, 45, 46, 47, 48, 49, 50, 52, 53, *60*, *62*, 195, 199
McCranie, E. W., 31, *38*
McDougall, J. M., *113*
McGill, H. C., 215, *226*
McGilley, B., 12, *18*, 104, *111*, 175, *192*
McIlvain, H. E., 96, 109, *114*
McKelvain, R., 26, 66, *88*
McKinney, M. E., 91, 96, 109, *114*
McLeroy, K. R., 172, *193*
McNamara, P. M., 215, 216, *224*, *225*
Medley, D. M., 12, *18*, *36*, 85, 197, 199, *204*
Mednieks, M., 200, *204*
Meehl, P., 138, *146*
Magargee, E. I., 33, *38*
Meilhan, E. N., *225*
Melmon, K. L., 222, *227*
Melosh, W., 75, *89*, 197, 198, 199, *205*
Menninger, K. A., 23, *28*
Menninger, W. C., 23, *38*
Merriman, J. E., 106, *112*
Messinger, H. B., 119, 132, *146*
Mettlin, C., 104, *114*, 175, *193*
Miller, E. W., 219, *225*
Miller, J. Z., 96, *114*
Miller, S. M., 12, *19*, 104, *114*
Miner, M. H., 96, 109, *114*
Mischel, W., 98, 99, *114*, 137, *146*
Mittlemark, M. B., 28, *39*, 66, *88*, 91, *114*, 118, *147*
Mobley, P. L., 200, *204*
Moergen, S., 12, *20*, 104, *115*
Moos, R. H., 178, *193*
Moss, A. J., 28, *36*, 91, *110*
Mueser, K. T., 106, *116*
Mulder, P., 165, *166*

Subject Index

241

Coronary heart disease (CHD)
  anger, 41, 42
  assessment, 58
  anxiety, 158, 164
  behavior patterns, 2–5
  biological mechanisms, 195–204
    cognitively mediated, 196–200
    noncognitively mediated, 200–204
    prevention, 202–204
  dangerous situations hypothesis, 13–16, 17
  development, 197, 198, 199
  depression, 157–158, 164
  emotions, 22–23, 42, 149–166
  extroversion, 158
  female protection from, 214–216
  heart rate responsivity, 208–223
  hostility, 32–35, 69–80
  hyperresponsivity hypothesis, 5–12, 16–17
  job stress, 169–191
  monkey study of, 198, 207–223
  neuroticism, 33–35, 42, 43, 48, 53
  nonverbal correlates, 154
  parasympathetic nervous system, 201–202
  personality correlates, 157–158, 164
  physiologic reactivity, 6–11, 95–98, 170
  prediction, 32–33, 157, 165, 202–203, 207, 209
  risk factors, 21–35
  risk models, 100–102
  speech style and, 80–84
  structural weakness hypothesis, 2–5, 16
  sympathetic nervous system, 197, 198, 199, 200, 219
  testosterone production, 72–76, 197, 199, 200
  transactional approaches to, 109 (*see also* Coronary artery atherosclerosis; Hostility; Job stress)
Coronary-prone behavior, *see* Type A behavior pattern
Cynomolgus monkey study of atherosclerosis, 207–223
  atherosclerosis assessment, 210, 212
  diet, 210, 211, 218
  endothelial injury, 218–223
  female monkeys, 214–218
    ovarian dysfunction, 217–218, 219
  heart rate, 208–223
  hemodynamic factors, 218–223
  male monkeys, 208–214
  social behavior, 209, 213, 218
  social grouping, 210, 217

D

Defense Mechanism Inventory (DMI), 50
Dictionary of National Biography, 22, 36
Dictionary of Occupational Titles (DOT), 179, 180, 181, 182, 183, 184, 194

E

Emotional expression
  AHA syndrome, 153
  coronary heart disease, 149–166
  depression, 157–158
  empirical studies, 158–164
  measurement of, 151–152
  non-Type A, 157
  nonverbal correlates, 154–155, 161, 162
  observation of, 164
  style, 162
  theoretical concepts, 151–153
  Type A subgroups, 152

F

Framingham Type A study, 22, 59, 156

G

Guilford-Zimmerman Temperament Scales (GZTS), 50

H

Hopkins Symptom checklist, 162, 164
Hostility
  agreeableness vs. antagonism, 41–60
  anger, 55, 196, 199, 207
  assessment of, 12, 15, 31, 34
  coronary heart disease, 69–80
  coronary occlusion, 14, 66
  factors, 56
  kinds, 43, 73
  measurement of, 29–32
  multidimensional nature, 33–35
  neuroticism, 42, 43, 48, 53, 57, 70
  Potential for Hostility, 29, 32, 41, 43, 44, 51–59, 197, 200, 207
    empirical links, 51–59
  prediction of CHD, 32–33
  scales, 12, 15, 31, 33, 34, 42–43
  social supports, 15–16